PEARSON ALWAYS LEARNING

Situated Writing at UIC

First Custom Edition

Taken from:
In Context: Reading and Writing in Cultural Conversations, Second Edition by Ann Merle Feldman, Ellen McManus, and Nancy Downs

Cover Art: *Mural in Pilsen* by Candice Rai.

Taken from:

In Context, Second Edition
by Ann Merle Feldman, Ellen McManus and Nancy Downs

Published by Longman
New York, New York 10019

Pearson Learning Solutions, 501 Boylston Street, Suite 900, Boston, MA 02116
A Pearson Education Company
www.pearsoned.com

Printed in the United States of America

1 2 3 4 5 6 7 8 9 10 V011 16 15 14 13 12 11

000200010270765315

CS/CM

ISBN 10: 1-256-16624-3
ISBN 13: 978-1-256-16624-5

Copyright Acknowledgments

Grateful acknowledgment is made to the following sources for permission to reprint material copyrighted or controlled by them:

"Taggers Spray over Vandal Image," by Phat X. Chiem, reprinted from *Chicago Tribune*, September 12, 1996.

"Gnome 174 Works on the Mural at West 59th St.," courtesy of Chicago Tribune.

"Van Gogh's Chair," (1888), courtesy of Art Resource.

"The Millionaire in Vincent's Chair," (1999), courtesy of Marlborough Fine Art.

"Skin," by Esmeralda Santiago, reprinted from *Body*, edited by Sharon Sloan Fiffer and Steve Fiffer (1999), Alfred A. Knopf, a division of Random House, Inc.

"A Portfolio of Self," by Shane Madden.

"Representin' the Real," by Todd Boyd, reprinted from *Am I Black Enough for You: Popular Culture from the 'Hood and Beyond* (1997), by permission of Indiana University Press.

"Identity in the Age of the Internet," by Sherry Turkle, reprinted from *Life on the Screen: Identity in the Age of the internet* (1995), by permission of Simon & Schuster, Inc.

"Famous All Over Town," by Danny Santiago, reprinted from *Famous All Over Town* (1984), by permission of Simon & Schuster, Inc.

"Review of Famous All Over Town," by David Quammen, reprinted from the *New York Times Book Review*, April 24, 1983, The New York Times Company.

"A Noted "Hispanic" Novelist Prove to Be Someone Else," by Edwin McDowell, reprinted from the *New York Times*, July 22, 1984, The New York Times Company.

"Three young women, portrait, elevated," courtesy of Getty Images Inc.

"Goin' Gangsta, Choosin' Cholita," by Nell Bernstein, reprinted from *San Jose Mercury News,* November 13, 1994,YGS Group.

"Bringing Hip-Hop Style to the Mainstream," by Marc Spiegler, reprinted from *American Demographics,* (November 1996).

"Hip-Hop 101: The Placement Test," by Mark Spiegler.

"U2's Double Trouble," by Richard Harrington, reprinted from *The Washington Post,* December 18, 1991.

"Excerpts from *Island Records Ltd. vs. SST Records/Negativland*," reprinted from *United States District Court: Central District of California* (September 3, 1991), by permission of Seeland—Negativland.

"U2 Negativland: The Case from Our Side," reprinted from *Fair Use: The Story of the Letter U and the Numeral 2* (1995), by permission of Seeland—Negativland.

"In Fair Use Debate, Art Must Come First," by Negativland, reprinted from *Billboard,* December 25, 1993, by permission of Billboard Magazine.

"Sampling without Permission is Theft," by Andrian Adams and Paul McKibbins, reprinted from *Billboard,* March 5, 1994, by permission of Billboard Magazine.

"Build a Desktop Studio," by Tom Samiljan, reprinted from *Rolling Stone*, June 8, 2000.

"RTMARK Finds Bucks for Beck Rip-Off," reprinted from *RTMARK Deconstructing Beck Press Release*, February 17, 1998.

"Route 66 Sign," courtesy of Corbis Images.

"Bright boy from the Delta," by Clifton L. Taulbert, reprinted from *Watching Our Crops Come In* (1997), by permission of The Doe Coover Agency.

"Hampton plantation sign," by Clifton L. Taulbert, reprinted from *Watching Our Crops Come In* (1997), by permission of The Doe Coover Agency.

"School portrait," by Clifton L. Taulbert, reprinted from *Watching Our Crops Come In* (1997), by permission of The Doe Coover Agency.

"Outstanding achievement certificate," by Clifton L. Taulbert, reprinted from *Watching Our Crops Come In* (1997), by permission of The Doe Coover Agency.

"Man under loft bed," by Clifton L. Taulbert, reprinted from *Watching Our Crops Come In* (1997), by permission of The Doe Coover Agency.

"The Triumph of Burbopolis," by Michael Pollan, reprinted from the *New York Times Magazine,* April 9, 2000, by permission of Steven Barclay Agency.

"Understanding the Preservation Process," city of San Antonio.

"King William Seeing Red over Purple," by Susan Yerkes, reprinted with permission from *San Antonio Express News,* July 26, 1997.

"Now We Know Why It's Called Purple Passion," by Susan Yerkes, reprinted with permission from *San Antonio Express News,* July 30, 1997.

"Purple Debate Reaches Commission–Cisneros Agrees to Work with City Staff on Mutually Acceptable Color Scheme," by Mike Greenberg, reprinted with permission from *San Antonio Express News,* August 7, 1997.

"Letters to the editor," reprinted with permission from *San Antonio Express News.*

"Purple Politics–Our Tejano History Has Become Invisible," by Sandra Cisneros, reprinted with permission from *San Antonio Express News,* August 17, 1997.

"Purple Politics–Individuality Surrendered for Preservation," by Milton Babbitt, reprinted with permission from *San Antonio Express News*, August 17, 1997.

"The Purple House: interview transcript with Sandra Cisneros," by Lisa McRee and Michele Norris, reprinted from *ABC Good Morning America,* July 15, 1998, by permission of American Broadcasting Company (ABC).

"Conversation piece," courtesy of the Smithsonian Institution.

"Hate Radio: Why We Need to Tune In to Limbaugh and Stern," by Patricia J. Williams, reprinted with permission from *Ms. Magazine*, March/April 1994.

"Symposium on Minority Journalists and the Media," by Ray Suarez, Ellis Cose, Joie Chen, George de Lama, and Mark Trahant, reprinted from *Talk of the Nation,* July 8, 1999, National Public Radio.

"The FDR Memorial: Who Speaks from the Wheelchair?" by Rosemarie Garland-Thomson, reprinted from *Chronicle of Higher Education,* January 26, 2001.

"Snapshot in Vietnam War Memorial," courtesy of Corbis Images.

"Statement for her Memorial Competition Submission," by Maya Ying Lin, March 1981, by permission of The Pace Gallery.

"Vietnam Veterans Memorial," by Maya Lin, reprinted from *Boundaries* (2001), by permission of Simon & Schuster, Inc.

"Memorials, Monuments, and Meaning," by Robert Ivy, reprinted from *Architectural Record* 190, no.7 (July 2002), Architectural Record.

"The New Ground Zero: Finding Comfort in the Safety of Names," by Michael Kimmelman, reprinted from the *New York Times*, August 2003, the New York Times Company.

"Continuing Controversy over Construction of a Memorial at the World Trade Center Site," by Tony Cox and Allison Keyes, reprinted from *Tavis Smiley Show,* December 5, 2003, National Public Radio.

"Reflecting Absence WTC Memorial Proposal image," courtesy of Lower Manhattan Development Corporation.

"McDonald's" courtesy of Corbis Images.

"For This We Sent You To College?" by Robyn Meredith, reprinted from the *New York Times*, June 8, 1997, New York Times Corporation.

"William D. Lucy," courtesy of Redux Pictures.

"Linda C. Roman," courtesy of Redux Pictures.

"Rachel D. Gunderson," courtesy of Redux Pictures.

"Malane Rogers," courtesy of Redux Pictures.

"Rebecca E. Johnson," courtesy of Redux Pictures.

"Douglas M. Fischer," courtesy of Redux Pictures.

"Nickel-and-Dimed," by Barbara Erenreich, reprinted from *Harpers Magazine* (1999), by permission of International Creative Management.

"A Man's Place," by Victoria de Grazia, Claudia Goldin, and Jacqueline Jones, reprinted from the *New York Times Magazine*, May 16, 1999, The New York Times Corperation.

Brief Contents

Unit IV

Participating in Civic Conversations 191

Unit V

Adapting to the Changing Economy 253

Detailed Contents

We represent ourselves to others when we're absent—for example in a letter or photograph—but we also represent ourselves when we're present, for example in our clothes or language. Santiago explores how our very skin can represent our lives both to others and to ourselves.

Unit III

Creating a Sense of Place 143

A Genre Glossary 295

With the exception of the "UIC Award-Winning Projects" all of the content is taken from *In Context: Reading and Writing in Cultural Conversations*, Second Edition, by Ann Merle Feldman, Ellen McManus, and Nancy Downs.

Readings Listed by Genre

The readings for *Situated Writing at UIC* were selected to create conversations on issues and themes, as you can see in the Detailed Table of Contents. But as you can see in this listing, the readings also represent a wide range of genres. The readings are organized below according to the genres in the Genre Glossary, with some additional, more specialized genres—court document, exhibit catalogue, legislation, lyrics, mission statement, news article, press release, survey and transcript of radio and television show—represented as well. Of course the boundary lines between some genres—for example academic article, essay, feature article, and opinion piece—are not always clear. Rather than cross-listing readings, we have made the categorizations below on the basis of content, format, place of publication, and when possible the designation given to the piece in the original publication. But you might want to categorize differently.

Preface

Writing is a way of acting in the world; that is the idea that drives this textbook. *Situated Writing at UIC* focuses on how societies and individuals, including students, use writing and reading to do things in the world. It presents a series of contexts in which people use writing to create, sustain, understand, and change their worlds.

Although organized with the flexibility of a thematic reader, *Situated Writing at UIC* presents its reading selections as pieces of writing that emerge from specific situations. We want students to see themselves as participants in important public conversations, which means that they must see themselves as readers and writers in situations that engage their attention and response. We have chosen readings that can easily be put into conversation with each other, and we have included genres—for example academic articles, newspaper stories, and symposia of various kinds—that report on, comment on, or analyze situations, as well as genres—for example press releases, codes of conduct, legal documents, and the manifesto—that take more direct actions in situations. Similarly, the writing projects that accompany each reading invite students to reflect on issues raised in the readings, as well as to use genres that allow them to participate more directly in the situations referred to in the readings. The case studies in Chapters 5, 7, and 9, consisting of documents gathered around a specific moment in a larger conversation, give students particularly vivid opportunities to see themselves as agents—readers and writers—in well-defined situations.

Distinctive Features

Rhetorical Framework: Situation, Genre, Language, and Consequences

Situated Writing at UIC is organized around a set of concepts—situation, genre, language, and consequences—that consolidate important rhetorical ideas. This set of concepts is powerful for several reasons. Because students can use the concepts as both readers and writers, they help students see the connections between reading and writing. They help students see the complexities of reading and writing by drawing attention to the fact that any text and any act of reading or writing has many dimensions. And because students are already familiar with the everyday meanings of these words, the terms themselves are very user-friendly.

When we use these concepts in our classrooms, we find that they help students make a variety of connections. Whether reading an essay or writing a letter to the editor, students see that they must take into account the many situations involved, consider the implications of genre, recognize the language of a text as a range of choices guided by various constraints, and focus on the consequences of what they read and write.

We have designed *Situated Writing at UIC* so that instructors can use these concepts fully to guide the course but can also choose to make only occasional use of them for particular purposes or not use them at all. To allow for this range of choices, we use icons to highlight activities that focus on one of the concepts, but all activities can be used productively without reference to the concepts.

Situation. How histories, cultures, communities, and individual experiences influence the writing and reading of texts. This concept helps students consider the complex contexts from which a piece of writing emerges.

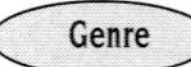

Genre. The forms—in writing, speech, or any other medium—that have evolved in response to repeated situations, needs, or desires. As readers, students learn to think about what genre a piece of writing belongs to and how that has shaped its way of representing the world. As writers, they understand that they choose and modify a genre in response to the situation they are in.

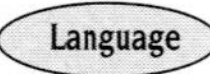

Language. The words, sentences, organization, and design of a text. Often the language of a text is considered only in terms of correctness on the one hand or as a matter of individual voice on the other hand. Our approach is to help students, as they read and write, see language issues in light of both genre and situation.

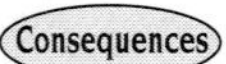

Consequences. The effects of writing in the world. Especially when writing in a classroom, it is easy to forget that writing has consequences, that this is why we write, and that these projected consequences guide our writing.

Guides to Analyzing Contexts for Writing and Analyzing Readings in Context

Perhaps the most distinctive feature of *Situated Writing at UIC* is the set of concepts we introduce to help students think about writing from a variety of perspectives. But such concepts remain "teacher talk" unless students have ways to use them on their own and to make such concepts part of their critical vocabulary and practical strategies. The Guide to Analyzing Contexts for Writing and the Guide to Analyzing Readings in Context help students do just that. Each guide poses a series of questions to help students use these concepts as either a reader or a writer. For example, from the Situation section of the Guide to Analyzing Readings in Context, questions such as the following help students gain an in-depth understanding of the effect of context on a particular reading:

> When and where was this text published? If it wasn't published, when, where, and how was it distributed? . . . Judging by the text itself and where it was published, what can I conclude about who the intended readers are? . . . Who is the writer? What relevant credentials and expertise does the writer have, including previous publications on the topic? . . . What events in the world was this text written in response to, and how might these or other events have influenced the writer? . . . How might my background affect how I respond to this text?

Similarly, questions such as the following from the Genre section of the Guide to Analyzing Contexts for Writing remind students of the genre-related issues they need to consider as they write:

> Does this writing situation call for a particular genre? . . . If not, what genre would typically be used for the situation I am in or the purpose for which I am writing? . . . What

> experience do I have with the genre I am expected to use or that I have chosen? . . . What is the typical form for this genre? How can I use or adapt it to fit my purposes? What form will my readers expect? . . . What content will my readers expect? Do I have access to this expected content? Is the content that I do have appropriate to the genre? . . . What language choices will help me achieve my purpose? . . . Do I need to adapt my language style or the genre?

In the activities and writing assignments throughout the book, icons indicate activities that focus on a particular dimension. Thus students can, either as part of the assignment or on their own, turn to the guides for help with the reading or writing assignment in terms of that particular dimension. Used in combination with the Genre Glossary, the guides are particularly powerful tools for helping students read and write in new genres.

Headnotes. The headnotes work along with other features of the textbook to provide context for students as they connect to an ongoing conversation. Unlike headnotes that offer only biographical information about the author, our headnotes connect students to the issues under discussion.

Activities. *Situated Writing at UIC* includes two kinds of activities that help students locate each reading in a wider social context, explore the relationship between situation and genre, and think about the consequences of writing. These activities enable the students to work both individually and collaboratively to prepare for the writing projects that follow each reading.

Preceding each reading are activities called "Connecting with the Conversation," which help students identify and create a variety of contexts in which to understand the reading. Working individually or in groups, students write about their own experiences with and knowledge of an issue; do research on an issue, author, or type of publication; and share their experiences and findings with a small group or the class as a whole. Often students use online resources to carry out these activities.

Following each reading, "Exploring Texts and Contexts" includes activities that guide students through a close examination of the language, composition, and design of a text; help students consider these textual features in terms of genre; and encourage students to make connections with other readings in the book, outside resources, and their own experiences and observations. Many of the activities ask students to reflect on one of the four rhetorical concepts and these activities are highlighted with the appropriate icon.

Writing Projects. Each reading is followed by two or three assignments that we call "Creating Texts," which are a key part of the book's overall effort to show the complexities of reading and writing in action. Many of these writing projects ask students to analyze texts, situations, and issues, often using traditional genres of academic discourse. Other writing projects ask students to use genres that intervene more directly in specific situations, for example a proposal to solve a problem, a code of conduct to shape behavior, a brochure to inform, a Web page to make connections, a speech to inspire action. Many sets of assignments invite students to reflect on the relationship between these different kinds of writing and more broadly on the many ways that we use writing to understand and do things in the world. Writing projects often ask students to draw ideas and information from other readings. Many projects involve using online resources of various kinds.

Genre Glossary

Students recognize genres much more easily than they can produce them. They easily distinguish television sitcoms, comedies, dramas, and talk shows and recognize written genres such as letters to the editor, essays, symposia, and feature articles. The "Genre Glossary" offers students a resource for producing writing in the wide variety of genres we ask for in *Situated Writing at UIC.* This very important tool reinforces the message of *Situated Writing at UIC* that writing emerges out of specific situations. To decide which genre, or even which aspects of a particular genre, might be appropriate, student writers must analyze possible situations and consequences as they plan and produce writing that will achieve their purposes.

The Genre Glossary contains more than twenty elaborated definitions of genres such as the dialogue, Web page, essay, manifesto, cover letter, code of conduct, and interview. Each entry describes the typical situations the genre emerges from, the form usually expected, the kinds of content typically included, and the range of language choices expected and accepted in that genre. These descriptions are meant to capture a sense of the genre, to show students where they are constrained and where they have latitude, and, most important, to show students that even within the most rule-bound genres they have decisions to make as they write.

Acknowledgments

We wish to acknowledge our debt most broadly to our colleagues in composition, English, and rhetorical studies whose theory, research, and pedagogy have informed our work. We are also indebted to the writers we include in the book, who have taught us much about writing as a social activity. We especially want to thank our colleagues at the University of Illinois at Chicago (UIC) and at Dominican University. At UIC we thank Patty Harkin, Jim Sosnoski, Marcia Farr, Ralph Cintron, Don Marshall, Walter Benn Michaels, Lennard Davis, Jerry Graff, Cathy Birkenstein-Graff, Stanley Fish, Jane Tompkins, Tom Moss, Toby Tate, Uday Sukhatme, Anne Cruz, Chris Messenger, Debra Hale, Julie Smith, Barbara Zusman, John Huntington, Gerry Sorensen, Richard Cameron, and Jessica Williams. At Dominican we thank Jeffrey Carlson; Robert Kaftan; Sister Jeanne Crapo, O.P.; Sister Mary Clemente Davlin, O.P.; Robert Greenwald; Sister Marci Hermesdorf, O.P.; Lisa Higgins; Mary Pat Radke; Chad Rohman; Donald Shaffer; Mary Scott Simpson; Mickey Sweeney; Sister Melissa Waters, O.P.; and Robbi Byrdsong-Wright. A special thanks to Barry Peterson at the Seton Hall University Institute on Work and Sharon Haar for her contributions to the section "Making a Home." Special thanks as well to Blondeen Jones, Michele Mancione, Kimberly Barba, and Lyæll Wallerstedt.

Graduate students and lecturers who help administer the UIC composition program, who have taken English 555, and who teach or have taught in the program, we thank all of you, and among you Paula Mathieu, Kelly Ritter, Bridget Harris-Tsemo, Nels Highberg,

Mary Biddinger, Beth Burmeister, Sharon Palo, Tina Kazan, Daiva Markelis, Diane Chin, Margaret Gonzalez, Rebecca de Wind Mattingly, Simone Meunch, Marianne Lyons, Jackie White, Brian Sheerin, John Martin, Grace Chan, Michael Badino, Amy L. Smith, Richard Kroeger, Susan Weinstein, Wendy Maland, Margaret Boyer, Mary Kay Mulvaney, Candice Rai, and Megan Marie. We also thank students in English 402 at Dominican University; Sue Cunningham, Kate Lyon, and Edith Villarreal. We also thank the members of our writing groups: Lauri Schaafner, Irma Olmedo, Ulrike Jaeckel, Sheila Kennedy, Martha Pacelli, and Linda Vavra.

This book could not have been completed without the detailed and wise commentary shared by members of our profession. Although their comments were anonymous at the time, we are pleased to recognize their fine work here: Michael Barry, University of Detroit-Mercy; Christina Bentley, University of Kentucky; Karen Lee Boren, University of Wisconsin-Milwaukee; Craig Branham, Saint Louis University; Brenda Brueggemann, Ohio State University; Ann Ciasullo, University of Kentucky; Gina Claywell, Murray State University; Deborah Coxwell Teague, Florida State University; Laurie Delany, Kent State University; Michelle Ephraim, Worcester Polytechnic Institute; Linda Ferreira-Buckley, University of Texas at Austin; Patricia Garcia Ocañas, Our Lady of the Lake University; Paul Heilker, Virginia Technical University; Shari Horner, Shippensburg University; Thomas Huckin, University of Utah; Alan Hutchinson, Des Moines Area Community College; Megan Knight, University of Iowa; Anna Laskaya, University of Oregon; Mark Mabrito, Purdue University at Calumet; Richard Marback, Wayne State University; Dennis M. Moore, University of Iowa; Matthew Parfitt, Boston University; Joe Pellegrino, Eastern Kentucky University; Pegeen Reichert Powell, Miami University-Ohio; Colleen Reilly, Purdue University; Abigail Robin, SUNY at New Paltz; Lance Ruben, Arapahoe Community College; Carolyn Stevenson, East West University; Gary Tate, Texas Christian University; Nancy Taylor, California State University at Northridge; Richard Taylor, East Carolina University; John Wegner, Angelo State University; and Abbey Zink, Northern Illinois University.

We have worked with an impressive group of publishing professionals throughout the development of this book, and we thank; Lynn Huddon, Katharine Glynn, Wendy Albert, Donna Campion, Joseph Vella, and Esther Hollander at Longman Publishers; and Mary Grivetti and Phyllis Padula.

Our families have sustained us throughout this process. We thank them and thank them again: Lawrence Gorman and Jack Gorman; Mary McManus and Jim, Kevin, Brian, and Terry McManus; Sheila Freeman and Colleen Hein; Philip Matsuhashi and Amy Matsuhashi; Robert, Jonah, and Aaron Meyerhoff; Florence Feldman; David and Bobby Feldman; Joel and Meryl Feldman; Tom Downs, Joseph Downs, and Thomas J. Downs.

Ann Merle Feldman
Ellen McManus
Nancy Downs

UIC
Award-Winning Writing Projects

Josh Bernstein—Instructor

Josh Bernstein, instructor.

Josh Bernstein designed the dialogue project below to engage students in a thoughtful and creative analysis of the role of politics in literature. Students were asked to take a position on whether or not writers should address current political issues in their fiction. Bernstein set up the dialogue project by asking students to read two essays written over 50 years apart. In 1940, George Orwell, who later produced the overtly political novels *Animal Farm* and *1984,* wrote a book review in praise of Henry Miller's somewhat scandalous novel, *The Tropic of Cancer.* Miller's novel offered a beautifully crafted first-person portrayal of the expatriate American life in Paris in the early 1930s. Orwell felt that this novel's unusual contribution was to reveal not what is strange, but rather to reveal what is typically unnoticed precisely because it is so familiar. Orwell wrote book reviews such as "Inside the Whale" to help him earn a meager living. He argued in "Inside the Whale" that the ordinary reader could find comfort from the perils of politics by entering the biblical belly of the whale.

More recently, in the early 1990s, Indian writer and essayist Salman Rushdie wrote a piece called "Outside the Whale" that responded directly to Orwell's earlier essay and that argued for the importance of politics in literature. Thus, Bernstein pointed out, the two writers were, in a way, already in dialogue. Each student's task was to imagine him- or herself in each writer's shoes, so to speak, and to create a conversation they might have. More important, though, the students in Josh's class had to determine for themselves their position on the role of politics in literature.

Agnes Weglarczyk—Writer

Agnes Weglarczyk, writer.

The dialogue project we include below gave Agnes Weglarczyk an opportunity to apply her creativity to an imagined conversation between two intellectual figures who lived at different times. Even though Salman Rushdie and George Orwell could not have met in real-time, Weglarczyk situated these characters, along with herself, at a local bookstore to pursue this dialogue about the role of literature in public life.

The most challenging feature of her first-year writing class, Weglarczyk smilingly told us, was getting there for the 8 a.m. starting time. A business major who also enjoys writing, Weglarczyk works part-time for a consulting business that helps entrepreneurs manage their emerging businesses while sustaining their quality of life.

Josh Bernstein's writing class was different from any class she had taken in high school: it moved faster and required much more writing. What Weglarczyk learned from this new approach to writing was to trust herself. In other words, she says, "be your own writer." While the idea behind this dialogue was interesting, the texts themselves—essays by Orwell and Rushdie—were among the most difficult she had ever read. Josh Bernstein took care to go over the readings in great detail, making sure that the class understood them. "Once we understood the essays," Weglarczyk told us, "we were able to get creative with our dialogues."

The Role of Literature: Politics or Pleasure?

A Dialogue by
Agnes Weglarczyk

On a calm Saturday afternoon, while standing in line waiting to pay for their selections, Rushdie and Orwell run into each other at a local bookstore. The line is moving slowly because Agnes Weglarczyk, the bookstore's owner, is putting up a poster for a sale on political novels. She's particularly pleased because she's been developing a series of promotions for the bookstore that will highlight what she sees as a very important relationship between politics and literature.

Rushdie, having met Orwell at a social gathering the previous year, recognizes the writer not by his appearance, but by the book he is holding. Orwell, known for being fond of literature written for the ordinary man, is holding a copy of Henry Miller's novel *Tropic of Cancer.* Rushdie, on the other hand, is holding Edward Said's book *Orientalism*. Even though Rushdie appears to be somewhat reluctant to approach Orwell, he does. As he comes up to Orwell from behind, he whispers into his ear:

Rushdie: "I accept" (Orwell 6).

Orwell: Excuse me?

Rushdie: "I accept," a phrase you admire and have grown fond of, isn't it?

Orwell turns around and is astonished to see who has whispered the phrase into this ear.

Orwell: Well, isn't this a surprise. I would imagine you to be the last person to speak those words, you who are always proactive and who demands that action be taken. What brings you to this part of the city?

Rushdie: I was passing through the neighborhood, and noticed the sign in the window saying there's a special on political literature today. You know me and my politics.

Orwell: Yes, you are rather fond of political action, aren't you?

Rushdie: Just like any other individual ought to be.

Orwell: Well, aren't you asking for a little too much? You know very well that most people have other problems to deal with; at the end of the day they would rather read something enjoyable and cheerful than something depressing and boring.

Rushdie: In other words, you mean they would rather go inside your so-called whale, accept everything that is happening, and read old Henry.

Orwell, noticing that Rushdie is getting irritated, decides to agitate his companion even more and answers his question with sarcasm.

Orwell: Exactly, I knew you would see my point of view one of these days. I didn't think it would be so soon, though.

Rushdie: Not so fast. I continue to disagree with your views and ideologies. And I will never believe that only "Miller-type of books" can speak with the people's voice as you have mentioned numerous times before.

Orwell: Well, what other books do you know of that get "away from the lies and simplifications, the stylized, marionette-like quality of ordinary fiction, even quite good fiction, and are dealing with the recognizable experiences of human beings" (Orwell 3)?

Rushdie, put on the spot to think of a book that would fit these criteria, is unable to come up with a title. Weglarczyk leans in toward the pair hoping to overhear their conversation. Seeing that his companion is struggling to find an answer, Orwell continues with his argument.

Orwell: Hard to think of one, isn't it? It's obvious that in Miller's books you are reading about "people living the exiled life, people drinking, talking, meditating, and fornicating." And, as you read his novels, "you have the feeling that all their adventures have happened to yourself" and that, my friend, is what you call "speaking with the people's voice" (Orwell 3).

As Orwell begins to lecture Rushdie about the people's voice and what it actually is, tension between the two men rises. Orwell knows he has touched on a serious topic and decides to continue, hoping to upset Rushdie even further.

Orwell: You see, unlike you, Rushdie, Miller gets away from the political animal and closer to the viewpoint of the ordinary person. He doesn't use politics or ethics in his writings because those aren't the characteristics of everyday people. For Miller "the ordinary man is non-political, non-moral, passive" (Orwell 6). He speaks to them for what they are, and if you haven't realized it yet, people are ordinary and nothing more. "During the past ten years, literature has involved itself more and more deeply in politics, with the result that there is now less room in it for the ordinary man than at any time during the past two centuries" (Orwell 6). Look around you and see what is happening. Laissez-faire capitalism and liberalism have broken up and we are in an age of totalitarian dictatorship (Orwell 3). Freedom of thought is nothing more than a meaningless idea. The ordinary individual has become a victim and is left only with a whale's belly to provide comfort and to fend off struggles that he or she has no control over.

Salesperson: Gentlemen, would you please move out of the line if you wish to continue having your conversation so other customers could pay for their purchases? Thank you.

As the two men move closer to the doorway, Rushdie bumps into the bookstore owner, Weglarczyk, knocking down all of her books as well as the ones in his hands.

Rushdie: Oh, I'm sorry. I didn't see you there. Please let me help you.

Weglarczyk: It's all right. Nothing to worry about. This happens to me at least once a week *(smiles politely).*

Bending over to pick her books off the floor, Weglarczyk notices a book that wasn't in her pile.

Weglarczyk: *Orientalism?*

Rushdie: You've read it?

Weglarczyk: At least two times. It's a great work, written with great passion. I especially liked the fact that the author questioned various paradigms of thought that are accepted on individual, academic, and political levels.

Rushdie: I'm so thrilled to come across another individual who shares the same passion for literature as I do. Isn't this great, Orwell? Orwell, Orwell, *[frustrated sigh]* you continue to be blinded by this theory that the whale exists and we need crawl inside. I'm sorry, but I can't stand here and agree with this nonsense. Actually, I'm not sorry. I won't be quiet and accept it, or even tolerate it. You know very well that there is no such thing as staying out of politics and you yourself said so. All issues are political issues. But still you attempt to construct this device, this whale, where the ordinary man can go for comfort. You know it's all baloney. Politics is a term that includes everything you hate, but especially the dogmatism and hypocrisy that politics brings. For this reason, you want desperately to keep it out of literature and you will do and say anything to make sure it happens (Rushdie 96).

Orwell: I see literature as an escape route for people. It should take them far away from the tyranny of politics, which, by the way, they can't control. Literature can provide some worthwhile pleasure, even if it lasts for a short time. It's an escape that people need. Why would anyone want to take that away from them?

Rushdie: Why? Because there is no whale. There is no comfort zone. And, quite frankly, there shouldn't be one. Being aware of the things that are happening around you and realizing that politics fills every aspect of your life is important. We, as individuals, understand the world through politics. The ordinary person shouldn't hide inside a nonexistent whale and keep quiet. Instead, he or she should strive to achieve change for the better by fighting back and making noise along the way. It's our responsibility.

Orwell, you must help people understand that politics is important and necessary in literature. Without politics, literature would create a universe in which "nobody needs to work, or eat or hate or love or sleep" (Rushdie 100). Ordinary men cannot survive without those fundamentals, just as they cannot survive without politics. Politics is a part of our lives and it has been since the beginning of time. It's what makes us grow as individuals and it defines who we are. History enlightens us, politics transforms us, and literature brings it all together to create a new reality.

Orwell: Rushdie, the last time we encountered one another, we had precisely the same discussion. And now we will leave with the same outcome. I will never join you to help incorporate politics—and the hypocrisy it brings—into literature. Literature should provide the comfort and refuge of a large whale where the ordinary, passive man can retreat to experience the pleasure of a good story. The world is a cruel place. Why would you want to take this gift away from ordinary people? Leave them be.

Rushdie: Being an intelligent person like yourself, I cannot believe you subscribe to this theory. . . .

Orwell realizes that this disagreement cannot be resolved, for both men are stubborn and will try anything in their power to change the viewpoint of the other. As Rushdie tries to finish his statement, Orwell looks at his watch and interrupts abruptly.

Orwell: Rushdie, I would love to continue this conversation. However, I have little time to do so. Please accept my apologies. Hopefully, we can finish this some other time. It was nice seeing you again.

Before Rushdie can say anything, Orwell walks out of the bookstore. As Rushdie walks up to the cash register, he noticed that Orwell had not purchased the book after all. Instead he left it on the counter. Walking out of the store, Rushdie gets the feeling that Orwell decided to leave because he couldn't continue the conversation anymore. Rushdie knows that deep down Orwell understands there is no whale. It was something he attempted to construct to keep politics out, but realized that politics cannot be blocked out, no matter how hard one tries. It's part of life. Ironically, the last time the both of them talked, Orwell ended the conversation the same way and walked out before Rushdie could say anything.

Weglarczyk: Mr. Rushdie, would you be willing to give a reading here? I agree that it is impossible to keep politics out of literature and I'd love to bring your message to the readers who spend so much time in my store. Let's set something up.

Works Cited

George Orwell. "Inside the Whale." *Inside the Whale and Other Essays.* London: Victor Gollancz Ltd., 1940 (page citations refer to the course packet).

Salman Rushdie. *Imaginary Homelands*. London: Granta Books, 1991, pp. 87–101.

Joseph Hicks—Instructor

Joseph Hicks, instructor.

In Fall 2006, Joseph Hicks taught a first-year writing course that aimed, according to Hicks, "to teach students the fundamentals of writing, such as thesis statements, arguments, counter-arguments, and utilizing evidence, while showing students how writing is used in everyday life to debate important issues and make both political and social decisions." The course emphasized the need to create strong, coherent arguments while accounting for the various sides of a given debate. Hicks used the newspaper article as his students' entry-point into a public debate, allowing his students to choose their own articles about a current issue that they would critique directly through their argumentative papers. Hicks's writing assignments advanced from the written dialogue to the letter to the editor, followed by the argumentative essay, the proposal, and a speech, in which students were required to take a position on a current debate and argue their views.

For this proposal project, each student chose a major social or political issue affecting Chicago and developed a program to address that issue. In creating the proposal, Hicks said that "students were required to state the problem they were addressing, argue why the problem needs to be addressed, give a detailed account of how the program works, and how they plan to implement the program, include a detailed budget that accounts for the cost of the program, and a final paragraph that argues why the funds should be approved." While it was a challenge to find successful and well-written examples of the genre to share with his students, Hicks said one of the many virtues of the proposal is the exposure it gives to the concept of writing within a well-structured template while still using the creative, critical-thinking, and argumentative skills developed throughout the semester.

Joel Ebert—Writer

Joel Ebert, writer.

In the midterm elections of November 2006, many of Joel Ebert's classmates failed to vote, believing that it was *only* a relatively inconsequential midterm election. Therefore, in the proposal assignment for Joseph Hicks's first-year writing course, Ebert decided to tackle the problem of voter apathy among registered voters. Ebert brainstormed ways to increase voter turnout in Chicago, and upon conferring with Hicks, he came up with the idea of a focus issue campaign combined with a cash lottery that would increase political awareness while providing a monetary incentive for all Chicagoans to head to the polls.

Ebert crafted his proposal after careful research into voter incentives programs practiced in other cities and countries. He tailored his project to Chicago, using the city's available resources while accounting for the additional tactics and costs needed to execute and promote his project. "The proposal was one of the most challenging types of writing I've done due to its basic structure," Ebert said. The proposal required him to give a realistic assessment of the costs, keeping well within Hicks's $3 million budget, while using compelling language and logic to sell his plan to the city of Chicago.

Ebert said he always chose "pretty heavy topics" to write about for Hicks's course, but he said the proposal was the most challenging and rewarding of all. "This project required me to do a lot more analytical thinking than any of the previous topics," Ebert said. Envisioning a career, or at least some level of involvement, in politics himself, Ebert said he's grateful for having gained the experience of proposal writing.

Improving Voter Turnout in the City of Chicago

A Proposal by Joel Ebert

I. Introduction

Voter turnout has been continually decreasing, not just in Chicago, but in the United States, over the last fifty years. One must consider why this is happening. Many reasons could include citizens' failure to identify with candidates, lack of time, or just general indifference to the whole process. Countries like Australia, Belgium, and Luxembourg have implemented compulsory elections. Compulsory voting requires citizens to vote, lest they face fines or jail time, among other penalties. These countries rank among the ten best for voter turnout, with over 90% going to the polls (Niemi and Weisberg 31). By using the system of compulsory voting, individual citizens feel a greater civic duty than those of voluntary voting systems. Voter turnout around the world has slid alarmingly over the past years. This may be due to civic disengagement or overall apathy towards the whole process. If voter turnout continues to slide, the question could arise whether this democracy's electoral process fairly and equally represents the people.

II. Problem

Chicago is among the many major U.S. cities that have yielded a low voter turnout in past years. Of the 2.8 million people that reside in Chicago, nearly 1.4 million are registered voters (CNN, BoEC). Based on the information given by the Chicago Board of Elections Commissioners, only 46% of those registered actually participated in the recent midterm elections. This means that only a little more than one-quarter of the population of Chicago voted. This trend has been continuing for several years. During the 2004 primary elections, only 38% of registered voters participated (BoEC).

The dwindling voter population in Chicago needs to be addressed so that the elections reflect accurately the views and needs of the citizens of Chicago. One reason for low voter turnout might be a lack of motivation to go to the polls. If an incentives program were adopted by the Chicago City Counsel, voter turnout for future elections could increase and provide a good example for other major cities as well.

III. Objectives

The objective of this proposal is to increase voter turnout in not only presidential elections, but in primary, midterm, and local elections as well, by implementing a program that would reward citizens for their participation. Increased involvement of Chicago's citizens would yield a more effective government that would, in turn, reflect the needs and desires of the people. The balance of equality among representation of the many cultures and demographics that make up the city of Chicago would be more accurately represented. In order to yield a more effective, citizen-reflective electoral process, Chicago's citizens must participate not only in the process of voting, but in preparing to vote as well. By implementing an incentives program, citizens would be motivated to head towards the polls out of desire and not out of obligation. One problem that exists with obligatory voting is that voters do not have very much incentive to vote for one candidate over another. If a citizen is required to vote by law, he or she may simply put forth only minimal effort in preparing to vote. By implementing an incentives program, we can hope to reinstitute desire into citizens that will result in higher approval of elected officials.

IV. Schedule

What needs to be done first is to properly and effectively get citizens prepared and aware of upcoming elections. Public awareness is a major key to gaining a more effective government. Public forums and debates would yield more voting citizens due to common interests and a feeling of involvement. Helping citizens learn more about the candidates, and giving them the opportunity to challenge the candidates before they take office, could give Chicagoans much-needed knowledge before entering the polls.

Secondly, a lottery system should be implemented that would give two hundred citizens the opportunity to win $1,000 from a random drawing that they would enter upon voting. A lottery drawing would raise interest in elections and give every Chicagoan a reason to look forward to the elections. Many needy and underprivileged citizens of Chicago, who might not vote otherwise, would then have a motivation to head towards the polls on Election Day.

The final part of this proposal is to give two voting citizens the opportunity to meet with elected officials and to express concerns that are important to their community. These concerns would be addressed with a mutual agreement between the politicians and the citizens to endorse $750,000 towards solving the issue. These citizens would also be chosen through the random lottery that would be taken from the polls. This would be effective because it would give the opportunity to yield the representation of communities and groups that feel they do not have a voice in the Chicago political process.

V. Budget

- Labor:
  Election Board Officials: (no additional cost)
- Facility Rental Space: (no additional cost)
- Office Supplies: (no additional cost)
- Advertising:
  1. Billboard ($2,500.00 per month x 6 months = $15,000.00)
  2. Flyers: ($1,000.00 per month x 6 months = $6,000.00)
  3. Newspaper: ($2,000.00 per month x 6 months = $12,000.00)
  4. Internet Banners: ($500.00 per month x 6 months = $3,000.00)
  5. Text Messaging: (no additional cost)
  6. E-Mail Messaging: (no additional cost)

- Lottery Money: ($1,000.00 x 200 winners = $200,000.00)
- Focus Issue: ($750,000.00)

Total Cost: $986,000.00

VI. Budget Justification

All funds for this project would become available through reallocation of the existing city budget. This would prevent any increase in taxes or any additional fees in order to implement this proposal.

Labor—The Board of Elections Commissioners for the City of Chicago would perform all additional labor for this project, with no additional compensation required. The five members of the Board of Elections Commissioners (Chairman, Secretary, Commissioner, Executive Director, Assistant Executive Director) would perform any additional labor for this project.

Facility Rental Space—No additional costs; labor would be performed in the existing space used by the Board of Elections.

Office Supplies—No additional costs; all office supplies would be available at the current Board of Elections facility.

Advertising—Billboards, handbill flyers, and newspaper advertising will be implemented throughout the city. Internet banners on highly visited websites would increase awareness. Mass text messaging would be supplied by any willing cell phone companies for free or a minor negotiable price. E-mail messages would be sent out to all registered voters that submit contact information.

Lottery Money—200 winners would receive $1,000 each. The odds of winning would be reasonable; of the 1.4 million registered voters, if 200 won the prize money, the odds of winning would be 1 in 7,000. A $200,000 lottery purse would be a sufficient amount of money to help with the overall purpose of this project without facing a major financial concern.

Focus Issue—This money would be evenly distributed among two focus issues that would be decided upon a random lottery. The amount used for this would be significant enough to help with a given issue, while at the same time, not creating a financial concern.

All funds for this project would become available through reallocation of the existing city budget. This would prevent any increase in taxes or any additional fees in order to implement this proposal.

VI. Conclusion

This project would set Chicago apart from other major U.S. cities by increasing voter turnout, while influencing other cities to follow its example. By implementing this project, Chicago would attract the interests of other cities that might consider a similar plan to boost voter turnout. This type of project would sustain Chicago's prestige among the major metropolitan cities in the United States today. While some may say that voter turnout is a large problem that cannot be easily fixed, this project would give some incentive to the average citizen to be interested in voting again. The objection could be made that public interest will not rise with the implementation of this project; however, if the average citizen feels more directly involved in the political process, voter turnout could indeed rise as a consequence.

Chicago is a large mix of many different people and it needs to close its social gaps through fair representation of all its citizens. By implementing this plan, this gap would lessen, due to the increased interest that smaller and unequally represented groups would have by going to election polls. This plan would create a greater collective identity of Chicago, that could be stronger than that of any other major city.

This plan would set a tone for other large metropolitan cities and may raise interest in their compliance as well. The implementation of this plan would prove that Chicago can be a political and economic leader among major U.S. cities. Raising voter turnout in Chicago could help gain interest in the implementation of this process nationally as well and could yield a better, more effective national government that would cater more towards the interests of the citizens. After all, a higher voter turnout would reflect a better picture of democracy, due to an accurate depiction of whom citizens want to represent them.

Works Cited

"Best Places To Live." *CNNMoney*. 8 Nov. 2006. <http://money.cnn.com/magazines/moneymag/bplive/2006/snapshots/PL1714000.html>.

Niemi, Richard, and Herbert F. Weisberg. *Controversies in Voting Behavior.* Washington: CQ Press, 2001.

United States. Board of Election Commissioners for the City of Chicago. 8 Nov. 2006. <http://www.chicagoelections.com/>.

United States. Board of Election Commissioners for the City of Chicago. 8 Nov. 2006. <http://www.chicagoelections.com/who_votes_in_chicago.html>.

Tim Henningsen—Instructor

Tim Henningsen, instructor.

According to Tim Henningsen, his first-year writing course, "Writing in the Real World," helps students to write academically about non-academic topics. In bridging the academic and non-academic, students learn how to write about topics that are important in the real world. Students are then able to find similarities between academic argument and take a position from the evidence they gather in real-world situations. As a baseball fan, Henningsen recognized that steroid use implies a number of issues (ranging from ethical to economic to health-related) incorporating a number of arguments. Designing an argumentative writing project allowed students to carefully select information and assert their arguments.

Meghan Fleming's argumentative essay surfaced from that assignment. To prepare students for the writing project, Henningsen encouraged students to note the public forum in which their arguments would take place and to be aware that the issue was one that was not "cut and dry." Henningsen says, "Approaching a hotly-contested issue with clarity and persuasion is a tough challenge, no matter the genre or situation." Students who met and exceeded the challenges of talking and writing about the various angles in this situation were most successful.

Meghan Fleming—Writer

Meghan Fleming, writer.

Assigned an argumentative essay for her first-year writing course, Meghan Fleming chose to take the position that hard work is preferable to steroid use in Major League Baseball. Fleming wanted to show that steroid use gives players an unfair advantage that also shifts the concerns of the game from fan entertainment to players' financial gain. To help build her argument, her instructor recommended that she look at other well-known players in the past. Fleming, in her research, discovered that players like Hank Aaron were successful not only without performance-enhancing drugs, but additionally were able to overcome issues of racism.

In addition to researching baseball history, Fleming's interest in health and biology also helped inform her argument and research. Fleming says, "I also knew steroids were unhealthy and even caused thoughts of suicide, which I learned in health in high school. I therefore did research and found all the side effects, both mentally and physically, regarding the use of steroids." In her revision, Fleming paid close attention to grammar, worked on paraphrasing relevant quotes, and perfected the transitions between paragraphs throughout the paper.

Fleming states that the writing project helped her with future papers because she learned how to better incorporate her own voice and interests to strengthen her argument, as well as how to use data and statistics as a form of support. Likewise, she learned how to anticipate a naysayer to make her own argument stronger.

Baseball Should Get Tough on Steroids

An Argumentative Essay by
Meghan Fleming

The legacy of America's favorite pastime, baseball, has been called into question because of the increased use of drugs. Performance-enhancing drugs, formally known as anabolic steroids, are being used by athletes everywhere to get an edge and to bulk up. Even star players like Rafael Palmeiro tested positive for steroids. Palmeiro was on his way to the Hall of Fame with more than 3,000 hits and 500 home runs, until he was proven guilty of using this illegal drug. Now anabolic steroids' place in Major League Baseball has become an issue of concern. On the one hand, anabolic steroids are illegal and the use of an illegal drug in MLB tarnishes the legacy of the game. On the other hand, more home runs are made due to the number of players allegedly using steroids, which inevitably attracts more fans. However, by taking steroids, players may be viewed as lazy and taking the easy way out. After all, athletes like Hank Aaron obtained a place in the Hall of Fame without using steroids by working hard. Therefore, there is no need for steroids, especially if players have not used them in the past. The professional baseball players who use steroids are cheating, which tarnishes baseball's legacy, damages players' health, and sets a bad example for adolescents. Steroids should be banned from MLB, and those guilty of using them should be suspended for an entire season.

Many great players have left their mark through hard work and determination. Their work ethic and talent started an MLB legacy. Players like Babe Ruth and Hank Aaron set the standard for players like Palmeiro. In the past, however, players had to endure multiple complications. Struggling with racism, Hank Aaron received 3,000 threatening letters claiming an African American could not beat Babe Ruth's record of 714 home runs. On April 8, 1974, Hank Aaron passed Babe Ruth's record and eventually set a new record of 755 home runs. Hank Aaron received the All-Star, National League Most Valuable Player, and Gold Glove award through hard work and training. He played in an era when everything was about fair play.

Around the year 2002, the word "fair play" started to lose its meaning. Players are more concerned about getting an edge the quickest way possible, so they turn to steroids. Instead of putting that extra time and effort into their workout, they cheat and inject themselves with steroids. According to Jose Canseco, as many as "eighty-five percent of major leaguers use steroids" (Caple 1). Because many players use steroids, the playing ground has been altered and other professionals feel that is unfair. Pitcher Tom Glavine of the New York Mets states, "Those of us who don't do it, we feel like we aren't on an even playing field and that's something that shouldn't happen" ("Anabolic Steroids: An Issue in MLB" 1). If a player is doing well, then suspicion of steroid use often arises, which is not fair for those players who choose to work hard and follow the law. In fact, steroids are illegal, unless prescribed by a doctor. The players who use anabolic steroids are criminals because they tested positive to an illegal substance. For these reasons, those who abuse steroids destroy the fun, good-natured legacy of Major League Baseball.

It is a well-known fact that home runs lure more fans to games, which brings in more money for players and for the organization. Is one willing, however, to put his health at risk just for fame and fortune? Steroids have many harmful side effects. In order to understand the side effects, one must understand what anabolic steroids are. In sum, steroids are a form of testosterone that allows one to quickly build muscles ("Anabolic" 1). However, one of the many problems with steroids is that users may not experience side effects until years later. These internal side effects include liver damage, elevated cholesterol levels, clotting disorders, and, most importantly, premature heart attacks and strokes (ibid 3). External effects for males include reduced sperm count, impotence, development of the breasts, shrinking of the testicles, and difficulty or pain while urinating (ibid). Men are not the only ones using steroids. Women's side effects tend to bring about male characteristics. For instance, women may develop facial hair growth, deepening of the voice, breast reduction, and menstrual cycle changes (ibid). Less-serious effects include acne, bloated appearance, rapid weight gain, and weakened tendons (ibid). Players who use steroids put their health at risk just to be more competitive.

Steroids also have psychological risks. They can cause severe aggression, otherwise known as "roid rage." Steroids can also cause hallucinations, anxiety, and panic attacks, severe mood swings, paranoia, depression, and suicidal thoughts ("Steroids" 2). In fact, Denise Garibaldi, a mother suffering the loss of her high school son Rob, told a House committee, "there is no doubt in our minds that steroids killed our son"(Livingstone 2). The use of steroids in MLB may have contributed to the increase of steroid use among adolescents. The use of steroids among high school students has increased twofold since 1991 and continues to rise (ibid). This issue became a major concern around 2002, however, when it was reported that 42,000 students in Texas used steroids (ibid). There seems to be a correlation between the steroid use in MLB and that among high school students. MLB players are role models, and when students see that the professionals are hitting home runs and signing multi-million-dollar contracts with the help of steroids, then students may feel compelled to use steroids like the professional players. Young athletes get the impression that they should use steroids to get an edge, which will help them to win games and get sport scholarships.

The fact that steroids are an illegal drug and are constantly being used by professional baseball players, has ultimately destroyed the legacy of the game. Baseball should be about playing hard and doing one's best without anabolic steroids. MLB should not be about the money, especially if an individual risks his health just to make an extra buck. Increased steroid use in MLB not only affects the legacy of baseball but also affects younger generations. Professional baseball players should set an example for students and show them that with hard work, massive training, and a healthy diet, they could be truly great athletes.

Works Cited

"Anabolic Steroids." 6 Sept 2005. 28 Sept 2006 <http://www.espn.com/special/s/drugsandsports/steroids.html>.

"Anabolic Steroids: An Issue in Major League Baseball." *University of Michigan* 2002. 1 Oct 2006 <http://sitemaker.umich.edu/mkschmidt/should_there_be_rules_in_the_mlb_against_steroids_>.

Caple, Jim. "It's Time for Steroid Use to Finally be Addressed." *ESPN* 29 May 2002. 28 Sept 2006 <http://sports.espn.go.com/espn/print?id=1388196oftypescolumnist>.

Jenkins, Lee. "Popular Steroid Is at the Center of Palmeiro's Case." *The New York Times* 3 August 2005. 28 Sept 2006 <http://www.nytimes.com/2005/08/03/sports/baseball/03steroids.html?ei...>.

Livingstone, Seth. "Fight Against Steroids Gaining Muscle in High School Athletics." *USA Today* 8 June 2005. 28 Sept 2006 <http://www.usatoday.printthis.clickability.com/pt/cpt?action=cpt&title=USA...>.

"Palmeiro Docked 10 Days for Steroids." *ESPN* 1 Aug 2005. 28 Sept 2006 <http://sports.espn.go.com/espn/print?id=2121659&type=story>.

Schwartz, Larry. "Hank Aaron: Hammerin' Back at Racism." *ESPN* 2005. 1 Oct 2006 <http://espn.go.com/sportscentury/features/00006764.html>.

"Steroids: Play Safe, Play Fair." 1 Oct 2006 <http://www.aap.org/family/steroids.htm>.

Caroline Gottschalk-Druschke, instructor.

Bridget Sullivan, instructor.

Caroline Gottschalk-Druschke and Bridget Sullivan—Instructors

In Fall 2006, Caroline Gottschalk-Druschke and Bridget Sullivan co-taught a first-year-writing course called "Writing about Civic Engagement." The idea behind such "community-based" or "community-oriented" writing classes, explains Gottschalk-Druschke, "is not 'the city as laboratory,' but having students think about how their writing can contribute to the community, to write something that's useful not just in the classroom."

From their very first project, a feature-story, students were expected to write with a public audience in mind. Instructors encouraged students to submit articles to the student newspaper. At the beginning, Gottschalk-Druschke says, the students were nervous about the idea of writing "in, about, and for" specific communities, rather than simply for a grade. By the end of the semester, however, several had produced work—in a variety of genres—good enough to donate for use by the organizations themselves.

Kim Dwan's feature story, "Band Members Win With Respect," emerged in response to that first project, "Investigating Local Communities." To prepare Dwan and the other students, Sullivan drew on her own experiences conducting interviews and writing articles for a Chicago magazine. The two teachers also had students find examples of the feature genre to discuss in class and had them practice writing their own "openers." They encouraged students to write about communities in which they already had credibility and special knowledge. The biggest teaching challenge, Sullivan says, was getting students not only "to demonstrate expertise in what they were writing about, but also to make it translatable to those without that experience."

Kim Dwan—Writer

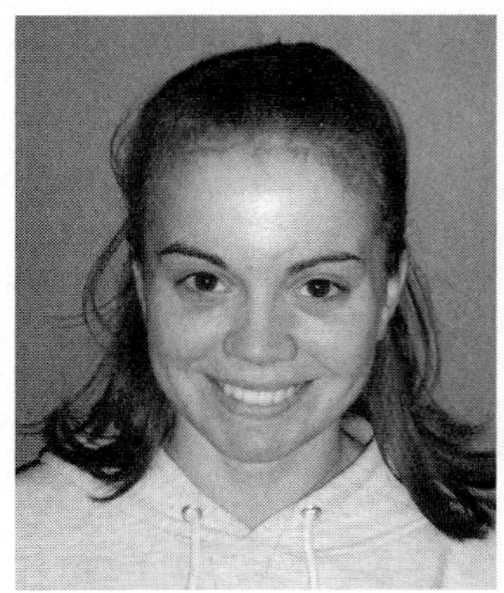
Kim Dwan, writer.

Assigned to write a feature about a local community for her first-year writing class, Kim Dwan decided she wanted to tweak people's perceptions about a group she'd been a part of in high school. "I thought it would be a cool way to approach writing about marching band—that we're competitive, but that we're not all about winning trophies. I wanted to make marching band interesting to those who don't care much about it."

To that end, Dwan interviewed a current member of the Andrew High School Marching Band, Ellen Brett, asking her about the nuts-and-bolts of practices and performances and about the students' motivations for practicing so hard. Dwan herself, now a freshman in movement science at the University of Illinois-Chicago, had been a saxophonist for three years in the same band. As her instructors had suggested, this familiarity made her writing more credible. But it also created challenges. Dwan had to do a follow-up interview to get Brett to elaborate on statements Dwan had taken for granted, like the band's motto, "Eyes With Pride," and she had to revise her feature to make it accessible to a wider audience. "I had to explain more, and not assume everyone would know what a 'set' or an 'opener' was. I never thought that much about it while I was doing it. It turned out to be a lot to write."

Later in the semester, Dwan was able to explore similar rhetorical concerns in a different genre of writing. She created a brochure she plans to give to the band to use to promote awareness and recruit new members.

Band Members Win with Respect

A Feature Story by Kim Dwan

How do you like to spend your Saturday mornings? Sleeping in until noon, watching some television, lying around until one of your friends calls you to go out?

How would you like to start your Saturday morning at 7:00 or 8:00 with this: "Everyone run two laps around the field, then get into the block for stretches, then we're going to do half an hour of basics, then line up on the first page of the opener and we're going to clean the opener a set at a time, then by the end we want to do run-throughs of the entire show."

This is a normal routine for the members of the Victor J. Andrew Marching Band of Tinley Park. This award-winning marching band has been known throughout the years for its interesting shows, respect towards other bands, a winning-isn't-everything attitude, and a policy that everyone marches. There are no bench-warmers.

According to Ellen Brett, a senior and a section leader of the saxophones, Saturday mornings are not the only time the band rehearses. "We practice on Tuesdays from 3:30 to 5:45, Wednesdays from 6:00 to 9:15, Thursdays from 3:30 to 5:45, and Friday the saxophones have sectionals from 3:30 to 4:30, plus football games. Saturdays are from 8:00 to 2:00, or 7:00 to 1:00," she said.

The band has a seven- to eight-minute field show that consists of a fast piece called an "opener," a slow piece referred to as a "ballad," and another fast piece known as a "closer."

All of the different pieces in the show are made up of sets, which specify where to march and what measures to play. During practice, the sets must be "cleaned": first students practice the march, counting out loud, then they practice the music for the set, then they put the marching and music together. Once that set is clean, the students move on to the next set until they get through the entire movement. At competitions, the band is judged on music, their marching, general effect, and visual effect. In other words, the judges are observing to see if everyone is marching in step. Are they using the same technique? Are their toes high enough? Are the members' postures correct and uniform? Does the music sound melodic? Are the formations readable from the skybox? And how does the color guard help with the visual aspect of the show?

What drives these students to put so much time and effort into this organization? When Ellen was asked this question, she simply replied, "The legacy of our band has been 'Eyes With Pride' from the beginning, and we have always wanted to teach and earn respect more than win trophies. The Andrew Marching Band has a reputation that has grown over the years. People know who we are."

What exactly does "Eyes With Pride" mean? Ellen paused to think about her response. Finally she explained, "Eyes With Pride represents the attitude that we bring onto the field. An attitude that shows people 'you can't touch us, we're Andrew High School.' When you look into our eyes before we perform, people can tell that nothing can stop us from owning the field."

Members of this organization feel that it's different from any other group at Andrew High School. "You work through the entire summer and fall towards a common goal; you work as a team and become more of a family," Ellen said.

In this organization, members have to do more than just show up to practice. Each member has a number of responsibilities, and if these responsibilities are not fulfilled, the entire band will suffer. Ellen elaborated: "The responsibilities of each member are that they arrive on-time and ready-to-work. They also must memorize their charts and music. If a person is unable to do this, it brings down the entire band."

In other words, if somebody is not in his or her correct position on the field, everyone will be off in the formation. Everybody depends on everybody else.

With all of these practices and responsibilities, what about their academic responsibilities? Ellen smirked and brought up one of the members' favorite expressions: "School is not an excuse for band, and band is not an excuse for school."

The members are not allowed to make excuses for their academic performance, and the staff, some of who work as faculty at the high school, will find out if the students' grades are dropping or if students are using band as an excuse not to do their school-work. So between the practices, football games, parades, and competitions, homework still must be done, and grades must be kept up.

Though the band sounds like it is its own separate community, it's still a major part of the Tinley Park community as a whole. "This organization brings 160 students to the Andrew population that know how to respect their teachers and community, and it brings a sense of pride to the school that so many students work together as a team," Ellen said.

This group of high school students has made this organization something special. They work together to create an amazing field show not to win trophies, but to earn respect and to learn the value of hard work.

Being a member of this organization, "I get to make 160 best friends," said Ellen, "and I get a family that I can always count on. I also learn respect, integrity, and the value of working hard."

Charlyne Sarmiento—Instructor

Charlyne Sarmiento, Instructor.

As a means to establish an understanding of the argumentative essay genre, Charlyne Sarmiento used the genre of dialogue as the assignment immediately preceding. This was an opportunity for students to begin developing the conversation they would be entering for their later argumentative essay. The goal of the dialogue assignment was to get students to understand that making an argument also means acknowledging what other people are saying. In other words, the objective was for students to explore and listen not only to their own arguments, but also to what others are saying in this conversation. The situation students responded to revolved around the complex subject of art and misrepresentation—the responsibility of an artist or author to their audience, and the consequence of blurring the line between art and politics. Charlyne's students read and discussed articles addressing controversies stemming from the misrepresentation of race or gender in the media, and the responsibility that authors or artists have to their audience. The students' first goal was to identify their argumentative position in response to controversy.

The assignment allowed students to take creative license in imagining with reason how naysayers or supporters would respond to their thesis, as well as to each other. Charlyne describes the process: 'As my English class focused in on concepts of rhetoric, I explained that by setting up a fictional dialogue between themselves and their sources, they would be practicing the art of rhetoric, an important tool that would prepare them to write their next writing assignment—the argumentative essay.' The learning goals for this project dovetailed from their basic understanding of rhetoric: Finding the available arguments suited for the given situation. 2.) Clearly communicating the perceptions of each character that you decided to include in your dialogue. 3.) Understanding that as human beings we all perceive the world differently, and disagreements are inevitable.

Essentially, the purpose of this project was to get students to understand that their argumentative essay is not writing for writing's sake. Instead, she urged students to consider that writing is consequential and that by entering a conversation with others who both support and counter their argument, they are making academic moves that create complex and meaningful writing. Charlyne says that Daisy's dialogue 'succeeds because not only does she fairly represent her characters, but she also actively referees the conflicts among them, which drives her to articulate her own stance in the conversation that takes place, a step that takes her closer to creating an argumentative thesis.'

Daisy Soto—Student

Daisy Soto, Student.

In her dialogue, 'Toys and Culture', Daisy Soto chose to respond to the article written by Joe Piasecki, 'The New Americana: David Gonzales and his Homies pay a visit to the Pasadena Museum of California Art.' David Gonzales, the creator of the Homies, argues that his toys—like any toys—were meant to entertain. Others have criticized Gonzales for the influence the dolls might have on young children, some going so far as to suggest that the dolls celebrate gang life and violence. Daisy, meanwhile, wonders about what sorts of influence Barbie might have on the same children. In her eyes, the Homies dolls represent parts of Hispanic culture, and she says 'they resemble the people we have grown up around and are accustomed to seeing in our neighborhoods.'

In class, Daisy had read an article by Joe Piasecki that dealt with Gonzales and the Homies, and she wanted to dig deeper into the subject, because of what she thought of as a 'common misconception that if Latinos, or members of any other ethnicity, look as if they are part of a gang and do not dress according to the social norms then they cannot have a positive effect on the community.'

The experience of writing and thinking about this issue has taught her something about misrepresentation in the media. 'Back in the old days the only thing toys were good for was to entertain children. Now they are turning into a form of art or ways to represent culture. People are not used to this idea and it scares them that the world is changing so much that even the little things that seemed to be of no significance before are evolving into a more complex issue.' As the ending of her dialogue indicates, she believes that 'it is the job of the parents to monitor what their child is exposed to,' and her dialogue suggests that parents will have the final word on the matter.

Toys and Culture

A Dialogue by Daisy Soto

On a bright Saturday afternoon, Lety planned a birthday party for her daughter who had just turned seven. Among her guests were the creator of the Homies characters, David Gonzales, and the creator of Barbie, Ruth Handler. At around 6 o'clock in the afternoon, the children attending the birthday party start to become restless and bored. In an effort to regain the children's interest, Samantha's mom, Lety, decides it was time to open the gifts. The children sit on the floor surrounding Samantha as the adults huddle close behind them in order to get a better view of the gifts. Ruth Handler and David Gonzales, accidentally bump elbows and turn to apologize:

Gonzales: Excuse me, I'm so sorry. Ruth, what a pleasant surprise.

Handler: Oh, David I hadn't recognized you. How are you?

Gonzales: Fine, thank you. I'm just here trying to get a better view of the gifts.

Handler: So was I.

At that point, Samantha opened the gift that came from Handler. It was a Barbie doll with a convertible car. After applause from the children, she handed it to her mother to put in the rest of the pile. The next gift came from Gonzales. He had given her a couple of Homie character figures and some Homie school supplies. There was the same applause and again, and Samantha handed the toy to her mother in order to continue with the gifts.

Handler: Do you believe that is an appropriate toy for a six year old child?

Gonzales: Why wouldn't it be? There is nothing wrong with it. It is just a toy.

Handler: Yes, but it is a toy that glorifies gang life. Is that the message you are trying to give little children? That gang life is so cool, they are making toys about it?

Gonzales: None of my characters are gang members. If you were to look at my website you can see that each character has a positive influence on the community. They just decide to look a different way from what is expected, which is more than I can say for your Barbie doll.

Handler: Barbie also has a positive effect on the community. I 'invented an American icon that functions as both a steady outlet for girls' dreams and an ever changing reflection of American society.' (Ament) Barbie gives girls a sense of security and the possibility of developing a secure future just like Barbie's.

Gonzales: That is true. Barbie does represent a positive lifestyle, but it does not represent the only one. Latino people did not grow up around people who looked like Barbie or Ken. We grew up with people who looked like the Homies.

Lety: He's right.

Gonzales and Handler had become so involved with their conversation, they failed to realize that the opening of the gifts was over. The kids were already going crazy with Samantha's new toys and Lety who had been nearby overheard their conversation and decided to join it.

Lety: Growing up, I played with Barbie. I always thought that she was so beautiful and perfect that I wanted to be just like her. Of course that was just a dream. The reality is that not everyone looks like that or lives that life.

Handler: That is the point. Barbie gives girls something to dream about.

Lety: What happens when the dreams don't come true? Should they keep trying until it does?

Gonzales: That is why I created Homies. They are a reality. They are people you see all over the countries in different communities. People I grew up with who did not turn to gang life to get what they wanted. Instead, they made something out of themselves. The only difference is that they dress and look a certain way not acceptable to society and often stereotyped in a negative way. That is exactly what I wanted to show when creating these figures. I wanted people to see the other part of society not just the traditional side. Each one of my characters has a story behind it. If you go online, you can see that they each have a job that has a positive affect on our community.

Handler: But not everyone knows who these characters are trying portray. Six year old children can not access the internet or even read the profiles for these characters.

Lety: That is where we, the parents, come in. It is up to us to monitor what our children are exposed to. We are living in an ever-changing world. This means were are going to be exposed to a number of things over the years that we are not accustomed to and instead of shutting it out, we should try to understand it. Not everyone is the same and we shouldn't be scared of the things we don't know about.

At that moment Lety's eldest daughter calls her from inside the house and she leaves the creators conversing.

Handler: I know we shouldn't be afraid of change, but we shouldn't embrace it so openly. The idea that these toys are on display in the Pasadena Museum of Art is ridiculous. What were you trying to convey with this. Did you think that if you can pass these things off as art that you would start a movement of some sort in favor of the Latino community?

Gonzales: 'It's a toy, not a social movement, not a political movement. It was meant to entertain, to make people smile and laugh' (Piasecki). Society has taken it upon itself to turn my creation into a cultural controversy. I only used my Hispanic background to defend my Homies. They shouldn't be seen as a negative example for children.

Handler: Then you shouldn't have dressed your characters as hoodlums who look like they dropped out of school and are doing nothing productive.

Gonzales: Actually that just goes to show that you shouldn't judge a book by its cover. My Homies are trying to encourage kids to stay in school. I even have images of my Homies on school supplies. 'I've got Homies in a classroom setting. So now Homies make school cool.'

Handler: Do you really think that having these characters are going to help children want to stay in school?

Gonzales: I do. It helps students to see ordinary people, people they see around their communities', progressing in life and doing what parents are trying to make them do.

Lety comes out of the house with the cake in her hands and walks over to where Gonzales and Handler were still holding their conversation.

Lety: Well, I hate to cut things short but I believe it is time to cut the cake. I do wish you could both join us in singing Happy Birthday to my impressionable young child.

Works Cited

Ament, Phil. 'BARBIE® DOLL.' The Great Idea Finder. 1 Mar. 2006. 27 Oct. 2008 <http://www.ideafinder.com/site/author.htm>.

Piasecki, Joe. 'The New Americana.' Pasadena Weekly, January 3, 2008.

Aaron Krall—Instructor

Aaron Krall, Instructor.

In Fall 2008, Aaron Krall taught a first-year writing course focused on 'Locating Writing in Urban Life.' The course created opportunities for writing through an examination of the tensions that structure contemporary urban life and explored the ways these tensions demand certain kinds of texts. The idea was to study how writing positions individuals in social life and how these positions are mapped onto the environments of modern cities. Krall's students investigated controversies in Chicago, including the city's bid for the 2016 Olympics, the construction of urban memorials, and the funding of the CTA.

The argumentative essay asked students to consider the use of 'historical district' designations as a strategy for maintaining economic viability and community cohesion, as well as a site of struggle between individual and social rights. The context for this examination was an article for the magazine Preservation Chicago about a conflict between homeowners in the neighborhood of Lincoln Park. The Sheffield Landmark District had been proposed to prevent the destruction of old residential buildings and the development of new high-rise condominiums, but neighborhood support was not unanimous. After reading essays on the benefits and limitations of 'historical districts,' students developed their own position on the Sheffield proposal.

Oliver Codd—Student

Oliver Codd, Student.

Oliver Codd's essay is effective because it skillfully navigates the complexity of the situation, while making a strong and well-supported argument. It contextualizes and analyzes the available evidence to explain multiple perspectives, and it reaches a well-reasoned conclusion that specifically targets its audience in the preservation community. In short, the essay successfully mobilizes writing to intervene in an urban conflict that involves conflicting interests and competing understandings of the common good.

After doing research as a class about the Sheffield Landmark district, Aaron Krall's students had to take a position on the issue and then argue why they had chosen the better side. Oliver learned from his research that there is a long and tedious process that goes into making a neighborhood a historic landmark district and that there are many conflicts surrounding this issue. Landmark designations offer many benefits but also create restrictions; this conflict is what divides people on the issue of preservation. While Oliver recognizes the validity of both positions, he chose, after extensive research, to make a persuasive argument in favor of historical preservation.

Oliver found Aaron Krall's focus on Chicago in English 160 enjoyable. He learned 'a lot of interesting things about Chicago that I didn't already know.' The curriculum's focus on civic and urban issues forced Oliver to expand his understanding of his city. Oliver's advise to new 160 students? Find a way to write about something you are interested in: 'It's a lot easier to write a strong and compelling paper when you actually believe in what you're writing about and feel passionate about the issue.'

The Sheffield Landmark District: Let's Preserve the Idea of Preservation

An Argumentative Essay by Oliver Codd

Early in 2004 a group of DePaul University neighborhood residents proposed the creation of a landmark district after many of them had voiced concerns about the increasing development and construction in their area coupled with the destruction of several historic buildings. According to Preservation Chicago, a city-wide non-profit organization supporting historical protection, these concerns were not unfounded. The Sheffield National Register District was among the largest and best preserved neighborhoods displaying urban Victorian architecture in the Midwest until the recent development ('Chicago's' 2). Although the district's title is the result of being nationally recognized as an area of historical and architectural importance, Preservation Chicago points out that this designation does not regulate development or prohibit the destruction of buildings in the area ('Chicago's' 1). On the other hand, a landmark district designation in the city of Chicago is the only one that prevents demolition of buildings erected within the 'period of significance,' the time frame of historical importance that is characteristic of that area (Preservation Chicago, '31' 2-3). Despite the undeniable need to protect the remaining historic buildings in the DePaul neighborhood, there is considerable debate among its residents as to whether to push for the creation of a landmark district. It is clear that passing the Sheffield Landmark District would benefit the local community and Chicago as a city, yet many residents resist preservation because of unfounded fears and misinformed concerns. The debate continues partly because the residents have not had access to all the facts surrounding the issue, but also because community organizations and leaders are unwilling to take a firm, unified position on the matter.

In the 1970s two community organizations—the Sheffield Neighborhood Association and the RANCH Triangle Association—were founded in that area to preserve the historic district. But ironically, now neither one of these groups is willing to take a stance on the proposed creation of the landmark district, which means neighborhood supporters of historical preservation must fend for themselves (Preservation Chicago 'Chicago's' 1). Alby Gallun reports in 'Lincoln Park historic plan cheers landowners; But preservationists boo alderman's proposal, cite tainted process,' that preservation supporters face opposition with a large number of residents who are backed by the community group Voters and Owners Coalition against Landmarking (VOCAL 1). In addition, 43rd Ward Alderman Vi Daley has taken a neutral position on the issue. Although in 2003 she acted to preserve the commercial part of the neighborhood by creating the Armitage/Halsted Landmark District, she is not currently supporting the proposed Sheffield Landmark District. This time around, Daley only pushed for landmark status for four city blocks in the neighborhood: the 800 block of West Belden, the 2100 block of North Bissell, and the 2100–2200 blocks of North Fremont. And 32nd Ward Alderman Theodore Matlak is not in favor of landmarking for his portion of the proposed district (Gallun 1).

So where does this leave the residents, both supporters and opponents of the designation, and how should this matter ultimately be resolved? Creating the Sheffield Landmark

District in Lincoln Park would undoubtedly benefit the community and its members and to some extent, the entire city of Chicago by preserving real and clearly identifiable assets. The only loss to the community would be one of potential: new development. On the other hand, not creating the landmark would result in the loss of many of the historical buildings, and it is currently unclear how the community would benefit from this decision. Tearing down historic buildings in the name of new development would permanently scar the integrity of the neighborhood and eventually erode its unique charm. Once these buildings are gone, they are gone forever and they can only be replicated, never brought back. In addition, residents and businesses in the neighborhood would only benefit financially from the landmark designation in the long term, as a result of the maintenance of property values and the promotion of economic development in a historically recognized area, as stated in the Chicago Landmarks Ordinance (cityofchicago.org 5). But perhaps most importantly, it seems that many residents of the area have not had the opportunity to hear both sides of the debate, resulting in opponents of the designation basing their decision on inaccurate or incomplete information (Gallun 1).

One of the reasons people argue against making the area a historic district is they fear it would limit home owners' freedom to decorate and renovate according to their individual tastes. But this is not necessarily the case. The Chicago Commission on Landmarks (CCL) was founded in 1968 by the City Council and assigned the responsibility of recommending and designating specific buildings and districts in Chicago for historic preservation and legal protection (cityofchicago.org). The Landmarks Ordinance and the Rules and Regulations of the Commission on Chicago Landmarks is a 50-page booklet published by the CCL with excerpts from the Municipal Code of Chicago pertaining to landmarks. The booklet outlines specific guidelines for homeowners of landmarked buildings regarding what they may or may not do to their properties. Preservation Chicago posts a summarization of these guidelines in '31 Landmarking FAQs' and points out that only buildings designated as historically significant are affected by the rules, and only those parts of the buildings open to public view are restricted. Therefore, home owners have the freedom to do anything to any part of their house that is not in public view, which means the backs and sides of buildings are an open canvas. Furthermore, the commission has no set color palette so home exteriors can be painted any color and the interiors are also open to any kind of renovation or decoration. Landscaping and sidewalk construction is allowed as long as any historic fences or garden walls remain intact (2-3, 8).

Another potential concern for residents is that of expense. One might assume that a homeowner of a landmarked building would be expected to make repairs to the home that he or she might not otherwise make. And while it is true that if your home has a broken window, for example, it must be replaced with one that matches its original style and form, it is not the case that a homeowner would be required to restore his or her home to its original state at the time it was built. Preservation Chicago makes it clear that the only requirement is that the home be maintained according to the minimum building code standard, but this rule applies to all homes in the city of Chicago, regardless of landmark status ('31' 5). Moreover, if a homeowner chooses to make major restorations that are consistent with the designated time period, not only will the CCL provide guidelines and assistance, but the homeowner would most likely qualify for at least one tax break. Depending on the extent and nature of the renovations, homeowners may be entitled to tax breaks administered by the Illinois Historic Preservation Agency for up to 8 years (Preservation Chicago, '31' 2-3, 5).

Perhaps more important, there are many who believe the residents of the neighborhood in question have not had the opportunity to hear both sides of debate. Preservation Chicago President Jonathan P. Fine believes that in meetings held by Alderman Daley to discuss the issue, not all the homeowners involved heard arguments in favor of landmarking the area. He states, 'The playing field was not level, and the alderman allowed a climate of misinformation to exist' (Gallun 2). Gallun reports that members of VOCAL have expressed concerns that passing the designation would place too much power in the hands of city administrators (1). But the Landmarks Ordinance lays out very clear guidelines and rules on landmarking to which bureaucrats and homeowners alike would be expected to adhere (cityofchicago.org). Before the city makes any definitive decision on the landmarking issue, additional meetings should be held by local aldermen so that community members can be given the opportunity to hear all relevant information surrounding the matter.

The proposed designation of the Sheffield Landmark District remains a topic of heated debate, with one alderman unwilling to take a firm position, the other opposing the preservation, and community members divided over the issue. To complicate matters further, some residents who would be affected by the designation have not had the opportunity to hear all the information surrounding the issue, particularly the arguments in favor of landmarking. Creating a landmark district is not only beneficial to the designated area, but to the entire city. The historic districts embody the heritage and culture of Chicago and give it a unique flavor. Properties increase in value in landmarked districts because they are much desired, owing to the beauty and reputation of the area. Establishing and maintaining these districts is vital because it attracts business, prospective homeowners, and tourists, all of which contribute to the city's economy. The community has clearly identifiable assets to preserve if the designation is approved, and very real treasures to be lost if it is not. On the other hand, the potential losses to the community from landmarking are only hypothetical, and the gains from not passing the designation are equally uncertain. Therefore, it is reasonable to propose that additional meetings be held so that community members can make an informed decision.

Works Cited

Cityofchicago.org. 'Landmarks Ordinance and the Rules and Regulation of the Commission on Chicago Landmarks.' 10 Sept. 2007. 30 Sept. 2008. <http://www.cityofchicago.org/Landmarks/pdf/Landmarks_Ordinance.pdf>.

Gallun, Alby. 'Lincoln Park historic plan cheers landowners; But preservationists boo alderman's proposal, cite tainted process.' *Crain's Chicago Business* 14 Oct. 2005.

Preservation Chicago. 'Chicago's Seven Most Threatened Buildings: Sheffield Historic District.' 2005. 18 Sept. 2008. <http://www.preservationchicago.org>.

Preservation Chicago. '31 Landmarking FAQs.' 1 Nov. 2005. 30 Sept. 2008. <http://www.preservationchicago.org>.

Jennifer Moore—Instructor

Jennifer Moore, Instructor.

In teaching the manifesto in her English-160 course Writing Across Culture, Jennifer Moore emphasizes not only that the genre implies a necessity for public engagement, but also that it stems from a group's desire to achieve greater visibility. According to Moore, 'each manifesto makes a claim about the necessity for (often radical) change.' In her view, the manifesto project encourages students to provoke change from within their own everyday situations, affording writers the opportunity to directly engage an audience.

'For this project,' Moore mentions, 'I encouraged students to consider a group or cause of interest to them and to compose a manifesto that speaks to the situation and goals of that group.' By prompting the members of her class to think deeply about how the needs of one's readership will influence how one writes, in the manifesto project, she expects students to identify a problematic issue. The end goal of such a writing project, according to Moore, is to give this issue 'greater visibility in the world.'

The effectiveness of 'The First Immigration Manifesto' lies in the way that Agnieszka Koleczek sheds light on the issue of immigrants' rights by carefully considering the subject at hand, the conventions of the genre, and the appropriate language with which to engage her audience. 'What makes Agnieszka's manifesto successful,' according to Moore,' is its level of directness, its clarity of construction and logical framework, and its sense of its own argument; she also anticipates her reader's reactions and questions, and responds in kind.' Undoubtedly, Koleczek's manifesto succeeds because its author is attentive to the situation of those for whom she speaks, as well as to the consequences that her writing will enact.

Agnieszka Koleczek—Student

Agnieszka Koleczek, Student.

By writing her manifesto 'as a response to the diverse, multicultural city that Chicago is, and to its large population of immigrants,' Agnieszka Koleczek hopes that, 'people will become more aware of the issue and truly realize how difficult life can get for an illegal immigrant.' For Koleczek, 'The First Immigration Manifesto' follows directly from her own situation and experiences in the city of Chicago, and she mentions that she can sympathize with those immigrating to the United States.

'From my own personal experience and from people around me,' says Koleczek, 'I know how hard the process of migrating is and how hard people struggle to achieve their American Dream.' Identifying an issue that has significantly shaped her everyday life in Chicago, she hopes that this manifesto will work as a call-to-action, perhaps even sparking debate on both sides of the issue.

So for this assignment, Koleczek examined her own situation as well as the consequences that 'The First Immigration Manifesto' might have. The outcome of her careful planning and thinking is a manifesto that opens 'some people's eyes to an issue that our nation is currently facing and to the bigger problems that will evolve in the future,' and that thoughtfully illustrates her argument. Reading over Koleczek's manifesto, one cannot help but sympathize with those immigrating to the United States, perhaps because her work is so clearly informed by the situation from which she writes and the consequences that she hopes to produce.

The First Immigration Manifesto

The United States of America was formed under the **American Constitution** and by its rights this country was supposed to be a ***FREE COUNTRY***. Indeed, it is a free nation, but only to its legal citizens. It is clearly stated in the Declaration of Independence that **'All men are created equal.'** Thus, why is this country **not *FREE* to everyone?** By everyone we meant to include not only legal but also illegal citizens. Why are the borders constantly being closed to new visitors who are without a visa? Why is the illegal immigrant population of the United States estimated to be ***12 MILLION PEOPLE*** (Knickerbocker 2)?

The main reason is that the government does not accept illegal immigrants and those people are forced to wait for years and years in order to receive their legal papers. We do not want to wait for a ***CHANGE***, we want a change now and we want the law to be changed ***TODAY!*** We are a group of illegal citizens of the United States and we are speaking not only to the illegal population of this country but to the population as a whole! **WE ARE DETERMINED TO HAVE A**

Revolution!!!

All people living in the United States are immigrants. Even the people who call themselves American are the ***DESCENDANTS OF IMMIGRANTS!*** This country started to function economically because of immigrants coming here from all over the world. When the pilgrims came to the new land, there was no order and no **one was required to have American citizenship.** Later on, when the government was well established, people needed to make regulations and in order to do so they introduced the idea of ***visa, green card, and citizenship***. Yes, the government was thinking in a way that many of you might think right now: **WE CANNOT HAVE AN OVERPOPULATED COUNTRY.** But **WHY** was the process of waiting for a green card so much shorter in the past than it is now? As the population grew larger we needed to make more restrictions in the laws, and by having people wait longer, we assumed that fewer people would be willing to come to our country. As a result, do **YOU** know what happens **NOW?** Thousands of illegal immigrants are waiting to receive legal papers for even as long as ***FIFTEEN YEARS!***

Furthermore, the US government wants to **get rid of all of the illegal citizens** without fully taking to a consideration the huge **impact** that immigrants have on the **American economy.** Did **YOU** ever imagine how a day would look like without immigrants and who would take over their jobs? The jobs that many of them take for a **minimum wage** are the building blocks of our economy. Those kinds of jobs involve tasks like **housekeeping, cleaning, landscaping,** and many more. Who else will work for minimum wage, which is $7.75 in the state of Illinois and $6.55 at the federal level ('Minimum' 8)? Well educated Americans with bachelor's degrees? Would **YOU** work as a housekeeper for $7.75? In this case, salaries would need to be brought up to at least an average wage, and today's average pay would need to be increased to a higher pay, and so on. This would **ruin the economy!**

Therefore, there are many **problems** that the **general public does not recognize.** The **life** of an illegal immigrant **looks** no better than this. **JUST IMAGINE.** You wake up ***every morning,*** worrying that someone will come to your house and deport you to your country. You go through the day, worrying that you have an ***illegal job*** and that you have to work for ***minimum wage.*** You are extra careful to not get sick because you realize that without a legal job there is ***no insurance.*** You worry that when your children grow up, they might **not** be able to get a ***higher education,*** even though they might have a desire to do so. There **are** many universities across the United States that ***REQUIRE*** **legal papers** in order to be **accepted** to the school. Even if an illegal student is accepted, just imagine trying to pay for college without any extra source of money, and without any help of ***scholarships or loans.*** Many illegal students deserve scholarships because of their high grades and academic accomplishments, but they are not eligible to apply for any financial aid! On top of everything, you **CANNOT** go anywhere; you **CANNOT** cross the border to another country, because you will **NOT** be allowed to come back. Taking everything to a consideration, the life of an illegal immigrant is **full of worries** and ***NO PRIVILEGES.***

The First Immigration Manifesto: The Declaration of October 3, 2008.

Here is what we demand from the government to change TODAY!

- Let illegal immigrants work legally.
- Let their children be educated with the help of scholarships and loans for any children with the greatest needs and highest grade point average.
- Do not deport anyone to their own country for no reason.
- Make all illegal immigrants legal citizens of the United States of America, within five years of applying for citizenship. Shorten the period of waiting for legal papers to two years.

We need a REVOLUTION! We need a CHANGE! We need more organizations! We need to **UNITE** in order to make a difference! As a united group, we can make a difference in the lives of those who live besides us. We need to **ACT NOW!** We need to start a massive strike and do it just before the eyes of the government. If we do not make it obvious, the government might be as blind to our needs as an owl is blind in the daylight. We need to give other people the opportunity to live where they want to live! Why not make a difference ***TODAY?***

The First Immigration Manifesto was written by Agnes Koleczek.

Below are signatures of people who contributed their efforts and worked on the above manifesto:

Yashmine Christner

Ivann Mckinston

Elwood Clewett

Ellery Parkinson

Julia Endsley

Martha Ring

Ellis Gonterez

Luke Sadley

Shaw Hawkins

Isa Schrader

David Holmeno

Dara Stontewer

Ásta Lopez

Alexander Warren

And many others . . .

Works Cited

Knickerbocker, Brad. 'Illegal immigrants in the US: How many are there?' *The Christian Science Monitor.* Posted 2006. Retrieved 01 Oct. 2008. <http://www.csmonitor.com/2006/0516/p01s02-ussc.html>.

'Minimum Wage Laws in the States—July 24, 2008' *U.S Department of Labor.* Posted 2008. Retrieved 01 Oct. 2008. <http://www.dol.gov/esa/minwage/america.htm>.

'US law relating to dual citizenship' *Dual citizenship FAQ.* Posted 2008. Retrieved 01 Oct. 2008. <http://www.richw.org/dualcit/law.html#INA>.

Jason Schneider—Instructor

Jason Schneider, Instructor.

In the Fall of 2008, Jason Schneider led an English 160 course which asked students to consider the ways in which language and rhetoric shape the situations and conversations of our everyday lives. The course touched on issues ranging from intellectual property in the music business to life in the workplace to the effectiveness of the college curriculum. In each case, Schneider challenged his students to view writing in various genres as an opportunity to clarify and complicate the way they saw themselves as an integral part of society. One of the central goals of Jason's teaching, then, involved helping students 'learn to think carefully about the situated nature of all uses of language and to develop some of the resources needed to communicate effectively in various contexts.'

To this end, students were asked to submit a portfolio at the end of the semester as evidence that they were prepared to move forward in their writing study. As a part of this final portfolio students were asked to include a cover letter explaining the progress they had made in the course, the subject matter, and the merit of their work. This piece, in many ways, came to represent the kind of situation Schneider's class was designed to prepare students for: a real situation in which effective communication has real consequences. As you can see, Jaime Gamboa's letter represents a particularly successful act of dealing with such a situation using both the conventions of a given genre, and the combination of personal and public conversations.

Jaime Gamboa—Student

Jaime Gamboa, Student.

Jaime Gamboa's motivation for writing a quality cover letter came from a rather unexpected place. When sitting down to write the letter he was reminded of the handful of times he had picked up a CD, looked at the cover art, and put it down because it was not what he expected. He figures 'if this artist is not willing to create a well-thought out cover, what can I expect from their music?' This is exactly the mentality he brought to writing his cover letter, understanding that this first impression could make or break the First Year Writing Program Portfolio Committee's decision to approve or deny his work.

Initially nervous about the process, Gamboa stuck to what he had learned in class. He explains that 'English 160 taught me how to always find a personal point of interest while writing so I decided to write about myself and my English 160 class in a natural and honest way, instead of forcing words into the letter trying to get the committee to like it.' The outcome of this decision resulted in not only the approval of his portfolio, but a cover letter that is clear, interesting, and effective.

Gamboa has since taken full advantage of his acceptance into English 161 and continues to reap the benefits of bringing personal interests into the writing process. Teamed up again with Jason Schneider, Jaime, an avid karate instructor, is currently working on an academic research paper which argues that inner-city youth should have better access to extra-curricular activities like martial arts. His advice to other writers is to 'always find a point of interest on any topic in order to write in a natural way, just like if you were having a one on one conversation with someone.'

Portfolio Cover Letter

By Jaime Gamoa

Jaime Gamboa
123 Composition Lane
Chicago, Illinois 65432

May 11, 2009

First Year Writing Program Portfolio Review Committee
University of Illinois at Chicago
601 South Morgan Street
Chicago, Illinois 60607

Dear Portfolio Review Committee:

I had always thought that college English would be extremely difficult. This was especially the case when I moved to America from Mexico just before entering high school and was placed into an ESL program during my freshman year there. Now, four years later, I have almost completed my first college writing class and can say that, although it was hard, the experience has been both very rewarding and enjoyable. Frankly, I would have never imagined that I could become so interested in writing about topics such as intellectual property, the college curriculum, and the music industry—just to name a few. Plus, in spite of the short time I have been living in America, I can honestly say that with a good deal of diligent practice and the help of my instructor I feel that have successfully made it through the process of learning and exploring a new language that I have now adopted as my own. The enclosed portfolio represents this success and includes two samples which, in my opinion, best embody my interests and talents as a writer.

The first piece is an argumentative essay which claims that universities could help their students prepare for the difficulties of academic and professional life in a more detailed way. The essay begins with an outline of what I see as the current plan for student preparation focusing in on three areas which I feel are problematic: use of freshman orientation and placement tests for choosing coursework, the existence of non-credit courses, and an overabundance of general education courses. I then propose that by better selecting admission criteria, eliminating placement essays, replacing general orientations with 'vocational orientations,' and increasing major-specific courses while decreasing the general education course load, universities could more efficiently and effectively prepare their students for the professional world

The second sample is an opinion paper, which turned out to be my favorite piece of writing from English 160. The topic for this work is intellectual property as it relates to the music industry. I have been very passionate about music my entire life, and this piece gave me the opportunity to write on a recent issue that I find truly disturbing for this field. I argue that record companies have taken sole possession of the music industry and, as a result, artists and bands are not getting what is rightfully theirs. In this piece, I explain how not only the record companies, but also promoters, concert managers, and ticket sellers have damaged the music industry by inflating prices and decreasing music quality. Ultimately, I am of the opinion that music should be considered an art form instead of a global business and end by pointing out some of the benefits of treating it that way. By putting music back in the hands of the artists, the profit-oriented business model that I feel is responsible for inflated prices and lowered quality would diminish and the industry could thrive.

In the end, these papers represent more than just the product of my work, they are evidence that I have come a long way in learning what it takes to write a good academic paper. In each case, these essays benefited a great deal from the drafting process because each revision of my original work allowed me to brainstorm about my ideas in new and creative ways. The process of writing and rewriting my ideas got me to the point where I could describe exactly how I thought college could create better prepared students and how music could be seen as an art form. I believe this sustained effort to edit and rethink my work with each new draft is reflected in the quality of my writing and is a habit I intend to keep.

In sum, I respectfully request that the committee consider these two writing pieces as both fulfillment of the English 160 requirement and opportunities for me to express my opinions and offer solutions to a set of complex problems that exist outside of the classroom. Thank you for your time and effort in reviewing my work and I look forward to hearing from you.

Sincerely,
Jaime Gamboa

UNIT I

Reading and Writing Rhetorically

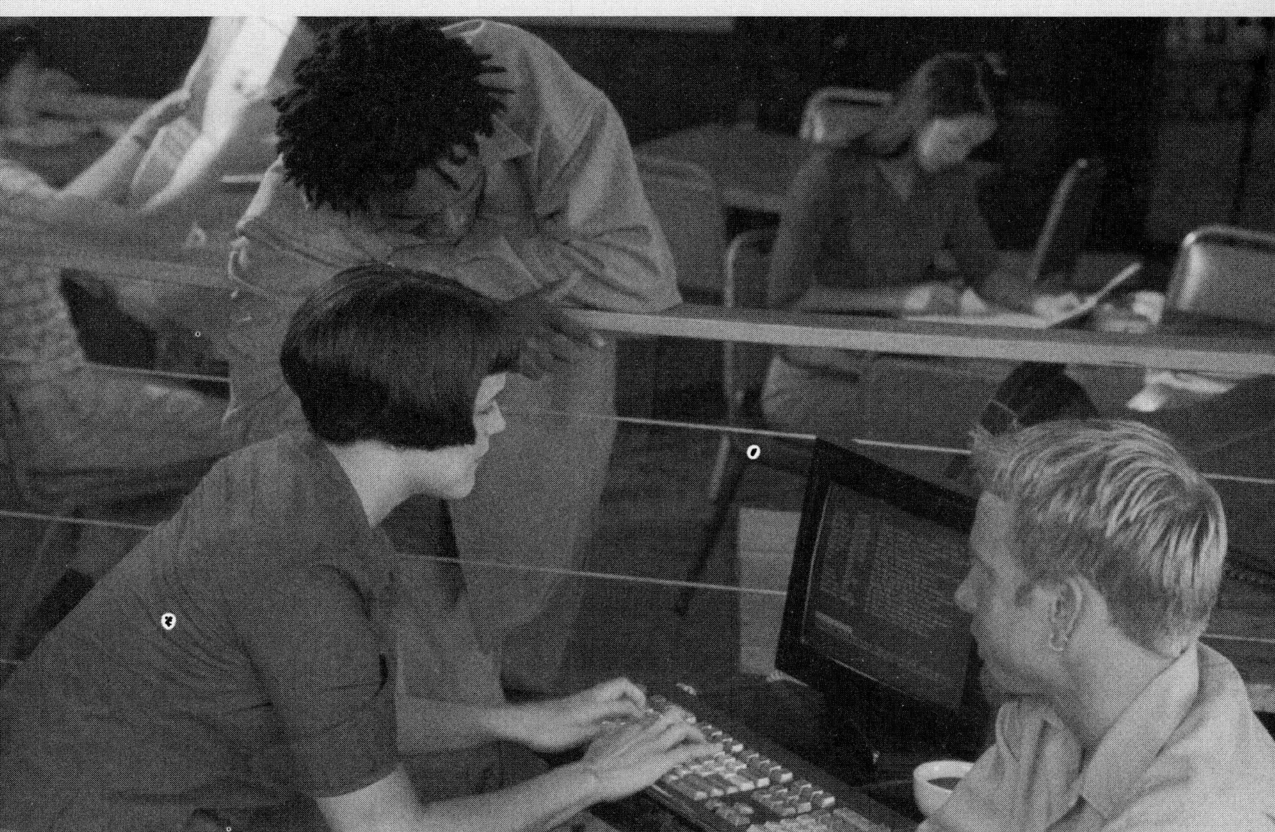

Every day we talk to each other about our common concerns and shared interests. Some conversations are as private and immediate as families talking around the dinner table, two friends exchanging e-mail messages, or a class discussing an assigned reading. Other conversations are as public and wide-ranging as an exchange of remarks by politicians through the mass media, a series of articles in a newspaper or magazine with opinion pieces and letters written in response to it, or a national "town meeting" broadcast on television.

Notice that we are using the word *conversation* here to refer to written as well as spoken communication and even to situations in which participants may not be in direct contact with each other; this is the sense with which politicians and pundits sometimes refer to "a national conversation" or your philosophy teacher might say that thinkers today are still "in conversation" with Plato and Aristotle. Often what we call a conversation is a combination of local and wide-ranging conversations.

Situated Writing at UIC invites you to explore how such conversations get started, what keeps them going, what forms they take, who participates and who doesn't, and how they affect us and the world. We focus on four ongoing conversations that have an impact on events in the world and that affect the way we see ourselves: what it means to be authentic, how we create a sense of place, how to get people involved in civic dialogues, and how the increasingly global economy affects us as workers and consumers. The essays, dialogues, editorials, newspaper articles, and other documents included in this book reflect moments in these conversations, and the activities and assignments throughout the book invite you to join the conversations through your reading and writing.

Consider, for example, this scenario. In your composition class, you read a piece by Richard Rodriguez, an essayist and cultural commentator, and you are assigned to write an essay about the issue he discusses. In the piece included in this book, Rodriguez discusses the impact of AIDS on gay culture and the gay community. But Rodriguez has written about other controversial topics, including multiculturalism, diversity, and assimilation, arguing most recently that our celebration of multiculturalism is shallow and doesn't recognize that assimilation is the much more powerful force in American culture. As you're trying to think of how to begin your essay, you remember that in one of the online forums you sometimes visit there's an ongoing debate about Rodriguez. You didn't pay attention to this debate before because you'd never heard of Rodriguez, but now you go into the forum and reread some of those exchanges. Rodriguez, you find, has taken controversial positions that you strongly agree (or disagree) with. You post some comments in the forum, to which you get several responses, both agreeing and disagreeing, and you soon find yourself an active participant in this forum's ongoing debates about multiculturalism and assimilation.

Meanwhile, you now have a much better sense of how to write your essay. You begin by referring to the ongoing controversies about Rodriguez, and the conversations you've been having in the online forum help you develop a stronger voice and a much more detailed argument. At the next class, one of your peer group members, reading your draft, remarks that Rodriguez once spoke at the university a friend attends and that members of a Latino student group protested his visit. You do some research to check this out, and then you integrate this information into your argument, adding a couple of new paragraphs about the role of universities in civic debates and cultural change. Later in the semester, there's a discussion on your own campus about whether or not to invite a controversial politician to speak at commencement, and you use some of the ideas from your essay to write a letter to the editor supporting (or opposing) the invitation of this speaker. In reshaping the material to address a different audience and purpose, you give greater emphasis to some of the ideas you included in your essay and you leave others out, and in this process you get different insights into the issue and your own response to it.

This is a hypothetical scenario but not an unrealistic picture of how private and public conversations intersect and, more importantly, how you might get involved in them. In order to participate in the complex civic and cultural conversations that help to shape our world, you must read with alertness to context, make connections between different things that you read, pay attention to your own responses, be willing to use writing to follow through on those responses, and shape your writing to particular purposes and audiences. That is, you must read and write rhetorically, with attention to how writing grows out of and responds to particular situations. Rhetoric is the study and practice of shaping communication to particular purposes, and *Situated Writing at UIC* invites you to read and write rhetorically in order to enter the civic and cultural conversations that are important to you.

In this opening unit, we illustrate our belief that reading and writing are multidimensional activities, and we introduce a variety of strategies to help you read and write with more complex understanding. Chapter 1 opens with a newspaper article from which we draw a set of rhetorical concepts—situation, genre, language, and consequences—that can help you read and write with more complexity and power, and we provide a set of guides that will help you use these concepts in very practical ways. In Chapter 2 we look at how one writer entered a conversation about a community issue, and then we introduce a variety of reading and writing strategies designed to help you get interested in and eventually join such conversations yourself.

CHAPTER 1

Contexts for Reading and Writing

Analyzing a Feature Story: Graffiti *as Art or* Vandalism

This feature story from the *Chicago Tribune* illustrates how contexts influence how we read and respond to what we read.

Taggers Spray Over Vandal Image

Phat X. Chiem

Ramiro makes no excuses for how he has spent much of the last nine of his 22 years. He is a graffiti bomber, a tagger, a vandal in the eyes of police and an artist to those like him.

"I basically do it because I grew up with it, and I feel really strongly about it," he said, "I don't care about the police. That's the whole point of graffiti: bombing and getting chased. That's how we get our respect."

For Ramiro, as for many graffiti "writers," his scribbling and scrawling on city viaducts and subway lines has become less a hobby and more a way of life. The possibility of arrest only adds to the thrill, said the burly Ramiro, who has been arrested five times on vandalism charges.

Wearing his "work uniform" of denim shorts and a black T-shirt, Ramiro has come to paint two huge retaining walls on West 59th Street between Damen and Western Avenues. About 30 graffiti artists have been commissioned by two community groups, the Southwest Community Congress and the Southwest Youth Service Collaborative, to create a 12,000-square-foot mural on the pristine walls.

5 Called "Pieces of Chicago," the graffiti mural depicts the history of Chicago, with individual sections devoted to events such as the Great Chicago Fire, the civil rights movement and the Columbian Exposition. With an $8,500 grant from the Chicago Community Trust, organizers have bought over a thousand cans of paint and hope to have the piece completed by this weekend.

From the *Chicago Tribune*, September 12, 1996. Metro Section, pp. 1–2.

A 22-year-old artist called Gnome 174 works on the mural at West 59th Street between Damen and Western Avenues.

For many of these inner-city youths, graffiti represents an art form born of urban squalor and frustration. Graffiti became a part of the rap and hip-hop culture that spread across the country from cities such as New York, Philadelphia, and San Francisco during the late 1970s and early '80s.

"People who think we're vandals are ignorant of the whole hip-hop culture," said Glenn Johnson, the 18-year-old artistic director of the mural project. Graffiti, along with rap music, breakdancing and deejaying, or spinning records, has always served as an expression of hip-hop culture, said Johnson, who has been a graffiti artist since he was 13.

"Graffiti has never been about tagging," said Johnson, a freshman at the American Academy of Art, where he hopes to major in computer animation. "Some people just want to be known as vandals. But me, I'm an artist."

10 Joe Damal, a project organizer, hopes the mural will educate the public about "one of the few indigenous forms of art for urban youth." Many graffiti artists who paint big pieces such as the one on 59th Street differentiate themselves from taggers who simply want to spray their signature across as many public surfaces as possible, he said.

"When it is completed, I will consider this mural graffiti art," Damal said. "But not all graffiti is art. There's some that's really vandalism. That's an important distinction."

Not everyone makes that distinction—certainly not the Chicago Police Department, which has committed a special tactical police unit to keep the city's walls from becoming overnight canvases. Members of the unit are derisively called the "graf squad" by the taggers.

The tension between the two groups was shown when a pair of undercover officers approached the muralists while they were working last week. After Damal refused to leave as an officer questioned one of the artists, he was arrested and charged with disorderly conduct. Later released, he faces a court date next month.

Police said they had every right to question the muralists, even though the graffiti wall had been approved by city officials and the Englewood District police had been notified.

15 "The police were there because they noticed six well-known taggers working on a wall," said Patrol Officer Patrick Camden, a police spokesman.

Police may be critics of so-called permission walls such as the South Side mural, but the concept of channeling graffiti artists' creativity has its supporters. The Chicago Transit Authority began a scholarship program four years ago for mural contest winners.

CTA spokeswoman Noelle Gaffney said the permission-wall program has saved the agency up to $20 million in cleanup costs over four years because vandals tend not to tag walls with murals. But the CTA continues to spend about $20 million annually to fight graffiti elsewhere.

The Streets and Sanitation Department spends about $4 million a year to clean up graffiti. Department spokesman Terry Levin said permission walls only deter illegal graffiti at that particular spot.

"I don't see any sign that [permission programs] are a deterrent for taggers to go somewhere else and vandalize," Levin said.

Allen Tyson, a West Side resident who has had his garage vandalized twice with graffiti, had stronger sentiments.

"I find it offensive to call these guys artists," Tyson said. "I don't think they deserve to be called artists when they're destroying public property."

Meanwhile, Johnson spent Tuesday afternoon at 59th Street using his Krylon paint sprays to depict a civil rights scene from the 1960s. One of his figures had one fist in the air and the other holding a sign reading "Equalitee."

"In the 1960s, there was a lot of segregation at first," Johnson said. "Then there was a lot of integration. People began to wake up and understand that, before we're white human or black human, we're human."

A few yards away, Ramiro was working on his piece, which he said pays homage to artists throughout Chicago, especially those whose outside work is removed by city crews.

"That's the whole basic struggle of graffiti: to keep it up," he said.

Four Ways to Look at Reading and Writing

This article, like any piece of writing, has multiple dimensions. There are, of course, the words on the page, but consider also the situations in which the article was written and will be read, the particular form or genre of this piece of writing, and the consequences this writing may have. Identifying these different dimensions of writing reveals a powerful set of rhetorical concepts with which we can think about what we read and write. These concepts help us see this piece of writing as part of a conversation, or several intersecting conversations, and help us think about what we bring to these conversations and how we might want to continue them.

Situation

The young people in the article see their work on the mural as an important form of artistic and political expression. But the city resident quoted in the article sees all graffiti as damage to property, and the police who arrest the artists working on the mural see it as a violation of laws that they must enforce. These opposing views emerge from different understandings of the situation. By **situation** we mean the immediate circumstance in which an act of reading or writing takes place, recognizing that the immediate circumstance, as well as the participants' understanding of it, is shaped by histories, cultures, communities, institutions, ideas, experiences, and other written texts. Our responses to this article will depend on the immediate circumstance in which we read the article as well as our individual histories, our social and economic background, our experiences with and ideas about graffiti, and perhaps things that we have read about graffiti, art, or vandalism.

Genre

But the controversy over the mural might also be seen as a question of **genre**. Genres are ways of doing things that, over a period of time and in response to repeated situations, needs, or desires, have evolved into recognizable forms. In this book we are concerned mainly with genres of writing and speech, but people also use the term to talk about music, art, movies, TV shows, and other forms of expression. Genres are a kind of social agreement about what forms and conventions are expected in particular situations. For example, if we want to express a strong opinion publicly, we know that one way of doing this is to write a letter to the editor and that our letter needs to follow certain rules and conventions. All genres have their own rules and conventions, but writers (or speakers, musicians, artists, etc.), depending on the situation or their particular goals, may choose to follow those rules, bend them, or break them. Using a graffiti mural to tell the history of Chicago may disrupt, and maybe eventually change, our expectations about the genres of graffiti, murals, and history writing. Similarly, in reading the newspaper article, we might be surprised if the reporter suddenly expressed a strong personal opinion about the mural or graffiti in general because we expect newspaper articles, with the exception of editorials and opinion columns, to be reasonably objective.

Language

When you look at this article, what do you see first? Even before you see the text, you notice the overall look of the article on the page, which includes its heading and byline, its overall layout and length, and the accompanying photo and caption. All of these elements contribute to the overall impact of the article. We use the term **language** to refer not only to the words and sentences but also to the organization and design of a text. In the case of a newspaper article, the reporter may not make visual design decisions, but in other kinds of texts such as brochures, comics, and graffiti murals, the same person may control all these elements. In addition to design elements, this dimension also refers to the overall organization and specific sentences and words of a text. Phat Chiem, the reporter who wrote the article, has organized it to describe the mural project first from the young people's perspective, then from an antigraffiti perspective, and again from the perspective of the mural painters. Notice also that he often describes the muralists and their work by using their own words—"writers," "work uniform"—but puts these words in quotation marks to show that they do not necessarily represent his perspective. All of a writer's choices contribute to the overall effect of a piece of writing. Individual word choices express nuances of meaning, and the combinations of words into phrases, clauses, and sentences build the complexities of meaning that create the overall impact of the work.

Consequences

A graffiti artist quoted in the article says that "the whole point of graffiti" is "bombing and getting chased." But Joe Damal, an organizer of the graffiti mural project, says that the purpose of the mural is to "educate the public about 'one of the few indigenous forms of art for urban youth.'" But whatever the goals of different graffiti artists might be, the police and property owners may see all graffiti in the same light—as vandalism—whereas other present or future readers of its messages might be affected in completely different ways. Depending on the contexts you bring to your reading of this article, you might think differently about graffiti or you might decide to take action by writing a letter to the editor or by joining your neighborhood's clean-up effort. The notion of consequences can help you think about these different intentions and results. By **consequences** we mean the effects of writing in the world. If we think of writing only in terms of school assignments, we may not take into account the important concerns about ethics and responsibility that writing can raise. Writers intend their writing to have particular effects on the world, and they work very hard to ensure that it will have those effects, but the effects of a piece of writing are not always controlled by what the writer intended.

Although each of these four dimensions—situation, genre, language, and consequences—has its own particular meaning and emphasis, they overlap and interact with each other. For example, the **situation** in which an act of writing takes place—participating in a chat room or wanting to express your opinion on a local issue—suggests which **genres** are appropriate to use, though writers might choose to use an unexpected genre or to reshape the expected genre. Genres, that is, have rules and conventions that to some extent determine the **language** choices that are acceptable. And decisions that the writer makes about genre and language, as well as the situation in which the text is ultimately read, will help determine the **consequences** of the text.

In the next two sections we look more closely at how you might use the concepts of situation, genre, language, and consequences to think in more complex ways about your own reading and writing.

Reading the Graffiti Article

Perhaps you are reading the newspaper over breakfast, and you come across Phat Chiem's article about the graffiti mural. How you read and respond to the article will depend on your own particular background and experience. Any time you read, you're already in a **situation** that influences the way you read. For instance, you may have some interest in this issue. You may be a graffiti artist yourself, a homeowner whose garage has recently been "tagged," or a student who partly admires and partly disapproves of graffiti artists.

Your reading might also be influenced by what section of the paper this article appears in. When you read a front-page article, you expect a conventional form that includes facts about a current, ongoing situation or event presented in an even-handed way. When you get to the feature section of the paper, you expect a human-interest piece that tells a story rather than just giving the facts. You bring a set of expectations to whatever you read that influences how you understand it. Although you may not be thinking of this word, the fact that you have these expectations means you are already bringing your **genre** knowledge to bear on your reading. To see this more clearly, imagine that an article about the graffiti mural had appeared on the front page of the paper. You would bring different expectations to it, and it would most likely be a different article. A front-page news article on the mural might focus on an aspect mentioned in passing in the feature article by Chiem, the arrest for vandalism of artists involved in the project. This focus would give the story a quite different meaning.

As you read the article, you will continue bringing various contexts to bear on your understanding of it. You might notice that the Chicago Community Trust is mentioned, and your knowledge of other Community Trust projects might reassure you that the mural is a worthwhile project. Or you might recall that the city has recently passed antigang and antiloitering laws, and you might hope that such laws will put a stop to things like graffiti murals. In other words, you are beginning to connect this story with the many contexts in which we find discussions of graffiti. You also bring to bear, probably unconsciously, other contexts such as your knowledge of how this newspaper has covered similar stories in the past. All these aspects of context contribute to the different **consequences** that this article might have. Did your ideas about graffiti change in any way after you read the article? Perhaps you concluded that graffiti murals are not the best choice for public art. Or did you come away with a feeling that such murals can have a positive impact on a particular community as well as the city as a whole? Was this article good publicity for the youth group? What effect do you think the story had on the neighborhood in which the mural appeared? Could the article have brought people to the neighborhood to see the mural?

The consequences of this article have to do partly with what you bring to it and partly with the social context of the article, but they also have to do with how the writer has crafted it. The **language** choices Chiem makes help us speculate on the effects he wanted the article to have. For instance, what effect is created through introducing the artist, Ramiro, by both quoting him—"I basically do it because I grew up with it, and I feel really strongly about it"—and describing him—"Wearing his 'work uniform' of denim shorts and a black T-shirt"? These choices suggest that Chiem wants the reader to see Ramiro in a sympathetic light and think about the situation from his point of view. Or consider the sentence: "For many of these inner-city youths, graffiti represents an art form born of urban squalor and frustration." By beginning the sentence with a qualifying phrase and by using the verb "represents," Chiem communicates a complex message: that he offers this description of graffiti as a potentially legitimate definition but not necessarily his own. What if the sentence had begun "Graffiti is" or "Many inner-city youths believe that graffiti is"; how would the message be different? Every decision about word choice or sentence structure can make a difference in the overall impact of a piece of writing.

We read every day in many circumstances and for many purposes. Although we don't necessarily think of what we read in terms of situation, genre, language, and consequences, we bring some awareness of all these concepts to our reading. Any act of reading, even of a newspaper article over breakfast, is far more than decoding words on a page; it is a complex activity that takes place within a variety of social contexts and involves a variety of intellectual operations.

Exploring a Writing Scenario

Chiem's article describes a series of events in which writing plays an important part. One of the most important instances of writing involved here is the grant proposal to the Chicago Community Trust that resulted in a grant of $8,500 to buy paint, which is what allowed the project to be completed. Imagine how a person writing a grant proposal—perhaps one of the organizers of the youth collaborative—might approach this task. This writing scenario is not unlike the reading and writing assignments you will encounter in this book: complex situations in which writing interacts with many other factors.

Let's imagine that the organizer has already gotten the youth collaborative interested in the project; maybe she's even contacted city officials for approval to use a specific space for the mural. But she realizes that her organization's budget cannot possibly cover the amount of paint needed for the huge surface. One way to get funding is to write a grant proposal to a foundation or agency to subsidize the project.

Our community organizer knows the proposal will be distributed to the board members of the funding agency to which she is applying. Thus she considers who these people are and what their expectations might be. She might also think about her own credentials and what she still needs to know about her project in order to write a persuasive proposal. In other words, she begins to define the immediate **situation** and its shaping contexts as she sits down to plan and draft her proposal.

While the writer is deliberating about the complex situation in which she writes, she is also aware that the situation demands a specific **genre** of writing—the grant proposal. She knows what sorts of information to include because funding agencies often give out guidelines for writing proposals. In situations in which genre guidelines do not exist, writers might look at other texts in the same genre. In this case, the agency's guidelines direct the project organizer to begin with an abstract that summarizes the project; to review the background of the situation and articulate a problem that must be solved; to offer a solution to the problem; to show how the proposed project will provide that solution; and to include a budget for the project. For all of these requirements, she has to determine whether she has the necessary information. For the most part she will probably follow the rules of the proposal genre, but she may find that in some respects her purposes don't match the expectations of the genre.

She might then need to consider whether she should change her purpose or adapt—or even break—the rules of the genre. She knows that in order to make her proposal effective, she must make careful **language** choices. In the case of a grant proposal, organization and design are usually predetermined; in fact, sometimes the writer simply fills out a form. Also, with a proposal, standard usage is expected; our project organizer knows she cannot make mistakes in grammar, punctuation, or spelling. And the proposal reviewers also expect the writer to speak in a professional voice, using precise and formal language. However, the project organizer also wants to convey how the teens think of themselves and how they describe themselves and their work. For example, should she refer to the teens as "graffiti artists," which is how the reviewers might think of them, or should she call them "writers," which is how the youths refer to themselves? How would you solve this problem? When you write, you are constantly making language decisions that determine the overall meaning and effect of what you write.

A writing project can be so absorbing that you think of little besides getting the writing finished. You may not think ahead to its **consequences**. But much writing takes its meaning from its consequences. In this situation the consequences will be very real: whether or not the money is granted will make a big difference in the lives of the teens the project organizer works with. As she writes, our organizer must remember that she needs to plan and draft her writing with its intended consequences in mind. It may seem that some writing activities—for example, journal entries—don't have significant consequences. But an idea that you write in your journal may in fact have consequences, if only for yourself and your future writing and thinking. Even if only your own mind is changed, that is a real consequence.

If you think of situation, genre, language, and consequences as conceptual tools to help you read and write with more awareness, think of the following guides as toolkits. These guides are sets of questions organized around these concepts, and they are designed to help you in both your reading and your writing. In the activities following each reading in this textbook, you will see icons that symbolize the four concepts of situation, genre, language, and consequences. When you see one of these icons, turn to the relevant section in the Guide to Analyzing Readings in Context or the Guide to Analyzing Contexts for Writing, and use the questions in that section to help you approach your reading or writing with more complexity and depth. Experienced readers and writers, mostly unconsciously, ask themselves similar kinds of questions when they read and write. As you use these guides, you'll discover which questions you find most useful, and you'll begin to ask yourself these questions whenever you read and write.

Questions to Ask as You Read and Write

A Guide to Analyzing Readings in Context

Situation

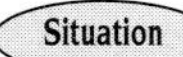

By situation we mean the immediate circumstance in which an act of reading or writing takes place, recognizing that the immediate circumstance, as well as the participants' understanding of it, is shaped by histories, cultures, communities, institutions, ideas, experiences, and other written texts.

- When and where was this text published? If it wasn't published, when, where, and how was it distributed? What costs were involved in publishing or otherwise distributing this piece of writing, and who paid those costs? What does this information suggest about the text and how I or others might respond to it?
- Judging by the text itself and where it was published, what can I conclude about who the intended readers are? What do I know about these readers, their beliefs and values, what they might know and feel about this topic, and how they might respond to this text? How might these facts have influenced the writing of the text?
- Who is the writer? What relevant credentials and expertise does the writer have, including previous publications on the topic? What other facts about

the writer's personal, cultural, social, intellectual, or political background might be relevant to understanding his or her perspective on the issue?

- What events in the world was this text written in response to, and how might these or other events have influenced the writer? What larger historical events, philosophical issues, or social concerns relate to this issue? How was this text a response to other writing or discussion of this issue?
- How might my background affect how I respond to this text? How does my background compare with what I know or infer about the backgrounds of the writer and the intended readers? How familiar am I with the issues, persuasive strategies, and vocabulary of this text? What can I do to help myself better understand this text?

Genre

Genre

Genres are ways of writing that have evolved, in response to repeated situations, needs, or desires, into recognizable forms. Genres are a kind of social agreement about what forms and conventions are expected in particular situations. Some examples are thank-you notes, short stories, graduation speeches, college essays, and rap songs. Each genre has rules—some strict, others loose—that tell what is expected and acceptable in both form and content. Writers may choose to follow the rules strictly, adapt them, or break them, possibly developing new genres. Some genres seem unchanging; others, such as electronic communications, are currently evolving.

- Do I recognize the genre of this text? If so, what do I know about this genre? How can I find out more?
- What are the purposes of texts in this genre? Does this text seem to accomplish those purposes? How does it do so? How effectively?
- In what situations do writers typically use this genre? What do I know or what can I guess about the situation in which this text was produced? Is it the appropriate genre to use in this situation? What other genre options might the writer have had?
- What is the typical overall form of texts in this genre? In what ways does this text fit or not fit the typical form?
- What is the typical content of texts in this genre? What kinds of information, arguments, or sources are included? Is the content what would be expected in texts of this genre?
- What kind of language is typically used in this genre? Is the language in this text what would be expected? Is it effective?

(*continued*)

Language

Language refers to the words, sentences, organization, and design of a text. It is thus the sum of a series of choices the writer makes that in turn may reflect many things, including the writer's personality and intentions, the subject matter, the context, the rules of the genre, and the sounds of particular words and combinations of words.

- What is the text's overall design? How does it use such features as fonts, margins, line spacing, justification, headings, lists, bullets, numbering, and white space or such visuals as charts, photos, or drawings? How does the design contribute to the overall effect? Should the design be changed in any way?
- What is the text's overall organization? What would an outline of the text look like? Do the paragraphs follow an identifiable order? Is the main point of each paragraph clear and sufficiently developed? Is it easy to follow the logic from one sentence or paragraph to another? Are there helpful transitions between sentences and paragraphs? How does the organization contribute to the overall effect? Could the organization be changed in any way to make the text more effective?
- What kinds of sentences does the writer use? Long, short, simple, complex, choppy, smooth, or a variety of types? Do they follow standard rules of grammar, are they clear, and do they have appropriate emphases? If not, does it seem that the writer has done this intentionally or has made mistakes? How does the writer use the ideas of others—direct quotes, indirect quotes, or paraphrasing—to make a point? How do the sentence structures contribute to the overall effect? Should they be changed in any way?
- What kinds of words does the writer use? Common, unusual, formal, informal, slang, or jargon? Do the words seem precise, imprecise, strong, weak, surprising, or predictable? What tone do the words create? Do the words and combinations of words sound pleasing or unpleasing? Are the words grammatically correct and spelled correctly? If they seem incorrect or inappropriate, does it seem that the writer has done this intentionally or has made mistakes? How do the word choices contribute to the overall effect? Could the words be changed in any way to make the text more effective?

Consequences

By consequences we mean the effects of writing in the world. Consequences can be intended or unintended, they can be ideas or actions, and they can be immediate and local or long-term and wide-ranging.

- What effects did this text have on me? Did it change my opinions or ideas in any way? Did it inspire me to act in any way? What specific features of the text contributed to this effect?

- Based on both the text itself and any context information I have about the text or the writer, what consequences do I think the writer intended this text to have? What specific things has the writer done to ensure these intended consequences and avoid unintended ones?
- How might this text affect other people? Could it help or hurt someone? Do you think the writer has thought about his or her responsibility to others in producing this piece of writing? How could, or did, this writing change something in the world, and would this be, or was this, a good change?
- Do I know of any other specific consequences this text has had—intended or unintended, ideas or actions, immediate and local or long-term and wide-ranging? What specific features of the text do I think contributed to these consequences?

A Guide to Analyzing Contexts for Writing

Situation

Situation

By situation we mean the immediate circumstance in which an act of reading or writing takes place, recognizing that the immediate circumstance, as well as the participants' understanding of it, is shaped by histories, cultures, communities, institutions, ideas, experiences, and other written texts.

- Where would I want to publish/distribute this text? Could I, in reality, publish this text where I want to? How much, if anything, will it cost for me to reach the audience I want to reach? How will these factors influence my writing?
- Who are my intended readers? What are they likely to know/not know about my topic? What position are they likely to take? How might their expectations influence how I write this text?
- Do I have the credentials and/or authority to make my audience hear my message? How might I achieve these? What more do I need to know about the topic? How can I find out this additional information?
- What events in the world am I writing in response to? How have these or other events influenced my thinking about the topic? What other historical events, philosophical issues, or social concerns relate to this issue? How have I been influenced by what others have said or written about the topic?
- How does my background influence my thinking and writing about this topic? How does my background compare with that of my intended readers? What facts about my personal, cultural, social, intellectual, or political background might influence my readers' response to my text?

(*continued*)

Genre

Genres are ways of writing that have evolved, in response to repeated situations, needs, or desires, into recognizable forms. Genres are a kind of social agreement about what forms and conventions are expected in particular situations. Some examples are thank-you notes, short stories, graduation speeches, college essays, and rap songs. Each genre has rules—some strict, others loose—that tell what is expected and acceptable in both form and content. Writers may choose to follow the rules strictly, adapt them, or break them, possibly developing new genres. Some genres seem unchanging; others, such as electronic communications, are currently evolving.

- Does this writing situation call for a particular genre? If not, what genre would typically be used for the situation I am in or the purpose for which I am writing? Do I want to use this expected genre or do something else?
- What experience do I have with the genre I am expected to use or that I have chosen? Have I written or read other texts in this genre? What do I need to know before I can write effectively in this genre? Why have people written in this genre historically? What about this genre has changed over time?
- What is the typical form for this genre? How can I use or adapt it to fit my purposes?
- What content will my readers expect? Do I have access to this expected content? Is the content that I do have appropriate to the genre? Will I need to adapt the genre in response to my content?
- What language choices will help me achieve my purpose? What sort of language does the reader expect? Do I need to adapt my language style or the genre?
- See the Genre Glossary for descriptions of genres you'll be asked to produce in this textbook.

Language

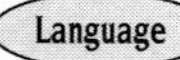

Language refers to the words, sentences, organization, and design of a text. It is thus the sum of a series of choices the writer makes that in turn may reflect many things, including the writer's personality and intentions, the subject matter, the context, the rules of the genre, and the sounds of particular words and combinations of words.

- How should I organize the text? Does the genre of the text, the subject matter I am writing about, the context in which I am writing (including audience and purpose), or my own experience suggest a particular organization? Can I make a tentative outline for the text? Does each paragraph have a clear and well-developed point? What transitions would help the reader? Does the organization contribute to the text's overall effectiveness? What organization changes might a reader suggest, and would these be helpful?

- What do I want my sentences to sound like? Fast-paced, smooth and flowing, or a mixture? Should they be long, short, simple, complex, or a variety of lengths and structures? Do my sentences follow standard rules of structure and grammar? If not, is this to achieve a desired effect, or should I make corrections? Do the sentence structures contribute to the overall effectiveness of the text? How might I use the ideas of others—direct quotes, indirect quotes, or paraphrasing—to make my point? What sentence structure changes might a reader suggest, and would these be helpful?
- What tone do I want the text to have, and what kinds of words would create that tone? Formal, informal, casual, intimate, slangy, professional, serious, or humorous? Does the genre, subject matter, context, or the persona I want to project suggest which words I should use? Do the words express my meanings precisely and effectively? Do the words and combinations of words sound pleasing? Do my word choices contribute to the overall effectiveness of the text? What word changes might a reader suggest, and would these be helpful?
- How can I use design elements to contribute to the overall meaning of the text? What do I want the text to look like, and what design elements would achieve that look? Does the situation, genre, language, or intended consequences suggest a design? How can I use such features as fonts, margins, line spacing, justification, headings, lists, bullets, numbering, and white space or such visuals as charts, photos, or drawings? Does the design contribute to the overall effectiveness of the text? What design changes might a reader suggest, and would these be helpful?

Consequences

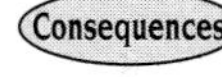

By consequences we mean the effects of writing in the world. Consequences can be intended or unintended, they can be ideas or actions, and they can be immediate and local or long-term and wide-ranging.

- What consequences do I want my text to have? Ideas or actions, immediate and local or long-term and wide-ranging? What consequences would I like to avoid?
- How might this text affect other people? Could it help or hurt someone? Have I thought about my responsibility to others in producing this piece of writing? How could my writing change something in the world, and would this be a good change?
- What specific things can I do to ensure these intended consequences and avoid unintended ones?

CHAPTER 2

Strategies for Writers at Work

In Chapter 1 we saw how the grant writer for the graffiti project evaluated the situation, considered the demands of genre, looked closely at language, and anticipated the possible consequences of her writing. We also saw how she employed a variety of strategies to help her do those things. For example, she did library or online research and talked with people in order to get a fuller sense of the particular situation she was working in. She knew that in order to get a clear sense of the requirements of the grant proposal genre she would also have to study proposal guidelines from the agency she was applying to, as well as proposals for similar projects. At various times throughout the process, she jotted down ideas and drafts in a notebook, brainstormed with co-workers, engaged in e-mail discussions with people involved in the project, worked with others to draft parts of the proposal, and asked people for feedback at different stages of the writing. The procedures, resources, and people that were part of her situation all provided her with specific strategies for planning, researching, drafting, and revising the proposal.

As suggested in the introduction to Unit I, students also engage in a range of strategies to help them carry out writing projects, but students may not be aware of all the strategies available to them. In this chapter we describe a variety of strategies that will help you carry out writing projects. Because different strategies work for different writers in different situations, the second part of this chapter describes a wide range of such strategies, including strategies to help you connect with a context, explore a reading and the issues it raises, and tackle those issues yourself in a writing project of your own.

A How-To List for Reading and Writing

The readings in this book are designed to help you similarly identify and shape contexts for your writing, and the activities that accompany each reading suggest specific strategies to help you write. This section gives you an overview of those strategies, organized into three categories according to the sets of activities that accompany each reading. The first group helps you connect to the larger context in which your reading and writing will take place. The second group helps you look closely at the readings and make connections with other readings and related issues. The third group helps you get started with and follow through on a variety of writing projects by helping you make the best use of the stages of the writing process. The following section is designed as a reference guide to be used as you need it, but you might want to look through it now to see which kinds of strategies are covered and think about how you might use them.

Before You Read: Connecting with the Conversation

The more you bring to a reading, the better you will understand it and be able to connect with it. Thus before each reading in the textbook, we ask you to think about your own knowledge of and experiences with the situations and issues described or referred to in the reading. These connections will help you create a context as you begin to write about the issues yourself. Consider the following strategies as ways to help you approach your reading, whether it's the morning paper, assignments for another class, readings in this book, or reading that you do on your own.

Consider Your Own Related Experiences. Use your experience to help you think about the broad context of and the specific situation presented in the text. Notice differences between what an author says and what you believe to be true or likely based on your experience. Also, use your experience with different kinds of writing to think about issues related to the genre of a reading, for example its overall form and design, organization, and language.

Pay Attention to Discussions in the Media. Newspapers and magazines are important forums for detailed reports on and extended discussions of issues. You and your family may regularly read a newspaper and a few magazines, and you may be familiar with the particular interests and biases of those periodicals. Reading other newspapers and magazines can give you different perspectives on issues or introduce you to new issues and ideas.

Some assignments might ask you to look at newspapers or magazines you are already familiar with; others might ask you to explore unfamiliar newspapers and magazines. In the case of the latter, you might go to the current periodicals section of a large library, to a large newsstand, or to the periodicals section of one of the large chain bookstores. Select a few periodicals that you don't usually read, from a variety of categories—dailies, weeklies, monthlies, quarterlies, news, financial, entertainment, general interest, special interest, scholarly, or literary. Browse through your selections, making notes about the overall look of the periodical and the kinds of writing, topics, and attitudes that seem typical for each. Pay special attention to genres, topics, or ideas that are new to you. Consider what kinds of conclusions you can draw about the writing practices in the familiar or new periodicals you have looked at.

Radio and television programs and advertising can give us interesting examples of how language is used in our society. Again, some assignments ask you to listen to or watch familiar stations or programs; others ask you to explore new ones. Make notes about the kinds of programs and advertising and about topics, attitudes, and uses of language, paying special attention to those that are new to you. Review your notes and consider what conclusions you can draw about the language practices you have heard or observed.

Search the Topic Online. Searching a topic online is a wonderful way to get basic information or a quick overview, and many young people today, by the time they get to college, have already developed strategies for getting information quickly from the Internet, whether for school projects or other purposes. But as you probably learned in high school, doing a quick search just to get a preliminary picture of a topic is not the same as doing systematic research in order to write a paper or complete a project. In order to help you connect with the context of a reading or a new topic, your teacher may ask you to follow certain steps or may simply allow you to do your own search. If you do your own search, be sure to keep track of the sites from which you take information so that you can provide references later if required or return to the same site for more information.

Talk to People with Relevant Knowledge or Experiences. You can enhance your understanding of any event or issue by talking with people who know something about it. You may want to start with someone you already know, or you can call an appropriate agency or office, explain your project, and ask whether there is someone appropriate who might have time to speak with you. When you first contact your interviewee, whether by phone or in person, remember to introduce yourself and explain your project. Try to tell the person what kind of information you're looking for and what kinds of questions you might want to ask. If that person is too busy or doesn't think she will be of much help, ask if she knows anyone who might be willing to be interviewed for your project. See the Interview entry in the Genre Glossary.

As You Read: Exploring Texts and Contexts

Each of the readings in this book comes out of a specific situation, which is itself part of a larger context. Activities following each reading help you explore both the text itself and the situations and conversations that surround it, and this in turn should help you think about how you might enter one of those conversations through your own writing.

Understand the Writing Situation. The following questions will help you explore how the writer's situation shapes the meaning of the text. What is the writer's background and experience? What larger conversation is the writer responding to? Does the writer mention a specific situation that sparked the writing? How does the writer's purpose and situation influence the form of the writing?

You might be able to intuit answers to some of these questions. Answers to other questions will be found in introductory material. But for other answers you may need to do other kinds of analysis, research, and observation.

Identify and Analyze the Genre of the Text. If you are used to reading and writing mainly personal narratives or essays, you may be surprised at the range of genres included in this book. Activities that follow each reading will help you identify the genre of the reading and think about how the genre helps shape meaning. This in turn may help you think about genres that you want to use as you write about these issues.

Analyze the Language of the Text. Carefully examining the language of a text will help you think more specifically about how a piece of writing works. Here are some specific strategies.

- Think about the significance of the title.
- Identify key terms—words that the writer uses in a special way, a way not easily explained by dictionary definition alone, especially words used in ways that puzzle you.

- Notice figurative language—images, metaphors—and consider how it shapes the meaning of the text.
- The questions posed in the Guides on pages 12–17 will help you look more closely at the language of a text. As you develop into a more active reader, you will learn which questions are most useful to you, and you will also develop your own questions.

Consider the Consequences of the Text. When we write in school to fulfill assignments, the most immediate consequence we can imagine for our work is the grade assigned to our work by the teacher. But as you become an engaged reader and writer, you will begin to think about writing that has consequences beyond the classroom. The news article about graffiti artists in Chapter 1 gets us thinking about all the ways in which writing might enter a situation and helps us to imagine all the ways in which consequences might play out. The grant writer we introduce later in Chapter 1 is hoping that her proposal will be funded, but she hopes for other consequences as well. For instance, she wants the Chicago Community Trust to fund her project for what she thinks is a good reason—supporting a culturally significant form of local art. This consequence—more subtle than being given funding—involves changing the funders' minds. Perhaps they began reading the proposal thinking that the money would be useful as a deterrent, keeping graffiti artists busy and away from the alleys and garages of local citizens. The grant writer hoped to change their view of graffiti, and this too is a potential consequence.

As you probably know, writing can have unintended consequences. An editorial you write for a school newspaper might not be understood as you intended it. An assignment is returned to you for revision because, the teacher explains, you did not complete it as he or she expected. A diary you have been keeping for some time, including very personal information, is found and read by someone discussed in the diary. We leave these consequences to your imagination!

Even when you are writing just to fulfill an assignment, thinking about the potential consequences of your writing will help you see it in a more complex way.

Compare the Text with Other Texts. Any individual text is part of a situation or history that includes other texts. Thus it makes sense to ask how particular texts relate to each other. Comparing one text to another makes it possible to notice things you might not have noticed looking at it in isolation.

- How do the perspectives of different writers change the way they treat an issue?
- How do different genres change the treatment of an issue?
- How do different language choices shape what writers communicate about an issue?
- How do writers' differing purposes and goals for writing affect what they say about an issue?

Search the Library and the Internet for Related Texts. Research usually grows out of and is an extension of classroom work, but it is more open-ended in the sense that you are usually working on your own, and neither you nor the teacher may know what you are going to find.

Research is a crucial part of learning because it allows you to make connections between what you have learned in the classroom and what you yourself have observed or what others have said about an issue, and it allows you to take more responsibility for your learning. The following kinds of activities will require you to do research in the library or online.

Search Reference Materials for Context Information. Some activities will ask you to look for information on the context or background of an issue or a person. Searching the Internet may produce a lot of material, but it may not be the information you need, and you'll have to evaluate it carefully. You might instead want to use library reference materials, which are materials that can't be taken out of the library, including dictionaries, encyclopedias, almanacs, resource guides, and other books in which you can "look things up." The reference librarian can help you find the most up-to-date source for the information you need.

Search Popular Magazines and Academic Journals for a Particular Topic. Some activities ask you to find out and compare what different kinds of periodicals are saying about a topic. Popular magazines are those that are read by general readers; they are usually published weekly or monthly. Academic journals are written and read by specialists in particular academic disciplines; they usually come out four times a year. Both can be searched by using either print or electronic indexes. Articles in popular magazines can be found by using general interest indexes, most of which can be found online, including FirstSearch or Wilson Select Plus. Articles in academic journals can be found by using various specialized indexes. Many electronic indexes and databases contain the full text of articles, usually more recent ones.

Search the Internet. Other assignments will ask you to do a search of a topic on the Internet. As with library research, there are tools that will help you find information, such as Yahoo and Google. Although each of these has its own procedures, which may change over time, all of them basically allow you to type in a keyword, and then they search for any documents on the Internet that contain this keyword. This usually results in a list of hundreds or thousands of documents, most of which may not be at all relevant to what you are looking for. Many handbooks on electronic research contain tips for choosing the best search tool and using it effectively to narrow or broaden your search so that you find the range of information you need. An assignment may ask you to find specific information, in which case you may want to narrow your search strategies, or to get an overview of an issue, in which case you may want to broaden your search strategies.

Explore a Web Site. Some activities ask you to go to a specific Web site to find information or to explore the site. (In these cases, the URL for the Web site will be provided, though note that URLs, like phone numbers, can become outdated.) In exploring a Web site, notice the kind of information it contains, including how up-to-date it is and whether sources for the information are provided; notice the graphics used and how they interact with the text; and check out the various links. The assignment may ask you to retrieve specific information or to analyze the composition of the site.

Visit a Real or Electronic Bookstore. An assignment may ask you to browse in a bookstore to see what is currently available on a particular topic. Many large bookstores these days—in addition to Amazon.com, which exists only online—have Web sites that allow you to shop for books online. This is a very good way to get an overview of the most recent publications on a topic. Browsing in a real bookstore will allow you to actually take the books off the shelf and look through them. Browsing in an electronic bookstore, on the other hand, allows you to see titles and descriptions of books that are too old or obscure to be given space on a shelf but which may be relevant to your topic. Thus you may want to browse in both places to get the best overview.

Evaluate Sources. Since we now use computers to search for both library materials and online materials, it's easy to confuse the two kinds of research. But it's important to understand the difference between online sources and library sources, for two reasons. First, there are differences in reliability between the two. Statements made in formally published books, periodicals, and other print documents may not always be true, and some published materials are less reliable than others, but it is usually at least possible to identify the publisher and author of such materials and take that information into account in doing your own assessment of the material's reliability. With material published on the Internet, it's often difficult to track down the source of the material, and it's easy for online materials to be misrepresented. The second reason to understand the difference is simply that there are different ways of citing print materials and online materials.

When you do online research, you will be using materials from Web sites, listservs, e-mail, and data banks of various sorts that sometimes exist only online. In all of these cases, you will have to do your best to identify the origins of the material and assess its reliability using that information and the judgment that you use in assessing the reliability of any materials. A number of recent guides and handbooks will help you find, identify, evaluate, and use these online sources. They will also explain the new and still-developing systems for documenting online sources, which are also available in most recent standard handbooks.

On the other hand, when you go online to access library catalogs, indexes, or databases of published print materials, you should think of yourself as doing library research. Thus, you should make sure that you can identify the traditional print publication information and use traditional print documentation systems when you incorporate parts of the material into your own work. On the other hand, if you use an article that you find on a Web page, you should determine whether it has only been published on that Web page or is reprinted from a print periodical; if the latter, make sure you cite the periodical. And when you use an online index such as FirstSearch, remember that the articles listed are from print periodicals and should be documented as such.

Getting Down to Writing: Creating Texts

Each reading in this book will be followed by at least two writing projects, which may include an essay as well as one of the other genres we describe in our Genre Glossary. In the following pages you will find strategies and processes that will help you complete writing projects assigned in this book as well as other writing for school or for work.

Identify a Situation and Purpose for Writing. One of the most helpful things you can do to get started writing is to think of yourself as participating in a situation and imagine how a piece of writing can have an impact on the situation. Review the Guide to Analyzing

Contexts for Writing to generate new ways to think about the situation in which you are writing. Consider carefully what you bring to the situation and what you have learned from similar situations. Consider also who your readers are and what experiences they might have had in similar situations. Then think about what kind of impact you would like your writing to have and how you can help assure that it will have that impact.

Take Advantage of the Writing Process. Even though you are often by yourself when you write, the process does not take place entirely in your head. Instead, your writing emerges from interactions with other people, with readings, with the world as you experience it, and with your own previous writing. Therefore, writing well depends on seeing yourself in a particular situation that will help shape your writing process.

In the pages that follow, you will find general descriptions of the writing process—planning, drafting, revising, and editing. But keep in mind that the particular process you use will be shaped by the situation you are in, and that the four phases of the process overlap and recur. After completing a draft and even after revising it, you may need to return to the prewriting phase to reconsider an aspect of the issue you had not previously considered. Some of the strategies described here will work better than others in particular writing situations. Through practice and experience you'll learn which strategies work best for you.

Planning. Imagine that you have been reading and writing about a particular issue that interests you, and you have decided to work through one of the writing activities suggested in this textbook. Here's a list of suggestions. Choose the ones that are most effective in pushing your process forward.

- *Review the Guide to Analyzing Contexts for Writing.* What is your writing situation and how will it shape your writing? What form will your writing take? Will it be an essay, a dialogue, or a report? How does genre influence your approach? What stylistic choices do you anticipate making? How will your voice emerge in your writing? What consequences do you want your writing to have for yourself and others? Who will read your work? What kind of impact do you want it to have?
- *Review and supplement previous work.* Reread all of your journal entries. Reread, annotate, and take notes on material that you think will contribute to your writing project. Consider where you might get more information. Do you need to read more, search the Internet, or conduct interviews? Do you need to take another trip to the library to search out journals, magazines, or documents?
- *Develop your ideas.* Engage in mind-stretching activities that encourage you to consider your information in different ways. Brainstorming, listing, and diagramming are all ways to identify, organize, and reorganize ideas and information. Initially you might want to brainstorm with yourself or others to generate as many ideas as possible. A special kind of brainstorming is freewriting, in which you write without stopping for a period of time. Next you may want to organize these ideas into lists. Or you could use a diagram to explore the relationships among these ideas. These activities might help you to determine whether your topic is too broad or too narrow.
- *Reflect on your project.* A valuable technique at any point in the process is to step back and reflect on your writing project as a whole. One of the best ways to do this is to

use a journal. Not only will you want to reread all the journal entries you have written up to this point, but you will also want to keep writing in your journal to reflect on your current thinking about your project. Try explaining to someone else the purpose for your writing. Try writing a memo to your teacher with key questions you have yet to answer. Or try writing a progress report and exchange it with a friend.

Drafting. Moving from notes to a complete first draft can be the most challenging aspect of a writing project. Remember that you are producing a *first* draft. It doesn't have to be perfect; it just has to emerge in some form so that you can continue working on it. The following suggestions offer a variety of approaches to crossing this bridge from notes to first draft.

- *Review the section on genre in the Guide to Analyzing Contexts for Writing.* This section of the guide encourages you to think about the relationship between the situation for writing and the typical forms that writing takes.
- *Consider your time frame.* When is this writing project due? Estimate how long it will take you to get started and complete a draft. Create a time line that includes time for prewriting, drafting, revising, and editing. If you work better doing small portions of a project on a day-by-day basis, schedule your work in this way.
- *So you have only four hours!* Here's a plan for generating a draft, developed by Peter Elbow (*Writing Without Teachers*, Oxford University Press, 1973). This plan works best for certain kinds of writing, usually writing that depends primarily on your own personal experience and not on a lot of outside research. Still, it provides a useful way to push yourself into completing a first draft.

  Divide your four hours into units of one hour each. During the first 45 minutes of the first hour do some freewriting; write everything that comes into your head; dump it out onto the page. During the last 15 minutes of the first hour read over what you have written and evaluate it. What seems important? What could you be moving toward? What big idea or ideas emerge? Sum up this idea in a sentence or two.

  This first version is your starting point for the next hour, in which you write for 45 minutes, continuing to discuss the main idea you identified in the previous version. Once again, take the last 15 minutes to reread and see what important ideas you can pull from this version. Sum up the main idea again; try to take it further than the last version suggests. Try this same process one more time during the third hour you have allotted. If you can see an organization emerging, try to use it to guide this version. Again, during the last 15 minutes ask yourself what you are trying to say. Write it as if you are telling it directly to a specific person that you imagine as part of your audience. Use the last hour to revise and shape the piece; during the last 15 minutes give the piece a final editing.
- *Develop an Outline.* An outline helps you to structure your draft, a substantially different approach from the one just described. You may find that your writing style makes one of the two approaches more comfortable for you. Or you may find that one of the approaches works better for a particular writing project.

In developing an outline, consider what the genre section of the Guide to Analyzing Contexts for Writing suggests for your writing project. Next consider your main idea for the project. What do you intend to explain or argue in this project? How might you develop the main idea? How can you divide this project into sections? What is the relationship among the sections? When you have answered these questions, you should proceed to develop an outline.

An outline is a hierarchical approach to organizing information. You can adopt a formal approach in which you organize your main topics and supporting details alphanumerically, labeling your main ideas with Roman numerals, letters, and numbers; or you can take a more informal approach, simply listing all main topics and supporting details. In either case, you write under each major section heading and subheading a sentence that you will include in that section and explain how it contributes to the project as a whole. When you finish your outline, share it with a partner and discuss where it works and where the organization isn't clear. Writing an outline challenges you to group your ideas in units that help you explore your topic in an interesting and compelling way.

Revising. Revising provides an opportunity to shape and refine the paper so that it says to others just what you want it to say. This is the point in the writing process when you focus on how the project hangs together. If you have time, put the project aside for a day or two in order to look at it again with fresh eyes. Often you can get the best feedback on how successful your draft is by sharing it with another writer. Here are some strategies for revising:

- *Collaborate with Others to Review Your Work.* At any point in the writing process, it helps to talk to someone else and get feedback on both your plans and your draft. Try to guide your reader's response in order to elicit the most useful response possible. A useful response will help you to understand the text as others do and decide what aspects need revision. Look on the peer review situation as a kind of interview; you need to ask questions that will give you the information you need to know. You may want to design a feedback sheet for your reader to work with. On the next page you will find an outline of a peer review worksheet that you can customize to suit your particular writing project.
- *Consider your project as a whole.* Reread the Guide to Analyzing Contexts for Writing and ask yourself how your perspective shapes what you have written. Ask yourself whether you are following the conventions of a genre or changing it in some way. Are your genre choices appropriate? Ask how design, organization, sentences, and words contribute to or detract from your paper in view of its goals. Finally, consider the consequences you hope it will have. Try to determine how to avoid unintended consequences.
- *If you wrote your introduction first, take an especially hard look at it.* Sometimes when you finish your paper you end up thinking differently about your project than when you began. You might read your paper over completely, put it aside, and write a new introduction. Compare that introduction to the rest of the paper and make the appropriate changes.

Peer Review Worksheet

Writer's Name ______________________

Writer's comments: In the space below summarize the main point of your text. Comment on its purpose. Tell your reader what you think works best in the paper and what you think needs more work. Tell your reader what you would do if you had a few more days to work on the text. Finally, write down a few questions that you would like your reader to consider.

Reader's Name: ______________________

Reader's Comments:

1. **Overall response:** Summarize the text's main point. Comment on how your reading differs from or confirms the writer's comments.
2. **Consider issues of situation and genre.** What events in the world is the writer responding to? How have these events influenced the writer's work? Does the writer offer enough background information and supporting material to help the text succeed in its purpose? What genre has the writer chosen? Does the shape of the text fit its purpose? Is the writer speaking with authority? Do you believe what the writer is telling you?
3. **Consider issues of language and consequences.** Outline the text briefly. How does the organization contribute to the overall effect? Do the writer's language choices seem appropriate? Does the introduction help you get started reading the text? What effect does the text have on you? Do you think this is the intended or an unintended effect? What specific things could the writer do to avoid unintended effects?
4. **Examine the text for correctness.** Do you see any problems with sentence structure, quoting and paraphrasing, usage, or spelling? Note these for the writer.
5. **Tell the writer about one strength in the text.**
6. **Suggest ways in which the writer can improve the text.**

- *Write an outline for your paper as it is currently organized.* Think hard about this plan. Might a different plan work better? How would moving sections around help your project succeed?
- Determine whether you have enough information to successfully complete this writing project. Do you need to gather more information to bolster a particular point you want to make?
- *Examine your language choices.* Do your stylistic choices further the points you are making? Does your personal voice come through the way you want it to? Do you use transitions appropriately to develop the path you want your project to take?
- Finally, revisit your main idea or argument and make certain that it will be clear to your readers. Is it supported fully throughout the project?

Editing. Never underestimate the impact that surface errors can have on your readers. One final step is editing your paper for style and usage, punctuation, and other mechanics. Here are some techniques for catching errors that may cause readers to undervalue your work:

- Read your essay aloud from beginning to end. Listen to the way individual sentences sound and the way paragraphs hold together.
- Did you title your work? Did you pay attention to other design issues, for example how the text is formatted on the page?
- Did you check for correct usage, paying particular attention to problems you have had in your writing before? Have you used your handbook to resolve editing questions?
- Have you documented sources correctly using the appropriate citation system? Have you correctly punctuated quotes?

In the previous sections we identified strategies that might be used in any writing project. The following sections provide information on some special strategies that you may use in particular kinds of projects: writing arguments, integrating material from other texts, creating visual texts, and collaborating with others on the writing of a text.

Writing Arguments

Whether you are writing in school or in a public context, you will often be asked to take a position, develop a thesis, and support your thesis with evidence. This thesis-driven writing underlies many of the genres we present in the Genre Glossary. Speeches, reviews, proposals, and, most obviously, the argumentative essay require you to place yourself in a context, evaluate an ongoing conversation, and develop your position within that conversation. We do this naturally as we participate in daily activities, but sometimes when asked to take a position in a classroom setting, we forget all the competencies we have developed over the years of taking positions in contexts outside of school.

You may be comfortable generating a lot of reasons for any given claim that you make, but as a writer, in school or out, you'll want to think carefully about how to support a particular position. When you gather evidence, consider its source. Consider also how reasonable it is to use that evidence in support of the particular thesis you want to support.

Integrating Material from Other Texts

Summarizing. Summarizing a text will help you understand it better and prepare you for thinking critically about it. Experienced readers go through a text several times before summarizing it. In an initial reading, focus on questions of content and meaning. Then, on a second pass, focus on the way the content is related to the structure of the text. Consider, also, the writer's goals.

Writing a summary requires that you restate the text in your own words. Remember, though, that it will not be enough to simply restate the message of the text in the order the material is presented. Consider which ideas are most important. This will help you decide what information is key and what can be left out. Consider also how the text is organized and how that influences its meaning. Most important, consider your purpose for summarizing the text. Consider these questions as you plan your summary:

- For what occasion did the writer produce this text?
- What is the purpose for writing?
- What is the genre of the text?
- What is the main point?
- Which parts develop the main point?
- Which parts provide the support and examples?
- How has the writer organized the parts?

Paraphrasing. Paraphrasing means *putting someone else's ideas or statements into your own words.* To summarize, you reduce a larger body of material to a smaller size; paraphrasing allows you to restate material fully while not quoting it exactly. Many of the same questions posed for summarizing apply to paraphrasing. Ask yourself why you need to use this information and how it contributes to your ideas. As you practice putting someone else's ideas into your own words, you'll get a better sense of what the text means and how best you can express its ideas.

Quoting. Often you will want to repeat *exactly* what another writer or speaker says, especially if the language is particularly compelling or if you cannot put the language in your own words. Be aware, however, that if you quote too often, you risk losing your own voice and your own point of view. The use of quotes requires appropriate punctuation, which will be explained in your handbook.

Avoiding Plagiarism. As you write, you may rely on the work of other writers. When you use the ideas of others, you'll want to include in-text citations to signal to your readers where the information comes from. When you work with exact language from your source, be sure to use quotation marks to set off this language. When you restate others' ideas, be sure to use your own words and syntax. If you don't give credit to other writers when you use their words and ideas, you will be accused of plagiarism. Plagiarism also includes turning in a paper that contains another's writing without acknowledging that other writer by quoting, citing, and listing the work in a reference list. This, however, does not mean that you should avoid using others' ideas and words in your own writing. But you must identify the work of those writers you are in conversation with.

Creating Visual Texts

More than ever before, we now communicate through visual texts; for this reason many projects in this book ask you to try your hand at comics, brochures, Web pages and other visual texts. Creating such texts draws on everything that you have learned about communicating a message but asks you to do so in an electronic or visual medium. Here are some things to think about as you prepare for such projects:

- Does the visual image tell a story? Will viewers be able to tell you what story they can draw from your visual text?

- If your visual text departs from viewer expectations, will viewers be able to make sense of your text in some new way?
- Can viewers interpret your visual text based on what they already know?
- Have you thought about who your audience is? Have you composed your visual text for, perhaps, fellow students, teachers, an audience with specific musical or artistic tastes, or a specific group of consumers?
- Have you represented the people in your visual text to reflect the diversity that exists in the larger society?
- Consider how realistic you want your visual text to be. You can work along a wide continuum—from close imitation of reality to imaginative representations that will ask your reader to make use of his or her interpretive powers.

Collaborating with Others on the Writing of a Text

As you use this textbook, you may be asked to write as a member of a team. A writing team may be helpful when you need to include other perspectives in your work. Sometimes a project or writing task is simply too large for one person, or you don't have enough time to complete the project on your own and you need to divide up the work. Or members of a group may have special expertise on different aspects of a topic.

There are several ways to work with a team. In a one-author team, the team discusses the project, and team members may draft portions of the document, but in the end one person writes the final document. In a multiple-author team, each team member contributes a specified portion to the project, and the pieces are then combined to create the final document. In a collaborative team, all members of the group contribute to the process and work together to produce the final product. This is one of the most challenging team situations because it may require the group to write as if one author has produced the document.

How to Handle the Writing Process

- Writing together differs from writing alone in many ways. Talk with your group about how you will divide up the work. Determine whether you will all be writing one document or whether you each will contribute parts of the final product.
- Brainstorm about ideas for your project.
- Set up a schedule and a way for the team to keep track of its progress.
- Identify ways to help each other with the writing—both finding information and reviewing drafts.
- Determine how you will evaluate the project once it is done.

How to Handle Conflict and Difference

- Sources of conflict: Personality differences, insensitivity to gender or ethnic difference, lack of clear team procedures, different ideas about the team's purpose or goal, and different ideas about how to get things done
- Conflict resolution: Determine how your team will make decisions—by consensus or by majority? Talk about the behavior in specific, concrete terms, and discuss what effect

it is having on the team. Discuss possible alternative behaviors and how they might influence the team's work. Learn to use reflective listening, which means repeating to a person what that person has said so that the team has the opportunity to understand that person's position or approach. Ask enough questions so that the team can determine a way to resolve a conflict.

How to Handle Leadership and Communication Skills

- Build into your process ways to observe yourselves. For instance, set aside a portion of every meeting for discussing the group's process.
- Assign leadership roles and discuss how those roles might be carried out. Members of teams can be assigned tasks as leader, secretary, and evaluator.
- Plan to play different roles in different team situations. See whether you can discover how you function best and whether your response in some roles surprises you.

The Multiple-Author Team. Kelly Ritter, an assistant professor at Eastern Connecticut State University, used a very structured, multiple-author approach to guide her students through the process of making a group presentation on their work. Her writing class was exploring film studies, and each group of four or five students was to make a presentation and turn in a report. Students, working individually, had already identified a topic and were writing a paper on it. Ritter grouped together students who were working on similar topics. Some of the groups' presentation topics included minorities in films, praise and blame in Hollywood, film genres and society, and stars and studios. The group presentations were to take 10 to 15 minutes, and students would be graded on both their oral and written contributions. As you work in groups, consider the following guidelines for class presentations and for handouts:

Oral Class Presentation

- Each writer summarizes his or her paper.
- One group member offers an overview of how the group members' topics are related to each other and how they differ. In addition, this member explains how these topics relate to the issues discussed in the course.
- Another group member reports on the group's process: what students learned from each other, how they identified and shared resources, how they helped each other sharpen the focus of their papers, and how they solved any problems the group had.

Handouts for the Presentation

- One group member should prepare a handout listing the group members and the topics they will discuss and summarizing the relationship of the presentation to the coursework.
- Another group member should write a summary of the entire group presentation in essay form. The essay might be two to three pages in length.
- If appropriate, another group member should provide film clips or visual material. This presenter should make it clear how the visual is necessary to a discussion of the topic.

The Collaborative Team. Maya Luna Books (2000) published an erotic thriller, *The Student Body*, under the pseudonym Jane Harvard. In reality, it was written by Michael Francisco Melcher, Faith Adiele, Julia Sullivan, and Bennet Singer, four Harvard grads. In a recent feature article in the *Chicago Tribune*, writer Patrick Reardon describes how the group went about writing this novel together. Initially, the four friends thought they would get together for a weeklong vacation and start the book. Melcher, the only one of the four who was not a writer, thought the entire project could be done during that week. Adiele, who is an English professor, knew that writing a novel in a week was unrealistic but looked at the project as a way to spend time with her closest friends and, at the same time, come to closure about their Harvard experience.

Here's how Reardon described the group's process:

> They wanted to produce a book that didn't read like it was written by four people. So they made sure that no one person had responsibility for any particular character or for any particular chapter. Adiele might start to draft a chapter, but when she'd get stuck, Melcher or Sullivan would step in.
>
> On vacations—yes, there were several other working vacations—they had their computer terminals set up next to each other, and, in between times, they communicated via e-mail and conference calls. Singer, who did relatively little of the initial writing, functioned as the group's editor, carried out research, and made business contacts with agents and publishers.
>
> Finally, they completed the book they wanted to write—a book about close friends from many backgrounds who helped one another struggle through the growing pains of reaching maturity at Harvard. The prostitution ring angle was in there to give the work a commercial hook. They turned it in to their publisher.
>
> And it was kicked back.
>
> There was too much talking and not enough action. Not enough plot. So a heavy rewrite took place. "We cut 250 pages and added 200 pages," Melcher said.
>
> And—voila—*The Student Body*, an erotic thriller.
>
> —"Designed by Committee" by Patrick Reardon, *Chicago Tribune*, Friday, May 15, 1998, p.5.

What do you make of the differences between these two descriptions of writing teams? Under what circumstances would you choose the more structured approach offered first, and when might you want to follow the procedures of the group writing a novel?

In this how-to list we provide a variety of strategies to help you prepare for reading, analyze and make connections with what you read, and most importantly get down to writing. Think of it as a resource that you can return to for help with specific projects, for example visual texts or group projects. Or you may turn to this list when you are stuck at any point of a project. Browse around in the list until you find a strategy that will help you get past that particular roadblock. Eventually you will be able to use the strategies you need without consulting the list!

UNIT II

Searching for Authenticity

Source: (*left*) *Van Gogh's Chair by Vincent van Gogh*, 1888, *National Gallery, London*, NG 3862; (*right*): *The Billionaire in Vincent's Chair*, by R. B. Kitaj, 1999, Marlborough Fine Art, London.

How do these two paintings talk to each other? The one on the left, painted by Vincent van Gogh in 1888, might be considered an ironic self-portrait: The striking presence of the empty chair, the tobacco and pipe left behind, draws our attention to the absence of its owner. In the painting on the right, on the other hand, the figure in the chair is the most striking presence in the painting: It seems to fill not only the chair but the whole room as well as the painting itself. In the late 1990s, the British Museum asked a number of artists to create a work that "conversed" with any of the paintings in their collection. R. B. Kitaj painted "The Billionaire in Vincent's Chair" as a comment on the huge sums needed to purchase famous works of art. The conversation between these two paintings helps us reflect on the different meanings of authenticity. In the art world, authenticity means the certainty that a work was truly created by the artist whose name is on it. In a world of technologically produced copies, authenticity is associated with uniqueness, which makes an object or experience more valuable. But some artists have responded to our technological environment by playing with the idea of the copy, as Kitaj plays with the image of van Gogh's chair. The conversation thus set up between the earlier work and the new one becomes part of our larger cultural conversation about the meaning of authenticity.

CHAPTER 3

Representing and Misrepresenting the Self

Situation: Have you seen *Spiderman?* What is the movie about? Are you familiar with the original *Spiderman* comics?

Genre: What do you know about the genre of the superhero story? How would you describe the rules or conventions of movies or comics that involve a superhero who switches identities?

Consequences: In any superhero story, what are the consequences of switching identities?

Have you ever described a movie to a friend who hadn't seen it? Did you focus on the plot, the theme, or the look of the movie? If you focused on the plot, did you tell the whole story or just describe a few particular scenes? If you told a different friend about the same movie, did you describe it differently? Did you ever worry that you were not describing it accurately or that you had misunderstood something about it?

If you've done any of these things, then you know what it means to represent something. To represent something means to re-present it, make it present again, or make it present in a new place or a new way. Different people can represent the same thing differently, and the same person can represent the same thing in different ways. We might tailor our representation to the audience or the situation. When we represent something, we have to make decisions about it.

Thus as soon as we begin representing, we have to think about form. The thing itself is not present, and to make it present again we have to embody it in a new way or give it a form. How will we shape our representation of a movie we've seen: a very detailed account of the plot, a description of the characters, a philosophical discussion of the theme, a dramatic recreation of a specific scene, a comparison of this movie to another of the same genre? To represent something is to make decisions about form or genre.

It follows, then, that as soon as we represent something, we also need to think about the possibility of misrepresenting it. Each decision we make has the potential to be a kind of misrepresentation. If we emphasize plot, are we misrepresenting the whole? If we describe the same movie differently to different people, is one of these descriptions a misrepresentation? Suppose you misrepresent the movie—describe it inaccurately—but in doing so you give your friend an accurate sense of what the movie is like. These complications suggest that the relationships between representing and misrepresenting, and thus between representation and authenticity, are not as clear-cut as we might think at first.

We represent things all the time: movies, books, events, experiences. But perhaps the thing that we represent most often is our self. To represent yourself is to make yourself present in a place where you are not or to make yourself present in a different form, for example when you give a picture of yourself to someone, send an e-mail, write a college application essay, or create a personal Web page. In all these cases you are representing yourself, yet each representation is different, and the difference is determined by the situation, the audience, and the form itself. Are all of these representations authentic?

In the reading and writing you do in this chapter, you will explore the complicated relationship between representation, misrepresentation, and authenticity, particularly in connection with the self and with the complicated things that we do when we represent or misrepresent ourselves.

Skin

Esmeralda Santiago

Although in this chapter we focus mainly on representation as a stand-in for something that is not present—the picture of yourself that you give to someone, the e-mail message that you send, the application essay that you write—it can be said that we represent ourselves even when we are present. That is, the ways we *present* ourselves—how we look, the things we say, the clothes we wear, the ways we behave—cause others to form impressions of us. In this sense of representation, our body plays a complicated role. Our body makes us physically present, but it also represents our self to others. In such situations of "presence," our body is usually the first thing about our selves that people encounter, and it's the most concrete possible representation of our selves, yet we all know that our body can misrepresent us in various ways.

Our skin is both the most public and one of the most private parts of both our bodies and our selves. Parts of our skin—our face, our hands—may be the first things that people notice about us, but other parts of our skin are covered up and private, and in fact the amount of skin that we show is often a significant aspect of how we represent ourselves to others. This essay by Esmeralda Santiago explores how our skin might help us represent our selves to ourselves. Santiago, the author of the novels *When I Was Puerto Rican, America's Dream,* and *Almost a Woman,* sees her skin as a form of memory, a record of significant events and experiences in her life. This record—her scars, her wrinkles—has significance mostly for Santiago herself, but she also recognizes that it is an important part of what others see and know about her, and she rejects the idea of plastic surgery because she knows that it would erase the evidence of experiences that make her who she is.

This essay appeared in a book called *Body,* a collection of personal essays about body parts written by poets, fiction writers, playwrights, essayists, and journalists. The collection's editors, Sharon Sloan Fiffer and Steve Fiffer, have edited two similar collections, *Family: American Writers Remember Their Own* and *Home: American Writers Remember Rooms of Their Own.* The assumption behind these collections is that, because it is the business of writers to perceive and record the world with clarity, they may describe our experiences even when they are writing with most intimate detail about their own. As you read Santiago's essay, consider how well she succeeds in doing this.

Connecting with the Conversation

1. English has a number of expressions that refer to skin: skin deep, thin skinned, it makes my skin crawl, and I almost jumped out of my skin. Working in small groups, think of other such expressions, and then explore what each suggests about how we see the relationship between our skin and ourselves.
2. Our skin is just another organ, like a liver or a kidney, but much more than these, and even more than our heart, we tend to identify our skin with ourselves, at least in terms of how we present ourselves and relate to the outside world. Write in your journal about how you see the relationship between your skin and yourself.

My skin is richly toned, soft brown, *trigueña* we say in Puerto Rico, wheat-colored. Not white, not black, *trigueña* is not a race. It is a blend of all the races that have contributed to my brownness. *Trigueña* is what, in the United States, makes me "Other."

There are spots on my *trigueña* skin, birthmarks and scars, blemishes, wrinkles, veins that refuse to be contained in deeper tissue and have made their way to just below the surface. I often find unexplained bruises on my limbs, dark blue, angry splotches that turn purple before they fade. Below my eye there is a red dot that appeared one day, a punctuation to something I saw, perhaps. On my neck, around my torso there are small chocolate brown tags that materialized during my first pregnancy. Or maybe they were always there and I didn't notice them before. Lately they seem to be creeping toward my face, and I imagine it is the darker me emerging, taking over the lighter skinned Esmeralda.Maybe I'm becoming other than "Other."

I need not look hard to read history etched on my skin. There, along the arch of my left foot, is the scar left when I stepped on the sharp barbs of a wire fence. On the outside of my left knee is another scar, formed when a nail that protruded from the balusters of our porch cut a deep wedge that took weeks to heal. A smile hovers over my pubic hair, the wound through which doctors delivered my two children. Right in the center of my forehead is a dash, all that remains of the bloody mess when Chago, my childhood playmate, threw a rock that found its mark. That scar has been swallowed by the deep wrinkles left by surprise and worry.

Each line, each spot, each scar is a story, forgotten by almost everyone else involved, but not by me. That scar on top of my foot? It was not an accident, as I told Mami. We were living in the city, in two rooms behind a bar. My brother Raymond's foot had been

From *Body,* Edited by Sharon Sloan Fiffer and Steve Fiffer. New York: Avon Books, 1999, pp. 61–72.

injured in an accident—my fault, I thought, because I'd been left in charge and wasn't careful enough. Raymond, then four years old, was in and out of hospitals for weeks. Nights, he cried because his foot hurt so much. Days, he limped, and whimpered pitifully with every step. Doctors thought he'd never heal and that he should be amputated.

5 Curled at the edge of my foot, my smallest toe looked silly and useless. I pinched it, stuck pins into it, placed it under the metal leg of a chair, then pressed hard with all my weight. It hurt, but not nearly as much as I thought it should, and it didn't bleed. Raymond's foot bled, and angry bubbles of pus formed around the wound the doctors cleaned again and again.

One day, while Mami was outside de-feathering a chicken, I went into the bedroom, rummaged through her sewing box, and found the heavy scissors she took to work in the bra factory. They were black and silver, weighed on my hand solid and menacing. They were very sharp, and I was certain they could slice through that useless little toe in a neat cut.

I straddled the windowsill, my left leg dangling outside, my right knee pressed up to my chest. It was mid-afternoon, and shadows crept from one end of the yard to another. I held the scissors, cool to the touch, opened and closed them a couple of times as if they were jaws. I was not afraid. I'd been cut, scraped, or bruised hundreds of times. My skin was, even then, spotted with scars on every limb. They had all been accidents, but this was the first time I deliberately hurt myself.

I placed the sharp blades of the scissors around my toe and squeezed the handle, but didn't have the strength to cut clear through. The skin opened and a bubble of blood sprouted then trickled down to my sole. It hurt, but not nearly enough. I hopped down from the windowsill, was about to put the scissors away and take care of the wound when I noticed how my bare feet provided a perfect target. I dropped the scissors, point down, an inch above my middle toe. It hurt more than I could have imagined, and I screamed and hopped around as the scissors twinked onto the cement floor. Everyone came running. Mami, her hands and hair clumped with chicken feathers. My sisters and brothers, who had been playing in the shadows under the mango tree. Even Raymond limped over, and screeched when he saw the blood spurt from my foot, the same foot that hurt him so much.

Mami took care of it right away, so the wound didn't fester, and there was no threat that my foot would be amputated. But it hurt a lot, almost as much, I thought, as Raymond's must have. The scar that was left is round, less than a quarter inch in diameter, a tiny crater where I store guilt.

10 AN ACTIVE CHILD WILL GET HURT, a competitive one will hurt others. I was both, and my skin confirms the many falls and tumbles of a childhood in motion. I never broke a bone, but scrapes, cuts, stings, and punctures have left their mark on me, and I have inflicted them on others. My ten sisters and brothers can each point to what's left of the arguments that turned into fights that drew blood.

I was eighteen when I chased my brother Héctor up the stairs. I caught up to him on the top step, reached out, grabbed a handful of his hair, and yanked. We tumbled down, causing a racket that brought my mother, stepfather, grandmother, her boyfriend, my nine other sisters and brothers, and a neighbor to the hallway, where Héctor and I lay sprawled, punching one another. Mami pulled us apart, yelled at me that as the eldest, I should stop acting like a little kid, and at Héctor that at fourteen and almost a man, he should not hit girls. I threw one last punch, and so did he, and we had to be separated again. I stumbled off, blood dribbling down my leg, a thin red ribbon from a gash below my knee.

I don't remember what Héctor said or did that made me chase him up the stairs, and probably neither does he. But I'm reminded of that humid afternoon every time I shave my legs because there is a round, flat scar on my right shin, its surface lighter than the skin around it. On that scar there is no hair, just as now, thirty-two years later, there is no hair atop Héctor's head. Within the uneven borders of the scar on my shin I hold the course of time, the physical changes it has wrought on me and my loved ones.

In my rural childhood, toys were not purchased, they were made. As children, we sought Y-shaped branches of various sizes, set them to dry and harden in the hot Puerto Rican sun. A discarded bicycle inner tube cut into strips made the perfect tensile straps and cradle for a slingshot. A battered bucket was my first target, the pings of a hit resonating with a satisfying echo that no one could argue with. As I gained skill, the targets became smaller—a bottle, a tomato sauce can, a mango still on its branch.

Not allowed to wear pants, I insisted Mami put pockets in the cotton dresses she made for me and my sisters so that I could carry pebbles in them. The sash at my waist that tied into a bow in the back of the dresses held the slingshot at my side, and I practiced drawing it out like a cowboy a six-shooter. No one could outdraw me, or outshoot me.

15 An iguana scurrying into the shade of the annatto bushes had no chance against me. A bird in mid-flight would plummet to the ground, stunned by a well-aimed rock. Snakes slithering under piles of kindling for the stove, lizards scuttling from branch to branch on the avocado tree, mice scampering toward the kitchen—not one reached their goal. Their death came as a soft hiss through the humid air followed by a sharp thwack to their narrow heads.

"Girls shouldn't play with slingshots," the neighbors muttered, but if I killed the rat that ate into their sack of rice, they sent Mami a bowl of candied papaya or a bagful of fresh pigeon peas.

It was a well-aimed slingshot stone that left a scar I never see. My neighbor and playmate, Chago, claimed to have seen an *ardilla,* a Puerto Rican mongoose, in the hill behind his house. We set out to hunt it, but on the way down the road we got into an argument about who was the best shot. Everyone knew I was, and I reminded him of this, but his response was to mumble "*Tu madre,*" under his breath. *Mencionar la madre,* to mention another person's mother as a curse, is a major insult in Puerto Rico, and I did what anyone would have done. I punched him in the mouth. After he recovered from the surprise of a girl striking out, he backed up, bent over, picked up a fist-size rock, and threw it at me. I fell on my face, my forehead covered in blood. As he ran off, he called out a few more specific insults about my mother. When he looked back to see if I was following him, a stone from my slingshot found its mark, square on his left eye. The scar I never see was formed when doctors sewed his eyelid shut. And while there were welts left after the beating administered by my mother, who did not care I was defending her when I shot Chago's eye out, they healed soon after we moved from the barrio. The scar Chago left on me closed into a hyphen that divides and connects the right side of my face from the left. Inside it I store power.

Another scar invisible to me was found by a hairdresser. WALK-INS WELCOME the sign on the window of Tami's Hair and Nails stated. Inside was Tami herself, redheaded, green-eyed, long orange nails in the shape of spades. She tried to talk me out of cutting my waist-length hair. "If I cut it to shoulder length," she offered, "it will be enough of a change." It had taken over seven years to grow, seven years in which I fell in love with, and was betrayed by, a man who loved my long hair. "I want it really short," I insisted. Tami gathered a long ponytail at the base of my neck, tightened a rubber band around it, and cut. The strands that were freed from the weight of the hair below the cut line came to attention into a fuzzy halo around my face. "More," I ordered. "Chop it all off."

"Boy," Tami giggled, "you must be really mad at him."

20 The more she cut, the more liberated I felt, until she stopped, gently tipped my head forward, and parted the stubble. "Oh, honey," she murmured, "this must have hurt." She traced a line from just above the nape of my neck toward the crown of my head.

That one was caused by my mother. Quique and I had been discovered behind the outhouse with our hands on each other's private parts. His mother used a switch that left puffy red stripes on his legs and back. But Mami grabbed the first thing she could get her hands on, a cast-iron frying pan. She chased me around the yard, screaming that I had no shame. Inside the scar she left on the back of my head I store desire.

The scars on my skin are only the most painful traces of my life. There are also the stamps I was born with, the freckles that dot my cheeks and nose, the birthmark shaped like the island of Hispaniola that floats just under my navel, the dark dot on the back of my neck that I thought was sexy. Those birthmarks are my disappointment. Why do I have freckles? Why did no lover ever kiss that spot on the back of my neck?

As a child fascinated with geography, I loved the fact that the middle of the Greater Antilles was represented on my belly. I searched for Cuba and Puerto Rico, but neither was visible on my skin. Superstitious enough to believe anything, I thought the birthmark meant that someday I was destined to live in Santo Domingo or Port au Prince. But when I did leave Puerto Rico, it wasn't for another island. I studied a map of the United States, wondering which had the same shape as the birthmark under my navel. None do, but I'm still superstitious enough to believe there is some significance to it, some reason why the shape of the island near my navel looks like Haiti and the Dominican Republic but not Puerto Rico. I've concluded that it is because I will die there. Within the ragged borders of that birthmark I hold fear.

My cousin Corazón has a birthmark on the inside of her right knee. It is round, chocolate brown, the size of a plain M&M. I once asked her about it, and she told me her mother wished for it when she was pregnant, and that's why Corazón was born with one. I didn't believe her, so I asked her mother.

25 "There is a reason," Titi Ana said, "that it's called a *lunar.*"

When she was pregnant with Corazón, Titi Ana confessed to her midwife that if her child were a girl, she wished she would have a birthmark near her lip, just like Maria Félix, the Mexican movie star. The midwife assured Titi Ana that the moon would not deny a pregnant woman an *antojo,* and told her what she had to do to make her wish come true. Titi Ana followed the midwife's instructions, but at the last minute, realized that the birthmark might not look as good near the lip if the child were a boy. So she wished for it where it would be invisible to everyone else. Titi Ana could not have predicted that someday Corazón would wear miniskirts and that people would compliment her on the moon-shaped dark spot near her knee.

Years later, when I became pregnant and modern medicine assured me I was having a girl, I remembered Titi Ana's story, and decided to test the moon. Would it fulfill my wish for a pretty *lunar* on my daughter? Titi Ana had died years earlier, but I'd never forgotten her soft voice repeating the midwife's instructions for ensuring a birthmark on a child.

On the seventh month of my pregnancy, I stepped outside on the first night of a full moon. "You must invite the spirit of a woman in your family to help you," Titi Ana had said, and so I closed my eyes and called upon her, until I felt her presence, cool and silent near me. My hands on my belly, I rubbed circles counterclockwise, spoke to my child until I felt her moving. "Tonight you will receive a gift," I said, "from the moon and from your Great-aunt Ana, who watch over you."

I faced the moon, opened my eyes, and was about to put my right index finger near my lip when, like Titi Ana before me, I worried that a *lunar* would not look good there. I changed my mind, but then it occurred to me that, now that I was outside, facing the full moon, having summoned both my unborn child and the ghost of Titi Ana, I had to make a wish because spirits didn't like to be disturbed for no reason at all. If I didn't make a wish, it might mean bad luck for my daughter. I pressed the tip of my index finger halfway up my left thigh, and wished for a *lunar* there, a much more intimate place than where Corazón has hers. Two months later, when Ila was born, she had a dark chocolate birthmark on the inside of her left thigh. As soon as the doctors saw it, they took a biopsy, and on subsequent exams, her doctor has studied it, measured it, scraped the center of it, concerned it might be malignant.

But it's not a precancerous lesion. It is a gift from me, Titi Ana, and the moon, a spot where Ila can gather knowledge of the mysteries of woman.

When I stand naked before a mirror, I see how skin has evolved from the tight, firm, bouncy sheath that held me in, to the looser, softer, more textured canvas on which I sketch my life. Except for the ones I was born with, there are no marks on my skin that have not come from experience. But even the birthmarks and freckles on my body have meaning, imposed on them by superstition.

Wrinkles, engraved time on my skin, reveal themselves in unexpected ways at surprising times. I noticed the lines across my forehead as a teenager, after reading an article in *Glamour* magazine. As the writer instructed, I faced the mirror to determine if I had dry, oily, or combination skin, and there they were, two faint inverted vees over my eyebrows, and one line that ran temple to temple above the scar left by Chago's rock. When I looked closer, there were more; two tiny vertical lines where my nose met my forehead, two more beside my lips.

It was the first time I realized that I was not just growing up, I was growing old. Old like my grandmother and the man who owned the candy store. Old like my social studies teacher and the school principal. Old like my uncle Chico and great-aunt Chía. The first signs of mortality were etched on my skin, faint but visible, wrinkles formed by an often too expressive face. Should I stop frowning, smiling, squinting, puckering my lips? No, the beauty magazines only advised I moisturize.

Years later, and in spite of thousands of dollars spent on beauty products that promised to keep the skin on my face looking younger, firmer, more supple, I am wrinkled. Were I to slather moisturizer on every part of my body, my skin might not reveal its fifty years. But would moisturizer keep away the wrinkles I recently noticed around my breasts? How about the folds over my knees, and over my elbows? Would several more thousand dollars have erased the deep lines around my neck? The beauty industry would say yes. Plastic surgeons would argue that a nip here, a tuck there, would accomplish more than truckloads of creams. I could look twenty years younger, they promise.

Twenty years! I can erase the wrinkles caused by the final frantic days before my wedding. The puffy folds around my eyes can be cut away, so that it looks as if I never cry. The saggy skin around my breasts can be excised, eradicating three years of nursing babies. The skin around my middle can be tucked so as to deny the pregnancies, the distention caused by too many rich meals, the aversion to sit-ups.

But what about the scars? Would they too be erased? Where would I hide despair? Would each and every birthmark locate to a different spot now that the skin has been pulled, nipped, pinched? What do I do with superstition? And if these new scars, the ones created by plastic surgery, the ones that will erase experience from my body, come to me while I'm unconscious on an operating table, what will they contain?

* * *

My skin scars easily, but it also heals fast. It has been an advantage in life, this skin that has taken such abuse but still responds to a caress. In spite of all the scars, or maybe because of them, I'm thin-skinned and sensitive. This skin that has held me in but has loosed so much it's had to fold into itself, still feels, still bleeds, still stores who I am, have been, hope to become. *Trigueña,* wrinkled, spotted, bruised, marked, and scarred, my skin is the surface on which I read sorrow, superstition, the passage of time. Its texture, color, and tone have changed over the years, but within its confines I have survived a half century of life, each moment indelibly carved into my flesh.

Exploring Texts and Contexts

For activities with icons, refer to the Guide to Analyzing Readings in Context.

1. Santiago's essay is carefully structured with an introduction and conclusion framing four sections in which she examines four different marks on her skin, and within each of these four sections she interweaves description, narration, and metaphor to help us understand what each mark means to her. See if you can divide the essay into its six main sections (some but not all of which are marked off with double spaces), and then within each of the four middle sections, see if you can identify the movements of description, narration, and metaphor.

2. Santiago identifies herself as a 50-year-old Puerto Rican woman. How might her essay have been different if she had been Caucasian, African American, Native American, Asian, a man, 20 years old, or 80 years old?

Creating Texts

For activities with icons, refer to the Guides to Analyzing Contexts for Writing and Analyzing Readings in Context. For additional help with these writing projects, read the description of **Essay** and **Comics** in the Genre Glossary.

1. In the collection from which Santiago's essay was taken, other writers such as National Public Radio host Jacki Lyden, novelists Francine Prose and Jane Smiley, cartoonist Lynda Barry, and short-story writer Chris Offutt write about such parts of the body as the brain, the nose, the belly, the teeth, and the knee bone. Using Santiago's essay as a general model, write a personal essay that might be included in such a collection.
2. In this personal essay Santiago uses language to explore a very physical phenomenon: how marks on the skin represent life experiences. Visual artists, almost conversely, may use visual images to express ideas or concepts. In Connecting with the Conversation Activity 1 on page 43, there is a list of expressions that refer to skin: skin deep, thin skinned, it makes my skin crawl, and I almost jumped out of my skin; you may have thought of others. Choose two or three of these expressions and draw a set of comics that visually convey the meanings of these expressions. Genre

A *Portfolio of Self Representations*

Shane Madden

In the last few years, you have probably created at least some of the following: a college application essay, a resume and cover letter, a profile of yourself for an online forum, a description of yourself for a yearbook, a Web page, a username, or a voice mail greeting. In all of these ways you have used language, written or spoken, to represent yourself to others. It might seem to you that what is being represented—your self—stays the same, yet each of these representations is different because each arises out of a different situation and thus takes a different form; that is, each one is a different genre.

People use a surprisingly wide array of genres to represent themselves, and in contemporary American culture, young people represent themselves in more complex ways than they themselves might be aware of. Just within the last few years, for example, Shane Madden, a college freshman, has filled out numerous college applications, most of which requested a personal statement; composed a statement about himself for his high school yearbook; submitted brief profiles of himself for some of the chat rooms and online forums that he participates in; created two different personal Web pages, one that he made with the help of some friends when he was in high school and one that he had to make for one of his fall semester college classes; written a resume and cover letter for a summer job; and recorded a voice mail greeting for the phone in his dormitory room. This is in addition to the many essays, and occasional stories and poems, that he wrote for high school and college classes; the e-mails, posts, and instant messages that he writes almost every day; the thank you notes that his mom made him write after his graduation party; and the "video letter" that he made for a friend attending a different college, all of which—although they are not "self-portraits" like a resume or a Web page—are certainly acts of self representation.

Here we include three of Madden's self representations:* parts of the Web page that he created in high school and still sporadically maintains, one of his college application essays, and the resume and cover letter that he recently wrote for a summer job. How does Madden represent himself in these different genres? What significant common ground and what interesting differences do you find between them? How do the conventions of the different genres both open up and limit possibilities for expressing himself? Do the three different self-portraits seem to be separate, different portraits or pieces of a larger whole? Does any one of them seem to be more authentic than the others? Do you think Madden would describe them as representations or misrepresentations of himself?

Connecting with the Conversation

1. Bring to class an object that you see as representing yourself and be prepared to discuss why you chose it.
2. Put together a mini portfolio of self representations—for example, your high school yearbook picture and caption, your dorm room application, your voice mail greeting, or an introduction of yourself that you had to write for a college orientation activity or for one of your classes—and discuss how you see them as representing or misrepresenting you.

*Details have been changed to protect the privacy of the author.

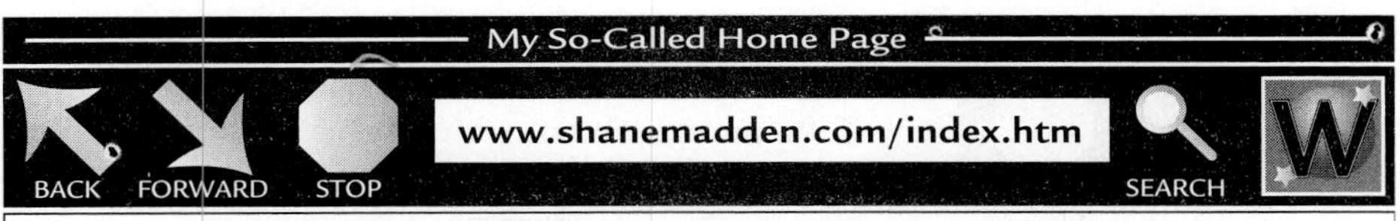

My So-Called Home Page

If you really want to hear about it...

My name is Shane Madden, I'm fifteen years old, and I live in Chicago with my dog, my parents, my cat, and my sister, in that order. I go to Thomas Paine High School but I won't bore you with the details. Here's what I like, more or less in this order: movies, music, and politics. My favorite director is David Lynch, but I'm interested in all kinds of movies, even one or two made in Hollywood. My favorite music is punk rock, but any kind of real rock and roll is fine by me. Politically, I'm pretty leftwing, but I enjoy reading about all kinds of political perspectives; some of them are very entertaining. I could tell you what I look like, but here's a couple pictures instead. You could click to enlarge them, but why would you want to? Thanks to Sandy for both of them.

But if you want to know who I really am,
check out my favorite web sites

www.theonion.com
www.indymedia.org
www.imdf.com
www.allmusic.com
http://news.yahoo.com
www.fourthwall.org

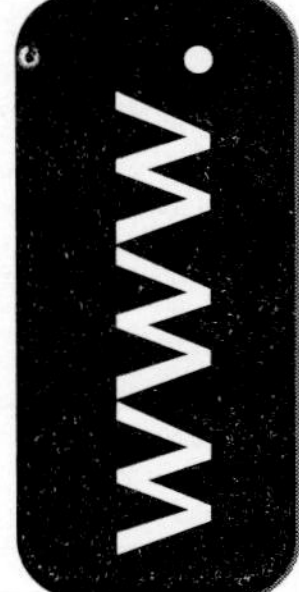

If you'd rather read about my life as it happens, click here

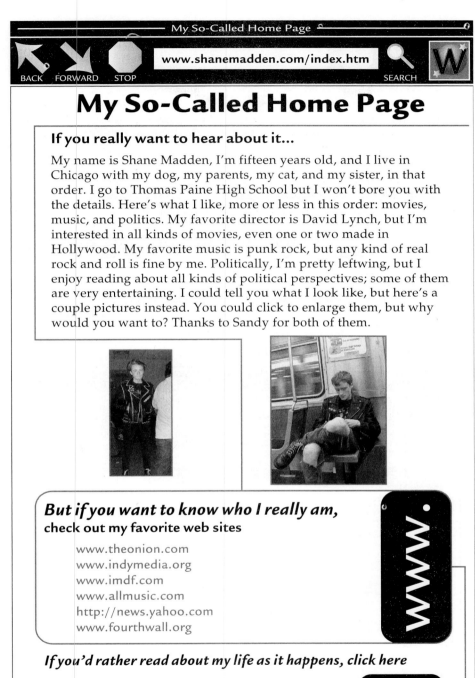

BLOG

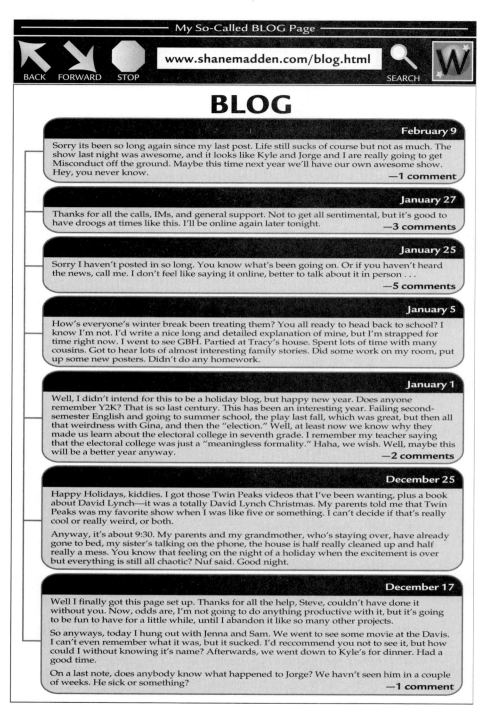

My So-Called BLOG Page

www.shanemadden.com/blog.html

BLOG

February 9

Sorry its been so long again since my last post. Life still sucks of course but not as much. The show last night was awesome, and it looks like Kyle and Jorge and I are really going to get Misconduct off the ground. Maybe this time next year we'll have our own awesome show. Hey, you never know.

—1 comment

January 27

Thanks for all the calls, IMs, and general support. Not to get all sentimental, but it's good to have droogs at times like this. I'll be online again later tonight.

—3 comments

January 25

Sorry I haven't posted in so long. You know what's been going on. Or if you haven't heard the news, call me. I don't feel like saying it online, better to talk about it in person . . .

—5 comments

January 5

How's everyone's winter break been treating them? You all ready to head back to school? I know I'm not. I'd write a nice long and detailed explanation of mine, but I'm strapped for time right now. I went to see GBH. Partied at Tracy's house. Spent lots of time with many cousins. Got to hear lots of almost interesting family stories. Did some work on my room, put up some new posters. Didn't do any homework.

January 1

Well, I didn't intend for this to be a holiday blog, but happy new year. Does anyone remember Y2K? That is so last century. This has been an interesting year. Failing second-semester English and going to summer school, the play last fall, which was great, but then all that weirdness with Gina, and then the "election." Well, at least now we know why they made us learn about the electoral college in seventh grade. I remember my teacher saying that the electoral college was just a "meaningless formality." Haha, we wish. Well, maybe this will be a better year anyway.

—2 comments

December 25

Happy Holidays, kiddies. I got those Twin Peaks videos that I've been wanting, plus a book about David Lynch—it was a totally David Lynch Christmas. My parents told me that Twin Peaks was my favorite show when I was like five or something. I can't decide if that's really cool or really weird, or both.

Anyway, it's about 9:30. My parents and my grandmother, who's staying over, have already gone to bed, my sister's talking on the phone, the house is half really cleaned up and half really a mess. You know that feeling on the night of a holiday when the excitement is over but everything is still all chaotic? Nuf said. Good night.

December 17

Well I finally got this page set up. Thanks for all the help, Steve, couldn't have done it without you. Now, odds are, I'm not going to do anything productive with it, but it's going to be fun to have for a little while, until I abandon it like so many other projects.

So anyways, today I hung out with Jenna and Sam. We went to see some movie at the Davis. I can't even remember what it was, but it sucked. I'd reccommend you not to see it, but how could I without knowing it's name? Afterwards, we went down to Kyle's for dinner. Had a good time.

On a last note, does anybody know what happened to Jorge? We havn't seen him in a couple of weeks. He sick or something?

—1 comment

College Application Essay

Write an essay of about 500–750 words in which you answer this question: What idea has most influenced your life and why?

As cliched as it might sound, I think that the idea that has most influenced my life is the oft-repeated creed: question everything. In a society where public debate seems limited to a very few voices, many of which have obvious financial interests, ideas put forth in the mainstream are likely to have flaws and benefit a small minority. I feel that in order to maintain a clear mind, a mind where you have more control over your own opinions, it is necessary to look rationally at everything you're told and to examine it with extreme scrutiny.

All too often in today's world, I see people blindly swallowing any idea that is given to them. When there are incredible amounts of evidence against something, they'll believe it if it's drilled into their heads long enough. This includes everything from religion to political issues. And, often, when it comes to the most important things, things that could sway votes and change public opinion, the people who put forth the false ideas have their own interests in mind. Whether it's a pundit who tells it on a network that owns a corporation that would be affected by the issue, or it's a politician whose power is at stake, the loudest voices don't necessarily have the best interest of the public in mind. This is why I believe it's important to question everything.

But I have to say that the influence of this idea on my life has been complicated. On the one hand it sometimes means that it's not easy for me to get involved in things, even things that I believe in. For example, I am definitely and strongly anti-war. Recently I went to an anti-war rally with some friends. The speeches were great, and I pretty much agreed with everything they said. But there was a part of me that kept thinking, Okay, but what about this, or Do I really believe that statement? Then when everyone started marching and shouting slogans, I just couldn't bring myself to join in. Of course I was marching with everyone else—I couldn't help it—but I wasn't shouting slogans and getting all excited. I kept wondering what the people who disagreed with us thought about the arguments against the war, what kinds of arguments they would make in favor of it, and what kinds of questions they might ask us—especially if they also believed in "question everything"! My friends had a great time during the march, but I was a little bored by it and would rather have gotten into a discussion with the people standing on the sidewalk watching us.

So it seems as if the idea of questioning everything limits my ability to get involved. But on the other hand it makes me more interested in everything. I like reading about other perspectives and other political and religious beliefs. I probably spend as much time on Web sites that I disagree with as on the ones that I agree with. I like going to the Web sites of really fundamentalist religious organizations or the various pro-Bush Web sites. I'm usually not convinced by their arguments, but they do tend to make me more skeptical about the arguments that I thought I agreed with. Although people think of me as someone with strong opinions, I get along pretty well with people who have different beliefs because I'm interested in finding out why they believe what they do, even if I don't agree with them.

So I still think that "question everything" is one of the most important ideas in the world, even if it makes your life more complicated. Thinking for yourself and questioning things will lead to further understanding of the world around you. If you understand something because you yourself sought to educate yourself about it, then it will resonate that much more in your head, and you will understand it that much more. Besides, if you blindly accept any idea, you may become prone to accepting falsehoods, whether they're falsehoods created with malicious intentions or just false common beliefs that are rarely questioned.

I feel that I understand many more things by thinking about them myself. I feel that if I did not set about trying to understand things for myself, my understanding of the world would be much more shallow, and would be limited to the opinions of others. My vision of the world might be vulnerable to the selfish desires of others. I feel that I am all the more intelligent and better for being naturally inquisitive. I feel that I would not be the person I am if I did not realize the importance of questioning everything.

Shane Madden

Shane Madden
4625 W. Cooper
Chicago, IL 60613

March 10, 2004

Leslie Stephens
Director of Counselors
Timberland Theater Camp
Timberland Lake, WI

Dear Ms. Stephens:

I am writing to you because I heard about your camp from my teachers at The Fourth Wall Theater Ensemble. They feel that I should apply for a counselor position at your camp this summer.

I was a member for five years of the Youth and Teen Ensembles at the Fourth Wall Theater. This involved acting classes as well as taking part in two or three productions a year. I have had parts in productions ranging from *Macbeth* to plays written and staged by the ensemble members. I have also had parts in several high school productions.

For the last five years I have attended the High Tower YMCA summer camp in Chicago, and last summer I worked there as a Junior Counselor. In this position I supervised children aged 6 through 10. I initiated and taught a playwriting and acting class, and at the end of the summer the kids put on a production of a play that they had written themselves. This was a great experience, and I would very much like to do this kind of work again.

I have good skills working with children and can help them further develop their acting talent, as well as help them feel comfortable in a summer camp environment. I am also good at the other various tasks involved with being a camp counselor.

I am currently a freshman at State University, and I will be finished with my spring semester by May 15. The fall semester begins on September 4. I will be available any time between those two dates. I can be reached at 773 234-5678, and I would be able to come to Timberland for an interview any weekend. I am very much looking forward to discussing the counselor position with you.

Sincerely,

Shane Madden

Shane Madden

4625 W. Cooper
Chicago, IL 60613
773 234-5678

Objective	To obtain a counselor job at a summer theater camp.
Education	
Fall 2003 – Present	Enrolled at State University Anticipated major: Philosophy Anticipated graduation date: May 2007
Fall 1999 – Spring 2003	Thomas Paine High School Graduated June 2003 GPA: 3.2 (on a 4-point scale)
Work and Other Related Experience	
Fall 2003 – Present	Assistant in the archives at the State University library. Catalogued documents and other materials; assisted in organizing materials in a newly designed document room.
Summer 2003	Junior Counselor at the High Tower YMCA Summer Camp. Supervised children aged six to ten; initiated and taught a class in playwriting and acting; assisted the children in writing and planning the production of a play; directed the play and supervised its production as part of the end-of-summer parents weekend.
Fall 1999 – Spring 2003	Acted in several productions at Thomas Paine High School.
Fall 1998 – Spring 2003	Member of the Fourth Wall Theater's Youth and Teen Ensemble. Acted in two or three productions each year; participated in writing of several productions; and participated in the stage design of all productions.
Other Skills	Computer skills including Word, Access, and HTML. Studied French for eight years and Latin for four years. Play guitar.
References	Available upon request.

Exploring Texts and Contexts

For activities with icons, refer to the Guide to Analyzing Readings in Context.

1. Describe the conventions of each genre included in this portfolio and discuss how these conventions might have shaped Madden's self representations. 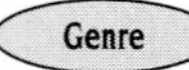

2. What were Madden's purpose and audience in each of these self representations, and how did these considerations shape the representation? How successful do you think each of these pieces is? If you were responding to any of these pieces as a peer reviewer, what suggestions for improvement would you make? Consequences
3. Discuss the different ways that Madden represents himself. What kind of person do you think he "really" is? Do you think any of these is more accurate or truthful, more authentic, than the others? Why?

Creating Texts

For activities with icons, refer to the Guides to Analyzing Contexts for Writing and Analyzing Readings in Context. For additional help with these writing projects, read the descriptions of **Personal Essay, Web Page, Resume/Cover Letter**, and **Cover Letter/Reflective Essay** in the Genre Glossary.

1. Add to the mini portfolio you put together for Connecting with the Conversation Activity 2, on page 51, a personal essay, a personal Web page, a resume and cover letter, and one or two other self representations that you choose.
2. Write a Cover Letter/Reflective Essay in which you discuss the relationship between each of the pieces of self representation in the portfolio and what you see as your authentic self or true identity, if you think there is such a thing. Do you see some as more accurate representations than others, and why? Do the conventions of any of these genres require you to represent yourself in ways that seem like distortions? On the other hand, do the rules of any of these genres allow you to represent yourself in ways that you otherwise are not able to express? Do you feel that you learned anything about yourself by representing yourself in any of these forms? Genre

Representin' the Real

Todd Boyd

Suppose that you represent yourself in different ways in different situations, say when you are with friends as opposed to with your parents or a teacher. Which is the real you? We tend to think that authenticity is a question of expressing our true self, finding our true voice. But what if you have more than one true self? What if your true self changes according to the context? Have you ever been in one of those situations where you had to interact with two people, or two groups of people, who knew you in different contexts and had different expectations about your behavior? How do you feel in such a situation, and how do you handle it?

Todd Boyd, an assistant professor of critical studies in the School of Cinema-Television at the University of Southern California, takes up this question in connection with writing, specifically academic writing. Boyd has written extensively about popular culture, in particular black popular culture, and he wants to make his writing accessible to ordinary people who are interested in and affected by the things he writes about. At the same time, in order to have professional credibility, he must write and publish for other experts in his field and academic readers in general. Because different audiences measure authenticity differently, Boyd has a complex sense of the hazards of trying to sound authentic to two different audiences. In this excerpt from his book *Am I Black Enough for You? Popular Culture from the 'Hood and Beyond*, Boyd both discusses and illustrates the struggle to develop an authentic style in this situation.

Connecting with the Conversation

1. In your journal, answer the questions posed in the first paragraph of the headnote above.
2. You've probably had a few occasions—for example, in writing a research paper—to read academic writing, that is, not a textbook written for students but a book or article written for other people in the field, other experts. And of course you've read popular media articles, for example in newspapers and magazines. In your journal, describe the differences between academic and popular writing. Discuss how you respond to these two kinds of writing.

One of my most vivid childhood memories is the constant presence of neatly though conservatively dressed Black men in dark suits with bow ties, sporting closely cropped hair, or a "Quo Vadis," as it was called at the time. These men were of course members of the Nation of Islam who sold *Muhammed Speaks* from the street corners of downtown Detroit. Their polite manner of speaking and dignified appearance were always interesting to me, and I looked forward to encountering them, if for no other reason than that they would often refer to me, a little boy, as "Sir" or sometimes "young brother," terms of acknowledgment and respect that had lasting meaning.

I guess in hindsight I was impressed by their pride and dignity, the fact that they looked you straight in the eye when talking, that they did not scratch when they did not itch, that they did not laugh when things were not funny, and that they seemed to

---

From *Am I Black Enough for You: Popular Culture from the 'Hood and Beyond.* Bloomington: Indiana University Press, 1997, pp. 1–12.

remain stoic at all times, regardless of the circumstances. They appeared fearless and the embodiment of what people now refer to as "hard."

Later on in life I began to understand why this was the case. As I learned about the Nation, or the Black Muslims as they were called in that day, it became clear that the reason for their stunning appearance was that the teachings of the Honorable Elijah Muhammed had given them the self-esteem that so many Black men are deprived of. While I have never been interested in being a Muslim, as their religious code of honor is unappealingly restrictive, the restoration of pride and dignity to their mostly male followers was laudable. Upon further investigation I discovered that many of the members of the Nation were ex-convicts or recovering substance abusers who found solace in this particular place.

Indeed, the Nation had established as its primary target for membership the neglected souls of our ghettoized society. These individuals are best summarized by Marx's description of the lumpenproletariat or, more concisely, what Frantz Fanon later described as the "wretched of the earth." Considering the fact that so few people are truly interested in assisting these depressed and deprived individuals, I have to commend the Nation for their assistance, even though I still have problems with their overall beliefs.

5 This "respect" for the Nation of Islam eventually led me to write a chapter of my doctoral dissertation on their current leader, Louis Farrakhan, and his place in popular culture and political discourse. At the time I was interested in finding a strident aesthetic of Blackness, somehow related to Black nationalism, but updated from its last incarnation in the late 1960s and early 1970s. I innocently called what I was searching for "Afrocentricity." Since that time the notion of an Afrocentric discourse has all but disappeared from my thought process. This is due to a lived politics of location that not only informs what I write but, in essence, defines the subject.

When I started the project, I was finishing my graduate studies at the University of Iowa, and upon completion I worked at my first academic job, as a professor at the University of Utah. The placement of a Black man in either one of these settings would be bad enough, but together, one behind the other, they were certainly a feat deserving of additional compensation. I have often called this my "fly in the buttermilk" tour. Nonetheless, my thoughts during that time were indicative of being marginalized in a sense that I am sure most cultural theorists have never thought of. Thus my writing was in defense, a justification for African American culture, as opposed to dealing with any substantive matter. While this process proved a good exercise, it was ultimately draining. African American culture does not need to be defended, as its impact on American culture is undeniable.

So as I began rethinking these ideas in the contested spaces of Los Angeles, I slowly realized that the battle lines were drawn somewhat differently. Here there was no doubt about the presence of African American culture; the point of reference had to do with its reception. I can vividly recall a member of the interview team at USC asking me to justify my critical inquiry into Louis Farrakhan. In the interviewer's mind, anything short of a pure dismissal was unacceptable. Not only was this attitude counterproductive in a scholarly environment, but as the public reaction after the October 1995 Million Man March would demonstrate, the refusal to treat the issue of Louis Farrakhan seriously remains a problem in American society. This dismissive attitude is still prevalent as I am writing this preface: one-time presidential hopeful Governor Pete

Wilson of California in the spring of 1995 led a vote by the University of California Board of Regents to end affirmative action. Wilson and others, including the interviewer, want to dismiss Black people in a way much more direct than a simple critical dismissal, though.

I moved to L.A. shortly after a jury in Simi Valley tried to disregard the fact that several police officers, who are charged with upholding the law, decided that they were above that law in their beating of Rodney King. I was a true resident of L.A. by the time a second jury conceded the bare minimum in sentencing two of the officers, though a judge decided that their punishment was too severe.

By then it was no longer a novelty to see members of the Nation of Islam standing on the corner of Crenshaw and Vernon selling newspapers and beanpies, nor was it a rarity to see Black men and women dressed in Afrocentric garb as I traveled around the area where USC is situated. No, these things were no longer abstract intellectual concerns, as they were in Iowa or Utah, but real live artifacts that were not as romantic or as distant as my state of denial might have made them seem before moving to L.A.

10 What was real was the way in which I often oscillated between being surrounded by the gang members of South Central and the Hollywood "niggaz" with whom most of my social time was being spent. I was constantly transposed between the "gangstaz" that Ice Cube rapped about, and the "gangstaz" themselves—or for that matter Ice Cube himself. Black men were once again real, as they had been for so much of my life. Thus I had to approach my subject with the same determination with which I would approach a real Black man. Romanticized theoretical concepts would no longer be privileged over real interaction.

In all this, my subject matter began to change. No longer was I searching for an Afrocentric position in Black popular culture. Instead I was in search of what held these competing tenets together: how Black men navigated the treacherous terrain of L.A., and how my own identity was being transformed in the process. No longer was I the novelty image; I had become real as well.

My move to L.A. also underscored another reason why Afrocentricity no longer seemed a relevant concern. This new evaluation of Afrocentricity had to do with commodification at the highest level. In Hollywood, where commercialization is so deeply ingrained, the selling out of Black political discourse in popular culture was readily evident—not only in the way that numerous individuals wore Afrocentric clothing for style, though having little knowledge of the politics, but in that the whole political process seemed empty. The media had simply found a way of co-opting everything, from the picture of Malcolm X on Roc's wall, to the emblematic X on baseball caps. Nothing appeared to be sacred.

Though Hollywood and commodity have never been enemies, there was a time when culture and politics that deviated from the mainstream were viewed as threatening. When there was a political theme that ran through popular culture, it was bounded by the real-life threat of a strong political presence. For instance, Les McCann and Eddie Harris's challenging political tune "Compared to What" was informed by the fact that the Black Panther Party was asking some of the same questions in society. Whereas politics at one time prompted popular culture, now popular culture exists in a world where politics has been completely displaced. Politics can exist only to the extent that it is replicated in the media, and even then this is short-lived.

This began to occur to me while listening to Gil Scott-Heron shortly after the riots in the spring of 1992. His tune "The Revolution Will Not Be Televised" is a concise deconstruction of the uselessness of media in a world where the people have decided to address their fate. Media, in this construction, would be obsolete. They could in no way alter the demands of history. Yet in 1992 the revolution was televised, and it proved quite entertaining at that. Not only did it displace Cosby, but the prevalence of home video cameras proved that we no longer had to be satisfied with a dominant version of the news, either. Most of the best footage came from amateur filmmakers, whose street ethnography became more valuable than the normally sophisticated news crews and their footage. The revolution was televised, and the availability of video equipment at the personal level made it that much more of a media event. Up close and personal took on an entirely different meaning.

15 So with the need for more and more authentic footage, the people in the street became simultaneously their own best friend and worst enemy. On one hand, they used the instruments of technology to momentarily halt their own materially motivated rampage through the streets, or in some cases to demonstrate it. On the other hand, they functioned as their own publicist by foregrounding their own images, totally ignoring, while ultimately falling into, the same traps that the mainstream media normally set for impoverished minorities. Is this what Buggin' Out, the character in Spike Lee's *Do the Right Thing,* meant when he said, "Put some brothers on the wall"?

What we saw in those streets was a true expression of urban politics in the postmodern world. All pretense toward social revolution was displaced by the more immediate goal of accumulating the commodities that were often advertised but normally denied to these oppressed people. Watching this and the cultural events that followed showed me that this was the state of contemporary politics for the urban poor: the imitation of crass materialism, by any means possible. This made me realize that we had entered a new day, when chaos as a way of life was forced onto the mainstream agenda for the first time. So any attempt on my part to argue about the politics of popular culture as it was linked to any overriding ideological theme, particularly Afrocentricity, would be a total waste of time.

As far as cultural representations of African Americans are concerned, we are in a seller's market. As mainstream representation requires more and more images to fill the ever-expanding visual space, it is inevitable that there will be a minority presence. Though the overall control of the media lies in the hands of the real "other," I would be remiss if I did not point out that African Americans do have some control over their image. Considering that excess sells in general, the more excessive the African American image, the stronger the likelihood that it will be accepted. The politics of negotiated conformity, focusing on excess, dominates the representation of contemporary Black popular culture. For this reason, Snoop Doggy Dogg is more relevant today than Spike Lee.

I MAKE THESE POINTS to emphasize what it means to analyze Black male culture in the context in which it is being produced. While the West Coast is not known for its intellectual acumen, it is known for the vast entertainment complex that produces the culture we all consume. "Hollywood" is the generic term that we often associate with this mode of production and the ensuing discourse that it brings. Considering all this, I am confronted with the task of being intelligent with respect to Black culture, while being an integral part of it. Those on the cultural side say that there is no meaning to what they do, that their work is often misinterpreted. They denounce both cause and effect. The academic side says that there is much meaning being produced, that cause and effect are parts of larger cultural systems, and that these cultural producers are simply agents of a much larger process. In Hollywood one has to listen to both sides. The writing in this book is a demonstration of these two approaches.

The entertainment world generally has little regard for academic pontification. The academic world, on the other hand, has much regard for entertainment, yet in such a distanced way that seldom do the twain meet. Being that I get paid for academic pontification—though some find it entertaining that a Black man could do such a thing—I will begin by explaining how I see my position in this larger arena.

20 As cultural critics, we should aim to explain the various processes of culture in relation to aesthetics, the economy, and the political systems that define the larger world around us. Our goal is much like that of the country preachers I used to hear as a child who would be encouraged by a church member to "make it plain!" In the process of making it plain, we have to evaluate and deconstruct our subjects so as to speak to others about our interpretation of the material. So often, though, we make it plain only for the already converted, the huddled masses of other academics in our respective fields. We make it plain to people who already understand. This is a problem. There are so many people outside the academy who never read our books, attend our conferences, or take our classes. Yet these people are often more interesting to talk to and learn from than those of us who are supposedly educated.

This propensity toward isolation in academia is currently being challenged by a new generation of African American scholars who have internalized the fundamentals of the academy, but have chosen to pitch their ideas to a larger audience. Unfortunately, there are still many in the academy who assume that by being accessible, one is somehow less serious. As Black intellectuals gain a stronger foothold in the marketplace, however, such pronouncements are becoming common. Often this debate is placed in the opposition between the terms "journalism" and "scholarship," the former clearly being less substantial than the latter. Thus, Black public intellectuals are considered journalists, while those intellectuals who deal in esoterica are considered scholars, and in some way use knowledge, like a country club membership, as an exclusionary resource. At the end of the day we must ask ourselves, Who does this help, and who does it hurt?

This dichotomy is similar to the old racially coded debate in sports that describes African American athletes as "natural" and white athletes as "hard-working." It is assumed that African American athletes are born with the skills to play and excel at sports, a clear reference to an assumed physical prowess that defies mental capacity, while white athletes are regarded as industrious, in keeping with the ideology of the American work ethic. In the same way, it is assumed that Black scholars are somehow less well equipped, or as former Los Angeles Dodger general manager Al Campanis once said, they do not have the "necessities" to do the job.

These concerns are representative of the racism that is operative in code words offered by liberal whites in the form of a compliment that is really defined by traditional racist tenets being expressed in a new era. African American cultural criticism has more to do with a mission of access to a large enough audience that the words can possibly mean something to the world in which we live, than with any lack of necessities. This is especially true when you consider that the academic credentials of African American cultural critics are indeed valid, if for no other reason than that they were earned according to the rules set in place by an overwhelmingly white academy.

It is my intention to fuse the formal and the vernacular in such a way that it informs both sides, as opposed to being limited to one or the other. As African American discourse has always been defined in conjunction with its audience, so too will be the scholarship that emanates from this position. Those African American scholars who are redefining the academy are like the African American musicians who constantly redefined American music throughout the twentieth century. They are forces that must be dealt with in the same way that blues, jazz, soul, and now rap must be dealt with. The key is being accessible without losing one's critical edge—to, in the immortal words of George Clinton, "dance underwater and not get wet."

If living in L.A. has taught me one thing, it is that entertainment sells, esoterica does not. Many would consider my stance to be a sellout. So as not to be misunderstood, let me say that insights on culture should be arrived at with nothing less than rigorous detail to attention. What I am suggesting, though, is that the work of scholars who make a living dealing with popular culture should in some sense be concerned with the popular in all its manifestations.

Recently the media have become interested in what are now called "public intellectuals"—all of whom, interestingly enough, have been Black. Since the beginning of 1995, several major publications have commented on the emerging Black intellectuals who seem to be taking the academy by storm. Among others, the *New Yorker, Atlantic Monthly, Village Voice,* and *Los Angeles Times Magazine* have done cover stories on the Black intellectual in the 1990s. Names which continually pop up are Henry Louis Gates Jr., Cornel West, bell hooks, Houston Baker, and Michael Eric Dyson. These names have been bandied about in both positive and negative ways in sectors normally off-limits to academics. This popularity is coupled with a rise over the last five years in the number of publications by Black authors who study popular culture. At least for the time being, Black academics are in the mix. So the path has already been trod. Now is the time to till some new ground.

One of the most prevalent themes that inform the field of cultural studies, especially popular culture, is the tendency toward politicizing the objects we study. It is as though our interest in things that other people consider frivolous is somehow justified by the political dimension that we bring to them. Yet I have long had a problem with the phrase "popular culture," as there seems to be a hierarchy with respect to those things that we choose to study. The artifacts that receive the most attention are those that carry the most obvious progressive political baggage. If ever the demands of political correctness were a factor, it is in the study of popular culture. Why have I never read an intense study of the films of Rudy Ray Moore, the novels of Iceberg Slim or Donald Goines, the music of Tyrone Davis, etc.? Why? Because they do not fit in so easily with what we consider acceptable, and because they are works of the lower class that have never transcended the world of folk culture in which they exist. In addition, their politics are a huge stumbling block in light of the resulting contradictions. Nonetheless, they still need to be studied.

This is also true of contemporary culture. Though several people make cursory mention of rap music, few fully explore its possibilities. Those who do seem interested only to the extent that they can make rap into an artifact of political discourse. I am not suggesting that rap transcends this political dimension, but rather that it is a product of political circumstances in America; it is a defense of and a response to certain historical and social conditions. It need not be defended, though it is constantly under attack; its presence signifies a defense that can come only from the product itself.

As academics, we need not defend rap, though the pressures of intellectual life and the superstructure of the university profession strongly urge us to do so. As practitioners of culture studies, we are encouraged to find the political as a way of linking us with an academic community—e.g. Marxist, poststructuralist, feminist. Without these labels we are constantly dismissed, our work disregarded. And notice that this is the reaction that we receive from the so-called left side of the academic spectrum. So the pressure is on to do a Marxist reading of Ice Cube, or a feminist reading of Salt n Pepa, so as to prove to our colleagues that we are one with them, that we are ultimately no threat. We are like Rodney King, in that we want only to get along.

30 Though you will find the influence of both Marxist thought and poststructuralist discourse in my work, I consider myself a follower of neither. In addition, I must constantly remind myself not to fall into the trap of articulating a Black nationalist party line. Criticism, like the best of the jazz tradition, should be an improvisation on cultural studies itself. Though I may borrow from the intellectual styles mentioned earlier, it is the context in which the thoughts arise that propels the project. The art of improvisation is informed by many components but driven by one, an abiding notion of African American oral culture and its effects. In the same way, the improvisers of jazz nuanced existing meanings, while on the bandstand their primary function was the articulation of the oral impulses that have always defined Black life in America. In this process it is the appropriation of other forms and their usefulness in furthering the African American oral project.

Thus quotations are used as just that, quotes, appropriated thoughts that strengthen my points. This is similar to rappers' use of sampling, where preexisting forms of music are incorporated into the contemporary as a way of enhancing the overall project. As with improvisation, the original is useful not as an object of sacred devotion but as a way of motivating contemporary expression. In this process, the improviser and the sampler are judged on their ability to recontextualize, not on their acumen in imitating the original.

In jazz you are required to improvise, to create your own form of expression by using other bits of information as they inspire you. The emphasis is not on the original but on one's own articulation. In this way jazz and rap are very similar. As jazz improvises, rap emphasizes the freestyle, an impromptu lyrical explosion that is defined by its spontaneity. These are the oral forms I hope to express through my writing, to improvise on the canon of popular culture and freestyle my way through the idiom of African American life in the late twentieth century, doing both at the same time, without missing a beat.

Exploring Texts and Contexts

For activities with icons, refer to the Guide to Analyzing Readings in Context.

1. Working in a small group, identify the passages where you think Boyd is trying to appeal to his popular audience, where he is trying to appeal to his academic audience, and where he is trying to appeal to both. Because Boyd is a good writer who is consciously trying to create a blended style that can appeal to both audiences, you won't find obvious shifts in style; rather look for subtle shifts in content and tone. You might find these shifts between paragraphs, within paragraphs, or even within a single sentence. Discuss the different strategies that Boyd uses to appeal to his diverse audience.

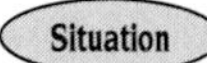

2. Working with the class as a whole—and making use of online resources if they're available—try to identify all the writers, musicians, filmmakers, critics, and intellectuals that Boyd refers to, and discuss what these references tell you about the contexts in which Boyd is writing and the audiences that he is trying to speak to.
3. What is Boyd's central argument in this piece? Is it stated directly anywhere in the piece, or do you have to figure it out?

Creating Texts

For activities with icons, refer to the Guides to Analyzing Contexts for Writing and Analyzing Readings in Context. For additional help with these writing projects, read the descriptions of **Essay, Feature Article**, and **Cover Letter/Reflective Essay** in the Genre Glossary.

1. Using Boyd's piece as both a source of ideas and a model, write a personal essay about experiences you've had in which you had to behave differently or represent yourself differently to different groups. Describe your experiences in such a way that your readers can share your experiences, but also analyze the wider implications of these experiences, either in terms of the idea of authentic identity or in terms of the social consequences of different kinds of behavior. Using Boyd's piece as a model, interweave description and analysis.

Genre

2. With your teacher's guidance, find an article in an academic journal on some topic that you are interested in and/or have some knowledge about. You'll be surprised at the wide range of "popular" topics that academics have written about, from hairstyles to lowriders, from science fiction to romance novels. Identify the most important ideas and rewrite them as a feature article for a popular magazine read by nonacademic people who are interested in that topic. Then write a cover letter discussing the kinds of changes you made.

Identity in the Age of the Internet

Sherry Turkle

Technology has given us new possibilities for self representation. While e-mail, for example, is an extension of letter writing, which has been around for centuries, the personal Web page and the voice mail greeting seem to be completely new forms of self representation. In this piece, Sherry Turkle describes how people have begun to use new technology to misrepresent themselves, and she discusses the risks and possibilities of these new forms of misrepresentation.

People have always found ways to misrepresent themselves or to pretend to be someone else. Plays, games, and pageants, for example, have allowed people to pretend to be someone else for fun, while costumes, disguises, makeup, and more recently surgery have helped people carry out these socially acceptable activities as well as engage in various kinds of fraudulent activities—pretending to be someone else in order to harm someone or benefit oneself. In addition to their own bodies, people have also used writing—forgeries, for example—to misrepresent themselves. In her book *Life on the Screen: Identity in the Age of the Internet,* Turkle discusses how computers and the Internet allow people to use writing to engage in extremely complex forms of misrepresentation. She interviews a variety of people who use MUDs, Multiple User Domains, to create alter egos, alternative worlds, and whole new virtual lives for themselves online. She discusses how some are able to use these alternative realities to explore and develop aspects of themselves that they haven't been able to develop in real life (RL) but how these alternative realities can also become means of escape from and excuses for not facing RL problems. For some MUD participants, online life becomes more real than real life, and their online personae become their most authentic selves.

Turkle argues that, for good or ill, these online activities are changing the way we think of the self and identity. Whereas we once thought of the self as singular, well-integrated, and with clear boundaries, today we tend to think of the self as multiple, changing, and fluid. Perhaps most interestingly, she argues that you don't need to participate in MUDs to be involved in these changing attitudes toward identity: Simply by using Windows—which allows you to simultaneously work on a document, check your e-mail, surf the net, play a game, and engage in an instant messaging conversation—you are in a sense splitting your self into multiple selves. Thus even in our most ordinary routines, we may be participating in an extraordinary change in the human understanding of identity, and we should be alert to both the possibilities and the dangers of this change.

Sherry Turkle is Professor of the Social Studies of Science and Technology at the Massachusetts Institute of Technology and has been one of the most perceptive thinkers about how computers are changing human life and even human nature. Her 1984 book, *The Second Self: Computers and the Human Spirit,* was the first in what she calls her "computational trilogy" of books about humans' interactions with computers and other kinds of artificial intelligence and artificial life. The excerpts here are from the second book in the trilogy, the 1995 *Life on the Screen.* The first excerpt is from Chapter 6, in which she describes how a variety of people, especially people in their teens and early twenties, interact in online environments; the second excerpt is from the book's final chapter, in which she looks at the larger social implications of our involvement with computers. Turkle is currently working on the third book in her computational trilogy

Connecting with the Conversation

1. Have you ever participated in a chat room, online forum, or online game, or do you know someone who has? Do you ever do anything to disguise or change your identity online? Write in your journal about your experience or the experiences of others. What does it feel like to misrepresent yourself online?
2. American popular culture seems preoccupied, almost obsessed, with the idea of alter egos, imposters, double identities, switched identities, and assumed identities. Consider, for example, the movies *Fight Club, The Nutty Professor, The Talented Mr. Ripley, Tootsie,* and *The Bourne Identity;* the singers Eminem and Prince; the phenomenon of professional wrestling; or any movie, comic book, or TV show about superheroes. Working with a small group, choose a movie, TV show, book, singer, or other artist or form of expression that embodies or explores the phenomena of alter egos, imposters, double identities, switched identities, or assumed identities, and make a presentation to the class about how that person or form of expression explores that phenomenon.

In the early 1970s, the face-to-face role-playing game Dungeons and Dragons swept the game culture. In Dungeons and Dragons, a dungeon master creates a world in which people take on fictional personae and play out complex adventures. The game is a rule-driven world that includes charisma points, levels of magic, and rolls of the dice. The Dungeons and Dragons universe of mazes and monsters and its image of the world as a labyrinth whose secrets could be unlocked held a particular fascination for many members of the nascent computer culture. The computer game Adventure captured some of the same aesthetic. There, players proceeded through a maze of rooms presented to them through text description on a computer screen.

The term "dungeon" persisted in the high-tech culture to connote a virtual place. So when virtual spaces were created that many computer users could share and collaborate within, they were deemed Multi-User Dungeons or MUDs, a new kind of social virtual reality. Although some games use software that make them technically such things as MUSHes or MOOs, the term MUD and the verb MUDding have come to refer to all of the multi-user environments. As more and more players have come to them who do not have a history with Dungeons and Dragons, some people have begun to refer to MUDs as Multi-User Domains or Multi-User Dimensions.

From *Life on the Screen: Identity in the Age of the Internet.* New York: Simon & Schuster, 1995, pp. 180–186 and 255–269.

Some MUDs use screen graphics or icons to communicate place, character, and action. The MUDs I am writing about here do not. They rely entirely on plain text. All users are browsing and manipulating the same database. They can encounter other users or players as well as objects that have been built for the virtual environment. MUD players can also communicate with each other directly in real time, by typing messages that are seen by other players. Some of these messages are seen by all players in the same "room," but messages can also be designated to flash on the screen of only one specific player.

The term "virtual reality" is often used to denote metaphorical spaces that arise only through interaction with the computer, which people navigate by using special hardware—specially designed helmets, body suits, goggles, and data gloves. The hardware turns the body or parts of the body into pointing devices. For example, a hand inside a data glove can point to where you want to go within virtual space; a helmet can track motion so that the scene shifts depending on how you move your head. In MUDs, instead of using computer hardware to immerse themselves in a vivid world of sensation, users immerse themselves in a world of words. MUDs are a text-based, social virtual reality.

5 Two basic types of MUDs can now be accessed on the Internet. The adventure type, most reminiscent of the games' Dungeons and Dragons heritage, is built around a medieval fantasy landscape. In these, affectionately known by their participants as "hack and slay," the object of the game is to gain experience points by killing monsters and dragons and finding gold coins, amulets, and other treasure. Experience points translate into increased power. A second type consists of relatively open spaces in which you can play at whatever captures your imagination. In these MUDs, usually called social MUDs, the point is to interact with other players and, on some MUDs, to help build the virtual world by creating one's own objects and architecture. "Building" on MUDs is something of a hybrid between computer programming and writing fiction. One describes a hot tub and deck in a MUD with words, but some formal coded description is required for the deck to exist in the MUD as an extension of the adjacent living room and for characters to be able to "turn the hot tub on" by pushing a specially marked "button." In some MUDs, all players are allowed to build; sometimes the privilege is reserved to master players, or wizards. Building is made particularly easy on a class of MUDs known as "MOOs" (MUDs of the Object Oriented variety).

In practice, adventure-type MUDs and social MUDs have much in common. In both, what really seems to hold players' interest is operating their character or characters and interacting with other characters. Even in an adventure-type MUD, a player can be an elf, a warrior, a prostitute, a politician, a healer, a seer, or several of these at the same time. As this character or set of characters, a player evolves relationships with other players, also in character. For most players these relationships quickly become central to the MUDding experience. As one player on an adventure-type MUD put it, "I began with an interest in 'hack and slay,' but then I stayed to chat."

The characters one creates for a MUD are referred to as one's personae. This is from the Latin *per sonae* which means "that through which the sound comes," in other words, an actor's mask. Interestingly, this is also the root of "person" and "personality." The derivation implies that one is identified by means of a public face distinct from some deeper essence or essences.

All MUDs are organized around the metaphor of physical space. When you first enter a MUD you may find yourself in a medieval church from which you can step out into the town square, or you may find yourself in the coat closet of a large, rambling house. For example, when you first log on to LambdaMOO, one of the most popular MUDs on the Internet, you see the following description:

> The Coat Closet. The Closet is a dark, cramped space. It appears to be very crowded in here; you keep bumping into what feels like coats, boots and other people (apparently sleeping). One useful thing that you've discovered in your bumbling about is a metal doorknob set at waist level into what might be a door. There's a new edition of the newspaper. Type "news" to see it.

10 Typing "out" gets you to the living room:

> The Living Room. It is very bright, open, and airy here, with large plate-glass windows looking southward over the pool to the gardens beyond. On the north wall, there is a rough stonework fireplace, complete with roaring fire. The east and west walls are almost completely covered with large, well-stocked bookcases. An exit in the northwest corner leads to the kitchen and, in a more northerly direction, to the entrance hall. The door into the coat closet is at the north end of the east wall, and at the south end is a sliding glass door leading out onto a wooden deck. There are two sets of couches, one clustered around the fireplace and one with a view out the windows.

This description is followed by a list of objects and characters present in the living room. You are free to examine and try out the objects, examine the descriptions of the characters, and introduce yourself to them. The social conventions of different MUDs determine how strictly one is expected to stay in character. Some encourage all players to be in character at all times. Most are more relaxed. Some ritualize stepping out of character by asking players to talk to each other in specially noted "out of character" (OOC) asides.

On MUDs, characters communicate by invoking commands that cause text to appear on each other's screens. If I log onto LambdaMOO as a male character named Turk and strike up a conversation with a character named Dimitri, the setting for our conversation will be a MUD room in which a variety of other characters might be present. If I type, "Say hi," my screen will flash, "You say hi," and the screens of the other players in the room (including Dimitri) will flash, "Turk says 'hi.'" If I type "Emote whistles happily," all the players' screens will flash, "Turk whistles happily." Or I can address Dimitri alone by typing, "Whisper to Dimitri Glad to see you," and only Dimitri's screen will show, "Turk whispers 'Glad to see you.'" People's impressions of Turk will be formed by the description I will have written for him (this description will be available to all players on command), as well as by the nature of his conversation.

In the MUDs, virtual characters converse with each other, exchange gestures, express emotions, win and lose virtual money, and rise and fall in social status. A virtual character can also die. Some die of "natural" causes (a player decides to close them down) or they can have their virtual lives snuffed out. This is all achieved through writing, and this in a culture that had apparently fallen asleep in the audiovisual arms of television. Yet this new writing is a kind of hybrid: speech momentarily frozen into artifact, but curiously ephemeral artifact. In this new writing, unless it is printed out on paper, a screenful of flickers soon replaces the previous screen. In MUDs as in other forms of electronic communication, typographic conventions known as emoticons replace physical gestures and facial expressions. For example, :–) indicates a smiling face and :–(indicates an unhappy face. Onomatopoeic expletives and a relaxed attitude toward sentence fragments and typographic errors suggest that the new writing is somewhere in between traditional written and oral communication.

MUDs provide worlds for anonymous social interaction in which you can play a role as close to or as far away from your real self as you choose. For many game participants, playing one's character(s) and living in the MUD(s) becomes an important part of daily life. Since much of the excitement of the game depends on having personal relationships and being part of a MUD community's developing politics and projects, it is hard to participate just a little. In fact, addiction is a frequently discussed subject among MUD players. A *Newsweek* article described how "some players attempt to go cold turkey. One method is to randomly change your password by banging your head against the keyboard, making it impossible to log back on."[1] It is not unusual for players to be logged on to a MUD for six hours a day. Twelve hours a day is common if players work with computers at school or at a job and use systems with multiple windows. Then they can jump among windows in order to intersperse real-world activities on their computers with their games. They jump from Lotus 1-2-3 to LambdaMOO, from Wordperfect to DragonMUD. "You can't really be part of the action unless you are there every day. Things happen quickly. To get the thrill of MUDs you have to be part of what makes the story unfold," says a regular on DuneMUSH, a MUD based on the world of Frank Herbert's science fiction classic.[2]

In MUDs, each player makes scenes unfold and dramas come to life. Playing in MUDs is thus both similar to and different from reading or watching television. As with reading, there is text, but on MUDs it unfolds in real time and you become an author of the story. As with television, you are engaged with the screen, but MUDs are interactive, and you can take control of the action. As in acting, the explicit task is to construct a viable mask or persona. Yet on MUDs, that persona can be as close to your real self as you choose, so MUDs have much in common with psychodrama. And since many people simply choose to play aspects of themselves, MUDs can also seem like real life.

Play has always been an important aspect of our individual efforts to build identity. The psychoanalyst Erik Erikson called play a "toy situation" that allows us to "reveal and commit" ourselves "in its unreality."[3] While MUDs are not the only "places" on the Internet in which to play with identity, they provide an unparalleled opportunity for such play. On a MUD one actually gets to build character and environment and then to live within the toy situation. A MUD can become a context for discovering who one is and wishes to be. In this way, the games are laboratories for the construction of identity, an idea that is well captured by the player who said:

> You can be whoever you want to be. You can completely redefine yourself if you want. You can be the opposite sex. You can be more talkative. You can be less talkative. Whatever. You can just be whoever you want, really, whoever you have the capacity to be. You don't have to worry about the slots other people put you in as much. It's easier to change the way people perceive you, because all they've got is what you show them. They don't look at your body and make assumptions. They don't hear your accent and make assumptions. All they see is your words. And it's always there. Twenty-four hours a day you can walk down to the street corner and there's gonna be a few people there who are interesting to talk to, if you've found the right MUD for you.

The anonymity of most MUDs (you are known only by the name you give your characters) provides ample room for individuals to express unexplored parts of themselves. A twenty-one-year-old college senior defends his violent characters as "something in me; but quite frankly I'd rather rape on MUDs where no harm is done." A twenty-six-year-old clerical worker says, "I'm not one thing, I'm many things. Each part gets to be more fully expressed in MUDs than in the real world. So even though I play more than one self on MUDs, I feel more like 'myself' when I'm MUDding." In real life, this woman sees her world as too narrow to allow her to manifest certain aspects of the person she feels herself to be. Creating screen personae is thus an opportunity for self-expression, leading to her feeling more like her true self when decked out in an array of virtual masks.

20 MUDs imply difference, multiplicity, heterogeneity, and fragmentation. Such an experience of identity contradicts the Latin root of the word, *idem,* meaning "the same." But this contradiction increasingly defines the conditions of our lives beyond the virtual world. MUDs thus become objects-to-think-with for thinking about postmodern selves. Indeed, the unfolding of all MUD action takes place in a resolutely postmodern context. There are parallel narratives in the different rooms of a MUD. The cultures of Tolkien, Gibson, and Madonna coexist and interact. Since MUDs are authored by their players, thousands of people in all, often hundreds at a time, are all logged on from different places; the solitary author is displaced and distributed. Traditional ideas about identity have been tied to a notion of authenticity that such virtual experiences actively subvert. When each player can create many characters and participate in many games, the self is not only decentered but multiplied without limit.

Sometimes such experiences can facilitate self-knowledge and personal growth, and sometimes not. MUDs can be places where people blossom or places where they get stuck, caught in self-contained worlds where things are simpler than in real life, and where, if all else fails, you can retire your character and simply start a new life with another.

As a new social experience, MUDs pose many psychological questions: If a persona in a role-playing game drops defenses that the player in real life has been unable to abandon, what effect does this have? What if a persona enjoys success in some area (say, flirting) that the player has not been able to achieve? In this, chapter and the next I will examine these kinds of questions from a viewpoint that assumes a conventional distinction between a constructed persona and the real self. But we shall soon encounter slippages—places where persona and self merge, places where the multiple personae join to comprise what the individual thinks of as his or her authentic self.

These slippages are common on MUDs, but as I discuss MUDs, it is important to keep in mind that they more generally characterize identity play in cyberspace. One Internet Relay Chat (IRC) enthusiast writes to an online discussion group, "People on [this mailing list] tell me that they make mistakes about what's happening on cyberspace and what's happening on RL. Did I really type what's happening *ON* Real Life?" (Surrounding a word with asterisks is the net version of italicizing it.) He had indeed. And then he jokingly referred to real life as though it, too, were an IRC channel: "Can anyone tell me how to/join #real.life?"[4]

* * *

Identity Crisis

Every era constructs its own metaphors for psychological well-being. Not so long ago, stability was socially valued and culturally reinforced. Rigid gender roles, repetitive labor, the expectation of being in one kind of job or remaining in one town over a lifetime, all of these made consistency central to definitions of health. But these stable social worlds have broken down. In our time, health is described in terms of fluidity rather than stability. What matters most now is the ability to adapt and change—to new jobs, new career directions, new gender roles, new technologies.

In *Flexible Bodies,* the anthropologist Emily Martin argues that the language of the immune system provides us with metaphors for the self and its boundaries.[5] In the past, the immune system was described as a private fortress, a firm, stable wall that protected within from without. Now we talk about the immune system as flexible and permeable. It can only be healthy if adaptable.

The new metaphors of health as flexibility apply not only to human mental and physical spheres, but also to the bodies of corporations, governments, and businesses. These institutions function in rapidly changing circumstances; they too are coming to view their fitness in terms of their flexibility. Martin describes the cultural spaces where we learn the new virtues of change over solidity. In addition to advertising, entertainment, and education, her examples include corporate workshops where people learn wilderness camping, high-wire walking, and zip-line jumping. She refers to all of these as flexibility practicums.

In her study of the culture of flexibility, Martin does not discuss virtual communities, but these provide excellent examples of what she is talking about. In these environments, people either explicitly play roles (as in MUDs) or more subtly shape their online selves. Adults learn about being multiple and fluid—and so do children. "I don't play so many different people online—only three," says June, an eleven-year-old who uses her mother's Internet account to play in MUDs. During our conversation, I learn that in the course of a year in RL, she moves among three households—that of her biological mother and stepfather, her biological father and stepmother, and a much-loved "first stepfather," her mother's second husband. She refers to her mother's third and current husband as "second stepfather." June recounts that in each of these three households the rules are somewhat different and so is she. Online switches among personae seem quite natural. Indeed, for her, they are a kind of practice. Martin would call them practicums.

"Logins R Us"

On a WELL discussion group about online personae (subtitled "boon or bête-noire") participants shared a sense that their virtual identities were evocative objects for thinking about the self. For several, experiences in virtual space compelled them to pay greater attention to what they take for granted in the real. "The persona thing intrigues me," said one. "It's a chance for all of us who aren't actors to play [with] masks. And think about the masks we wear every day."[6]

In this way, online personae have something in common with the self that emerges in a psychoanalytic encounter. It, too, is significantly virtual, constructed within the space of the analysis, where its slightest shifts can come under the most intense scrutiny.[7]

30 What most characterized the WELL discussion about online personae was the way many of the participants expressed the belief that life on the WELL introduced them to the many within themselves. One person wrote that through participating in an electronic bulletin board and letting the many sides of ourselves show, "We start to resemble little corporations, 'Logins R Us,' and like any company, we each have within us the bean-counter, the visionary, the heart-throb, the fundamentalist, and the wild child. Long may they wave."[8] Other participants responded to this comment with enthusiasm. One, echoing the social psychologist Kenneth Gergen,[9] described identity as a "pastiche of personalities" in which "the test of competence is not so much the integrity of the whole but the apparent correct representation appearing at the right time, in the right context, not to the detriment of the rest of the internal 'collective.' "[10] Another said that he thought of his ego "as a hollow tube, through which, one at a time, the 'many' speak through at the appropriate moment. . . . I'd like to hear more . . . about the possibilities surrounding the notion that what we perceive as 'one' in any context is, perhaps, a conglomerate of 'ones.'" This writer went on:

> Hindu culture is rooted in the "many" as the root of spiritual experience. A person's momentary behavior reflects some influence from one of hundreds of gods and/or goddesses. I am interested in . . . how this natural assumption of the "many" creates an alternative psychology.[11]

Another writer concurred:

> Did you ever see that cartoon by R. Crumb about "Which is the real R. Crumb?" He goes through four pages of incarnations, from successful businessman to street beggar, from media celebrity to gut-gnawing recluse, etc. etc. Then at the end he says, "Which is the real one?" . . . "It all depends on what mood I'm in!"
>
> We're all like that online.[12]

35 Howard Rheingold, the member of the WELL who began the discussion topic, also referred to Gergen's notion of a "saturated self," the idea that communication technologies have caused us to "colonize each other's brains." Gergen describes us as saturated with the many "voices of humankind—both harmonious and alien." He believes that as "we absorb their varied rhymes and reasons, they become part of us and we of them.

Social saturation furnishes us with a multiplicity of incoherent and unrelated languages of the self." With our relationships spread across the globe and our knowledge of other cultures relativizing our attitudes and depriving us of any norm, we "exist in a state of continuous construction and reconstruction; it is a world where anything goes that can be negotiated. Each reality of self gives way to reflexive questioning, irony, and ultimately the playful probing of yet another reality. The center fails to hold."[13]

Although people may at first feel anguish at what they sense as a breakdown of identity, Gergen believes they may come to embrace the new possibilities. Individual notions of self vanish "into a stage of relatedness. One ceases to believe in a self independent of the relations in which he or she is embedded."[14] "We live in each other's brains, as voices, images, words on screens," said Rheingold in the online discussion. "We are multiple personalities and we include each other."[15]

Rheingold's evocation of what Gergen calls the "raptures of multiplicitous being" met with support on the WELL. One participant insisted that all pejorative associations be removed from the notion of a saturated self. "Howard, I *like* being a saturated self, in a community of similarly saturated selves. I grew up on TV and pop music, but it just ain't enough. Virtual communities are, among other things, the co-saturation of selves who have been, all their lives, saturated in isolation."[16] To which Rheingold could only reply, "I like being a saturated self too."[17] The cybersociety of the WELL is an object-to-think-with for reflecting on the positive aspects of identity as multiplicity.

Identity and Multiplicity

Without any principle of coherence, the self spins off in all directions. Multiplicity is not viable if it means shifting among personalities that cannot communicate. Multiplicity is not acceptable if it means being confused to a point of immobility.[18] How can we be multiple and coherent at the same time? In *The Protean Self,* Robert Jay Lifton tries to resolve this seeming contradiction. He begins by assuming that a unitary view of self corresponded to a traditional culture with stable symbols, institutions, and relationships. He finds the old unitary notion no longer viable because traditional culture has broken down and identifies a range of responses. One is a dogmatic insistence on unity. Another is to return to systems of belief, such as religious fundamentalism, that enforce conformity. A third is to embrace the idea of a fragmented self.[19] Lifton says this is a dangerous option that may result in a "fluidity lacking in moral content and sustainable inner form." But Lifton sees another possibility, a healthy protean self. It is capable, like Proteus, of fluid transformations but is grounded in coherence and a moral outlook. It is multiple but integrated.[20] You can have a sense of self without being one self.

Lifton's language is theoretical. Experiences in MUDs, on the WELL, on local bulletin boards, on commercial network services, and on the World Wide Web are bringing his theory down to earth. On the Web, the idiom for constructing a "home" identity is to assemble a "home page" of virtual objects that correspond to one's interests. One constructs a home page by composing or "pasting" on it words, images, and sounds, and by making connections between it and other sites on the Internet or the Web. Like the agents in emergent AI, one's identity emerges from whom one knows, one's associations and connections. People link their home page to pages about such things as music, paintings, television shows, cities, books, photographs, comic strips, and fashion models. As I write this book I am in the process of constructing my own home page. It now contains links to the text of my curriculum vitae, to drafts of recent papers (one about MUDs, one about French psychoanalysis), and to the reading lists for the two courses I shall teach next fall. A "visitor" to my home page can also click a highlighted word and watch images of Michel Foucault and Power Rangers "morph," one into the other, a visual play on my contention that children's toys bring postmodernism down to earth. This display, affectionately referred to as "The Mighty Morphin' Michel Foucault," was a present from my assistant at MIT, Cynthia Col. A virtual home, like a real one, is furnished with objects you buy, build, or receive as gifts.

40 My future plans for my home page include linking to Paris (the city has a home page), the bot Julia, resources on women's studies, Imari china, and recent research on migraines. I am not limited in the number of links I can create. If we take the home page as a real estate metaphor for the self, its decor is postmodern. Its different rooms with different styles are located on computers all over the world. But through one's efforts, they are brought together to be of a piece.

Within the psychoanalytic tradition, there have been schools that departed from the standard unitary view of identity. As we have seen, the object-relations theorists invented a language for talking about the many voices that we bring inside ourselves in the course of development. Jungian psychology encouraged the individual to become acquainted with a whole range of personae and to understand them as manifestations of universal archetypes, such as innocent virgins, mothers and crones, eternal youths and old men.[21] Jung believed that for each of us, it is potentially most liberating to become acquainted with our dark side, as well as the other-gendered self called anima in men and animus in women. Jung was banished from the ranks of orthodox Freudians for such suggestions. The object-relations school, too, was relegated to the margins. As America became the center of psychoanalytic politics in the mid-twentieth century, ideas about a robust executive ego became the psychoanalytic mainstream.

Through the fragmented selves presented by patients and through theories that stress the decentered subject, contemporary psychology confronts what is left out of theories of the unitary self. Now it must ask, What is the self when it functions as a society?[22] What is the self when it divides its labors among its constituent "alters"?[23] Those burdened by post traumatic dissociative disorders suffer these questions; here I have suggested that inhabitants of virtual communities play with them.

Ideas about mind can become a vital cultural presence when they are carried by evocative objects-to-think-with.[24] I said earlier that these objects need not be material. For example, dreams and slips of the tongue were objects-to-think-with that brought psychoanalytic ideas into everyday life. People could play with their own and others' dreams and slips. Today, people are being helped to develop ideas about identity as multiplicity by a new practice of identity as multiplicity in online life. Virtual personae are objects-to-think-with.

When people adopt an online persona they cross a boundary into highly charged territory. Some feel an uncomfortable sense of fragmentation, some a sense of relief. Some sense the possibilities for self-discovery, even self-transformation. Serena, a twenty-six-year-old graduate student in history, says, "When I log on to a new MUD and I create a character and know I have to start typing my description, I always feel a sense of panic. Like I could find out something I don't want to know." Arlie, a twenty-year-old undergraduate, says, "I am always very self-conscious when I create a new character. Usually, I end up creating someone I wouldn't want my parents to know about. It takes me, like, three hours. But that someone is part of me." In these ways and others, many more of us are experimenting with multiplicity than ever before.

45 With this last comment, I am not implying that MUDs or computer bulletin boards are causally implicated in the dramatic increase of people who exhibit symptoms of multiple personality disorder (MPD), or that people on MUDs have MPD, or that MUDding is like having MPD. What I am saying is that the many manifestations of multiplicity in our culture, including the adoption of online personae, are contributing to a general reconsideration of traditional, unitary notions of identity.

The history of a psychiatric symptom is inextricably tied up with the history of the culture that surrounds it. When I was in graduate school in psychology in the 1970s, clinical psychology texts regarded multiple personality as so rare (perhaps one in a million) as to be barely worthy of mention. In these rare cases, there was typically one alter personality in addition to the host personality.[25] Today, cases of multiple personality are much more frequent and typically involve up to sixteen alters of different ages, races, genders, and sexual orientations.[26] In multiple personality disorder, it is widely believed that traumatic events have caused various aspects of the self to congeal into virtual personalities, the "ones" often hiding from the "others" and hiding too from that special alter, the host personality. Sometimes, the alters are known to each other and to the host; some alters may see their roles as actively helping others. Such differences led the philosopher Ian Hacking to write about a "continuum of dissociation."[27] These differences also suggest a way of thinking about the self in terms of a continuum of how accessible its parts are to each other.

At one extreme, the unitary self maintains its oneness by repressing all that does not fit. Thus censored, the illegitimate parts of the self are not accessible. This model would of course function best within a fairly rigid social structure with clearly defined rules and roles. At the other extreme is the MPD sufferer whose multiplicity exists in the context of an equally repressive rigidity. The parts of the self are not in easy communication. Communication is highly stylized; one personality must speak to another personality. In fact, the term "multiple personality" is misleading, because the different parts of the self are not full personalities. They are split-off, disconnected fragments. But if the disorder in multiple personality disorder is the need for the rigid walls between the selves (blocking the secrets those selves protect), then the study of MPD may begin to furnish ways of thinking about healthy selves as nonunitary but with fluid access among their many aspects. Thus, in addition to the extremes of unitary self and MPD, we can imagine a flexible self.

The essence of this self is not unitary, nor are its parts stable entities. It is easy to cycle through its aspects, and these are themselves changing through constant communication with each other. The philosopher Daniel Dennett speaks to the flexible self in his multiple drafts theory of consciousness.[28] Dennett's notion of multiple drafts is analogous to the experience of having several versions of a document open on a computer screen where the user is able to move between them at will. The presence of the drafts encourages a respect for the many different versions while it imposes a certain distance from them. No one aspect can be claimed as the absolute, true self. When I got to know French Sherry I no longer saw the less confident English-speaking Sherry as my one authentic self. What most characterizes the model of a flexible self is that the lines of communication between its various aspects are open. The open communication encourages an attitude of respect for the many within us and the many within others.

As we sense our inner diversity we come to know our limitations. We understand that we do not and cannot know things completely, not the outside world and not ourselves. Today's heightened consciousness of incompleteness may predispose us to join with others. The historian of science Donna Haraway equates a "split and contradictory self" with a "knowing self." She is optimistic about its possibilities: "The knowing self is partial in all its guises, never finished, whole, simply there and original; it is always constructed and stitched together imperfectly; and *therefore* able to join with another, to see together without claiming to be another."[29]

50 When identity was defined as unitary and solid it was relatively easy to recognize and censure deviation from a norm. A more fluid sense of self allows a greater capacity for acknowledging diversity. It makes it easier to accept the array of our (and others') inconsistent personae—perhaps with humor, perhaps with irony. We do not feel compelled to rank or judge the elements of our multiplicity. We do not feel compelled to exclude what does not fit.

* * *

As we stand on the boundary between the real and the virtual, our experience recalls what the anthropologist Victor Turner termed a liminal moment, a moment of passage when new cultural symbols and meanings can emerge.[30] Liminal moments are times of tension, extreme reactions, and great opportunity. In our time, we are simultaneously flooded with predictions of doom and predictions of imminent utopia. We live in a crucible of contradictory experience. When Turner talked about liminality, he understood it as a transitional state—but living with flux may no longer be temporary. Donna Haraway's characterization of irony illuminates our situation: "Irony is about contradictions that do not resolve into larger wholes . . . about the tension of holding incompatible things together because both or all are necessary and true.[31] It is fitting that the story of the technology that is bringing postmodernism down to earth itself refuses modernist resolutions and requires an openness to multiple viewpoints.

Multiple viewpoints call forth a new moral discourse. I have said that the culture of simulation may help us achieve a vision of a multiple but integrated identity whose flexibility, resilience, and capacity for joy comes from having access to our many selves. But if we have lost reality in the process, we shall have struck a poor bargain. In Wim Wenders's film *Until the End of the World,* a scientist develops a device that translates the electrochemical activity of the brain into digital images. He gives this technology to his family and closest friends, who are now able to hold small battery-driven monitors and watch their dreams. At first, they are charmed. They see their treasured fantasies, their secret selves. They see the images they otherwise would forget, the scenes they otherwise would repress. As with the personae one can play in a MUD, watching dreams on a screen opens up new aspects of the self.

However, the story soon turns dark. The images seduce. They are richer and more compelling than the real life around them. Wenders's characters fall in love with their dreams, become addicted to them. People wander about with blankets over their heads the better to see the monitors from which they cannot bear to be parted. They are imprisoned by the screens, imprisoned by the keys to their past that the screens seem to hold.

We, too, are vulnerable to using our screens in these ways. People can get lost in virtual worlds. Some are tempted to think of life in cyberspace as insignificant, as escape or meaningless diversion. It is not. Our experiences there are serious play. We belittle them at our risk. We must understand the dynamics of virtual experience both to foresee who might be in danger and to put these experiences to best use. Without a deep understanding of the many selves that we express in the virtual, we cannot use our experiences there to enrich the real. If we cultivate our awareness of what stands behind our screen personae, we are more likely to succeed in using virtual experience for personal transformation.

55 The imperative to self-knowledge has always been at the heart of philosophical inquiry. In the twentieth century, it found expression in the psychoanalytic culture as well. One might say that it constitutes the ethic of psychoanalysis. From the perspective of this ethic, we work to know ourselves in order to improve not only our own lives, but those of our families and society. I have said that psychoanalysis is a survivor discourse. Born of a modernist worldview, it has evolved into forms relevant to postmodern times. With mechanistic roots in the culture of calculation, psychoanalytic ideas become newly relevant in the culture of simulation. Some believe that we are at the end of the Freudian century. But the reality is more complex. Our need for a practical philosophy of self-knowledge has never been greater as we struggle to make meaning from our lives on the screen.

Notes

1. Katie Hafner, "Get in the MOOd," *Newsweek,* 7 November 1994.
2. Frank Herbert, *Dune* (Philadelphia: Chilton Books, 1965).
3. Erik Erikson, *Childhood and Society,* 2nd rev. ed. (New York: Norton, 1963 [1950]), p. 52.
4. This communication was signed "The Picklingly herbatious one."
5. Emily Martin, *Flexible Bodies* (Boston: Beacon Press, 1994), pp. 161–225.
6. mcdee, The WELL, conference on virtual communities (vc.20.17), 18 April 1992.
7. The sentiment that life online could provide a different experience of self was seconded by a participant who described himself as a man whose conversational abilities as an adult were impaired by having been a stutterer as a child. Online he was able to discover the experience of participating in the flow of a conversation.

    I echo [the previous contributor] in feeling that my online persona differs greatly from my persona offline. And, in many ways, my online persona is more "me." I feel a lot more freedom to speak here. Growing up, I had a severe stuttering problem. I couldn't speak a word without stuttering, so I spoke only when absolutely necessary. I worked through it in my early 20s and you wouldn't even notice it now (except when I'm stressed out), but at

> 37 I'm still shy to speak. I'm a lot more comfortable with listening than with talking. And when I do speak I usually feel out of sync: I'll inadvertently step on other people's words, or lose people's attention, or talk through instead of to. I didn't learn the dynamic of conversation that most people take for granted, I think. Here, though, it's completely different: I have a feel for the flow of the "conversations," have the time to measure my response, don't have to worry about the balance of conversational space—we all make as much space as we want just by pressing "r" to respond. It's been a wonderfully liberating experience for me. (Anonymous)

8. spoonman, The WELL, conference on virtual communities (vc.20.65), 11 June 1992.
9. Kenneth Gergen, *The Saturated Self: Dilemmas of Identity in Contemporary Life* (New York: Basic Books, 1991).
10. bluefire (Bob Jacobson), The WELL, conference on virtual reality (vr.85.146), 15 August 1993.
11. The WELL, conference on virtual reality (vr.85.148), 17 August 1993.
12. Art Kleiner, The WELL, conference on virtual reality (vr.47.41), 2 October 1990.
13. Gergen, *The Saturated Self,* p. 6.
14. Gergen, *The Saturated Self,* p. 17.
15. hlr (Howard Rheingold), The WELL, conference on virtual reality (vr.47.351), 2 February 1993.
16. McKenzie Wark, The WELL, conference on virtual reality (vr.47.361), 3 February 1993.
17. hlr (Howard Rheingold), The WELL, conference on virtual reality (vr.47.362), 3 February 1993.
18. James M. Glass, *Shattered Selves: Multiple Personality in a Postmodern World* (Ithaca, N.Y.: Cornell University Press, 1993).
19. Robert Jay Lifton, *The Protean Self: Human Resilience in an Age of Fragmentation* (New York: Basic Books, 1993), p. 192.
20. Lifton, *The Protean Self,* pp. 229–32.
21. See, for example, "Aion: Phenomenology of the Self" in *The Portable Jung,* ed. Joseph Campbell, trans. R. F. C. Hull (New York: Penguin, 1971).
22. See, for example, Marvin Minsky, *The Society of Mind* (New York: Simon & Schuster, 1985).
23. See, for example, Colin Ross, *Multiple Personality Disorder: Diagnosis, Clinical Features, and Treatment* (New York: John Wiley & Sons, 1989).
24. Claude Lévi-Strauss, *The Savage Mind* (Chicago: University of Chicago Press, 1960).
25. Ian Hacking, *Rewriting the Soul: Multiple Personality and the Sciences of Memory* (Princeton, N.J.: Princeton University Press, 1995), p. 21.
26. Hacking, *Rewriting the Soul,* p. 29.
27. See Hacking, *Rewriting the Soul,* pp. 96ff.
28. Daniel C. Dennett, *Consciousness Explained* (Boston: Little, Brown and Company, 1991).
29. Donna Haraway, "The Actors Are Cyborg, Nature Is Coyote, and the Geography Is Elsewhere: Postscript to 'Cyborgs at Large'" in *Technoculture,* eds. Constance Penley and Andrew Ross (Minneapolis: University of Minnesota Press, 1991), p. 22.
30. Victor Turner, *The Ritual Process: Structure and Antistructure* (Chicago: Aldine, 1966).
31. Donna Haraway, "A Cyborg Manifesto," p. 148.

Exploring Texts and Contexts

For activities with icons, refer to the Guide to Analyzing Readings in Context.

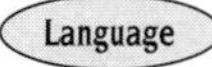

1. Throughout this excerpt, Turkle use the words "persona," "self," and "identity." How does she define or seem to be defining these terms and what is the relationship between them? Turkle also sets up a dialectic between the terms "multiplicity" and "unity" or "multiple" and "unitary." What's the relationship between these words and between these words and Turkle's overall argument?
2. What is Turkle's overall argument? Does she state her thesis anywhere in this excerpt? If not, can you sum it up in a sentence or two?

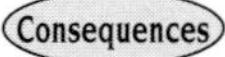

3. Turkle sees moral implications for the phenomena she discusses in this excerpt. What does she see as the possible consequences, and how would she like her book to influence these consequences?

Creating Texts

For activities with icons, refer to the Guides to Analyzing Contexts for Writing and Analyzing Readings in Context. For additional help with these writing projects, read the descriptions of **Dialogue/Symposium** and **Debate/Essay** in the Genre Glossary.

1. This is a group project with several stages. It involves creating a fictional character, or persona, using that persona to interact with others in an online environment, and then analyzing the interactions. Write a description of a persona that you would be interested in exploring. It might be simply a projection of yourself into the future or past, or it might be a persona that is very different from you in gender, ethnicity, or background. With your teacher's help, use the chat feature of an online course platform to set up a discussion topic or activity that everyone in the class will participate in as their personae. This works best if the group is given a task to carry out, for example deciding on the rules for an online game or the features of an online environment. This activity should be carried out over the course of several class meetings so that everyone gets a chance to "perform" his or her persona. The purpose of this activity is to give you a sense of what it might be like to participate in an online forum using a persona. Please remember, though, that this is a classroom activity, and the rules of civility and respect that are otherwise observed in your classroom should be observed in this activity as well. Print out the transcripts of these chat sessions so that the class can discuss the activity as it unfolded.

2. Write an essay in which you discuss your experiences in the activity described in Activity 1. You might begin by describing your persona and why you chose it. Then describe some of the significant interactions in the activity and your persona's participation, and discuss what these interactions felt like to you.

What was it like to participate in this activity as your persona? In what ways was your persona's "behavior" different from and similar to what would have been your own behavior in these situations, and what do you see as the significance of these differences and similarities? To what extent did it feel as if you had actually "become" your persona? Did the activity feel risky or liberating, and in what way? Did you feel that you learned anything from this experience about yourself or the nature of representation and misrepresentation? Discuss also what you see as the larger implications of this experience for our understanding of identity, the self, authenticity, and the possibilities and dangers of the Internet.

Famous All Over Town

Danny Santiago

In 1983, the novel *Famous All Over Town* was published to modest commercial success and great critical acclaim. It was the story of a 14-year-old boy, Rudy Medina, also known as Chato, growing up in a Mexican-American neighborhood of Los Angeles. The novel was hailed as a kind of barrio *Catcher in the Rye,* a coming-of-age story that also gave readers a glimpse into an ethnic American experience. A reviewer in the *Pittsburgh Press* said, "The 14-year-old Mexican-American point of view is authentic, funny, and tragic." A *New York Times* reviewer said, "*Famous All Over Town* is a classic of Chicano urban experience. And Danny Santiago is good news." But Danny Santiago, the author, remained somewhat of a mystery. There was no picture of him on the book jacket, and the brief biography simply said that he "grew up in Los Angeles."

Why the mystery? To find out, read the three pieces included here. The first piece is the first chapter of the novel. It will give you a good sense of the novel's narrative voice and a glimpse of the main characters and setting, though it won't convey the scope and narrative arc of the plot or the complex interactions of the characters; if you enjoy the first chapter, try to get a copy of the book and finish the novel. The chapter is followed by the *New York Times* review quoted here and then by an article about Danny Santiago published in the *Times* a little over a year later.

Connecting with the Conversation

1. Many first novels, especially if they are written in the first person, are assumed to be autobiographical at least to some extent. Have you read any of the following: *I Know Why the Caged Bird Sings,* by Maya Angelou; *The House on Mango Street,* by Sandra Cisneros; *Invisible Man,* by Ralph Ellison; *To Kill a Mockingbird,* by Harper Lee; *The Bell Jar,* by Sylvia Plath; *The Catcher in the Rye,* by J. D. Salinger; or *The Joy*

Luck Club, by Amy Tan? Did you wonder about the relationship between the author and the first-person narrator?

2. Many writers, for a variety of reasons, use pseudonyms or pen names: Mark Twain for Samuel Clemens, Lewis Carroll for Charles Dodgson, O. Henry for William Sydney Porter, George Eliot for Mary Ann Evans, Jules Verne for M. Olchewitz, for example. What are some of the reasons a writer might use a pen name, and how do you think the use of a pen name changes the relationship between a writer and his or her readers? Does it make a difference to you as a reader if a writer has used a pseudonym?

Slow, law-abiding and drunk, I cruised down North Main Street toward the river. It was way past the middle of the night. Frankie Martin's bar was dark, the last drinker long gone home. I passed by old familiar Eastside Brewery, took a left into Shamrock Street and switched off my headlights. I planned to dig up various long-buried corpses and didn't care for company.

Up ahead, one long block ahead were the S.P. tracks. I watched the signal tower blink red and green as it angled south toward skyscraping City Hall beyond. When the two of them lined up just right, I coasted to the curb. This would be the place exactly. I got out and looked and listened. Not a truck, not a car, not a sound. My patriotic bumper was the loudest noise in sight

"CHICANO POWER," it yelled. "BROWN IS BEAUTIFUL. FULANO FOR SHERIFF."

"Shut up," I told my bumper. "Be quiet."

5 I stood face to face with the enemy, a long line of trailers boxcar size with S.P. Railroad on their rumps. Nothing between me and them except a 10-foot chainlink fence with two strands of friendly barbwire at the top. I planted my feet and spoke the magic word.

"114."

Trailers and chainlink went up in flames. In their place a certain saggy picket fence sprouted from the ground, a certain squeaky front porch rose up behind, and the skinny little house where I lived half my life. Down the block up popped number 112 and 110 and all their brothers. Old Shamrock lived again and I was home.

Before the S.P. rolled us under asphalt we were the best street in all L.A. with cozy little homes on both sides solid. Maybe they weren't too new or too fresh-painted but they were warm and lively, and when the trains passed by, how those little houses used to shake, rattle and roll. Strangers would ask, How can you stand it? But to tell the truth, we barely noticed. It was like rocking a baby and very good for the circulation of the blood, people used to claim.

"Gimme the pelota, Stupid." "Pítchala, pendejo!" "Enrique, vente p'acá or else you're really gonna get it." My ears tuned in ghost voices and murdered Spanish and my father's well-known whistle that used to bring me running home.

From *Famous All Over Town,* by Danny Santiago (second edition). New York: Penguin Books, 1984, pp. 7–17.

10 One hour I stood there listening to the dead and gone. It was a bad time in my life. I couldn't see my next step, should it be Left or Right, or Up or Down? Maybe if I relived my yesterdays I could be surer of my tomorrows. So I spread out old memories like hopscotch on the sidewalk, took a running jump and landed in the square of my fourteenth birthday, which was the last I spent on Shamrock Street, and that's where let's begin.

It took place on a hot Saturday in September.

"Here's your present."

My father slapped his chicken-killer knife into my hand. It was ground down thin as a needle and had a razor edge. Nobody but him was allowed to touch it.

"Huh?" I asked.

15 "Fourteen years makes a man, so prove yourself."

"Me?" I asked.

"Why not?" he said. "You seen me do it often enough."

"When?" I asked.

"When I tell you to," he told me crossly, "and quit looking so green in the face."

20 My father was quite famous for his chicken killing. People came from up and down the street to watch. He made a regular rodeo of it, jumping up and down like a cowboy with chickens running every which way. He'd grab and miss in a dozen comical ways till his watchers ran out of laughs, then he'd make one quick snatch and there was his chicken-of-the-week scooped up in his arms with a cord whipped tight around her legs. Next my father would make love to that chicken, whispering in her ear, and she'd arch her neck and wink at him as flirty as any senorita while he waltzed her round the yard singing. Then the music would stop.

"Buenas noches, mi amor," he'd say. "Go to sleep, little chickie dear."

The American Way of twisting necks off or chopping heads never pleased my father. It left the meat tough and angry, he claimed. So, Mexican style, he hung his chicken from her feet and slipped the blade into her neck so nice and easy she never felt it. She'd flop her wings once or twice and her eyes would blank out very peaceful while she bled to death with a pan underneath to catch the blood.

That was my father's style and I only hoped I could do as well. In one way I was proud he trusted me, but in another way, Who knows? So then the mailman came with the insurance check for his shortened pinkie finger. That cheered my father up and he slapped me on the shoulder.

"Let's go cash it," he suggested, which was a wonder because my father always preferred to cash his checks in private. So we climbed into our famous '55 low-mileage Buick and away we went to García's Short-Change Department Store to check on the merchandise.

25 "You call these things boots?" he hollered in that bull-voice of his. My father is very loud in stores when speaking Spanish but in English you can barely hear him. "What you make them of, worm skin?" he asked and the clerk ran to bring the best boots money could buy, and triple-soled. My father dropped them on the floor. They hit like sledgehammers and he was more or less content.

"Fit my Junior here," he ordered. "Good heavy boots will put meat on those matchstick legs of yours," he preached for all who cared to listen, "only don't leave them around where your mother will trip on them in her condition."

"Si, señor," I said and stomped my boots around the store. I was crazy to wear them home but my father said, No, put neat's-foot oil first, and peeled off a 20. As usual they tried to short him a dollar, my father's arithmetic is not the best, but I caught them at it. So from there we stopped by the Brewery for a keg and rolled home at five miles an hour to keep the foam from rising.

What followed was a little argument. My sister started throwing little indirectos like "What a thoughtful present for a fourteen-year-old and will you invite his hoodlum friends?" And, "How charming for our mother to have a gang of drunkards in the house with the baby due any minute now." Her smart remarks failed to please my father. In our house it was the pants that ruled so when Lena said Shit right out loud in English, my father hit her. In the right way of course. He never closed his fist on any girl or woman, like some, or slapped in dirty places. But even so he had a heavy hand and Lena marched out swearing she would never enter my father's door again. Personally, I expected her back for dinner. She had the biggest appetite in the family but on her it didn't show. My sister was as skinny as me except here and there, but what a temper.

On Shamrock, like most other places, people drank privately in backyards, not my father. He set up his beer on the front porch for all the world to come help him drink it. He stood the keg in a tub with ice around and threw an old rug over for shade, then he shoved in the tapper. It stuck up shiny as a sword.

30 "Free blood," my father shouted to various passing friends and slipped off the bandage for all to admire his stump. Myself; I didn't care to look at it.

"How much they pay you?" was asked.

"Hundred-fifty," my father said, which was not bad for one tiny knuckle on his pinkie finger's end.

"What's your fat finger worth?" they inquired.

"The S.P. Railroad don't have that kind of money," my father bragged. Quite some crowd soon collected. Virgie's Arturo and various others from S.P. and of course Chuchu Madrigal that was in Construction. My father settled his big piledriver butt onto his Superchief silver train step which he bought it for twenty-five cents. There are always good bargains on Shamrock if you don't ask too many questions. He sat there solid as a fireplug with little brown eggs of flesh poking out through the holes in his famous air-condition T-shirt, enjoying his beer and king of everybody.

35 Up and down the street the paychecks had been cashed. Saturday night lay ahead, and after, Lazy Sunday. My father and his friends were in the mood to laugh at everything and I was proud to laugh along with them while I sat sunning on the steps. They were soft to sit on, spongy and not like new lumber, only you had to drive the nails back in once a week which was my regular job. So I sat there working the neat's-foot oil into my new boots. My fingers slided slick and smooth over the leather and deep into the creases till I found myself wondering if a girl or woman might feel like that.

"What you dreaming there boy?" my father asked. Maybe I jumped because the men couldn't quit laughing. "You got a little window in your head," my father told me, "and oh what I can see in there. You keep your hands out of your pockets, hear? or else we'll see hair growing on your palms."

I was ready for the subject to get changed.

"Still," my father said, "this Junior of mine, he's a pretty good boy, smart too, his teachers claim, with prizes for his handwriting. So stand up, son, and let's drink him a toast on his fourteenth birthday."

"Hey, look where he's taller than his dad," Chuchu pointed out.

My father doubted it so they stood us back to back. I had an easy quarter-inch on him, so Chuchu gave me a dollar, and everybody cheered except my father. "It's all in that skinny goose neck," he complained and gave my head a friendly shove that nearly tore it off, then preached barbells for my self-improvement while he went back to sharpening up the chicken-killer knife.

Out on the street my friends were busy shoving Fat Manuel's car in hopes to get it started, Gorilla, Hungryman, Pelón and a couple others. Los Jesters de Shamrock was our name and in those days we were Kings in Eastside, nobody cared to mess with us.

"Esé, Chato," they called, which was my street name, from being flat-nose like a cat. "Give us a hand, man," they hollered but I shook my finger No.

"What's this 'Chato'?" my father scolded. He hated that name. "You're Rudy M. Medina, Junior, and be proud of it."

"Sí, señor," I quickly told him and hoped to be forgotten, but Pelón was a genius for trouble and here he comes with his decorátеd shoeshine box, all silver stars and red reflectors.

"Buenos días, Padrino," he tells my father. "No quieres un free shoeshine?"

I sweated. Of all my friends Pelón was my father's least favorite. Three years back when the guy was orphaned, my father took him into our house and slept him on the couch with me like twins. Till that bad day when my father caught us doing something.

"Come on, Godfather," Pelón begged, on the sarcastic side, "I'll give you a real fine shine and you could lay back and tell us all about your cowboy days in Mexico when you were captain of one hundred horses."

"Get out of my nose, mocoso," my father shouted and started down the steps.

"Oh, indubitably," said Pelón, which was his favorite word, and off he went like a rabbit. My father knew better than to try and catch him.

"No-good hoodlums," he complained. "Where's Respect? Fight, steal, rob, make trouble, that's all those rat-packers know to do, light their pimpy cigarettes and blow the smoke in their fathers' face. When I was their age I was already doing a man's work down there in mi pueblo. And any time I came in the house I kissed my father's hand and any time I went out too. But when I come home these days who kisses my hand? Not even a dog or cat."

"They're all too educated," Arturo agreed, "with their twelve years in school and their television. But down there in my village we had our advantages. We were poor as dirt but there used to be a certain little dark-skin girl, a fine plump little morenita she was. We all went to school on her and nobody whined about their homework."

To hear my father's friends tell it, there was a girl like that in every village and always she seemed to be dark-skinned and generous. And while my father's knife sang on the stone, his friends' Spanish words came rolling out like on rubber tires and they all turned patriotic Mejicanos. Yes, they admitted, there was hunger down there but the food had such a taste on it. The beans themselves were better than the best prime steaks of the USA. And yes, maybe it was chilly sleeping nights on those little mats of straw, but the mornings, hombre, when you stood outside shivering against the adobe wall and then the big round Mexican sun came up to warm you. It was the blanket of the poor, they all agreed, and tequila was the other poor man's blanket. To hear them talk, you wondered why they ever left the place.

And the snakes, man, those snakes of Mexico which always raised their head by beer number 5, snakes that whipped you to death with their tails, and others that rolled after you like wheels, tail tucked into mouth. And still others, nighttime snakes that came sliding down out of the grass roof while your compadre's mother's cousin's wife was sleeping, and sucked her nipples till her baby pined away to skin and bones, but that snake grew fat as a fire hose and over 12 feet long. I found myself especially interested in that nighttime snake and its strange way of life, while I sat there on the steps working on my new boots. By now they had soaked up all the oil they could hold so I put them on and laced them up very carefully to keep the tongues from wrinkling.

"Stand up, son," my father told me.

My time had come. Everybody had their eyes on me. I was the Main Event.

"You're fourteen years today," my father said. "And old enough to be my right hand. Now for once don't mess up. And be sure you catch all the blood." He slapped the chicken-killer knife into my hand. I gripped it tight.

"Con permiso?" I asked.

"Pass," they told me in a chorus.

My new boots marched me like an army round the corner of the house, along the side fence and up the back steps to the kitchen. My mother with her swollen belly stood leaning on the stove. Her braids hung tired and heavy down her back and she didn't notice when I came in. Since last month she'd been like half-asleep with her eyes turned inside out to watch the baby grow inside her.

"Hey, where's the pan at?" I asked her.

"What pan?" she wanted to know.

"The one for the blood naturally," I told her and flashed my knife. She looked at it and looked at me.

"You?" she said.

"Why not?" I told her.

My mother groaned when she bended down to rattle the pan out from under the sink. What if she should die? flashed through my head. What if this giant baby killed her while my father and his friends sat drinking on the front porch?

"See you don't cut yourself," she said and tuned me out.

Our backest yard was where the chickens lived. We had nopales solid along the fence reaching up their prickly paws higher than your shoulders. Our tumbledown shed took up one corner. I stood by the gate, knife in hand and watched the stupid chickens peck-peck-pecking through the gravel and complaining about the hard life they had. It was our old red hen I wanted. She used to be a steady layer but now only gave eggs when in the mood.

"Hey Junior, you gonna kill the chickie?"

"Make a circus like your daddy, Junior, huh?"

It was those pesty little kids from next door. I ignored them. My plan was to imitate my father exactly. I opened the gate and started clowning but those dumb kids never laughed even one time. So then I got disgusted and went after that old hen for real, but she turned track star on me. Twice I missed her and fell against the nopale cactuses and tore my shirt.

"Should I call your daddy, Junior?"

Junior this and Junior that. "Shut up," I told those snotnose kids. Maybe I even threw my knife at them, I don't remember, anyway they left there running. Then I really grabbed that chicken and hit her a good one too, to learn her a lesson. The rope kept tangling. It took three tries to get her legs tied up. Next, I hung her upside down where my father always did and put the blood pan under. With my left hand I stretched her neck out long for the knife, but it felt very funny to me, like something I had possibly felt before, only with feathers on it.

I creeped the knife in till it just barely touched skin. Only one inch more, a half-inch even. But my muscles froze on me. My hand started in to shake. Out front the men were waiting. Out front my father trusted me. He had generously put his own special knife into my hand. There was no way in all this would I could possibly go back to the front porch with that chicken still alive.

We hung there, me and that old red hen, how long—who knows? Till suddenly it came to me: What's so great about my father's crazy Mexican way of chicken killing? Why not try something new for a change, something more up-to-date? In his closet, in a shoe box, my father had a revolver which he kept loaded just in case. It was another one of those Shamrock Street bargains and he paid $10 for it. For years my father always warned me, "Don't you ever touch that thing," but today I was fourteen years old which was a man, so I went for it.

75 God was good to me. My mother didn't notice when I sneaked through the kitchen with the .45 under my T-shirt. It seemed heavier than I remembered, and wanted to wave around when I took aim. So I steadied the barrel on the trash can just 6 inches away from that old chicken's throat. It was quite important not to miss. I might be criticized.

"SSAAAAHHHHSSS!"

It turned out to be the Shot Heard Round The World.

On Shamrock people can tell pistols from firecrackers any day, having heard plenty of both from time to time. No doubt they asked each other, "Did she finally shoot him? Or him her?" There were several well-known trouble spots. So they all came running to see the corpse. But of course it was my father that got to me first.

"Here's your chicken," I told him and held it up.

80 Nothing in this world was ever deader than that old red hen. It was a perfect shot, just one tiny thread of neck left and the head hanging down. I expected my father to be quite pleased with me. Instead he yelled. He grabbed the pistol. He slammed the chicken in the dirt. He slapped for my face but I ducked under.

"Hey," I told him, "what's wrong with you?"

"You wait!" he shouted and slung me into the shed and banged the door.

"What happened?" somebody outside asked. "Who's dead?"

"Medina's kid just shot a chicken."

85 "With a GUN?"

Then somebody hollered, "Yaaay, chicken-shooter!" It sounded like Pelón that used to be my friend. Others took it up. I heard that ugly word race up and down the block like a fire engine. But I ask you, "What's the difference how you kill a chicken as long as that chicken gets dead?" Possibly I was the first in history to use a gun. But that's people for you, try anything new and different and they're sure to criticize, my father especially. You had to do every least thing exactly his way or he blamed you for it.

I laid there in the dirt. The sun was shooting blades of light between the boards. There was a big new hole where the .45 blasted through. My hands were all over dirt and blood. My boots were bloody too. Who cared? Let it rot there. From outside I heard my father chasing people from the yard. I heard Chuchu arguing with him till my father ordered him out too. It got quite quiet. I heard the noise leather makes when you slap it on a wall. And then my father pulled the shed door open. His well-known belt squirmed in his hands like a snake.

Let him kill me. I'll never make a sound.

But behind him, through the door I saw my mother. She came waddling down the back steps. If she argued with him it would only make things worse. She didn't. Instead, she grabbed her belly and screamed a scream like no scream I ever heard before. My father dropped his belt and ran to catch her. I ran too, but it turned out to be a false alarm. The baby took two more days in coming. And I could almost swear I saw my mother wink at me while my father carried her inside.

Exploring Texts and Contexts

For activities with icons, refer to the Guide to Analyzing Readings in Context.

1. What do we know about Chato or Rudy, the narrator of the novel? For example, how old is he when the events of the novel take place and how old is the narrator when he is telling the story? How do we know? What else do we know about him?

Language

2. One of the great mysteries of literature is how a writer is able to use words on the page, ink on paper, to create a character that can seem like a real person, that can seem alive. How does this writer use language to create Chato? Which descriptions particularly help us to imagine Chato? How does the writer to create a "voice" for Chato? What are some of the distinctive characteristics of this voice?
3. A concept that critics use to discuss how fiction works is the "reliability" of the narrator. Is the reader meant to believe the narrator and accept the narrator's judgments and values? Does the narrator represent the values of the author? How reliable a narrator is Chato?

Review of Famous All Over Town

David Quammen

Few things are more cheering than to pick up a first novel by an unknown author and see immediately, after only a dozen pages, that the new novelist is a natural. A writer endowed as though genetically with the sure, pure sense of how to shape his material, just where to expand and where to elide, when to maintain pace and when to change it, how to select rather than merely amass details. A writer with the delicate, precious trick of keeping a reader off balance yet engaged, with not just a keen eye but a keen ear, a keen wit and a feel for those narrative contours that make a good novel quite different from a padded short story or a veiled diary. That may not sound like much to ask but, among first novelists, it is surprisingly uncommon. So it is cheering to be able to report that Danny Santiago is a natural.

His book is "Famous All Over Town" and very simple in program: It chronicles the 15th year in the life of Rudy Medina Jr., a.k.a. "Chato," a street-wise Chicano kid trying to live long enough to look back someday and say he grew up in the tough Eastside neighborhood of Los Angeles. Chato measures out on the school tests with a brilliant I.Q. but he nevertheless gets himself in enough idiotic and punk-daring trouble to make that 15th year a lively one. Besides being bright and warmhearted he is also a born comic, which to readers may be his greatest charm but to himself (in dealing with all levels of authority) is often his worst liability.

Chato's life as a schoolboy, his neighborhood and gang of friends, his immediate family and even the familial house itself all collapse during the course of this novel, yet Chato floats on through the flotsam, buoyed up only by a manic appetite for experience and his own detached humor. "Famous All Over Town" is full of poverty, violence, emotional injury, and other forms of major disaster, all vividly and realistically portrayed, yet, like a spring feast-day in a barrio, it is nevertheless relentlessly joyous. Best of all is its language; narrated by Chato, the novel employs a rich street Chicano English that pleases the ear like sly and cheerful Mejicana music.

"Famous All Over Town" is an honest, steady novel that presents some hard cultural realities while not for a paragraph failing to entertain. I am totally ignorant of the Chicano urban experience but I have to believe this book is, on that subject, a minor classic. And Danny Santiago is good news.

From *The New York Times Book Review* by David Quammen, April 24, 1983, section 7, page 12.

A Noted "Hispanic" Novelist Proves to Be Someone Else

Edwin McDowell

At the annual meeting of the American Academy and Institute of Arts and Letters last May, John Kenneth Galbraith presented a $5,000 award for an outstanding work of fiction published during the preceding 12 months.

The winner was "Famous All Over Town," a novel about a Mexican-American family in the Los Angeles neighborhood of Eastside. The dust jacket of the book described the author, Danny Santiago, as having grown up in Los Angeles.

But Mr. Santiago did not show up to receive the award. To this day, neither his agent nor his editor has ever seen him. In fact, hardly anyone else has ever seen Danny Santiago. For the author of "Famous All Over Town" is not a Hispanic American, as many critics assumed, but Daniel James, 73 years old, who grew up in Kansas City, Mo., graduated from Andover and says he was the only member of the Yale Class of 1933 to major in classical Greek.

"We figured there was something strange going on, having to write to him in care of a post office box and his saying he did not have a telephone," said Bob Bender, Mr. James's editor at Simon & Schuster. "But we figured he was probably in prison and didn't want anybody to know."

5 Mr. James said he never told the publisher that he grew up in Los Angeles. "In my letter I said 'Danny Santiago was a product of Los Angeles,' " he recalled in a telephone conversation from his home in Carmel, Calif. He described his name change as only a "mild deception" for which he feels no qualms, in part because he and his wife spent 20 years in the Los Angeles barrio as volunteer workers. In addition, Mr. James believed he might still have been blacklisted. In 1951 before a Congressional committee he was named as a member of the Communist Party.

The fact that Mr. James used the pen name of Danny Santiago has evoked mixed reactions from writers of Hispanic origin, some of whom regard the deception as serious.

Prof. R. W. B. Lewis of Yale University, chairman of the seven-member American Academy committee that voted the award, said the new information about Danny Santiago casts a different light on the matter.

"We were considering the ethnic dimension," he said. But he added that the prize, called the Richard and Hinda Rosenthal Foundation Award, "was given for its literary quality."

"I don't think when I was reading it I was too much concerned with whether the author was Chicano or not," he said, "but now that I know, I think I admire the novel all the more. But I would have to say that if we had known, it would have given us pause. We would not necessarily have rejected it, but we would have had to talk a little more about it. It does raise all kinds of interesting questions."

From *The New York Times,* article by Edwin McDowell, July 22, 1984, section 1, page 1.

10 Mr. James said in the telephone interview that a number of his friends had warned him against publishing as Danny Santiago.

"They said this can be very touchy, it could hurt a lot of feelings and you shouldn't do it," he recalled. "But I said the pen name is pretty well established, with Mark Twain, Rabelais, and so many others. I said nobody's going to be hurt if the book's any good."

One of the friends who warned Mr. James against using a Hispanic name was the writer John Gregory Dunne, who met Mr. James in 1966. Mr. Dunne has written an article, for the Aug. 16 issue of *The New York Review of Books,* about Mr. James and his use of the pseudonym.

What complicates matters among Hispanic Americans is that some of them think the book, which evolved from a collection of short stories, is quite good.

"I read one of the short stories Danny Santiago wrote about a part of town I grew up in, right on the same street, and I thought the characterizations were right on target," said Felix Gutierrez, chairman of graduate studies at the University of Southern California school of journalism. But Mr. Gutierrez added, "I think Dan James should write as Dan James, because a piece should stand on the merit of the writing, not the author's name."

15 To illustrate how sensitive the issue is, he said that last year his cousin, Ricardo Munoz, telephoned and excitedly told him to read "Famous All Over Town" because it was an authentic account of growing up Mexican-American in their old neighborhood.

"The very next day a friend of ours telephoned and I told him what my cousin said," Mr. Gutierrez said. "My friend said, 'You know what? It was written by an Anglo who used a pen name,' and so I never read it."

But Mr. Gutierrez added, "You don't have to be a Latino to write on the Latino experience, and Latinos should not write only on that. There's nothing to stop an Anglo from writing authentically about it if he spends the time. That's the key, get to know us."

Philip Herrera, executive editor of *Connoisseur,* a monthly magazine of culture and the arts, said, "It is possible for Anglos to write as Hispanics and vice versa." What offended him, he said, was that one of Danny Santiago's short stories—ironically, the one Mr. Gutierrez liked so much—appeared in *Nuestro,* a magazine founded by Mr. Herrera and Jose M. Ferrer 3d, who had been at *Time* magazine."

"We were taken," Mr. Herrera said, when told of Danny Santiago's identity. "We were trying to present the best image of Hispanics we could. We were not trying to publish Anglo writers with Spanish surnames."

20 Mr. Ferrer, now a senior editor at *Time,* also expressed mild annoyance. "Our magazine was intended as an outlet for Latin voices," he said.

But he added that there were two different issues – "the longstanding question for the philosophers to settle, about whether somebody who has not lived the experience of another can write accurately about it; and whether the motive in choosing the name Danny Santiago had to do with cachet, with trying to get onto the bandwagon of minority writers who might be more publishable these days. In other words, can you gain an advantage by changing your name?"

Thomas Sanchez, the author of "Rabbit Boss" and "Zoot-Suit Murders," the latter novel set in the Los Angeles barrio in the 1940's, is quoted approvingly on the jacket of

"Famous All Over Town." In a recent conversation he said he had heard a rumor "that Danny Santiago was an Anglo."

He added: "But you have to ask, was this intentional deceit? And it doesn't appear to be that, since he chose the Spanish equivalent of his name rather than going out of his way to call himself Raul Alameda, for example."

Besides, what matters, Mr. Sanchez said, is not the author but the art.

25 "A work must be judged by the work itself, not the political or ethnic orientation of the author," he said. "A lot of professional Chicanos, professional blacks, professional Jews, professional Anglo-Saxons say no one else can cut into their territory. I don't believe in terms of the human race there is any such thing as territory. What creativity and art are all about are the absolute freedom to cross all those lines and go into any point of view in terms of the context of the work."

Mr. James based the novel on people and places that he and his wife, Lilith, experienced in the 20 years they spent as volunteer workers in the Eastside neighborhood depicted in the book. That neighborhood forms the world of Chato Medina, the book's sensitive, 14-year-old protagonist, who becomes famous all over town because he spray-paints his name everywhere. "We went down to the barrio at the invitation of a social worker for the Los Angeles Church Federation," Mr. James said. Mr. James soon began writing short stories based on that experience. His reason for choosing a pen name was not to deceive, he said, but in part because he believed that he had been blacklisted after he was named before the House Committee on Un-American Activities in 1951 as having been a member of the Communist Party.

Mr. James and his wife were party members for 10 years, but quit in 1948, according to Mr. Dunne's article. In the war years, the article says, one of Mr. James's contributions to the Communist cause was a 1942 play called "Winter Soldiers," which played 25 performances at the New School for Social Research. It won a $1,500 prize given to a promising young playwright. Mr. Dunne said in a telephone conversation that it was pure propaganda. "It was a true Stalinist play," he said. "People actually say in it, 'That's what my tractor said to me.'"

Mr. and Mrs. James collaborated on a play that, after various revisions, became the libretto for "Bloomer Girl," a musical that opened on Broadway on Oct. 5, 1944, and ran for 654 performances. "When it was later done as a two-hour television spectacular," Mr. James said, "they removed our credits, apparently to protect the morals of the American people. But we still collected royalties."

Those royalties helped pay the bills. So did his work on the scripts of two monster movies, "The Giant Behemoth" and "Gorgo," written under a family name, Daniel Hyatt. The movies were a far cry from Charlie Chaplin's "The Great Dictator," on which he had worked for two years in the 1930s and for which he received a screen credit as an assistant director.

30 In 1966, Mr. Dunne, his wife, Joan Didion, and their daughter moved into the house in Hollywood owned by Mr. and Mrs. James. Eventually, Mr. James showed Mr. Dunne some short stories he had written in the 1950s under the name of Danny Santiago but had been unable to sell.

"I had published a book about Cesar Chavez and the grape strike," Mr. Dunne said, "and he knew I was interested in the Chicanos. He had also helped me by giving me some names when I wanted to see if the strike had any impact on urban Chicanos."

Mr. Dunne liked the stories but said he was troubled by the idea of the author presenting himself as a Chicano. But Mr. James said that he had been unable to write under his own name for nearly 20 years, because of the blacklist and because he had lost confidence in his own ability. In a letter to Mr. Dunne, written from Carmel, he said, "In any event, unless you feel too guilty about this mild little deception of mine, I'd like you to send on the stories to Brandt."

He referred to Carl Brandt, the New York literary agent for Mr. Dunne and other writers. Mr. Brandt placed the stories in various magazines, including *Playboy* and *Redbook,* but in all those years he neither saw nor spoke to his reclusive client.

"The first time he heard my voice was earlier this month," Mr. James said, "when I told him that I had agreed to let John Dunne write about my secret. All he could say was 'Oh my God, oh my God.'"

The book jacket's description of the author said: "Danny Santiago grew up in Los Angeles. He is the author of short stories published in *Playboy, Redbook,* and *Nuestro.* One of his stories, 'The Somebody,' was chosen for Martha Foley's annual collection The Best American Short Stories and has been widely anthologized. 'Famous All Over Town' is Danny Santiago's first novel." The book was issued in paperback last April by New American Library.

Mr. James said he had "one day of misgivings" that his identity was about to be disclosed. "I wondered if it was going to hurt my writing," he said. "And while I was happy with Danny Santiago, it was getting a little claustrophobic never being able to meet my agent or editor or people who wrote to me."

He is working on another book with a Mexican-American theme, also set in Los Angeles. It too will appear under the name of Danny Santiago.

"Dan James couldn't ever write that book," he said. "Besides, I now realize that I enjoy my hours as Danny Santiago more than I enjoy my hours as Dan James."

Exploring Texts and Contexts

1. In David Quammen's review of *Famous All Over Town,* written soon after the book was published, what assumptions does the writer make about the author of the novel? Did you share these assumptions?
2. In the article written by Edwin McDowell a year or so after the novel was published, what does McDowell reveal about the author of *Famous*? Were you surprised by this revelation?

3. According to McDowell, on what grounds has Daniel James been criticized on the one hand and defended on the other hand?

4. What do we know about Daniel James's motivation? Are you sympathetic or unsympathetic with what he did and his motivation for doing it?

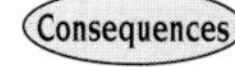

Creating Texts

For activities with icons, refer to the Guides to Analyzing Contexts for Writing and Analyzing Readings in Context. For additional help with these writing projects, read the description of **Cover Letter/Reflective Essay** and **Essay**.

1. Try your hand at writing a short story about a character who is very different from you in some way. You might, if you like, write about the persona that you created for the Creating Texts Activity 1 on page 81. This character should be the first-person narrator of the story and can be a reliable or unreliable narrator. Use description and dialogue to make the character as realistic, believable, and interesting as possible. After writing the story, or a portion of it, write a cover letter in which you discuss how you chose the character and how you tried to make that character come alive.

2. Write an essay in which you take and defend a position on the ethics, social implications, and artistic validity of Daniel James's authorship of *Famous All Over Town*. Should he have written the novel, and should he have published it under the name Danny Santiago? In developing your position on this issue, you should consider the following questions: Can writers create works of fiction about people who are different from them and whose experiences are different? Do such works of fiction have artistic validity and social value? Can they be considered authentic representations of the experiences they describe? Can readers learn anything from reading such works of fiction? What are the social and ethical implications of publishing works of fiction under a pseudonym that leads readers to believe one belongs to a different social or ethnic group or is a different gender? What are the social implications of imagining and writing about the experiences of others? If you know of other instances of impostorship that would illuminate this discussion, feel free to bring them in.

CHAPTER 4

Buying and Selling Authenticity

Situation: What aspects of contemporary culture does this photograph seem to refer to or draw on?

Genre: What kind of photograph is this? What clues help you decide?

Language: How does the angle the photograph was taken from affect its composition and impact? Describe the attitude of the three people in the photograph; which visual elements lead you to that description—pose, facial expression, clothes?

Consequences: If this picture were part of an ad in a magazine, how might you respond to it?

No true artist wants to sell out, but most artists would at least like to have the opportunity to resist selling out, because having that opportunity also means that you have reached an audience. There is a real tension for artists who would like to reach an audience—whether the art is folk craft or music or fashion—but remain true to their creative process. Is it possible for something to have mass appeal and still be genuine? What happens to the authenticity of art when it becomes a commodity?

The story of mediagossip.com—a personal Web site created by Jim Romenesko, a once-obscure journalist—raises questions about the nature of the creative process, the role of the artist, and the function of art in an increasingly commercialized culture. In 1999, Romenesko's work became the subject of feature stories and columns in national papers such as the *New York Times* and the *Wall Street Journal*. He was the focus of a panel discussion on new media at the University of California at Berkeley media conference and was interviewed for the Internet magazine Salon.com. Why all the attention?

At that time, mediagossip.com was one of the most popular of a new kind of Web site, which later became known as weblogs or blogs. At the time the most creative area of the Internet, such sites provided links to other stories and places on the Web that the blog's creator found interesting. The designers of these sites interspersed information with commentary and personal asides. Because they bore the personal stamp of their creators, they were unlike other lists of links. Part online journal, part referrer site, they were a wholly new form of expression, the products of irreverent writers whose independent spirit and subversive nature drew people who were looking for an authentic voice.

Romenesko's site recorded anywhere from 5,000 to 7,000 hits a day, a fact that drew the attention of businesses and corporations. If Romenesko linked a story to his site, it had the potential to reach thousands of new readers. But partly because of the increasing popularity of the site, Romenesko eventually decided to relinquish independence and agreed to have his site sponsored. Mediagossip.com is now Jim Romenesko's MediaNews, sponsored by the Poynter Institute, a nonprofit journalism education foundation.

The deal immediately inspired talk about the dangers of being co-opted. Most sponsored sites are not as popular as the independent sites, in part because they lack the strong personal voice and subversive element of many independent sites. Much of what they publish can be found in other sources such as the evening news and the mainstream press. In any case, Romenesko's creative process might already have been affected by all the attention he had been attracting and the knowledge that large numbers of people were viewing his site. What will happen to this new form of discourse, the weblog, as the original creators succumb to pressure to give up their independence? Can these sites keep their edge and their authenticity under corporate or more benign forms of sponsorship?

The tug-of-war between authenticity and commercial success, exemplified by the creation and subsequent development of weblogs, is played out in many forms of art, commerce, and self-expression, as we will see in this chapter.

Goin' Gangsta, Choosin' Cholita

Nell Bernstein

In "Goin' Gangsta, Choosin' Cholita," Nell Bernstein tells the stories of young people who use fashion and music to identify with a particular ethnic group. Bernstein's feature story grows out of her work with teens in the San Francisco Bay area. She edits a publication called *YO!* (an acronym for "youth outlook" and the Spanish word for "I"), a bimonthly news journal of youth culture produced by young people in the Bay Area. The young people profiled here are bored because they see their lives as conventional and "too bland," and they are attracted to lifestyles and cultures they perceive as more authentic than their own.

Whether exposed to ethnic difference in their own schools and neighborhood or through the media, these teens believe in their ability to identify with other lifestyles by listening to alternative music or wearing the clothes promoted by famous rap artists. Published in the mid-nineties, Bernstein's article was one of the first to document our growing fascination with the cultural phenomenon of the wannabe. Other newspapers, magazines, and radio and TV talk shows were also running stories featuring "wiggers," white youth who want to be black, and other teens searching for an authentic identity. Is this behavior merely rebellion for its own sake, or are these young people a vision of the future?

Connecting with the Conversation

For activities with icons, refer to the Guide to Analyzing Readings in Context.

1. Map out the cafeteria or hangout at your college or the high school you graduated from. In a journal entry, describe the seating arrangements. Who sits where, and how do clothing, hairstyles, and taste in music help identify the different groups?
2. What words do you and your peers use to describe people that you consider fake or phony? Do you also have words for people you consider genuine or sincere? In a small group, compare notes. Discuss how young people use language, including slang, to express their values and make judgments.

Her lipstick is dark, the lip liner even darker, nearly black. In baggy pants, a blue plaid Pendleton, her bangs pulled back tight off her forehead, 15-year-old April is a perfect cholita, a Mexican gangsta girl.

But April Miller is Anglo. "And I don't like it!" she complains. "I'd rather be Mexican."

April's father wanders into the family room of their home in San Leandro, California, a suburb near Oakland. "Hey, cholita," he teases. "Go get a suntan. We'll put you in a barrio and see how much you like it."

A large, sandy-haired man with "April" tattooed on one arm and "Kelly"—the name of his older daughter—on the other, Miller spent 21 years working in a San Leandro glass factory that shut down and moved to Mexico a couple of years ago. He recently got a job in another factory, but he expects NAFTA to swallow that one, too.

5 "Sooner or later we'll all get nailed," he says. "Just another stab in the back of the American middle class."

Later, April gets her revenge: "Hey, Mr. White Man's Last Stand," she teases. "Wait till you see how well I manage my welfare check. You'll be asking me for money."

From *San Jose Mercury News,* November 13, 1994. Reprinted in the *Utne Reader,* March–April 1995.

A once almost exclusively white, now increasingly Latin and black working-class suburb, San Leandro borders on predominantly black East Oakland. For decades, the boundary was strictly policed and practically impermeable. In 1970 April Miller's hometown was 97 percent white. By 1990 San Leandro was 65 percent white, 6 percent black, 15 percent Hispanic, and 13 percent Asian or Pacific Islander. With minorities moving into suburbs in growing numbers and cities becoming ever more diverse, the boundary between city and suburb is dissolving, and suburban teenagers are changing with the times.

In April's bedroom, her past and present selves lie in layers, the pink walls of girlhood almost obscured, Guns N' Roses and Pearl Jam posters overlaid by rappers Paris and Ice Cube. "I don't have a big enough attitude to be a black girl," says April, explaining her current choice of ethnic identification.

What matters is that she thinks the choice is hers. For April and her friends, identity is not a matter of where you come from, what you were born into, what color your skin is. It's what you wear, the music you listen to, the words you use—everything to which you pledge allegiance, no matter how fleetingly.

10 The hybridization of American teens has become talk show fodder, with "wiggers"—white kids who dress and talk "black"—appearing on TV in full gangsta regalia. In Indiana a group of white high school girls raised a national stir when they triggered an imitation race war at their virtually all-white high school last fall simply by dressing "black."

In many parts of the country, it's television and radio, not neighbors, that introduce teens to the allure of ethnic difference. But in California, which demographers predict will be the first state with no racial majority by the year 2000, the influences are more immediate. The California public schools are the most diverse in the country: 42 percent white, 36 percent Hispanic, 9 percent black, 8 percent Asian.

Sometimes young people fight over their differences. Students at virtually any school in the Bay Area can recount the details of at least one "race riot" in which a conflict between individuals escalated into a battle between their clans. More often, though, teens would rather join than fight. Adolescence, after all, is the period when you're most inclined to mimic the power closest at hand, from stealing your older sister's clothes to copying the ruling clique at school.

White skaters and Mexican would-be gangbangers listen to gangsta rap and call each other "nigga" as a term of endearment; white girls sometimes affect Spanish accents; blond cheerleaders claim Cherokee ancestors.

"Claiming" is the central concept here. A Vietnamese teen in Hayward, another Oakland suburb, "claims" Oakland—and by implication blackness—because he lived there as a child. A law-abiding white kid "claims" a Mexican gang he says he hangs with. A brown-skinned girl with a Mexican father and a white mother "claims" her Mexican side, while her fair-skinned sister "claims" white. The word comes up over and over, as if identity were territory, the self a kind of turf.

15 At a restaurant in a minimall in Hayward, Nicole Huffstutler, 13, sits with her friends and describes herself as "Indian, German, French, Welsh, and, um . . . American": "If somebody says anything like 'Yeah, you're just a peckerwood,' I'll walk up and I'll say 'white pride!' 'Cause I'm proud of my race, and I wouldn't wanna be any other race."

"Claiming" white has become a matter of principle for Heather, too, who says she's "sick of the majority looking at us like we're less than them." (Hayward schools were

51 percent white in 1990, down from 77 percent in 1980, and whites are now the minority in many schools.)

Asked if she knows that nonwhites have not traditionally been referred to as "the majority" in America, Heather gets exasperated: "I hear that all the time, every day. They say, 'Well, you guys controlled us for many years, and it's time for us to control you.' Every day."

When Jennifer Vargas—a small, brown-skinned girl in purple jeans who quietly eats her salad while Heather talks—softly announces that she's "mostly Mexican," she gets in trouble with her friends.

"No, you're not!" scolds Heather.

20 "I'm mostly Indian and Mexican," Jennifer continues flatly. "I'm very little . . . I'm mostly . . . "

"Your mom's white!" Nicole reminds her sharply. "She has blond hair."

"That's what I mean," Nicole adds. "People think that white is a bad thing. They think that white is a bad race. So she's trying to claim more Mexican than white."

"I have very little white in me," Jennifer repeats. "I have mostly my dad's side, 'cause I look like him and stuff. And most of my friends think that me and my brother and sister aren't related, 'cause they look more like my mom."

"But you guys are all the same race, you just look different," Nicole insists. She stops eating and frowns. "OK, you're half and half each what your parents have. So you're equal as your brother and sister, you just look different. And you should be proud of what you are—every little piece and bit of what you are. Even if you were Afghan or whatever, you should be proud of it."

25 WILL MOSLEY, HEATHER'S 17-year-old brother, says he and his friends listen to rap groups like Compton's Most Wanted, NWA, and Above the Law because they "sing about life"—that is, what happens in Oakland, Los Angeles, anyplace but where Will is sitting today, an empty Round Table Pizza in a minimall.

"No matter what race you are," Will says, "if you live like we do, then that's the kind of music you like."

And how do they live?

"We don't live bad or anything," Will admits. "We live in a pretty good neighborhood, there's no violence or crime. I was just . . . we're just city people, I guess."

Will and his friend Adolfo Garcia, 16, say they've outgrown trying to be something they're not. "When I was 11 or 12," Will says, "I thought I was becoming a big gangsta and stuff. Because I liked that music, and thought it was the coolest, I wanted to become that, I wore big clothes, like you wear in jail. But then I kind of woke up. I looked at myself and thought, 'Who am I trying to be?' "

30 They may have outgrown blatant mimicry, but Will and his friends remain convinced that they can live in a suburban tract house with a well-kept lawn on a tree-lined street in "not a bad neighborhood" and still call themselves "city" people on the basis of musical tastes. "City" for these young people means crime, graffiti, drugs. The kids are law-abiding, but these activities connote what Will admiringly calls "action." With pride in his voice, Will predicts that "in a couple of years, Hayward will be like Oakland. It's starting to get more known, because of crime and things. I think it'll be bigger, more things happening, more crime, more graffiti, stealing cars."

"That's good," chimes in 15-year-old Matt Jenkins, whose new beeper—an item that once connoted gangsta chic but now means little more than an active social life—goes off periodically. "More fun."

The three young men imagine with disdain life in a gangsta-free zone. "Too bland, too boring," Adolfo says. "You have to have something going on. You can't just have everyday life."

"Mowing your lawn," Matt sneers.

"Like Beaver Cleaver's house," Adolfo adds. "It's too clean out here."

35 Not only white kids believe that identity is a matter of choice or taste, or that the power of "claiming" can transcend ethnicity. The Manor Park Locos—a group of mostly Mexican-Americans who hang out in San Leandro's Manor Park—say they descend from the Manor Lords, tough white guys who ruled the neighborhood a generation ago.

They "are like our . . . uncles and dads, the older generation," says Jesse Martinez, 14. "We're what they were when they were around, except we're Mexican."

"There's three generations," says Oso, Jesse's younger brother. "There's Manor Lords, Manor Park Locos, and Manor Park Pee Wees." The Pee Wees consist mainly of the Locos' younger brothers, eager kids who circle the older boys on bikes and brag about "punking people."

Unlike Will Mosley, the Locos find little glamour in city life. They survey the changing suburban landscape and see not "action" or "more fun" but frightening decline. Though most of them are not yet 18, the Locos are already nostalgic, longing for a Beaver Cleaver past that white kids who mimic them would scoff at.

Walking through nearly empty Manor Park, with its eucalyptus stands, its softball diamond and tennis courts, Jesse's friend Alex, the only Asian in the group, waves his arms in a gesture of futility. "A few years ago, every bench was filled," he says. "Now no one comes here. I guess it's because of everything that's going on. My parents paid a lot for this house, and I want it to be nice for them. I just hope this doesn't turn into Oakland."

40 Glancing across the park at April Miller's street, Jesse says he knows what the white cholitas are about. "It's not a racial thing," he explains. "It's just all the most popular people out here are Mexican. We're just the gangstas that everyone knows. I guess those girls wanna be known."

Not every young Californian embraces the new racial hybridism. Andrea Jones, 20, an African-American who grew up in the Bay Area suburbs of Union City and Hayward, is unimpressed by what she sees mainly as shallow mimicry. "It's full of posers out here," she says. "When *Boyz N the Hood* came out on video, it was sold out for weeks. The boys all wanna be black, the girls all wanna be Mexican. It's the glamour."

Driving down the quiet, shaded streets of her old neighborhood in Union City, Andrea spots two white preteen boys in Raiders jackets and hugely baggy pants strutting erratically down the empty sidewalk. "Look at them," she says. "Dislocated."

She knows why. "In a lot of these schools out here, it's hard being white," she says. "I don't think these kids were prepared for the backlash that is going on, all the pride now in people of color's ethnicity, and our boldness with it. They have nothing like that, no identity, nothing they can say they're proud of.

"So they latch onto their great-grandmother who's a Cherokee, or they take on the most stereotypical aspects of being black or Mexican. It's beautiful to appreciate different aspects of other people's culture—that's like the dream of what the 21st century should be. But to garnish yourself with pop culture stereotypes just to blend—that's really sad."

45 Roland Krevocheza, 18, graduated last year from Arroyo High School in San Leandro. He is Mexican on his mother's side, Eastern European on his father's. In the new hierarchies, it may be mixed kids like Roland who have the hardest time finding their place, even as their numbers grow. (One in five marriages in California is between people of different races.) They can always be called "wannabes," no matter what they claim.

"I'll state all my nationalities," Roland says. But he takes a greater interest in his father's side, his Ukrainian, Romanian, and Czech ancestors. "It's more unique," he explains. "Mexican culture is all around me. We eat Mexican food all the time, I hear stories from my grandmother. I see the low-riders and stuff. I'm already part of it. I'm not trying to be; I am."

His darker-skinned brother "says he's not proud to be white," Roland adds. "He calls me 'Mr. Nazi.' " In the room the two share, the American flags and the reproduction of the Bill of Rights are Roland's; the Public Enemy poster belongs to his brother.

Roland has good reason to mistrust gangsta attitudes. In his junior year in high school, he was one of several Arroyo students who were beaten up outside the school at lunchtime by a group of Samoans who came in cars from Oakland. Roland wound up with a split lip, a concussion, and a broken tailbone. Later he was told that the assault was "gang-related"—that the Samoans were beating up anyone wearing red.

"Rappers, I don't like them," Roland says. "I think they're a bad influence on kids. It makes kids think they're all tough and bad."

50 Those who, like Roland, dismiss the gangsta and cholo styles as affectations can point to the fact that several companies market overpriced knockoffs of "ghetto wear" targeted at teens.

But there's also something going on out here that transcends adolescent faddishness and pop culture exoticism. When white kids call their parents "racist" for nagging them about their baggy pants; when they learn Spanish to talk to their boyfriends; when Mexican-American boys feel themselves descended in spirit from white "uncles"; when children of mixed marriages insist that they are whatever race they say they are, all of them are more than just confused.

They're inching toward what Andrea Jones calls "the dream of what the 21st century should be." In the ever more diverse communities of Northern California, they're also facing the complicated reality of what their 21st century will be.

Meanwhile, in the living room of the Miller family's San Leandro home, the argument continues unabated. "You don't know what you are," April's father has told her more than once. But she just keeps on telling him he doesn't know what time it is.

Exploring Texts and Contexts

For activities with icons, refer to the Guide to Analyzing Readings in Context.

1. Add your own voice to those in Bernstein's article. Andrea Jones, a young woman quoted in the article, sees the other young people in the article as

posers and their behavior as shallow mimicry. Do you agree? Or do you think that they are genuinely trying to create a new identity for themselves? Do you see the situation as yet one more attempt by companies to market overpriced reproductions of urban wear to adolescents? Or can you offer some other explanation?

Situation

2. Look closely at the last three paragraphs of Bernstein's article. Who is being addressed here? "Goin' Gangsta, Choosin' Cholita" was originally published in the Sunday supplement magazine of the *San Jose Mercury News*. Speculate on how the type of publication and its audience may have influenced Bernstein's conclusion to this article.

Creating Texts

For activities with icons, refer to the Guides to Analyzing Contexts for Writing and Analyzing Readings in Context. For additional help with these writing projects, read the description of **Essay, Opinion Piece,** and **Cover Letter/Reflective Essay** in the Genre Glossary.

Situation

1. In an essay, explore how three different writers portray young people who try to create an identity by adopting a particular look and attitude. Bernstein, as well as other writers in this unit such as Marc Spiegler and James Ledbetter, all discuss teens who make lifestyle choices to attain authenticity, but each author writes about this phenomenon within a different context. What conclusions can you draw about the connection between the author's context and his or her portrayal of young people?

Genre

2. The opinion piece is a familiar genre that appears in the editorial section of newspapers and journals. Typically, writers concerned about a particular social issue use opinion pieces to persuade readers to adopt a specific plan or idea. Feature articles like this one by Bernstein may also discuss larger social issues, but they are very different from opinion pieces. For one thing, because these feature articles often appear in Sunday papers, the writers have the space to use vivid descriptions, anecdotes, and pictures. What are some other similarities and differences between feature articles and opinion pieces? Rewrite Bernstein's feature article as an opinion piece. Then, in a cover letter to your teacher, discuss how genre influences the meaning and impact of a piece of writing.

Marketing Street Culture

Bringing Hip-Hop Style to the Mainstream

Marc Spiegler

When a company attempts to design clothes that appeal to a specific group of consumers, they conduct what is called *market research*. You may have participated in such research if you have answered questions on the telephone about your interests or filled out a survey in your local mall. It is in this transaction between your desires as a consumer and a company's desire to sell its product that authenticity finds itself being stretched and pulled almost beyond recognition. Corporations recognize that if their product is not seen as authentic, consumers will not buy it. Yet artists as well as consumers would like to believe that authenticity is not a commodity that can be sold.

In his article, "Marketing Street Culture: Bringing Hip-Hop Style to the Mainstream," Marc Spiegler explores the possibility that corporations can identify and sell authenticity if they have a more sophisticated understanding of the social processes involved in achieving authenticity. He relies primarily on survey data gathered by marketing or trendwatching firms and on observers of the hip-hop scene such as Upski Wimsatt to analyze what makes white surburban youth willing consumers. Spiegler has even produced a hip-hop quiz for you to determine for yourself how much you know. For instance, what does the term "sampling" mean in the context of hip-hop culture? Or "bombing trains"? How about "freestyling"? Understanding the inner circle of hard-core hip-hop culture, according to Spiegler, will allow corporations to design and market authentic products attractive to teens who want to identify with rappers.

Connecting with the Conversation

1. Visit two or three of the stores you usually shop at and ask to interview the manager or the buyer. Ask how that company or franchise makes decisions about what clothes to feature. What sorts of information do they need to make those decisions? How do they get that information? Write up what you find out and report to the class.
2. Go to your library and browse through several issues of *American Demographics* or look at the journal online at www.demographics.com. Look over at least two other articles that attempt to explain a trend or offer information on a cultural phenomenon. What are some common characteristics of this genre? Write a brief report and share it with the class.

The Scene: Martha's Vineyard, Massachusetts, a bastion of the white East Coast establishment. A teenaged boy saunters down the street, his gait and attitude embodying adolescent rebellion. Baggy jeans sag atop over-designed sneakers, gold hoops adorn both ears, and a baseball cap shields his eyes. On his chest, a Tommy Hilfiger shirt sports the designer's distinctive pairing of blue and red rectangles.

Once, this outfit would have been unimaginable to this cool teen: only his clean-cut, country-club peers sported Hilfiger clothes. What linked the previously preppy Hilfiger to jeans so low-slung they seem to defy gravity? To a large extent, the answer lay 200 miles southwest, in the oversized personage of Brooklyn's Biggie Smalls, an admitted ex-drug dealer turned rapper, who was killed in 1997.

During the mid '90s, Smalls and other hip-hop stars became a crucial part of Hilfiger's open attempt to tap into the urban youth market. In exchange for giving artists free wardrobes, Hilfiger found its name mentioned in both the rhyming verses of rap songs and their "shout-out" lyrics, in which rap artists chant out thanks to friends and sponsors for their support.

For Tommy Hilfiger and other brands, the result is *de facto* product placement. The September 1996 issue of *Rolling Stone* magazine featured the rap group The Fugees, with the men prominently sporting the Tommy Hilfiger logo. In February 1996, Hilfiger even used a pair of rap stars as runway models: horror-core rapper Method Man and muscular bad-boy Treach of Naughty by Nature.

5 Threatened by Hilfiger in a market he had profited from but never embraced, it hardly seems coincidental that Ralph Lauren signed black male super-model Beckford Tyson to an exclusive contract. Even the patrician perfumier Esteé Lauder jumped on the Hilfiger bandwagon, launching a new cross-promotion series with the clothing company. The name of one of Lauder's new perfumes said it all. "Tommy Girl" plays on both Tommy Hilfiger's name and the seminal New York hip-hop record label Tommy Boy. Hilfiger also launched a clothing line for teenaged girls in fall 1996, projected by the company to gross $100 million in its first year on retail racks.

On the surface, it seems Hilfiger and others are courting a market too small and poor to matter. The majority of true hip-hoppers live in inner cities, although not all urban youths embrace the culture. About 5 million U.S. teens aged 15 to 19 lived in central cities in 1994, or 28 percent of all people that age. Inner-city blacks aged 15 to 19 are an even smaller group. At 1.4 million, they are only 8 percent of all teens. They also have significantly lower incomes than their white suburban counterparts. The numbers of 20-to-24-year-olds and black 20-to-24-year-olds in central cities are also small, at 6.5 million and 1.6 million, respectively.

So why are companies pitching products to the hip-hop crowd? Because for most of the 1990s, hordes of suburban kids—both black and white—have followed inner-city idols in adopting everything from music to clothing to language. The most prominent examples are in evidence at suburban shopping malls across the country: licensed sports apparel, baseball caps, oversized jeans, and gangster rap music.

Scoring a hit with inner-city youths can make a product hot with the much larger and affluent white suburban market. But to take advantage of this phenomenon, you

---

From *American Demographics,* November 1996, pp. 29–34. Updated by the author, November 2000.

have to dig into how hip-hop culture spreads from housing projects to rural environs, understand why hip-hop is so attractive to suburban whites, and discern the process by which hip-hoppers embrace products.

Hip Hop Hits the Mainstream

In its early years, MTV drew jeers for being too "white," for shying away even from vanilla-flavored black pop stars such as Michael Jackson. Yet most pop-culture watchers agree that the cable channel's launching "Yo! MTV Raps" in 1992 was the pivotal event in the spread of hip-hop culture. Running in a prime after-school spot, and initially hosted by graffiti artist and rapper Fab Five Freddy, the show beamed two daily hours of inner-city attitude at adolescent eyeballs in even the most remote Iowa corn country.

10 "There's no question—'Yo! MTV Raps' was the window into that world for Middle America," says Janine Misdom of Sputnik, a Manhattan-based firm that tracks youth trends for clients such as Levi-Strauss, Reebok, and Pepsi. Other video-oriented media soon followed. Within a few years, an all-day viewer-controlled channel called The Box supplied a steady stream of harder-edged hip-hop to any kid within the viewing area of a major metropolis. In 1993, about a year after "Yo! MTV Raps" hit cable, more than six in ten teens aged 12 to 19 rated hip-hop music as "in," according to Teenage Research Unlimited (TRU) of Northbrook, Illinois.

Music and fashion went hand in hand, as teens adopted the looks sported by rappers. Most Americans first saw baggy jeans in music videos sagging around the hips of white rap star Marky Mark (now known as *Perfect Storm* film star Mark Wahlberg). Teens also got an eyeful of Mark's boxers-exposed backside in his beefcake ads for Calvin Klein jeans. By spring 1993, 80 percent of teens favored the style, up from two-thirds six months earlier. And the look has staying power. Seventy-eight percent of teens still say baggy clothes are "in," according to TRU's Spring 1996 survey, although the style's popularity may be waning slightly.

Today, elements of hip-hop culture appear in the mainstream media, from commercials using rapped slogans to hit films such as *Menace II Society* and *Boyz N the Hood.* Suburban record stores stock relatively extensive hip-hop sections, and with good reason. Among consumers aged 12 to 17, almost three in five (58 percent) either "like" or "strongly like" rap, according to SounData of Hartsdale, New York, which tracks sales and other trends for the music industry. The 1996 figure is equally high among 18-to-20-year-olds. And even among the solidly adult 21-to-24-year-old age group, almost two-fifths favor the genre. Not surprisingly, it has now become a music-industry maxim that for a rap record to go platinum, it must sell strongly among white youths.

What draws white teens to a culture with origins so strongly linked to the inner city, and so distant from their suburbia's sylvan lawns? Clearly, rebellion is a big factor. "People resonate with the strong anti-oppression messages of rap, and the alienation of blacks," says Ivan Juzang of Motivational Educational Entertainment, a six-year-old Philadelphia firm specializing in targeting urban youth. "All young people buy into rebellion in general, as part of rebelling against parental authority."

Embracing Fear

Gangster rap artists such as the late Tupac Shakur and Dr. Dre represent only the latest link in a long chain of anti-establishment American icons (Shakur was wounded in a drive-by shooting in Las Vegas in September 1996 and died a week later). American teens have always been fascinated with outsider heroes, who score money and fame without being cowed by societal strictures. Such idols run from John Dillinger and Dennis Rodman, to Marlon Brando's fictional biker in *The Wild One* to James Dean's *Rebel Without a Cause*.

Yet many argue that hip-hop's attractiveness transcends mere rebellion, placing it in a different category from past teen trends. For instance, punk, with its body piercing and mohawked heads, was often rebellion for rebellion's sake. Based on the urge to shock, it constructed a new reality for its adherents outside of societal norms. In contrast, hip-hop springs from the experiences of young blacks living in cities. It's based on a real culture, giving it more permanence than earlier teen trends. People who want a part of hip-hop culture always have something new to latch onto, because the culture is always evolving.

But perhaps more important to white teens, embracing hip-hop fashion, language, and music lets them claim to be part of black, inner-city culture. "By entering into the

Who's Got the Beat

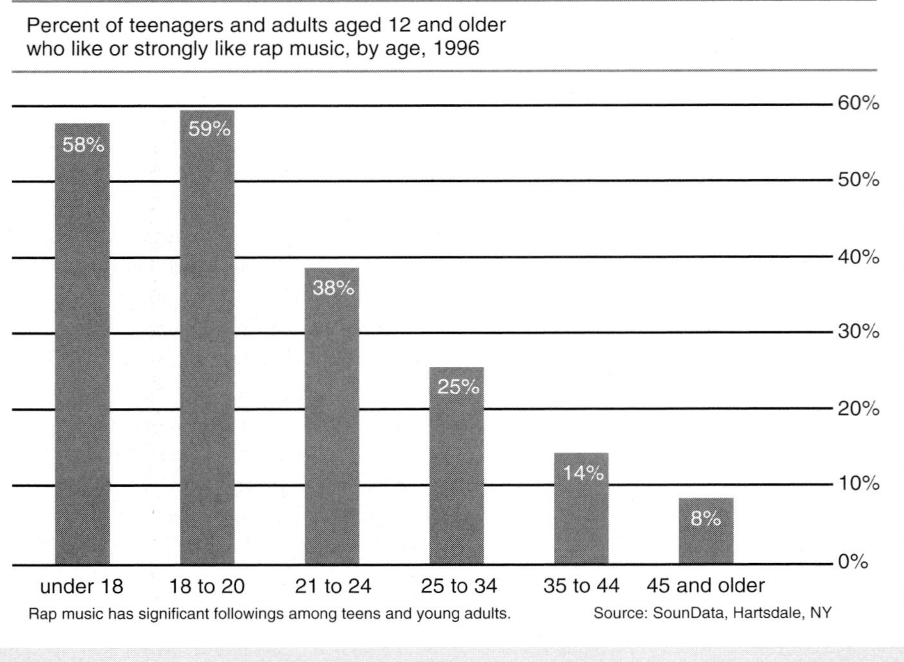

Rap music has significant followings among teens and young adults. Source: SounData, Hartsdale, NY

hip-hop sphere, I felt like I was opening a whole world that was closed to me before—it gave me a basis to meet all these people I had been scared of, whose main context for me was that they stole my bikes," says white 23-year-old William "Upski" Wimsatt, author of the memoir *Bomb the Suburbs*. The book in part details his trajectory from University of Chicago faculty brat to graffiti artist and journalist covering the rap music scene.

The attraction, he says, is part admiration, part fascination, and part fear. "A lot of white kids suspect they wouldn't make it through what inner-city blacks do, so there's an embedded admiration that's almost visceral," Wimsatt says. "Fear is one of our strongest impulses, and poor black men are the greatest embodiment of that fear."

Skateboarders, snowboarders, and other practitioners of nontraditional sports were among the first white teens to adopt the accouterments of hip-hop culture. Yet they are also some of the culture's least devoted adherents. "Most of them don't really understand hip-hop," says Chicagoan Tim Haley, a Midwest sales representative for snowboarding gear. "They want to come off as being bad ass, pumping their stereo around town," he says. "So you'll see a bunch of white kids in Podunk, Michigan, trying to dress 'hip-hop,' but really they're just jocks with rich parents."

Got to Be Real

Turning teens like these on to hip-hop styles begins with a much smaller group—hard-core hip-hoppers. "If we develop the hardest core element, we reach middle-class blacks, and then there's a ripple effect," says Juzang of Motivational Educational Entertainment. "If you don't target the hard-core, you don't get the suburbs." For example, marketers for the 1995 Mario Van Peebles film *Panther* misfired by casting it "as *JFK* for African Americans," Juzang says. The flick bombed. Soon after, the comedy *Friday* came out, pitched as a straight-up ghetto laugh-fest, and scored big both inside and outside

Music Video Generation

Percent of hip-hoppers* and all blacks aged 16 and older who watch selected types of television programs at least once a week, 1995

	Hip-hoppers	Bourgeois/Mercantile
Game Shows	44%	40%
Music Video Shows	42	34
Weekday Morning News	37	37
Dramas	36	40
Award Shows	35	29
Nighttime Comedies	31	32
Late-night Entertainment	29	24

*Hip-hoppers are young, urban blacks as defined by Yankelovich Partners.
Source: Yankelovich Partners Inc. Norwalk, CT.

city borders. The lesson here: core hip-hoppers display an almost fanatical obsession with authenticity. Sanitizing any element of hip-hop culture to make it more palatable for middle-class suburban whites is likely to result in failure, because the core hip-hop audience will reject it. And other groups look to this core for their cues. This wasn't always the case. The pop-music audience was responsible for the commercial success of artists such as faux rapper Vanilla Ice and thinly disguised pop star MC Hammer. Both scored major hits by unimaginatively sampling 1980s pop songs and rapping bland rhymes over them. Some critics would argue that Puff Daddy did the same thing only a few years later. But now, even peripheral hip-hop consumers have grasped the difference between real and rip-off. If white kids realize a product has been toned down in a bid to make it "cross over," they'll avoid it. Instead they go for music with a blunt, urban sensibility—the harder-edged stuff Chuck D of the rap group Public Enemy once described as "CNN for black America." Soundscan sales statistics bear this out. In 1994, three-quarters of hard-core rap albums were sold to white consumers.

The Inner and Outer Circles

20 The hip-hop market encompasses consumers with varying levels of commitment to the culture. Millions of people buy rap records, but can hardly be called hard-core. Strictly speaking, a person must do at least one of three things to qualify: rap or be a disc jockey; breakdance; or paint graffiti.

Few white teenagers meet these criteria. Some are afraid to venture into inner cities or cities at all, many are restricted by their parents, and others are content to absorb hip-hop culture through television and other media. "Lots of kids' parents won't let them cross certain borders. So they're watching videos to see how to dress, how to look, how to talk," says black urban-sportswear designer Maurice Malone. "They can visualize the inner city. But they don't go there, so they can't fully communicate with the heart of the hip-hop movement."

Wimsatt, the Chicago hip-hop writer, sees the white parts of the "hip-hop nation" as a series of concentric attitudinal rings. At the center lie those who actually know blacks and study the intricacies of hip-hop's culture. "These people tend to consider themselves the racial exception," says Wimsatt. "They have a very regimented idea of what's cool and what's not."

Next is a group that has peripheral contact with the culture through friends or relatives, but doesn't actively seek "true hip-hopper" status. They go to shows, but don't rap, spray-paint, or breakdance. "After that, you have people who play hip-hop between other types of music," Wimsatt says. "They're sort of free-floating fans." Most white suburban teens probably fall into this category, listening to accessible acts such as A Tribe Called Quest and De La Soul.

Finally, the people in the outermost circle are those Wimsatt documented in a controversial 1993 article for hip-hop's *Source* magazine. Touring America, he met rural "wiggers" who avoided cities, thought blacks complained too much about their societal lot, and spouted phrases such as, "We wear a lot of pro-black clothes." To Wimsatt, such kids "are pure consumers—they're really into rap, but don't know much, so they're easily manipulated."

Unlocking the Door

25 As hip-hop has made its mark on the mainstream, all but the most gullible fans have spotted a flurry of laughable bids to capitalize on the trend. Anybody with a drum machine and a rhyming dictionary, it seemed, could be presented as a true hip-hopper. "The history of semi-insiders trying to exploit hip-hop is an incredible comedy of errors," Wimsatt says. "I've seen so many commercials with some sort of hip-hop theme that are just transparent. You can almost see the creatives looking around the office and saying, 'Hmm . . . who do we know who's black and has a teenage cousin? Maybe that cousin raps . . . ' " If you're trying to reach the hip-hop crowd, he says, take the time to find and hire legitimate hip-hop players. Good places to start tracking down insiders include record stores, music venues, and recording studios. National magazines such as *Vibe, RapPages*, and *The Source* may also mention local players on their pages.

Sprite evidently did its homework. For a series of NBA-game commercials, Coca-Cola Company (makers of Sprite) hired two of hip-hop's legendary "MCs," wordsmiths KRS-One and MC Shan. Even better they had them face off in the sort of extemporaneous "freestyle battle" seen as any rapper's truest test of verbal skills and mental agility. The spot was roundly acclaimed, both inside and outside the rap world.

In the clothing arena, it's the same game. Mainstream designers such as Hilfiger and Lauren have scored. But smaller "underground" lines can also flourish in both city and suburb, says Misdom of Sputnik. "Even in places like [Minnesota's] Mall of America, you'll see kids who dress 'hip-hop' wearing grass-roots brands like Mecca,

Rappin' on the Web

Hip-hop enthusiasts maintain dozens of Internet Web sites. These are good sources of information on language, art, music, and figures in hip-hop. The following is a sampling. Most have links to other rap and hip-hop sites.

Gossip, commentary, insider news:
www.urbanexpose.com/

Vibe magazine
www.vibe.com

The Source magazine
www.thesource.com/

The Original Hip-Hop Lyrics Archive
www.ohhla.com

All purpose commercial hip-hop site
www.360hiphop.com

The Rap Dictionary
www.rapdict.org

Boss Jeans, and Phat Farm," she says. "They are embracing these brands because they are seen as 'true.' "

Not every company that wants to sell to the inner-city crowd has grasped this wisdom. Malone cites two design prototypes making the rounds recently. Both try to emulate the boxers-exposed-by-sagging-jeans look. One pair of pants sports an underwear-like band of cloth sewn directly into the jeans waist, to peek out in a risk-free risqué style. Another features two waists—the first hangs at pelvis height giving the impression of disdain for belts, the second sitting traditionally on the hips. Both models have yet to make any splash. As Malone points out mockingly, "The most successful crossovers don't try. People will cross over to you if you don't try to play to them."

An Ever-Changing Scene

There's another reason the phony jeans may have failed. In hip-hop, the baggy jeans look has started to fade, following the lead of the skate-boarding subculture that abandoned drowning in denim for a "cleaner," tighter look in 1995. Baggy clothes of all kinds reached their peak in popularity in Fall 1993 and Spring 1994, when 82 percent of teens aged 12 to 19 said baggy clothes were in. That share slipped to 78 percent in spring 1996, according to Teenage Research Unlimited.

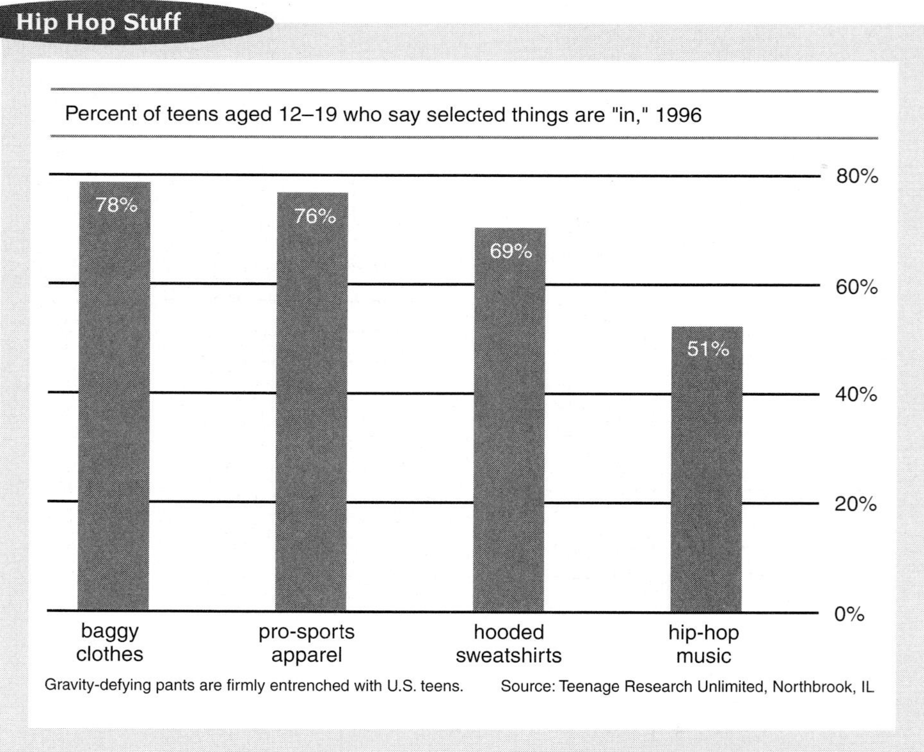

Gravity-defying pants are firmly entrenched with U.S. teens. Source: Teenage Research Unlimited, Northbrook, IL

Hip-Hop 101: The Placement Test

Although hip-hop's media prominence has risen, the culture's slang, dress, and music evolve so quickly that it's hard to track. Below, a little test of how much hip-hop knowledge has come your way over the years, broken down into three levels of difficulty.

Easy

1. When Will Smith was "The Fresh Prince," who was his partner?
   A. Jazzy Jeff
   B. Schooly D
   C. Big Daddy Kane
   D. Queen Latifah
2. Which of the following terms used to mean "cool" in hip-hop slang?
   A. "Dope"
   B. "Fat"
   C. "Stupid"
   D. All of the above
3. For hip-hop fans, the term "sampling" refers to:
   A. Any poll-taking method
   B. Reusing sections of an older song
   C. Shoplifting "gear" from malls
   D. Using rhymes from other artists
4. Deliberately "scratching" a record yields:
   A. An angry record owner
   B. A broken record needle
   C. New sounds for a musical mix
5. Run-DMC's lyrics promoted which shoe company?
   A. Nike
   B. Adidas
   C. Pony
   D. Converse

Moderate

6. The Beastie Boys started as:
   A. A breakdancing group
   B. Art-school students
   C. A 3-on-3 basketball team
   D. A hardcore-punk band
7. Two of the following pairs were partners. Two had famous feuds. Which are which?
   A. Scott LaRock and Kris Parker
   B. Canibus and LL Cool J
   C. Puff Daddy and Suge Knight
   D. Q-Tip and Phife
8. Which of the following white rappers are generally considered "legit" by their black peers?
   A. Eminem
   B. Marky Mark
   C. Vanilla Ice
   D. Everlast
9. "Freestyling" refers to:
   A. Impromptu breakdancing
   B. Spontaneous rapping
   C. Drawing graffiti without stencils
10. For the late Tupac Shakur, conviction and imprisonment on sexual-assault charges meant:
   A. The end of a budding career
   B. A temporary hiatus
   C. A huge boost in popularity
   D. A religious conversion
11. In 2000, which NBA team had two players who are rap recording artists?
   A. The L.A. Lakers
   B. Chicago Bulls
   C. The New York Knicks
   D. The Boston Celtics

12. In hip-hop slang, the term "bombing" refers to:
    A. Artistry
    B. Terrorism
    C. Insect extermination
13. Doctor Dre is:
    A. The ex-NWA member who scored a huge hit with "the Chronic"
    B. A movie actor and MTV VJ
    C. The man charged with recruiting dancers for Sisqo videos
14. A "B-Boy":
    A. Plays basketball well
    B. Wears baseball caps
    C. Breakdances
    D. Works as a bouncer at rap shows
15. Which of the following brands has never been embraced by hip-hop's fashion mavens? No partial credit will be awarded.
    A. Brooks
    B. Puma
    C. Timberland
    D. Bass
    E. Polo
    F. North Face
    G. Stetson
    H. Kangol
    I. Gucci
    J. Ferragamo

Answers:

1. A
2. D
3. B
4. C
5. B. The 1986 song "My Adidas" counts among the earliest of rap's frequent product "shout-outs."
6. D. (Kate Schellenbach, of Luscious Jackson, was their drummer)
7. The allies: A, as Boogie Down Productions; and D, in A Tribe Called Quest. The enemies: B and C.
8. A, D, though some will debate this. Our case: In 1999, mythic producer Dr. Dre oversaw production on Eminem's hit record "Slim Shady." And Everlast was featured on Prince Paul's critically acclaimed "Prince Among Thieves."
9. B
10. C, Shakur scored a No. 1 song, "Dear Mama," while behind bars in New York.
11. A. Center Shaquille O'Neal has cut several records, while guard Kobe Bryant rapped on R&B star Brian McKnight's 1998 single "Hold Me."
12. A. The "bomb" involved is an aerosol can used by graffiti artists
13. B. The DJ and producer is *Dr.* Dre, not *Doctor* Dre. And, yes, it's a trick question.
14. C
15. A, D, G, J

30 Hip-hop culture is constantly evolving, partly because of the commercial success of some of its elements. As Don DeLillo wrote in his novel *America*, "as soon as Madison Avenue breaks the code, Harlem devises a new one." But hip-hop music, language, and fashion also change because looking good and sporting the latest styles are very important to core members of the culture.

The 1995 Yankelovich African-American Monitor clusters black consumers into six segments based on attitudes and income. Its "hip-hopper" segment includes 27 percent of U.S. blacks. These single, urban blacks probably include members who are not authentic hip-hoppers. But their attitudes are telling, nonetheless. More than half of Yankelovich's hip-hoppers strongly agree that they feel the need to be fashionably dressed, compared with only 33 percent of all blacks aged 16 and older. These hip-hoppers are twice as likely as all blacks to strongly feel the need to keep up with new styles, at 42 percent.

To Sputnik's Misdom, hip-hop culture's emphasis on innovative fashion counts among its strongest selling points for teens, who demand a never-ending slew of status symbols to define them against both their peers and parents. "All the rock and grunge styles have stayed the same," she says. "But hip-hop always has a lot of styles coming out." Already her studies project a shift away from the preppier Hilfiger style toward "uptown," high-end designer labels such as DKNY, Versace, and Dolce & Gabana. Garments bearing these labels have a sleeker, more European look than brands such as Hilfiger. They also have higher price tags.

Recent rap videos support her observations. "Roughneck" styles featuring hunting and fishing apparel are on the wane. Another emerging hot style uses high-tech fabrics and styles that resemble those worn by scientists at the South Pole and by mountain climbers. Last summer, designer Donna Karan dressed many of New York City's fashionable young in DKNY Tech. This lower-priced line of clothing featuring high-tech fabrics represents the designer's nod to the trendsetting power of urban teens.

Hip-hop culture is in some ways the next page in the decades-long book of teenagers embracing the forbidden. Yet it's also more lasting, because it is based on the day-to-day experiences of millions of inner-city teens. Targeting this relatively small group of teens may open the door to the larger, more affluent, white, suburban market. But the niche has countless pitfalls. Companies that have successfully negotiated them know a fundamental truth of hip-hop culture: For a product to appeal to a rapper in south central L.A. or a white mall crawler in Des Moines, it's got to be real.

Exploring Texts and Contexts

For activities with icons, refer to the Guide to Analyzing Readings in Context.

1. Consider what you know about the genre of quizzes like the one that appears in this article. Why do you suppose quizzes like this commonly appear in popular magazines? Take Spiegler's hip-hop placement quiz and compare your answers with his guide. Write about your experience taking this quiz and how it affected your attitudes and understanding of hip-hop. Why do you suppose Spiegler included this quiz in his article? **Genre**
2. Spiegler explains that "Scoring a hit with inner-city youths can make a product hot with the much larger and affluent white suburban market." What does he think corporations need to know to take advantage of that process? What kinds of explanations and information does he rely on to guide those who want to market hip-hop fashions? How does he use the data from trendwatching firms to support his argument?
3. Examine the language of Spiegler's article. Are there any terms you are not familiar with? What words or phrases does he use frequently? How has he made language choices to fit the needs of his corporate readers? **Language**

4. In his article, Spiegler says, "If white kids realize a product has been toned down in a bid to make it 'cross over,' they'll avoid it" (page 109). The term *cross over* refers to the phenomenon in which a product or performer shifts from one category or market niche to another. What does Spiegler mean by the term? How has this term been used in discussions of authenticity? What are the broader implications of this term?

Creating Texts

For activities with icons, refer to the Guides to Analyzing Contexts for Writing and Analyzing Readings in Context. For additional help with these writing projects, read the descriptions of **Opinion Piece, Cover Letter/Reflective Essay**, and **Online Posts** in the Genre Glossary.

Genre

1. Write an opinion piece in which you respond critically to Spiegler's position on educating corporations to improve their marketing know-how. Imagine that you disagree with his approach. Consider who your audience will be and in what magazine or journal your opinion piece will appear. Choose one particularly strong area of disagreement with Spiegler and share it with your readers. After writing your opinion piece, write a cover letter discussing what you learned about genre in completing this project.

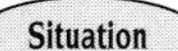

2. Divide into small groups. One group should use the dictionary, thesaurus, and a book of quotations to explore the definitions that are offered for the term "authenticity." Another group should look at the section of Spiegler's article subtitled "Got To Be Real" (pp. 108–109). What does Spiegler mean by "authenticity"? Each group should post the results of its work on the class listserv or message board, and then members of the class should respond to each other, contributing to a conversation about how a writer's context influences the way he or she defines authenticity.

CHAPTER 5

CASE STUDY
Contesting the Ownership of Music

The Case

If you're a college student, listen to music, and have a computer, you probably remember the controversies over Napster and Kazaa, the programs that allow users to download music for free from the Internet and that were challenged in court by musicians and record companies who argued that their music was being stolen. You probably also know that these programs were not the first technological innovation to cause controversy over the ownership of music. The practice of sampling—incorporating bits of recorded music by other musicians into one's own songs—has also been the subject of legal challenges, most famously in the 2 Live Crew case, in which the Supreme Court ruled in 1994 that the sampling was legal under the Fair Use clause of the U.S. Copyright Act. But you might not be aware that others have contested the ownership of music not just to make money but to make an artistic and political point. Here we look at the Negativland/U2 case in order to raise questions about art, ownership, and authenticity.

Negativland is a group of musicians who create works of art that make extensive use of already-recorded words and music from songs, advertisements, radio and television broadcasts, and other sources. Their work usually comments in some way on technology, the media, business, and mass consumer culture. In 1990 Negativland created a 13-minute single that included, among other things, computer-modified segments of the song "I Still Haven't Found What I'm Looking For," by the Irish rock group U2, and other sampled bits related to the song and the music industry in general. Negativland did not obtain permission to use any of this material, and in August 1991—a few months before the real U2 was expected to release its album *Achtung Baby*—they released the single under the title "U2," in packaging that featured a picture of a U2 spy plane superimposed over a large letter U and number 2, and with their name, Negativland, printed across the bottom. Almost immediately, the record company and publishers of the band U2, Island Records and Warner-Chappell Music, filed a suit against Negativland and its record company, SST Records. A judge issued a restraining order requiring SST to recall and turn over all copies of the single and the original tapes and artwork, pay damages and legal costs, and publish explanations and apologies.

A series of complex legal maneuvers followed in the next few years, but Negativland has never been able to recover and release the copies of the single.

The Issues

The two central legal issues here are the concepts of copyright and fair use. Island Records/Warner Chappell base their legal arguments on the principle of copyright. One purpose of copyright laws is to protect the creative work of writers, composers, and other artists from intellectual and commercial exploitation by giving them exclusive control over their work for a specified period. To use all or a part of a copyrighted work, one must obtain permission from the holder of the copyright and often pay a fee. But the concept of copyright creates a tension. While the purpose of copyright laws is to protect writers, composers, and other artists, a very strict interpretation of the laws puts severe restrictions on anyone who wants to use copyrighted material. The concept of fair use, on which Negativland based its arguments, was developed to balance the needs of copyright holders against the needs of members of the public, in particular critics, reporters, researchers, scholars, and teachers, as well as other writers and artists. The fair use clause of the 1976 United States Copyright Act stipulates that in certain situations copyrighted material can be used without permission or fees. But, like most legal concepts and most laws, the fair use clause and the Copyright Act itself contain ambiguities, places where the law is open to different interpretations, thus requiring lawsuits and trials to clarify how the law should be applied.

The Negativland case illustrates the complexities involved in discussing authenticity in contemporary art and entertainment, especially popular music. Some critics of contemporary culture have suggested that traditional ideas about art and authenticity are no longer applicable when words, images, and sounds can be almost endlessly reproduced and distributed. This problem was noticed as far back as the 1930s in a famous essay, "The Work of Art in the Age of Mechanical Reproduction," which asked what would happen to the "aura" of unique works of art when photography and other techniques could make unlimited copies of an image.[1] In our time, digital technology has multiplied this copying ability so vastly and complexly that the very idea of originality is thrown into question; as cultural critic Mary Poovey says of the rock concert experience,

> [T]he familiarity of the art object [the album, album art, or music video] so completely anticipates the experience that the "event" as such only exists as a repetition, and there is never an "original," not even in the moment of supreme presence, the moment of performance itself.[2]

But what if we redefine both art and authenticity to fit with the technological conditions of our age? Rap music, with its use of sampling, might be considered one such redefinition. But this redefinition still leaves many questions about art, ownership, and technology unanswered. The case of *Island Records/Warner-Chappell Music vs. Negativland* allows us to explore some of these questions.

At the heart of the Negativland case, under layers of legal principles and arguments, is a set of claims and counterclaims about authenticity. One of the arguments against Negativland was that their work was not authentic art because it was not an original creation but rather a pastiche of things, some of them created by other, "authentic" artists. In their analysis of the case, cultural critics Andrew Herman and John Sloop argue that Negativland built their defense by redefining authenticity as "free appropriation" rather than individual expression:

> While Negativland initially attempted to defend itself using the logic of romantic authenticity (the artist as free-standing author of his/her own ideas, created solely by him or her), this logic was certain to fail as it could—and was—effectively deployed against the band's own practices, given that their performances are reassemblages of fragmented discourses.[3]

We can see this defense in Negativland's claim that

> Our work is an authentic and original "whole," being much more than the sum of its samples. This is not a form of "bootlegging" intending to profit from the commercial potential of the subjects appropriated. The law must come to terms with distinguishing the difference between economic intent and artistic intent.[4]

Herman and Sloop argue further that Negativland sees this new definition of authenticity as a necessary response to the problems caused by the "postmodern landscape" of unlimited reproduction and circulation of images.

---

[1]Walter Benjamin. *Illuminations.* Edited by Hannah Arendt. New York: Schocken Books, 1969, pp. 217–251.
[2]Mary Poovey. "Cultural Criticism: Past and Present." *College English* 52, p. 615.
[3]Andrew Herman and John Sloop. "The Politics of Authenticity in Postmodern Rock Culture: The Case of Negativland and The Letter 'U' and the Numeral '2'." *Critical Studies in Mass Communication* 15 (March 1998), p. 5.
[4]Negativland. "Tenets of Free Appropriation." *Fair Use: The Story of the Letter U and the Numeral 2.* Concord, CA: Seeland, 1995, p. 251.

The Documents

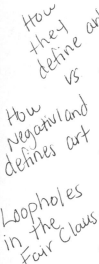

- Periodicals in the music industry and counterculture began covering the Negativland story in September 1991, just after the lawsuit was filed, but by December the mainstream press also picked up the story nationally. This ***Washington Post* article, "U2's Double Trouble" by Richard Harrington,** explains the case and the issues involved. Note which passages it quotes from the two documents that follow. After reading the next two documents, think about how you would have presented the story and the issues. What passages would you have chosen to quote?
- The next document is an **excerpt from the Island/Warner-Chappell Lawsuit** requesting a restraining order that would require SST Records to recall all copies of the single and turn them over to Island Records and Warner-Chappell Music. As you read the excerpts from this legal document, note how the lawyers build their argument and how they explicitly or implicitly define art in the process of making their case. How does the style of legal writing shape the way the case is made?
- Negativland and its record company were represented by lawyers in court, but Negativland also took its wider argument to the public in a variety of ways, for example in **"U2 Negativland: The Case from Our Side,"** a press release sent out soon after the case was filed. Compare Negativland's style of argument and implied definition of art with those in the Island Records/Warner-Chappell legal brief. What similarities and differences do you see?
- Both the Island Records/Warner-Chappell legal brief and the Negativland press release refer to the U.S. Copyright Act of 1976. Negativland makes particular reference to the fair use clause of the Copyright Act, included in the excerpt. As you read this **excerpt of the Copyright Act,** in particular the fair use clause, consider which parts of it seem ambiguous—open to different interpretations—and how these ambiguities might turn on assumptions about art and ownership.
- Since the court did not accept Negativland's underlying interpretation of fair use, Negativland took its argument directly to the public. In December 1993, they published a statement of their position in a guest commentary in *Billboard Magazine.* The following March, two music business executives published a response. This exchange of commentaries, **"In Fair Use Debate, Art Must Come First"** and Andrian Adams and Paul McKibbins' **"Sampling Without Permission Is Theft,"** presents two very different perspectives on art, ownership, and, by implication, authenticity. As you reach this point in the case study, you should be developing your own perspective on these questions. Where do you stand in relation to the positions presented by Negativland on the one hand and Adams and McKibbins on the other?
- Keep in mind that this case unfolded in 1993. Much has happened in the world of music and technology since then—for example the development of MP3 technology and the controversies over Napster and Kazaa—and your perspective is probably influenced by these developments. A software review in *Rolling Stone* magazine, **"Build a**

Desktop Studio," describes just one of these developments. **"RTMARK Finds Bucks for Beck Rip-off,"** a press release from the group ®RTMARK, suggests that the Negativland tradition of musical subversion continues. What other developments along these lines do you know of, and how do these developments influence your own ideas about art, ownership, and authenticity?

YOUR ROLE

The following writing projects are designed to help you think through the issues raised by the Negativland case, using writing both as a form of action and as a means of reflection. On the one hand we ask you to imagine yourself participating as someone who is immediately and actively affected by these issues, which some of you may indeed be. For example, you may be sampling some other Web pages in order to build your own home page. What kinds of artistic, ethical, and legal questions would you have to confront? In the first activity that follows, you write about the practical implications of these issues on your own campus. Another way of participating is as a critic or other thoughtful observer. In the second activity you analyze the larger issues suggested by this case study.

1. Your college probably has policies and codes of conduct related to the legal and ethical issues raised by the Negativland case, for example policies on downloading music and codes of conduct regarding plagiarism, the unacknowledged use of someone else's ideas or words. Do some research on those policies and on students' observation of and attitudes toward these policies, and write an opinion piece for your campus paper in which you express an opinion on those policies, students' observation of them, and your school's enforcement of them. As part of your argument, discuss what you see as the similarities and differences between sampling and other copyright violations, the illegal downloading of music, and academic plagiarism, perhaps in particular plagiarism involving online resources. (See **Opinion Piece** in the Genre Glossary.)
2. Write an essay exploring the nature of art, ownership, and authenticity, drawing upon the case study, as well as any other events, phenomena, or materials you find useful. Use the documents in the case study to help you think carefully about the relationship between ownership and authenticity in the context of art. You might consider how these terms have been traditionally defined and how this case study does or does not change your own definitions of these terms. Remember that you must consider the concepts of ownership and authenticity from the perspectives of both art and law. Working closely with the case study documents, consider how these perspectives influence, conflict with, or help define each other. (See **Essay** in the Genre Glossary.)

U2's Double Trouble

Richard Harrington, Washington Post Staff Writer

U2, whose new "Achtung, Baby" opened at the top of Billboard's album chart, has stomped down hard on California agitpopsters Negativland, which in September released a single titled "U2" that incorporated smidgens of the Irish group's hit "I Still Haven't Found What I'm Looking For." Island Records, to which U2 is signed, and Warner-Chappell Music, U2's publisher, filed suit against Negativland and SST Records, charging deceptive advertising, copyright infringement and "image defamation." Island and SST settled last month.

Indeed, Negativland's 12-inch single features a huge letter "U" and numeral "2" occupying 90 percent of its cover; there's also the shadow of the famous spy plane. "Negativland" is printed at the bottom. Indeed, the group, which has been in existence almost as long as U2, did not get (or seek) permission to sample the original. Indeed, U2's lyrics are drolly recited, the melody is solemnly hummed by a male chorus, and both elements are incorporated into the kind of socially sharp sound collage Negativland is know for (albeit in very small circles). Anybody but U2 and its lackeys would have a hard time not laughing at what Negativland calls "a work of art . . . created as parody, satire, social commentary and cultural criticism."

Right now, though, Negativland and SST are not laughing. The settlement requires all distributors that received the record be notified to return it; if they don't, or engage in "selling, advertising, promoting or otherwise exploiting" the record, they are subject to penalties, "which may include imprisonment and fines."

Once all copies are returned, SST must deliver them to Island, which will destroy them along with all of SST's on-hand stock. All artwork is also to be turned over to Island, which has been assigned the copyright to the song "U2" (with Warner-Chappell). SST also had to fork over $25,000 and half the wholesale proceeds from copies sold or not returned—SST estimates the settlement's total cost at $70,000, "more money than we've made in our 10 years of existence," the label said in a statement. SST said it settled the suit because it feared "the tremendous costs in fighting for our rights in court."

Eric Levine, senior director of business affairs for Island, said: "Record companies' primary assets are rights—copyrights, exclusive rights for recording services, names, trademarks etc. When certain of those rights were violated, we felt we had no choice but to act swiftly and, apparently, successfully."

One of the complaints in Island's original suit was that U2 fans might confuse Negativland's "U2" with "Achtung, Baby" and that SST would "be free to flood the shelves of record stores . . . creating massive confusion among the record-buying public." In fact, SST had shipped out 7,643 copies of "U2," and none of the five Negativland albums has sold more than 15,000 copies ("Achtung, Baby" sold 295,000 copies in its first week on the market).

"Our single deals, in part, with our perception of the group U2 as an international cultural phenomenon, and therefore particularly worthy

(continued)

From *The Washington Post,* December 18, 1991, Style section p. B7.

of artistic comment and criticism," the band noted in a statement. "Island's legal action thoroughly ignores the possibility that any such artistic rights or inclination might exist. Apparently Island's sole concern in this act of censorship is their determination to control the marketplace, as if the only reason to make records is to make money."

The Negativland/SST statement also insists that claiming economic gain as the sole criterion for legal deliberation "is to admit that music itself is not to be taken seriously. Culture is more than commerce. It may actually have something to say about commerce. It may even use examples of commerce to comment upon it."

The four members of Negativland explain their approach as "recontextualizing captured fragments to create something entirely new—a psychological impact based on a new juxtaposition of diverse elements, ripped from their usual context."

In terms of sampling, which remains one of pop culture's great unresolved issues, Negativland claims "fair use . . . as it was used for purposes of fair comment, parody and cultural criticism, which the copyright law specifically allows." As for the cover art, "Island's inference that U2 fans might actually assume that we are them upon hearing our record is simply ridiculous on the face of it, and another indication of their lack of respect for their own audience."

The original Island complaint also noted that U2 "has cultivated a clean-cut image, and its recordings never include expletives, curses and scatological language"—a reference to a bootlegged comment about U2 by Casey Kasem that can be heard on the Negativland single—"which will undoubtedly anger and upset parents of youngsters who purchase the 'U2 Negativland' record." Ironically, the back cover of "Achtung, Baby's" CD booklet had to be censored because it contained a frontal nude photo of bassist Adam Clayton. A discreet X was added.

Excerpts from the Island/Warner-Chappell Lawsuit

MILGRIM THOMAJAN & LEE
DANIAEL H. WILLICK, ESQ. (Cal. State Bar No. 58643)
2049 Century Park East, Suite 3350
Los Angeles, California 90067
(213) 282-0899

MILGRIM THOMAJAN & LEE P.C.
CHARLES B. ORTNER, ESQ.
53 Wall Street
New York, New York 10005-2815
(212) 858-5300

Attorneys for Plaintiffs

UNITES STATES DISTRICT COURT

CENTRAL DISTRICT OF CALIFORNIA

ISLAND RECORDS LTD. (a United Kingdom Corporation), ISLAND RECORDS, INC. (a New York corporation), WARNER CHAPPELL MUSIC INTERNATIONAL LTD., (a United Kingdom corporation), and WARNER/CHAPPELL MUSIC, INC. (a California corporation), Plaintiffs,	Case No. CV 91-4735AAH (GHKx)
vs.	DECLARATION OF ERIC LEVINE IN SUPPORT OF ORDER TO SHOW CAUSE, RE PRELIMINARY INJUNCTION, TEMPORARY RESTRAINING ORDER AND EXPEDITED DISCOVERY
SST RECORDS (an entity), SEELAND MEDIA-MEDIA (an entity), NEGATIVLAND (an entity), Gregory Ginn (an individual), Chris Grigg (an individual), Mark Hosler (an individual), Don Joyce (an individual), and David Wills (an individual), Defendants.	DATE: September ___, 1991 TIME: PLACE: Courtroom (Judge Andrew A. Hauk)

I.
PRELIMINARY STATEMENT

This Application seeks an *ex parte* temporary restraining order, preliminary injunction and related relief in order to halt the defendants' unlawful exploitation of a record entitled "U2 Negativland" by using deceptive and misleading packaging in violation of the plaintiffs' rights under Section 43(a) of the Lanham Trademark Act, 15 U.S.C. §1125(a), and by making unauthorized use of a sound recording and musical composition in violation of the rights of certain plaintiffs under the Copyright Act of 1976, as amended (the "Copyright Act"), 17 U.S.C. §101, *et. seq.*

The plaintiffs include (a) the affiliated record companies (Island Records Ltd. and Island Records, Inc.) which have the exclusive rights throughout the world to manufacture, distribute and sell (either directly or through authorized licensees) sound

(continued)

Excerpts from *Island/Warner-Chappell (Plaintiffs) vs. SST/Seeland/Negativland et al.* lawsuit, Sept. 3, 1991. Reprinted in Negativland, *Fair Use: The Story of the Letter U and the Numeral 2.* Concord, CA: Seeland, 1995, pp. 4–20.

recordings embodying the performances by the renowned musical group known as "U2," and (b) the affiliated publishing companies (Warner Chappell Music International Ltd. and Warner/Chappell Music, Inc.) which, directly or through affiliated corporations and licensees, have the exclusive rights to publish and administer the copyrights in U2's musical compositions. Plaintiffs are exclusively entitled to use the band's well-known name and mark "U2" in connection with the exploitation of those rights.

The defendants are violating the plaintiffs' rights by selling or otherwise exploiting the "U2 Negativland" recording in interstate commerce using cover artwork, packaging and labelling which is so deceptive as to create the false impression that the recording is a genuine U2 record album. This unlawful conduct—which will deceive consumers into believing that when they purchase "U2 Negativland" they are buying an album by U2—constitutes a violation of Section 43(a) of the Lanham Trademark Act, which prohibits the use of false and misleading packaging which may tend to deceive consumers.

Plaintiffs Island Records Ltd. and Island Records, Inc. have publicized the imminent release of U2's next record album. The defendants' "U2 Negativland" recording constitutes a transparent use of deceptive packaging designed to dupe U2's millions of fans throughout the United States into believing that this "new record" is the widely-anticipated new album by U2. It is not. "U2 Negativland" is nothing less than a consumer fraud, and a blatantly unlawful attempt to usurp the anticipated profits and goodwill to which plaintiffs are entitled from the exploitation of recordings and musical compositions by U2.

Moreover, one of the two songs contained in the "U2 Negativland" recording incorporates an unauthorized copy of a portion of U2's recording of the song "I Still Haven't Found What I'm Looking For," which is part of U2's hit album entitled "The Joshua Tree," released in 1987. The second song contains an unauthorized and mutilated instrumental version of "I Still Haven't Found What I'm Looking For" performed by persons other than U2. As discussed below, defendants' unauthorized use of the foregoing U2 recording and musical composition constitutes infringement of the rights of two of the plaintiffs (as evidenced by Certificates of Copyright Registration issued by the United States Copyright Office) in violation of the Copyright Act.

To prevent the irreparable harm which plaintiffs will suffer from the violation of their rights under the Lanham Trademark Act and the Copyright Act, the defendants should be immediately restrained and enjoined from manufacturing, distributing, selling or otherwise exploiting "U2 Negativland." And, defendants should be required to immediately disclose certain information, discussed below, pertaining to the extent of their infringing activities (and the involvement, if any, by others), and to submit to expedited discovery to permit plaintiffs to prepare for a preliminary injunction hearing without delay.

I, Eric Levine, hereby declare and say as follows:

1. I am the Senior Director of Business Affairs of Island Records, Inc., one of the plaintiffs in this action. I submit this declaration on personal knowledge in support of the motion by plaintiffs, brought on by Order to Show Cause, for a Temporary Restraining Order and Preliminary Injunction to prohibit the defendants from manufacturing, copying, marketing, advertising, promoting, distributing, selling or otherwise exploiting a sound recording entitled "U2 Negativland" (or derivatives thereof) on the grounds that defendants' conduct constitutes a violation of the plaintiffs' rights under, among other things, Section 43(a) of the Lanham Act and the Copyright Act. Plaintiffs also seek certain other relief, including expedited discovery, described below.

2. As set forth in the Complaint (a copy of which is annexed hereto as Exhibit A), and as discussed below in greater detail, since 1980 Island Records, Inc. and its affiliate Island Records Ltd. (and their authorized licensees) have been manufacturing, marketing, promoting, advertising and selling millions of records by the enormously popular recording group known as "U2" in the United States and abroad. The U2 band's name and trademark, "U2," have been prominently displayed on all album packaging, artwork and labels. The public has thus come to recognize and associate the name and

(continued)

mark "U2" with the band and its recordings released by Island Records, Inc., Island Records Ltd. and their authorized licensees.

3. Recently, plaintiffs learned that defendants* released a recording which, on the cover artwork packaging and record label (Exhibit B), is prominently labeled "U2 Negativland." "U2" is the dominant feature of the cover and label.** Defendants have falsely created the impression that "U2 Negativland" is a record album embodying performances by U2. On the face of the cover packaging artwork and labelling, it would appear to any consumer that "U2 Negativland" is a U2 recording, and nothing contained on the cover artwork or label indicates that it is not.

4. Such false and deceptive packaging and labelling is a clear violation of Section 43(a) of the Lanham Act, and the defendants should be restrained for that reason alone. However, as discussed below, the "U2 Negativland" recording also infringes the plaintiffs' copyrights, providing additional grounds upon which to restrain defendants from continued exploitation of "U2 Negativland."

BACKGROUND FACTS

5. Plaintiffs Island Records, Inc. (based in New York) and Island Records Ltd. (based in London) are affiliated companies. For ease of expression, both corporations and their authorized licensees will sometimes be referred to herein collectively as "Island Records."

6. Island Records has long been closely associated with the U2 band. Between 1980 and 1986, Island Records manufactured and distributed in the United States and abroad four long-playing albums, so-called "single" records, and two "extended play" recordings, prominently displaying the name and trademark "U2" on packaging, artwork and labels to denote that the recordings embodied the performances of the particular band known as "U2."

7. In 1987, Island Records released the band's album entitled "The Joshua Tree."*** That album—which was clearly labelled with the "U2" name and mark (see Exhibit C hereto, which is a copy of the compact disc packaging)—was released and distributed by Island Records throughout the world under a master sales agreement which granted Island Records the exclusive worldwide rights to U2's recordings, including the copyright and the exclusive right to use the band's name "U2" in connection with the exploitation of sound recordings.

8. "The Joshua Tree" album was an enormous artistic and commercial success. Island Records, Inc. sold over 5 million copies of that album in the United States alone, all clearly labelled "U2." Indeed, that was the first album in history to have been certified by the Record Industry Association of America as having sold at least one million copies in the "compact disc," or "CD," format.

9. The band's success was enhanced by the release of a single of U2's recording of one of "The Joshua Tree" album's songs—"I Still Haven't Found What I'm Looking For"—which was sold throughout the United States and abroad, and received widespread air-play on radio stations and television stations (including MTV).

10. The success of U2's "The Joshua Tree" album and U2's recording of "I Still Haven't Found What I'm Looking For" was highlighted when U2 was awarded a Grammy award on a nationwide award telecast in February 1989.

---

* Apparently, SST is a proprietorship owned by defendant Gregory Ginn, and affiliated with defendants Seeland MediaMedia and Negativland.

** The "U2 Negativland" recording is being distributed in interstate commerce. The copy obtained by plaintiffs, which alerted them to defendants' unlawful conduct, was purchased at a record store in Athens, Georgia.

*** As discussed below, SST (and apparently the other defendants) has recently unlawfully copied a portion of U2's recording of the song entitled "I Still Haven't Found What I'm Looking For" from "The Joshua Tree" album, and incorporated that unlawful and unauthorized copy into the "U2 Negativland" recording in violation of the Copyright Act.

(continued)

11. Thereafter, Island Records released throughout the world U2's next album, entitled "Rattle and Hum." That enormously successful album was also clearly labelled as a U2 recording (see copy of packaging for that album annexed hereto as Exhibit D).

12. Recently, numerous publications read by U2's fans, and the music industry trade press, have reported that U2 has completed a new album which will soon be released by Island Records. Annexed hereto as Exhibits E, F and G are copies of a few of the articles that have been published about the anticipated new U2 album. Given U2's enormous popularity, it is inescapable that U2's fans are anxiously awaiting the day when they will find U2's new album in record stores.

DEFENDANTS' INFRINGING ACTS

13. Island Records recently learned that the defendants, under the names SST Records and Seeland MediaMedia, have released a recording entitled "U2 Negativland." It is apparent that defendants are unlawfully seeking to capitalize upon U2's popularity and the anticipation by U2's fans of the release of U2's new album, by packaging and labelling the "U2 Negativland" recording in such a false, misleading and deceptive manner as to confuse consumers into believing that the defendants' recording is a "U2" album, which it is not.

14. As discussed above, Exhibit B hereto is a copy of the cover artwork for the "U2 Negativland" recording in the CD format, and the CD label itself.

15. On the face of the packaging artwork, it appears that the recording is an album by U2. Indeed, the name "U2" is displayed prominently on the cover, and nearly takes up the entire cover artwork. The cover clearly would lead any unsuspecting consumer into believing that SST's recording is a "U2" album, and nothing contained anywhere on the cover artwork or the CD label would disabuse a consumer of that erroneous belief.

16. Indeed, the artwork which appears on the reverse side of the cover, and the label on the CD itself, also fosters the false impression that "U2 Negativland" is a recording by U2 in at least two ways:

(a) First, the artwork identifies the song on the recording as "I Still Haven't Found What I'm Looking For"—the same title as one of the songs recorded by U2 on the band's "The Joshua Tree" album.

(b) Second, the inside packaging artwork and the CD label lists in two places the names of the members of U2—Paul Hewson, David Evans, Lawrence Mullen and Adam Clayton—falsely implying that the recording is by U2.

17. There can be no doubt that consumers will be deceived by the "U2 Negativland" artwork into falsely believing that it is a U2 album. Such false and deceptive packaging is precisely the kind of unfair and unlawful competition that Section 43(a) of the Lanham Act was designed to prohibit. Unless SST is immediately restrained and enjoined from further exploitation of "U2 Negativland," unwitting consumers will be duped into purchasing that record in the mistaken belief that it is the new U2 album.

18. The egregious nature of this consumer fraud is underscored by the content of the record itself, which contains only two songs (although the CD is deceptively packaged as an album, which in the popular record industry ordinarily contains approximately ten songs).

19. The first song is over seven minutes long. It contains approximately one minute's worth of portions of U2's recording of "I Still Haven't Found What I'm Looking For," unlawfully copied from "The Joshua Tree" album and incorporated into the "U2 Negativland" recording without the authorization or consent of Island Records.

20. In that regard, it should be emphasized that Island Records Ltd. is the proprietor throughout the world of the copyright in and to "The Joshua Tree" album, including U2's recording of "I Still Haven't Found What I'm Looking For." Accordingly, Island Records Ltd. obtained a Copyright Registration from the United States Copyright Office for the entire "The Joshua Tree" album. Annexed hereto as Exhibit H is a copy of the Certificate of Copyright Registration for the entire "The Joshua Tree" album as

(continued)

performed by U2—SR 78-949. This Certificate establishes, *prima facie,* that Island Records Ltd. is the copyright proprietor of U2's recordings contained in "The Joshua Tree" album, including U2's recording of the song entitled "I Still Haven't Found What I'm Looking For."

21. The unauthorized copying of a portion of U2's recording of "I Still Haven't Found What I'm Looking For," and incorporation of that recording into "U2 Negativland," constitutes a blatant case of copyright infringement. Under the Copyright Act, 17 U.S.C. § 101 *et seq.*, such infringement entitles Island Records to, among other things, a restraining order and injunction.

22. Equally outrageous is the content of the second song on the "U2 Negativland" recording. It is replete with expletives, curses and scatological language which many consumers will likely find offensive, and which will undoubtedly anger and upset parents of youngsters who purchase the "U2 Negativland" record.

23. It must be emphasized that U2 has cultivated a clean-cut image, and its recordings never include such language. The band's image will be tarnished, and the name and mark "U2" and the goodwill associated with it, will be substantially harmed as a result of defendants' deception which will lead consumers to purchase what they believe to be a U2 album, only to find a recording containing such lyrics.

24. "U2 Negativland" gives every indication that it is a U2 album, and there is nothing in the artwork or otherwise which indicates that that is not the case. Thus, some unwitting consumers, upon purchasing and listening to the "U2 Negativland" recording, might well conclude that U2 has made a poor quality and offensive recording, thus further unlawfully tarnishing the band's reputation and image, and the enormously valuable "U2" name and mark. This would undoubtedly diminish future sales of U2 recordings, to the detriment of both U2 and Island Records.

The Requested Relief

25. Plaintiffs have demonstrated a clear right to the injunctive relief which they seek in this action. There can be no doubt that the packaging, artwork, labeling and text employed by the defendants create the overwhelming impression that "U2 Negativland" is a recording by U2. There also can be no doubt that consumers will be confused by the prominent use of the name and mark "U2" on "U2 Negativland," and that the confusion and deception will be enhanced by defendants' use of the names of the members of U2 and the title of their hit song "I Still Haven't Found What I'm Looking For."

26. This strong showing of deceptive labeling and likelihood of confusion, compounded by a clear case of copyright infringement, establishes that plaintiffs will likely prevail on the merits.

27. Moreover, the balance of hardships tips decidedly in favor of the plaintiffs and against the defendants. If the requested injunctive relief is not granted, the defendants will be free to flood the shelves of record stores with the infringing recording on the eve of the release by Island Records of the new U2 album, thereby creating massive confusion among the record-buying public. Once the "horses" are out of the "barn door," the harm to Island Records will be done, and will be irreparable.

WHEREFORE, plaintiffs demand judgment against defendants, jointly and severally, as follows:

(1) Preliminarily and permanently enjoining and restraining the defendants, their officers, directors, agents, servants, employees, subsidiaries, affiliates, assigns, licensees, distributees, attorneys and all persons in active concert or participation with them or in privity with them from (a) manufacturing, distributing, promoting, advertising, marketing, selling or otherwise exploiting the sound recording entitled and labelled "U2 Negativland" or any derivatives thereof, or otherwise affixing or utilizing the name and mark "U2" in connection with any goods or services furnished by or on

(continued)

behalf of defendants or any of them; (b) suggesting or implying that any of defendants' goods or services are associated with, sponsored by or otherwise authorized by plaintiffs and/or the performing group known as U2; and (c) manufacturing, copying, recording, distributing, promoting, selling or otherwise exploiting the sound recording and musical composition entitled "U2 Negativland," or any derivatives thereof, or any other sound recording or musical composition embodying any portion of the sound recording by U2 and musical composition entitled "The Joshua Tree," including "I Still Haven't Found What I'm Looking For," or otherwise infringing the respective copyrights of Island Records Ltd. and Warner/Chappell.

(2) Awarding damages to plaintiffs due to defendants' violation of Section 43(a) of the Lanham Trademark Act in such amounts as may be determined by the Court, the amounts to be trebled in accordance with 15 U.S.C. § 1117, together with such punitive damages and trebled damages where authorized under applicable state law;

(3) Statutory damages under the Copyright Act of 1976, as amended, 17 U.S.C. § 504, for defendants' willful copyright infringement.

(4) Requiring defendants to account for all copies of "U2 Negativland" and all derivatives thereof manufactured, distributed, sold and/or otherwise exploited by or on behalf of defendants, their officers, directors, agents, servants, employees, subsidiaries, affiliates, assigns, licensees, distributees and all persons in active concert or participation with them or in privity with them;

(5) Requiring defendants to account for and pay over to plaintiffs all revenues derived from defendants' activities set forth above, received by or payable to defendants, their officers, directors, agents, servants, employees, subsidiaries, affiliates, assigns, licensees, distributees, and all persons in active concert or participation with them or in privity with them, the amounts thereof pertaining to violations of Section 43(a) of the Lanham Trademark Act to be trebled in accordance with 15 U.S.C. § 1117;

(6) Directing defendants to recall and withdraw "U2 Negativland" and all derivatives thereof from all radio stations and clubs, and from sale or distribution, and to deliver to the plaintiffs to be impounded during the pendency of this action, and for destruction thereafter, all copies of "U2 Negativland" and all derivatives thereof in all formats;

(7) Directing defendants to deliver to plaintiffs to be impounded during the pendency of this action, and for destruction thereafter: (a) all inventory of "U2 Negativland" and all derivatives thereof in all formats; (b) all advertising, sales, promotional packaging, labelling, and other materials, in connection with the distribution, sale or other exploitation of "U2 Negativland" in any media; and (c) all devices for manufacturing copies of "U2 Negativland" and all derivatives thereof, including, without limitation, all lacquers, plates, molds, masters, stampers and tapes in defendants' possession, custody or control;

(8) Directing defendants to publish in *Billboard Magazine* and other trade publications to be determined by the Court, a prominent announcement that it has withdrawn and recalled "U2 Negativland" and all derivatives thereof, and requesting the withdrawal of all copies of "U2 Negativland" and all derivatives thereof from play lists and store shelves;

(9) Awarding plaintiffs the costs of this action and reasonable attorneys' fees under the Lanham Trademark Act, the Copyright Act of 1976, as amended, and other applicable laws and rules; and

(10) Awarding plaintiffs such other and further relief as the Court deems just and proper.

(continued)

Dated: Los Angeles, California
September 3, 1991

MILGRIM THOMAJAN & LEE

By: *Daniel H. Willick*
Daniel H. Willick
Attorneys for Plaintiffs
2049 Century Park East
Suite 3350
Los Angeles, CA 90067
(213) 282-0899

Dated: Los Angeles, California
September 3, 1991

MILGRIM THOMAJAN & LEE P.C.

By: *Charles B. Ortner*
Charles B. Ortner
Attorneys for Plaintiffs
53 Wall Street
New York, NY 10005
(212) 858-5300

NEGATIVLAND'S FIRST PRESS RELEASE, NOVEMBER 10, 1991

U2 Negativland

The Case from Our Side

Negativland is a small, dedicated group of musicians who, since 1980, have released 5 albums, 4 cassette-only releases, 1 video, and now a single. This single, which is entitled "U2," was created as parody, satire, social commentary, and cultural criticism. As a work of art, it is consistent with, and a continuation of, the artistic viewpoint we have been espousing toward the world of media for the last ten years.

Island Records and music publisher Warner-Chappell Music, presumably acting on behalf of their group U2, have instigated legal action against our single and have succeeded not only in removing it from circulation, but ensuring that it cannot ever be released again. It is clear that their preference is that the record never even be heard again. The terms of the settlement that was forced on us include:

- Everyone who received a copy of the record—record distributors and stores (6951 copies), and radio stations, writers, etc. (692 copies)—is being notified to return it, and that if they don't do so, or if they engage in "distributing, selling, advertising, promoting, or otherwise exploiting" the record, they may be subject to penalties "which may include imprisonment and fines." Once returned, the records will be forwarded to Island for destruction.
- All of SST's on-hand stock of the record, in vinyl, cassette, and CD (5357 copies total), is to be delivered to Island, where it will be destroyed.
- All mechanical parts used to prepare and manufacture the record are to be delivered to Island, presumably also for destruction. This includes "all tapes, stampers, molds, lacquers and other parts used in the manufacturing," and "all artwork, labels, packaging, promotional, marketing, and advertising or similar material."

(continued)

From Negativland, *Fair Use: The Story of the Letter U and the Numeral 2.* Concord, CA: Seeland, 1995, pp. 21–25.

- Our copyrights in the recordings themselves have been assigned to Island and Warner-Chappell. This means we no longer own two of our better works.
- Payment of $25,000 and half the wholesale proceeds from the copies of the record that were sold and not returned. We estimate the total cost to us, including legal fees and the cost of the destroyed records, cassettes, and CDs, at $70,000—more money than we've made in our twelve years of existence.

Our single deals, in part, with our perception of the group U2 as an international cultural phenomenon, and therefore particularly worthy of artistic comment and criticism. Island's legal action thoroughly ignores the possibility that any such artistic right or inclination might exist. Apparently Island's sole concern in this act of censorship is their determination to control the marketplace, as if the only reason to make records is to make money.

This issue is not a contest among equals. U2 records are among the most popular in history: *The Joshua Tree* sold over 14,000,000 copies. Negativland releases usually sell about 10,000 to 15,000 copies each. Our label, SST Records, is a relatively small, independent label interested in alternative music. Neither of us could afford the tremendous costs involved in fighting for our rights in court. Island could. What we *can* do is try to bring as much publicity and attention to Island's actions as possible. This statement, we hope, is a more humane attempt at reasonable discourse about artistic integrity and the artless, humorless legalism that controls corporate music today.

We've included a small sampling (excuse the expression) from the large stack of legal documents that arrived from Island's attorneys dripping with the unyielding intimidation of money and power. That preliminary stack of documents, 180 pages in all, cost Island approximately $10,000 to produce (they ultimately spent over $55,000 to stop us). Preferring retreat to total annihilation, Negativland and SST had no choice but to agree to comply completely with these demands.

Companies like Island depend on this kind of economic inevitability to bully their way over all lesser forms of opposition. Thus, Island easily wipes us off the face of their earth purely on the basis of how much more money they can afford to waste than we can. We think there are

(continued)

issues to stand up for here, but Island can spend their way out of ever having to face them in a court of law. So some important ideas about what constitutes art, and whether those ideas can supersede product constraints, will not reach a forum of precedent. In this culture, the market rules and money *is* power. They own the law, and no one who is still interested in the supremacy of a vital and freewheeling art can afford to challenge this aspect of our decline. It is a telling tribute to this culture corporation's crass obsessions that Island's whole approach to our work automatically assumed its goal was to siphon off their rightful profits. These people lost their ability to appreciate the very nature of what they're selling a long time ago.

As you will notice from the accompanying legal documents, Island is able to bring certain existing laws to bear against our work under the assumption that any infringement of those laws is done for purposes of diverting their monetary return. Our question is: how and why should these laws apply when the infringement is not done for economic gain? For the law to claim that this alleged motive is the sole criterion for legal deliberation is to admit that music, itself, is not to be taken seriously. Culture is more than commerce. It may actually have something to say about commerce. It may even use examples of commerce to comment upon it. We suggest that the law should begin to acknowledge the artistic domain of various creative techniques which may actually conflict with what others claim to be their economic domain. Any serious observer of modern music can cite a multitude of examples, from Buchanan and Goodman's humorous collages of song fragments in the 50's to today's canonization of James Brown samples, wherein artists have incorporated the actual property of others into their own unique creations. This is a 20th century mode of artistic operation that is now nothing short of dramatic in its proliferation, in spite of all the marketplace laws designed to prohibit it. We believe that art is what artists do. We hope for laws that recognize this, just as the dictionary recognizes new words (even slang) that come into common usage.

At this late date in the mass distribution of capturing technology (audio tape recorders, samplers, xerox machines, camcorders, VCRs, computers, etc.) there should be no need to prove the cultural legitimacy of what we do with sound. And this is even more obvious when you look further back. We pursue audio works in the tradition of found-image collage which originated in the visual arts—from Schwitters and Braque to Rauschenberg and Warhol. In music, we

(continued)

refer you to the whole histories of folk music and the blues, both of which have always had creative theft as their modus operandi. Jazz and rock are full of this too. The music business can try to reach the end of this century pretending that there is something wrong with this, or they can begin to acknowledge the truth and make way for reality.

Perceptually and philosophically, it is an uncomfortable wrenching of common sense to deny that once something hits the airwaves, it is literally in the public domain. The fact that the owners of culture and its material distribution are able to claim this isn't true belies their total immersion in a reality-on-paper. Artists have always approached the entire world around them as both inspiration to act and as raw material to mold and remold. Other art is just more raw material to us and to many, many others we could point to. When it comes to cultural influences, ownership is the point of fools. Copycats will shrink in the light of comparison. Bootlegging exact duplicates of another's product should be prosecuted, but we see no significant harm in anything else artists care to do with anything available to them in our "free" marketplace. We claim the right to create with mirrors. This is our working philosophy.

Negativland occupies itself with recontextualizing captured fragments to create something entirely new—a psychological impact based on a new juxtaposition of diverse elements, ripped from their usual context, chewed up, and spit out as a new form of hearing the world around us. One of Negativland's artistic obsessions involves the media, itself, as source and subject for much of our work. We respond (as artists always have) to our environment. An environment increasingly filled with artificial ideas, images, and sounds. Television, billboards, newspapers, advertisements, and music/muzak being blasted at us everywhere we go (and that background hum of everyday life certainly includes top forty bands like U2). We follow our working philosophy as best we can amid the proprietary restrictions of a self-serving marketing system that has imposed itself on culture. In reality, that system of ownership is today's emperor's clothes, now casually subverted by every kid with a tape recorder. However, it is crucial to note that, as we plunder the ocean of media we all swim in, we believe in artistic responsibility. We do not duplicate existing work or bootleg others' products. We believe every artist is due whatever rewards he or she can reap from his or her own products. The question that must rise to the surface of legal consciousness now is: at what point in the process of found sound

(continued)

incorporation does the new creation possess its own unique identity which supersedes the sum of its parts, thus gaining artistic license?

One of Island's objections to our record is the unauthorized use of a sample from the U2 song that formed the basis for both of our pieces: *I Still Haven't Found What I'm Looking For.* We believe that what we did is legally protected fair use of the segment, as it was used for purposes of fair comment, parody, and cultural criticism, which the copyright law specifically allows. A relevant precedent was set earlier this year in 2 Live Crew's *Pretty Woman* case. The fact is that today there is no operationally workable way to reuse existing sound recordings in collage-based work and see that the original artists are paid for the use of their work. Those artists who only use a few samples and have the time, money, and inclination can have their record companies negotiate payments for "sampling clearances" to the labels that originally released the records containing the desired snippets. But this is cumbersome, arbitrary, and expensive enough to discourage advanced sound collage work where there might be anywhere from one to a dozen found sound elements present at any instant, dozens or hundreds over the duration of a record.

So much for content. It is clear that the more significant objection to our single was Island's concern about our cover graphics, which they claimed would cause "massive confusion," resulting in millions of U2 fans buying the wrong record. Does our packaging look like a new release by the group U2? *Yes, of course it does . . .* at first. But upon closer inspection it reveals itself to be something else. Closer inspection is one of the things we like to promote, while Island appears resigned to the entrenchment of stupidity and the inability of their audience to notice subtle cues such as our name on the cover or our label's logo on the back.

Further, the context in which any potential confusion would take place is a retail record store. The first clue to record store employees would be that our single arrives from SST, not Island, and in small quantities, not the hundreds Island would send. Ours would be located in the "Indies" bins common to most outlets, not the general "Rock" bins where U2 records are found. Ours would be filed under "N," not "U." These logistics aside, let's assume someone does buy our record thinking it's theirs. Does Island really believe that the U2 fan will be satisfied with such a mistake and, returning ours or not, not proceed to buy U2's new record? Accusing

(continued)

us of trying to make money off their name is one thing, but claiming that the money we would make would be money they would not make is not very realistic. Island's inference that U2 fans might actually assume that we are them upon hearing our record is simply ridiculous on the face of it, and another indication of their lack of respect for their own audience.

As to Island's point about scheduling our single to coincide with U2's new release, we must plead to interesting coincidence. Island should come to grips with the fact that not everybody in the world avidly soaks up every promo blurb that Island feeds to the mainstream rock press. We don't generally read that press and neither knew nor cared that U2 was about to release another chart-busting epic. Our single was scheduled for fall release because our market stems primarily from college radio airplay, and that's when school resumes and the listening population is largest. Fall is also a prime time to release throughout the record industry, which is probably why U2's new record was also scheduled for fall. It seems clear that both Island and SST were attempting to take advantage of the same situation, not each other.

So why would we want to simulate a U2 cover if not to swipe some of the big money that this big band attracts? Our real reasons are actually so reflective that they would never cross the corporate legal mind. The image on our cover was U2's namesake, the U-2: a high-altitude espionage plane which, prophetically enough, was shot down over the now-defunct Soviet Union in 1960 causing a huge, meaningless international flap. The only point of light in those dark days was that it gave a self-righteous and complacent America its first clear photo opportunity to catch its own president telling a blatant lie which the CIA assured him was plausible deniability. Our U2 was a spy full of secrets intruding into the self-righteous and complacent image-world of polite pop. We did it as an example of something not being what it seems to be. We did it because we're all subject to too much media image mongering. We did it because tricksters and jesters are the last best hope against the corporate music bureaucracies of good grooming that have all but killed the most interesting thing in popular music—grassroots inspiration. We did it for laughs—listen to it and try not to. We did it so you could read this. The fact that Island Records can't understand all this, or if they can understand it they can't appreciate it, or if they can appreciate it they can't allow themselves to acknowledge it, is precisely why they should not have the right to control the life of other people's art.

(continued)

One basic failing of the U.S. legal system is that it treats the plaintiff and the defendant as though they are equally powerful entities, regardless of the actual resources each may have. Further, it disregards the fact that the cost of preparing a legal defense for a trial is prohibitively high—unthinkable for any entity other than a wealthy individual or a good-sized corporation. Thus, when a corporation goes after a small business or low-income individuals, the conflict automatically rolls outside of the court system because of the defendant's inability to pay the costs of mounting a proper defense. The matter is resolved by the more powerful organization threatening to press the suit back into the courts unless the smaller party agrees to their terms unconditionally. The powerful crush the weak. Note that all of this is purely a *power* relationship, essentially without regard to the legality of the issue, let alone the morality.

What would be the solution to prevent the cruel squashing of interesting jokes such as ours? How about a thorough revamping of the antique copyright, publishing, and cultural property laws to bring them into comfortable accord with modern technology and a healthy respect for the artist's impulse to incorporate public influences? Marketer's constraints should be restrained in cases of valid artistic commentary. This is a huge and complex Congressional undertaking and would inevitably result in sticky legal decisions akin to deciding whether or not a particular work of art is pornographic. So be it.

Art needs to begin to acquire an equal footing with marketers in court. We can even imagine such changes extending all the way to recording contracts which, strange as it may seem, might actually be written so as to allow the artist, rather than the marketer, to own and control his or her own work. You might as well start thinking about these problems now because they're not going to go away.

Excerpts from Chapter 1 of the 1976 United States Copyright Act

PUBLIC LAW 94-553—OCT. 19, 1976 90 STAT. 2541

Public Law 94-553
94th Congress

An Act

For the general revision of the Copyright Law, title 17 of the United States Code, and for other purposes.

Oct. 19, 1976
[S. 22]

Be it enacted by the Senate and House of Representatives of the United States of America in Congress assembled,

Title 17, USC, copyrights.

TITLE I—GENERAL REVISION OF COPYRIGHT LAW

Sec. 101. Title 17 of the United States Code, entitled "Copyrights," is hereby amended in its entirety to read as follows:

TITLE 17—COPYRIGHTS

Chapter 1.—SUBJECT MATTER AND SCOPE OF COPYRIGHT

§ 101. Definitions

As used in this title, the following terms and their variant forms mean the following:

A "compilation" is a work formed by the collection and assembling of preexisting materials or of data that are selected, coordinated, or arranged in such a way that the resulting work as a whole constitutes an original work of authorship. The term "compilation" includes collective works.

"Copies" are material objects, other than phonorecords, in which a work is fixed by any method now known or later developed, and from which the work can be perceived, reproduced, or otherwise communicated, either directly or with the aid of a machine or device. The term "copies" includes the material object, other than a phonorecord, in which the work is first fixed.

"Copyright owner," with respect to any one of the exclusive rights comprised in a copyright, refers to the owner of that particular right.

A work is "created" when it is fixed in a copy or phonorecord for the first time; where a work is prepared over a period of time, the portion of it that has been fixed at any particular time constitutes the work as of that time, and where the work has been prepared in different versions, each version constitutes a separate work.

A "derivative work" is a work based upon one or more preexisting works, such as a translation, musical arrangement, dramatization, fictionalization,

(continued)

From 1976 United States Copyright Act, Public Law 94-553, Oct. 19, 1976.

motion picture version, sound recording, art reproduction, abridgment, condensation, or any other form in which a work may be recast, transformed, or adapted. A work consisting of editorial revisions, annotations, elaborations, or other modifications which, as a whole, represent an original work of authorship, is a "derivative work."

A "device," "machine," or "process" is one now known or later developed. To "display" a work means to show a copy of it, either directly or by means of a film, slide, television image, or any other device or process or, in the case of a motion picture or other audiovisual work, to show individual images nonsequentially.

A work is "fixed" in a tangible medium of expression when its embodiment in a copy or phonorecord, by or under the authority of the author, is sufficiently permanent or stable to permit it to be perceived, reproduced, or otherwise communicated for a period of more than transitory duration. A work consisting of sounds, images, or both, that are being transmitted, is "fixed" for purposes of this title if a fixation of the work is being made simultaneously with its transmission.

"Phonorecords" are material objects in which sounds, other than those accompanying a motion picture or other audiovisual work, are fixed by any method now known or later developed, and from which the sounds can be perceived, reproduced, or otherwise communicated, either directly or with the aid of a machine or device. The term "phonorecords" includes the material object in which the sounds are first fixed.

"Publication" is the distribution of copies or phonorecords of a work to the public by sale or other transfer of ownership, or by rental, lease, or lending. The offering to distribute copies or phonorecords to a group of persons for purposes of further distribution, public performance, or public display, constitutes publication. A public performance or display of a work does not of itself constitute publication.

To perform or display a work "publicly" means—

(1) to perform or display it at a place open to the public or at any place where a substantial number of persons outside of a normal circle of a family and its social acquaintances is gathered; or

(2) to transmit or otherwise communicate a performance or display of the work to a place specified by clause (1) or to the public, by means of any device or processs, whether the members of the public capable of receiving the performance or display receive it in the same place or in separate places and at the same time or at different times.

"Sound recordings" are works that result from the fixation of a series of musical, spoken, or other sounds, but not including the sounds accompanying a motion picture or other audiovisual work, regardless of the nature of the material objects, such as disks, tapes, or other phonorecords, in which they are embodied.

(continued)

17 USC 102. **§ 102. Subject matter of copyright: In general**

(a) Copyright protection subsists, in accordance with this title, in original works of authorship fixed in any tangible medium of expression, now known or later developed, from which they can be perceived, reproduced, or otherwise communicated, either directly or with the aid of a machine or device.

Works of authorship.

Works of authorship include the following categories:

(1) literary works;

(2) musical works, including any accompanying words;

(3) dramatic works, including any accompanying music;

(4) pantomimes and choreographic works;

(5) pictorial, graphic, and sculptural works;

(6) motion pictures and other audiovisual works; and

(7) sound recordings.

(b) In no case does copyright protection for an original work of authorship extend to any idea, procedure, process, system, method of operation, concept, principle, or discovery, regardless of the form in which it is described, explained, illustrated, or embodied in such work.

17 USC 103. **§ 103. Subject matter of copyright: Compilations and derivative works**

(a) The subject matter of copyright as specified by section 102 includes compilations and derivative works, but protection for a work employing preexisting material in which copyright subsists does not extend to any part of the work in which such material has been used unlawfully.

(b) The copyright in a compilation or derivative work extends only to the material contributed by the author of such work, as distinguished from the preexisting material employed in the work, and does not imply any exclusive right in the preexisting material. The copyright in such work is independent of, and does not affect or enlarge the scope, duration, ownership, or subsistence of, any copyright protection in the preexisting material.

17 USC 106. **§ 106. Exclusive rights in copyrighted works**

Subject to sections 107 through 118, the owner of copyright under this title has the exclusive rights to do and to authorize any of the following:

(1) to reproduce the copyrighted work in copies or phonorecords;

(2) to prepare derivative works based upon the copyrighted work;

(3) to distribute copies or phonorecords of the copyrighted work to the public by sale or other transfer of ownership, or by rental, lease, or lending;

(4) in the case of literary, musical, dramatic, and choreographic works, pantomimes, and motion pictures and other audiovisual works, to perform the copyrighted work publicly; and

(5) in the case of literary, musical, dramatic, and choreographic works, pantomimes, and pictorial, graphic, or sculptural works, including the individual images

(continued)

of a motion picture or other audiovisual work, to display the copyrighted work publicly.

17 USC 107. **§ 107. Limitations on exclusive rights: Fair use**

Notwithstanding the provisions of section 106, the fair use of a copyrighted work, including such use by reproduction in copies or phonorecords or by any other means specified by that section, for purposes such as criticism, comment, news reporting, teaching (including multiple copies for classroom use), scholarship, or research, is not an infringement of copyright. In determining whether the use made of a work in any particular case is a fair use the factors to be considered shall include—

(1) the purpose and character of the use, including whether such use is of a commercial nature or is for nonprofit educational purposes;

(2) the nature of the copyrighted work;

(3) the amount and substantiality of the portion used in relation to the copyrighted work as a whole; and

(4) the effect of the use upon the potential market for or value of the copyrighted work.

17 USC 114. **§ 114. Scope of exclusive rights in sound recordings**

(a) The exclusive rights of the owner of copyright in a sound recording are limited to the rights specified by clauses (1), (2), and (3) of section 106, and do not include any right of performance under section 106(4).

(b) The exclusive right of the owner of copyright in a sound recording under clause (1) of section 106 is limited to the right to duplicate the sound recording in the form of phonorecords, or of copies of motion pictures and other audiovisual works, that directly or indirectly recapture the actual sounds fixed in the recording. The exclusive right of the owner of copyright in a sound recording under clause (2) of section 106 is limited to the right to prepare a derivative work in which the actual sounds fixed in the sound recording are rearranged, remixed, or otherwise altered in sequence or quality. The exclusive rights of the owner of copyright in a sound recording under clauses (1) and (2) of section 106 do not extend to the making or duplication of another sound recording that consists entirely of an independent fixation of other sounds, even though such sounds imitate or simulate those in the copyrighted sound recording. The exclusive rights of the owner of copyright in a sound recording under clauses (1), (2), and (3) of section 106 do not apply to sound recordings included in educational television and radio programs (as defined in
47 USC 397. section 397 of title 47) distributed or transmitted by or through public broadcasting entities (as defined by section 118(g)): *Provided,* That copies or phonorecords of said programs are not commercially distributed by or through public broadcasting entities to the general public.

(c) This section does not limit or impair the exclusive right to perform publicly, by means of a phonorecord, any of the works specified by section 106(4).

In Fair Use Debate, Art Must Come First

By Negativland

As Duchamp pointed out many decades ago, the act of selection can be a form of inspiration as original and significant as any other. Throughout our various mass media, we now find many artists who work by "selecting" existing cultural material to collage with, to create with, and to comment upon. In general, this continues to be a method that both "serious" and "popular" arts incorporate. But is it theft? Do artists, for profit or not, have the right to "sample" freely from the already-"created" electronic environment that surrounds them?

The psychology of art has always favored fragmentary "theft" in a way that does not engender a "loss" to the owner. Call this "being influenced" if you want to sound legitimate. But some will say there is a big difference between stealing ideas, techniques, and styles that are not easily copyrighted, and stealing actual material that is easily copyrighted. However, aside from the copyright-deterrence factor prevalent throughout our law-bound art industries, we can find nothing intrinsically wrong with an artist deciding to incorporate existing art "samples" into their own work. The fact that we have economically motivated laws against it does not necessarily make it an undesirable artistic move.

All of music history has involved the fragmentary appropriation of existing works within "new" creations. Even material "theft" has a well-respected tradition in the arts, dating back to the Industrial Revolution. It first flowered in Cubist collages, then became blatant in Dada's found objects and concept of "detournment," and finally peaked in mid-Century with Pop Art's appropriation of mass-culture icons and mass-media imagery. Techniques of material appropriation bear a direct relationship to this century's *invention* of mass culture and the technologically-based barrage of information, imagery, and communication directed at the masses. Now, at the end of this century, it is in music where we find appropriation raging anew as a major creative method and legal controversy.

It's about time that the obvious aesthetic validity of appropriation begins to be raised in opposition to the assumed preeminence of historically recent copyright laws prohibiting the free reuse of cultural material. The prevailing assumption—that our culture, and all its cultural artifacts, should be privately controlled and locked away from any and all further creative uses by the audience they are directed at—is both undesirable and unworkable. Uninvited appropriation is inevitable when a population bombarded with electronic media meets the hardware that encourages people to capture those media. However, laws devised to protect the "ownership" of transmittable information have, for example, resulted in a music industry in which the very *idea* of collage is a dangerous one, and artists inspired by "direct reference" forms of creation do not have the "right" to decide what their own art will consist of. Has it occurred to anyone that the private ownership of mass culture is a bit of a contradiction in terms?

The urge to make one thing out of other things is an entirely traditional, socially healthy, and artistically valued impulse that only recently has been criminalized in order to force private tolls on the practice, or else prohibit it to escape embarrassment. Artists continue to employ appropriation because it's just plain interesting, and no law can keep artists from being interesting.

(continued)

From *Billboard,* December 25, 1993. Reprinted in Negativland, *Fair Use: The Story of the Letter U and the Numeral 2.* Concord, CA: Seeland, 1995, p. 154.

How many artistic prerogatives should we be willing to give up in order to maintain our owner-regulated culture? The directions artists want to take may sometimes be dangerous—that's the risk of democracy—but they certainly should not be dictated by what business wants to allow. Look it up in the dictionary: Art is not defined as a business! Is it a healthy state of affairs when laws of commerce get to lock in the boundaries of experimentation for artists, or is this a recipe for cultural stagnation?

Today, in a culture thoroughly colonized by private "property rights," the only solution for artists who appropriate other works rests with the legal concept of "Fair Use," which already exists within copyright law. The Fair Use statutes are intended to allow for free appropriation in certain cases of parody or commentary, and are the sole acknowledgement within copyright law of a possible need for artistic freedom and free speech. Unfortunately, the Fair Use Doctrine is now being interpreted conservatively and is being withheld from many "infringers." However, the beauty of Fair Use is that it is capable of overriding all the other restrictions.

Those of us who still value art over profit are now focusing on how to release the Fair Use Doctrine from its present commercial handcuffs. Both courts and Congress await the powerful suggestion that Fair Use issues are not about who is going to profit, but about who is going to determine what art might consist of. Until this adjustment in basic legal presumptions occurs, modern societies will find the corporate stranglehold on cultural "properties" continuously at war with the common sense and natural inclinations of their "user" populations.

Here is our main suggestion for updating the concept of Fair Use in order to accommodate the realities of recent technology, and to promote, rather than inhibit, "direct reference" art forms. Clear all restrictions—including requirements for payment and permission—on any practice of *fragmentary* appropriation. We would retain the present protections and fees for artists and their administrators only in uses of their *entire* works (cover versions) or for any form of usage at all by commercial advertisers. The test of whether a "fragment" is too close to the whole should be an artistic definition, not a commercial one. Namely: Is the material used superseded by a *new nature* of the usage itself—is the whole more than the sum of its parts? When faced with actual examples, this is not difficult to evaluate.

This one alteration in the Fair Use Doctrine would (for a change) serve to balance the will of commerce to monopolize its products with the socially desirable urge of artists to remix culture. If this occurred, the rest of copyright law might stay as it is (if that's what we want) and continue to apply in all cases of "whole" theft for commercial gain (bootlegging entire works).

The law *must* come to terms with the difference between artistic intent and economic intent. We believe that artistic freedom for all is more important to the health of society than the supplemental and extraneous incomes derived from private copyright tariffs that create a climate of art control and Art Police. No matter how valid the original intent of our copyright laws may have been, they are now clearly being subverted to censor resented works, to suppress the public's need to reuse and reshape information, and to garner purely opportunistic incomes. The U.S. Constitution clearly shows that the reason for copyright law was to promote a *public* good, not a private one. No one should be allowed to claim a private control over the creative process itself. Make no mistake: This is essentially a struggle of art against commerce, and ultimately about which one must make way for the other.

Sampling Without Permission Is Theft

By Andrian Adams and Paul McKibbins

A chill crawled up our spines upon reading the commentary on fair use by self-described "noisemakers" Negativland (*Billboard,* Dec. 25, 1993).

Through a series of wildly specious arguments, Negativland seeks to promote the idea that they should be able—through the technique of "sampling"—to use others' creative and interpretive work for their own commercial gain without the inconvenience of payment or permission. To those who put in the time, energy, creative effort, and money necessary to create their music in its original form, this is intellectual and physical theft.

The Supreme Court is considering the definitions of "fair use" and "parody" as they apply to the 2 Live Crew's use of the Acuff-Rose-owned song "Oh, Pretty Woman" on their album "As Clean As They Wanna Be." If the Court rules in favor of the publishers, some argue that it could have a dampening effect on other artists that employ parody (*Billboard,* Nov. 20, 1993). The ruling is expected this spring, and the case has spurred some artists, like Negativland, to call for dramatic alteration of the Copyright Act.

Negativland's position—"We believe that artistic freedom for all is more important to the health of society than the supplemental and extraneous incomes derived from private copyright tariffs"—actually negates the whole concept of music as a business. In Negativland's world, "art" and commerce are completely distinct entities. However, in our world of realism and logic, there is no distinction between art and commerce once the art is offered for sale. To insist otherwise is naive.

We feel compelled to address the other sides of the sampling issue. However, before we clean up the minefield of negativism and reseed it with positivism, let us state our view on sampling: If you use copyright-protected music for commercial gain, you must pay. Period.

In very practical terms—in fact, the Constitution guarantees it—intellectual property is no different than physical property regarding ownership. Just as one cannot take another's car without permission, one cannot take or use another's copyrighted creation without permission. Taking this one step further, no one, except a thief, would take another person's car and sell it without the proper, formal, legal arrangements. But this is exactly what happens when an artist appropriates a musical fragment and then profits from its use and sale. It's taking without permission.

Although Negativland justifies "fragmentary theft" (read: sampling) as an inescapable part of the artistic process, they defend this view *vis à vis* music with a historical reference linking Cubist collages to Dada and, finally, to Pop Art's use of mass-culture icons, i.e., Andy Warhol's Campbell's Soup can. Historical borrowing, says Negativland, supersedes modern copyright law.

But beyond the issue of art as commerce also lie the intrinsic moral and ethical responsibilities that come with the privilege of participating in a free-market system. In more colloquial terms, "doing the right thing."

With regard to music, the "right thing" is for users to pay the people who own the

(continued)

From *Billboard,* March 5, 1994. Reprinted in Negativland, *Fair Use: The Story of the Letter U and the Numeral 2.* Concord, CA: Seeland, 1995.

property, i.e., the copyright holders. In a civilized society, the rule of law, through legislation, rightfully plays an important role in codifying moral and ethical behavior. It also dictates the practical elements of the free market: The law defines who gets what and who has "the right to copy." Without laws to help guide a nation's citizens, there would be anarchy, although this seems to be the direction in which Negativland wants our nation to head.

Interestingly, Negativland claims that our "owner-regulated culture" prevents artists from partaking in their instinctive "urge" to create musical "collages" should they so desire. Furthermore, according to Negativland, "uninvited appropriation is inevitable" since our population is "bombarded with electronic media."

If the real issue is only that artists have the right to sample, we completely agree with Negativland's, and their "artist" friends', desire to sample. You may sample *anything,* as long as it is not for commercial gain. Since Negativland values "art over profit" and embraces a definition that "art is not a business," why should they care about selling their creations? Therefore, the point is moot. Sample away!

While determined to justify the appropriation of others' creative sweat, Negativland devises a bizarre interpretation of the "Fair Use" statute contained in current copyright law, which allows for free appropriation in instances that include parody, education, and commentary. Negativland benignly views these exceptions as a window for an "artistic freedom" and "free speech" interpretation of the Fair Use statute that would allow stealing for personal gain.

We believe that Negativland's position that "the private ownership of mass culture is a contradiction in terms" is nonsense. Mass culture is made up of an infinite number of distinct parts. It's the protection of those parts—that is, the copyrights—that continually stimulates creators to work in the arts. Without the stimulus of financial gain, how will artists survive? This brings us back to the idea of laws, morals, and ethical values.

While it is unlikely that Negativland's ideas will ever be implemented by Congress or the courts, we in the music business must be vigilant in protecting the copyrights we control. It is sad that there are growing numbers of Negativlands in our midst, people who want to steal from us in the name of "art." Like Negativland, these people want to "clear all restrictions—including payment and permission—on any practice of fragmentary appropriation." Whether it's one James Brown shout or the whole "hook" of a song, Negativland wants the right to have it in *their* music without paying the rightful owners of that music.

Make no mistake. This is not a struggle of art against commerce. It is about honest, hard-working people being compensated for the music they create and rightfully own.

Build a Desktop Studio

By Tom Samiljan

Previously the exclusive realm of professional studio musicians, music-creation software has become so simple that any amateur with a decent computer can start making noise. Two of the following programs—Acid and Mixman—are powerful enough to be used by professional DJs and musicians; Sounder is a Web-based diversion that lets duffers remix for free.

Mixman Studio Pro
(Windows and Mac, $90)

If you want to be making music within minutes of installing your software, try Mixman Studio Pro, a user-friendly suite of professional quality mixing tools. Mixman has more than 300 offerings in its library of presupplied tracks—everything from deep-house loops to funky guitar licks to classic-rock drumbeats. (You can make your own tracks as well.) Each selected track is assigned a different button on the keyboard; you can, say, lock in a salsa groove by triggering the correct track and holding down the space bar, then tap in little guitar flourishes wherever you please. You can port your remixes over to MP3 or WAV formats, or burn them onto a CD. Besides Mixman's ease of use, its other great advantage is its library of D-plates, which are Mixman-compatible songs by Luscious Jackson, Moby and others.

Acid 2.0
Sonicfoundry.com

Acid comes in three flavors: Acid Pro (for professionals), Acid Music (the intermediate-level software, for something called "prosumers") and Acid Style (for armchair DJs). Getting started is more difficult than with Mixman; Acid's interface, a huge grid in which each cell holds a different sound, looks more like a professional mixing program. First you preview loops of sounds (samples of drums, keyboards, bass, whatever). When you have enough sounds in your track list to make a song, you just drag sounds into the spreadsheet-like grid (each sound is color-coded so you can keep track). Prerecorded loops (which you can play and remix) can be gathered from a separate CD that comes with the program—choices vary from generic rock beats to jungle and house rhythms. If you want to focus on a particular kind of music, you can buy specialized versions of Acid in genres such as hip-hop, rock and dance ($60 each) or download loops off Sonic Foundry's site (individual loops can be purchased for $1 each). Of course, you can record and manipulate your own loops, too. Like Mixman, Acid makes it easy to use seemingly disparate samples: Place a rock & roll beat in the same song as a house beat and the software will automatically make it work, with no change in pitch. In addition, you can burn your tracks onto a CD or create MP3 and streamable tracks with simple mouse commands. Some major names (including Beck) have provided original loops from their songs for Acid users, but the program doesn't have the deep lineup of Mixman's D-plates.

Sounder
Sounder.com

A true original in the music-creation space, Sounder presents you with graphic animations-spheres, stars, rocks—that move around windows (called Sounder Spaces) on your desktop.

(continued)

From *Rolling Stone,* June 8, 2000, p. 529.

Each time an object hits the wall of a window, it plays a preassigned note. You can also assign different notes (A, B, C) and timbres (telephone ring, drum, wood block) to each object. To change the music, grab Sounder objects with your cursor and throw them around the window so that they move in different ways and at different speeds, creating the same sounds at different tempos. The result is usually something that resembles an ambient, abstract composition by the likes of Brian Eno or Aphex Twin - Sounder is half desktop diversion, half genius ambient-music generator.

RTMARK Finds Bucks for Beck Rip-Off

FOR IMMEDIATE RELEASE

February 17, 1998

Contacts: *info@rtmark.com* (http://www.rtmark.com/)
illegalart@detritus.net
(*http://www.detritus.net/illegalart*)

RTMARK FINDS BUCKS FOR BECK RIP-OFF

Group channels money for subversion, hopes to spark dialogue on corporate wrongs

RTMARK is pleased to announce the February 17 release of a new Beck CD: *Deconstructing Beck.*

Recording artist Beck might be less pleased. Why? Because it isn't really his work. *Deconstructing Beck* is a collection of brilliant but allegedly illegal resamplings of Beck, produced by Illegal Art with the help of $5,000 gathered by RTMARK from anonymous donors.

Deconstructing Beck is the latest of more than twenty successful sabotage projects made possible by RTMARK since its beginnings in 1991. RTMARK's aim is to further anti-corporate activism by channelling funds from donors to workers. Other recent and upcoming acts of RTMARK-aided subversion are documented on RTMARK's web site, http://www.rtmark.com/.

According to an anonymous RTMARK spokesperson, RTMARK was first approached by Illegal Art last November. "Using artwork illegally helps fight the stranglehold that corporations have on our lives, and that's what we're all about," the spokesperson said. "We weren't sure about this project at first, since RTMARK usually targets the crassest of mass-produced items. But while Beck may be a superb artist, his lucrative persona remains just another product that others get rich from, and one that we need to subvert."

Philo T. Farnsworth, the pseudonymous main force behind Illegal Art, says his label exists to provide "an outlet for artists interested in exploring an illegal palette. Corporations invade our lives with product but forbid us to use it—in our art, or in any way they don't want. This just doesn't make sense."

(continued)

RTMARK, Deconstructing Beck Press Release, Feb. 17, 1998, http://www.rtmark.com.

What does makes sense, given the corporate climate, is that record stores won't touch this CD. It is available only from Illegal Art (*illegalart@detritus.net*), and costs just $5, including US postage. Illegal Art was able to keep production costs low by packaging the CD in a plain white box and putting its liner notes on their web site. Even more importantly, the cost of the CD reflects a markup of only 100%, instead of the industry-standard 800%. (The page with the liner notes, *http://www.detritus.net/illegalart/beck/*, also features 30-second RealAudio(tm) clips of each track.)

Illegal Art's email and web service, incidentally, is provided by *detritus.net,* an Internet site dedicated to the artistic reuse of pre-existing culture. "We're happy to be helping out with the Beck project," said Steev Hise, Detritus webmaster. "Copyright laws are too restrictive, and they're counterintuitive. These laws in their present form are there just to funnel money to corporations, not to protect artists. As artists we need to fight that."

UNIT III

Creating a Sense of Place

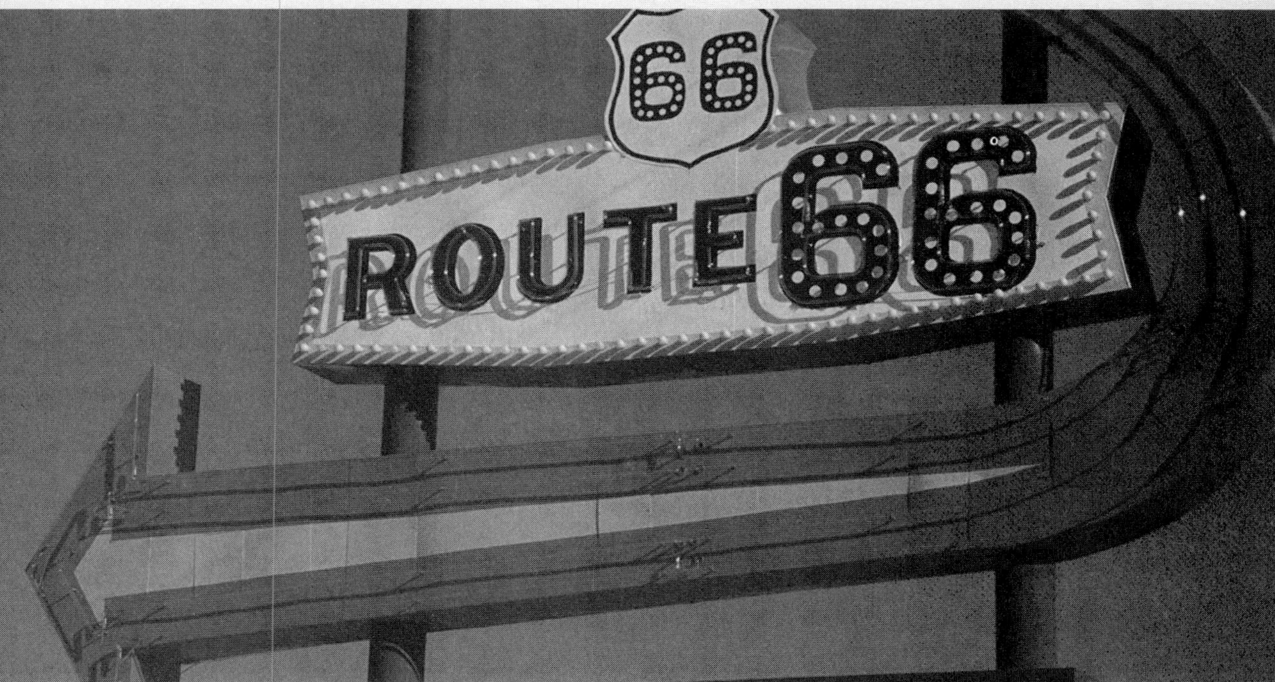

Route 66 was commissioned in 1926 to connect existing local roads into a single roadway between Chicago and Los Angeles. By the 1960s, partly because of movies, songs, and a TV series that celebrated it, Route 66 had become a symbol of freedom and adventure. But by the 1980s, the narrow, meandering road had been almost completely replaced by multilane expressways. Recently, though, the remnants of Route 66 have been rediscovered as a culturally richer alternative to the impersonal interstates. Route 66 has now come to symbolize a longing for the local sense of place that the interstates and fast food franchises seem to have taken away. For many people, photographs like this one of the motels, restaurants, gas stations, and tourist attractions along Route 66 are visual expressions of a dialogue between the local and the exotic. We go on the road to escape the familiar and find adventure, but travel is an adventure only if the places we travel to have retained their own local sense of place, the things that make them home to others. These are some of the complexities of creating a sense of place that you will explore in this unit. But before you turn the page, pause to read some of the meanings in this photograph. How do you "read" the sign on a motel to decide if you want to stay in that particular home on the road? How would you judge this motel if all you had to go on was this sign?

CHAPTER 6

Creating a Sense of Place

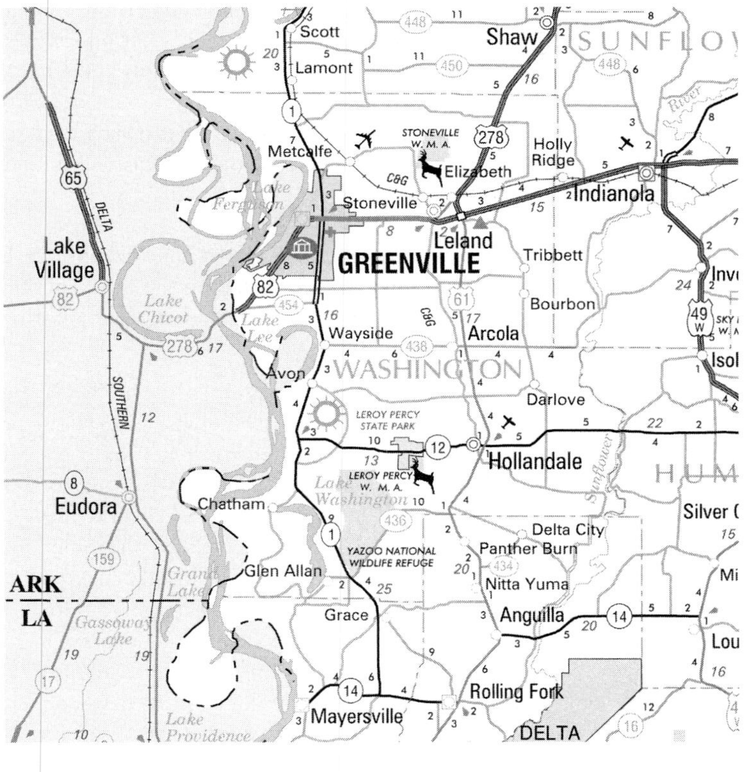

Situation: Can you visualize where the area represented by this map is located?

Genre: What are maps used for? How have maps changed over time? What different kinds of maps are there? How would you compare this map with other maps you've seen?

Language: How do maps combine visual language with the language of words? What do you do when you "read" a map? Have you ever drawn a map? What kinds of "language" did you use?

Consequences: Have you ever tried to get somewhere using an inaccurate map? How have maps changed the way we see the world?

When Audubon Naturalist Society guide Mark Garland published his book *Watching Nature, Washington Post* reporter Kevin McManus called him for an interview. Garland, characteristically, asked the reporter to meet him "in the field," in this case on the trail along the C&O Canal, rather than at his Chevy Chase office. Reflecting on the interview later, McManus wrote,

> I'm struck by how different our powers of perception are, out here on the trail. My brain has been registering much bird chirping, leafy trees and shrubs, many flowers, some frogs nearby. When I ask Garland what he's seeing and hearing, he says: "There's a pair of yellow-throated vireos, first ones I've heard today, calling on either side. Toads are still singing to the left—I just love that long, monotonous trill of theirs. Lots of other birds: There was a chestnut-sided warbler that just sang on the other side. You try and filter out some of the resident birds that you hear all the time—there's a tufted titmouse singing like crazy off to the right. Little buzzy notes of the blue-gray gnatcatcher.
>
> "So my ears are picking all of this up while my eyes are noticing things. Like there've been a couple of catbirds jumping in the bushes on the side. And I'm just marveling at the dogwood flowers on the other side. They're in full bloom right now . . ." (The *Washington Post,* July 4, 1997)

This short anecdote suggests a number of things about why we like to move about, take to the road, go into the field, return to nature, or otherwise change our perspective.

First, it suggests how much perspective influences perception. What we are able to see and hear depends on both who we are and where we are. When we change our situation—move to a different place, look from a different angle—we see the world anew, and this in turn changes us, renews us. Literary critics have a term for a related phenomenon: *defamiliarization* or *making strange,* the process by which art renews our perception of a world grown so familiar that we can no longer truly see it. This renewal of perception is one of the functions of art, but it can also happen through unaccustomed experiences, which is why we seek out these experiences, even though they can be frightening or dangerous.

The anecdote also points to the fact that many of us look for a renewal of perception in nature. There is an otherness in the natural world, an estrangement from human life that can shock us into seeing the world differently. But many travelers have found that visiting a strange culture can have a similar effect. Notice, in fact, that what challenges the reporter's perceptions is not simply an encounter with nature but a simultaneous encounter with the culture of the naturalist. Garland's skill at identifying many different sights and sounds depends not just on his ability to see and hear more but also on his knowledge of distinguishing names—yellow-throated vireo, chestnut-sided warbler, blue-gray gnatcatcher—and these names of course belong to culture, not nature. In fact, some philosophers argue that our encounters with nature are always "cultural" because we can see nature only through our culturally determined ideas about it.

But this is not to say that nature is just an extension of culture or that when we travel to new places we see only what we project there. Both nature and culture, both the new experience and our perception of it are real. Geographer Yi-Fu Tuan suggests that what we find at the intersection of nature and culture, or at the conjunction of a new experience and our existing structures of perception, is lucidity, a state of clarity and understanding that requires both a new experience and a perceptive faculty that is capable of change. Our encounters with the strange, whether in art, nature, or different cultures, can clarify both what we perceive and our own structures of perception: We see the world anew and are ourselves renewed.

We leave our accustomed places for many reasons—maybe just for fun, relaxation, a change of scenery, or, as with the reporter in the anecdote, as part of our job—but if we allow for an interaction between the strangeness of the new place and the insistence of our old ways of perceiving, we may bring back home with us a kind of lucidity. And if, as the reporter does, we can write about our experience, we can share that lucidity with others. This is one of the reasons why, even though it's easier and usually safer to stay put, we so often want to take to the road.

Bright Boy from the Delta

Clifton L. Taulbert

Watching Our Crops Come In is the third of Clifton Taulbert's memoirs chronicling his personal journey from his boyhood in the segregated Mississippi town of Glen Allen to the completion of his military tour as a classified airman with the Eighty-Ninth Presidential Wing. Earlier memoirs included *The Last Train North* and *When We Were Colored,* which was made into an independent film directed by Tim Reid and starring Felicia Rashad, Isaac Hayes, and Richard Roundtree.

"Bright Boy from the Delta" is the first chapter of *Watching Our Crops Come In* and finds Taulbert, in 1967, at Dow Air Force Base in Bangor, Maine. In Maine's blustery cold winters, Taulbert could not be much farther from the warm winds of the Mississippi Delta where he grew up. Of Glen Allen, even though Taulbert spent long, hard hours picking cotton and had to travel to another town to attend a segregated school, he has only warm memories of the times spent sitting on porch steps with his neighborhood's elders learning about trust and community. Cold winters or not, Taulbert tells us that he would rather be in Maine than in Vietnam, where young men one after another were being sent to fight for their country. This series of relocations encourages Taulbert to recall his upbringing in Glen Allen and how it had prepared him for his present challenges.

Taulbert, who consults and speaks internationally, has written a book, *The Eight Habits of the Heart: Embracing the Values that Build Strong Families and Communities,* which translates what he learned on the front-porch steps to lessons for getting along in a diverse society. These lessons form the basis for the consulting work that Taulbert does regularly with businesses and civic groups to help their members live and work together successfully.

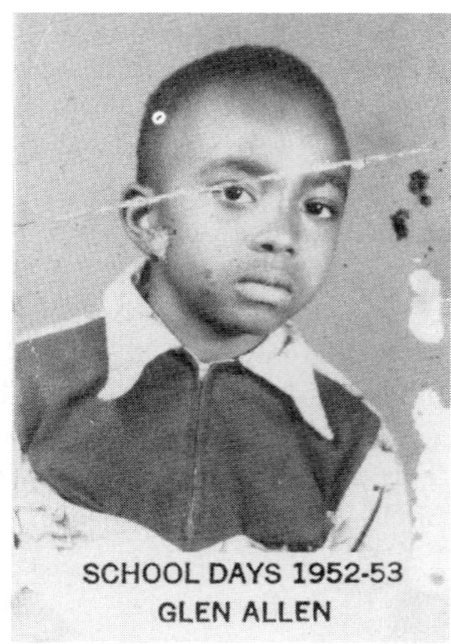

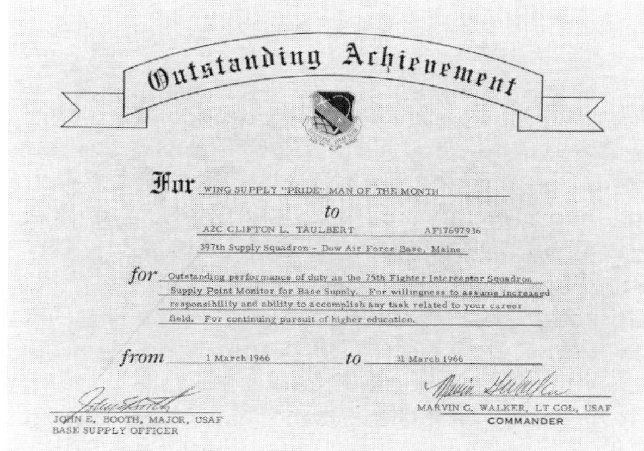

Outstanding Achievement

For WING SUPPLY "PRIDE" MAN OF THE MONTH

to

A2C CLIFTON L. TAULBERT AF17697936

397th Supply Squadron - Dow Air Force Base, Maine

for Outstanding performance of duty as the 75th Fighter Interceptor Squadron Supply Point Monitor for Base Supply. For willingness to assume increased responsibility and ability to accomplish any task related to your career field. For continuing pursuit of higher education.

from 1 March 1966 to 31 March 1966

JOHN E. BOOTH, MAJOR, USAF
BASE SUPPLY OFFICER

MARVIN C. WALKER, LT COL, USAF
COMMANDER

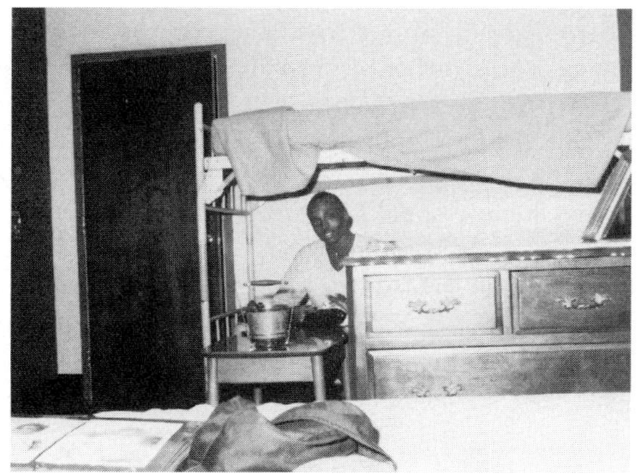

Connecting with the Conversation

1. Whom do you get advice from? Consider the people you accept advice from and the places you receive it. Do you accept advice from people who are your elders or your contemporaries? Consider generally the giving of advice: How is it portrayed on TV, in books and stories you have read, in movies? Write in your journal about what you have observed.
2. Consider how you would tell the story of your life up to this point. What key people and events contributed to who you are today? Write in your journal about key memories that you might include in an autobiography.

It was winter, 1967, early in the year. Like thousands of other soldiers, I had lived for months with the fear that I would one day receive orders that would carry me far from home, into the random terrors of the war in Vietnam, which we witnessed daily on TV. None of this had been my plan. In August of 1964, to circumvent the draft, I had joined the air force. After basic training at Lackland Air Force Base and technical school in Amarillo, Texas, I was assigned to Dow Air Force Base in Bangor, Maine, a place I had barely heard of and knew little about. By now, I had seen two hard northeastern winters and I wanted to see no more. But I wanted Vietnam even less.

However, on this midwinter day, I could hardly believe my good fortune. Standing outside the post office in the cold, bright air, I read again and again a letter that informed me that I had been selected to serve in a classified position at Andrews Air Force Base in Washington, D.C. "Congratulations," it said. Congratulations! All I could see was that word. I had survived an extensive background check, and now I could tell my great news to everyone except my best friend, Paul Demuniz, who had already shipped out for Vietnam. I was sad for Paul, but elated for myself. This was not a pipe dream. It was a real assignment, one that would make any airman proud. But it wasn't "any airman," it was me, Cliff, the little boy who had grown up in the village of Glen Allen, in the Mississippi Delta, living first with Poppa, my great-grandfather, and later with Ma Ponk, my great-aunt, under whose stern but loving eye I spent my high school years.

It was a long walk but a good one back to the barracks from the post office. As I moved along the quiet path, alone except for an occasional passing car, I recalled how badly as a child I had wanted to go north and how much I hated picking and chopping cotton. But as long as I was in Ma Ponk's care, I knew I had to work and be ready every morning to catch Mr. Walter's truck, which never broke down, no matter how much I prayed.

With the letter of my good news safely put away in my satchel, I walked and whistled as I thought about Ma Ponk and my childhood dreaming. "Boy, git off them steps, wash yore hands, and git back here to dis kitchen," I could still hear her yelling from the back of her small frame house. "You know we got to git up early to catch that darn field truck."

From *Watching Our Crops Come In.* New York: Viking Press, 1997, pp. 1–19.

5 Thus she would catch me resting on the front porch steps, still wet from the day's sweat but enjoying any breeze the evening swept my way, and I would hurry back to the kitchen so that I could eat, get the chickens in, and get ready for bed. Some nights, the sun would leave a trail of colors as it moved across the sky and would look as if it was going to fall right on top of our neighbor Miss Elsie's house. I dreamed of the day that I'd no longer have to eat fast, go to bed early, and get up before the roosters. I dreamed of going north, where there were no cotton fields, just good jobs.

Good jobs, I thought, as I walked up the small paved sidewalk to my barracks. I wanted to run into the building shouting the news of my good job, but instead I entered the back door by the fire escape, the one that was hardly used except as our weekend gathering place. Weekdays, our barracks were tense with the fear of impending orders. Most of the guys just went about their routine, watching the news, reading the bulletin board, and waiting for the weekend to arrive, when the mental war we waged could be put on hold. Since this was not the weekend, I hesitated to blurt out my news. I just walked up the inside stairs to the second floor and quietly approached the room that I shared with Airman Robuck from New Jersey.

Robuck was fearful of the war, but he had managed to adopt a "so what" attitude. If he had to go, I expected he would go and do what he was supposed to do. I wanted to talk to Robuck, but I hoped now to find the room empty. I needed time to reflect on this new assignment and what it could mean. In our hall, one guy stood talking on a pay phone, but everything else was quiet. I nodded at him as I got out my key to unlock my door.

When I opened the door, only the heavy smell of furniture oil and wax greeted me. Robuck wasn't back from work. I sat down in the green vinyl chair that was equally spaced between the single bed and the bunk beds, pulled the letter out of my satchel, and looked at it again. Only a few of my close friends knew how fearful I had been about the prospect of Vietnam. We seldom discussed fear, perhaps because refraining from such discussions seemed to be part of the rite of becoming a man. I just knew that I wanted to live to become a man, and I kept quiet when members of the group loudly discussed how they would handle a deadly situation. I would watch in silence as they pretended to crouch in foxholes, crawl through jungle brush, or wade through rice paddies with their imaginary weapons held high above their heads. Even though I was part of them, I never felt as "ready" for battle as they appeared to be. And I never felt I had the character and skills required to be the kind of soldier who could kill so as not to be killed. Fear had caused me to enlist to escape the draft, and I surprised myself when I not only made it through basic training but also made it with honors. However, once in, I still lived with the prospect of my being reassigned to a remote supply post in Southeast Asia. Now that prospect had itself become remote with this new assignment—an assignment I almost hadn't applied for.

Like the rest of the guys, I daily watched the bulletin board, praying not to see my name. I never dreamed that I would find there a notice that would save my life. The bulletin board was always surrounded at the end of the day, and Orell Clay, an airman from New York, was always there, his body blocking our view. Since he was big and mouthy, I felt it best to give him room, although some of the guys would elbow him aside. On the day I found my notice, I waited while Orell and Fred Crowly, his white roommate from Rhode Island, looked at every piece of posted information. When at last they left, I moved to the spot they had vacated and was relieved to see that there was no word of any need for additional troops in Vietnam. Just as I was about to walk away and join my friends at the mess hall, a small bulletin from Strategic Air Command (SAC) headquarters in Nebraska caught my eye. A new slot, a classified position, had opened at Andrews Air Force Base in Washington, D.C. Reading more closely, I realized that the job description fell under my air force classification. AF 17697936 was administrative supply, and they needed someone with my skills. For a brief moment, I fantasized that I could win this post, but I was also sure that I had no chance. Although the military was more integrated than any place I had ever seen, I somehow felt that this job would go to a white airman. I didn't want to apply only to be disappointed, but I wrote down the information anyway, and tucked it in my pocket as I walked from the barracks to the mess hall.

10 That night, I reconsidered. Maybe I did have a chance. After all, back home in Glen Allen I had applied and had been hired for a job in Mr. Hilton's grocery store that had historically been reserved for white boys. Believing that just maybe I could do it again, I completed the form requested and mailed it in. I told no one, not even my closest friends. I then planned to forget the exercise. I knew that thousands of airmen just like me would have read the same announcement and would be thinking, as I was, that this assignment could limit their chances of being shipped off to Vietnam. I returned to my routine of shipping aircraft parts from base to base and to my continuing fear of Vietnam. Days stretched into weeks, and weeks into months, and Dow Air Force Base was beginning to feel more like home than I wanted.

Home for me would always be Glen Allen, and it felt strange to find myself becoming comfortable in a place where the snow fell as frequently as rain. The Mississippi Delta was my home, and I wanted to live so that I could return to the house built by my great-grandfather Sidney Peter. Grandpa had come from Demopolis, Alabama, to the Delta, where he encountered other "colored" who had migrated from Natchez, from Louisiana, and from as far away as South Carolina. Only one generation removed from slavery, these people had held on to their dreams and had built their homes to give place to them. The front porches became the place where visiting relatives from up north would sit and spin their intoxicating tales of northern life. And as long as I can remember, the tales were told each summer. And I remembered them all.

Legal segregation kept the wonderful older people, on whose porches we sat, from using official meeting places such as the library and the community room at the town's clinic, but they seemed not to have cared. Their front porches became their centers of command, from which they welcomed us into a world and a life that had barely changed since the early days of Jim Crow, the system that evolved once slavery stopped.

Like many small towns throughout the south, ours was a cotton community whose social order set the course for both white and colored babies. Miss Lottie, the town's colored midwife, brought me into the world, a world that had already relegated me to an inferior position, but one that could not negate the welcome I felt as a child growing up in the big house with the long front porch. During my years in this rambling wooden house infused with hopes, I started school and began my youthful dreaming.

Glen Allen was a safe place to dream. Although we lived day to day with the harshness of the Jim Crow laws and the limitations imposed by legal segregation, the elders in our community still managed to instill in us the will to live, work hard, and study long because they believed that tomorrow was always the brightest day. They understood the necessity to leave home and do well, but they expected you to return. This safe, predictable world would one day pass into history. But as I grew, I had the benefit of three generations of wisdom, wisdom that years later would serve me well as I was finding my own way.

As I approached my seventeenth birthday in 1963, I found myself preparing to leave for my first train ride and my journey north. St. Louis was my destination. I would live there, get a job, go to school, and return home to Glen Allen every summer, just as my idols, Uncle William Henry and Aunt Dora, from Chicago, and other relatives had done before me. It was a grand plan: the train ride north, the colored porter, and the bright city lights and paved streets. But it was not to be. Immersed in my own dreaming, I hadn't paid close attention to the outside world and the changes taking place. At home in the Delta, I was insulated by fields of cotton and by those who picked it, by lakes of brim and catfish and those who caught them. No one had pulled me aside to tell me about the civil rights movement or the other delta, so far away in Vietnam. They left me to my chopping and picking cotton and dreaming on my own. Little did I know that the fantasy world up north I had created in my mind while working Miss Jefferson's fields would one day be derailed by the reality of war and a social revolution.

The unraveling began after I arrived in St. Louis, where I lived in a small room over a small store, in a city I had dreamed about but barely knew. Suddenly I found myself on my own, hundreds of miles away from the people who knew me best. Even though my natural father had paid for my ticket to St. Louis, I really did not know him. He had left the Delta as a young man, gone north, and created a new life for himself. I had been excited over the prospect of a relationship with him, but it never materialized as I had hoped. I don't question his joy in seeing me, but I soon learned that his life in St. Louis had little room for me. He had arranged for me to stay with relatives I had never met. For the first time in my life I found myself acting, thinking, and doing on my own.

At night, while sharing my small room with a younger cousin, I tried to sort out my feelings. Would I be able to find a good job? I had been led to believe that color was not a factor here, only skills, and I knew that I was skilled. After all, I had been given a white boy's job back home and had graduated as valedictorian of my small high school class. But the long-promised good life with the good job, where whites and blacks lived and worked together, was fraught with complexities that I hadn't understood. Still, I was determined to press forward in spite of all that wasn't there, to dig deep beneath that reality and to find a way to make my dreams come true.

For about a year, things went well enough. I was becoming a northerner. I had started school at the St. Louis branch of the American Institute of Banking and had almost lost my southern accent, a sure sign that I was becoming one of those who would one day return south to visit in the summer. However, as I moved toward social acculturation, the reality of a military conflict expanding into war invaded the world I knew. America was sending thousands of young men, mostly black, to Vietnam. I watched them leave St. Louis in the prime of their life, never to return. As the war wore on, I was sure that one day I would be drafted, too, and I was scared. Having just begun to live, I didn't want to die. But I was black, and it seemed as if black soldiers formed the ranks of the front line in Vietnam.

Although I had friends, I had no one to counsel me, not even my father, but I had grown up more than I realized as I faced the prospect of being drafted. In the quietness of my heart, a heart shaped in the Delta, I decided to enlist in the air force to escape an army draft and possible death in Vietnam. No one knew better than I that I was not guntoting soldier material. Though handling guns was a way of life in the South, I couldn't shoot straight and had never killed, bagged, or skinned anything. In light of what I knew, the air force seemed like the best place for me. And it was. Again, I boarded a train, this time the Texas Lone Star to San Antonio, where I started basic training. With a shaved head, five sets of white boxer shorts, and uniforms that didn't fit properly, I became an airman in August 1964.

Basic training was different. Unlike Glen Allen and even St. Louis, there were no nurturing front porches and caring people to hold my hand, just a stranger neatly dressed in a starched uniform and dark glasses, a drill sergeant who asked no questions and expected none. He only barked orders. However, with the help of such friends as Jerry Williams, James Rinderknect, and Airman Canty, I actually managed to adapt to the new and challenging world of "orders." We learned to march to them all. Too afraid to mess up, I did my best in basic training and even later became a junior barracks leader while in technical school in Amarillo, Texas. Still young and afraid, I was slowly becoming a soldier. Most of the men were as apprehensive as I was, although we all tried not to show it. We had started to learn that the military was there to make men out of us, not to deal with our idealistic views and youthful fears.

Amarillo was indeed a detour for me. I had dreamed only of going north to live, not of becoming a soldier in Texas, sitting in a barracks worrying about my orders. When my permanent orders came, I was relieved. My fate was not as bad as I had imagined. Some of the guys who seemed to have connections had found themselves with orders to Florida, but for Kenneth Cone, James Rinderknect, and me, it was the cold Northeast, a cause for sober thankfulness, if not for jubilation. We were going not to Vietnam but to Dow Air Force Base in Maine.

At first I dreaded the assignment, the remoteness of it and the chilling prospect that I could still be sent at any time to Vietnam. As the war continued and the numbers of dead and wounded increased, I began to accept that being cold and isolated was better than being warm and wounded. After making up my mind to give Dow my best shot, it wasn't long before I began to feel like the others, just doing my job, biding my time, and waiting for orders that I hoped would never come.

Sometime after I applied for the classified position, a letter came, telling me that I was among the ones selected for a background investigation. If it proved positive, I would be given orders for reassignment to Washington, D.C. I had never been investigated before and had no idea what it entailed. The letter contained a questionnaire. I was to provide information about the people I knew and the places I had lived. I carefully answered each question, wondering all the time if this was really happening to me. Maybe my porch people were right, and tomorrow was the brightest day. I didn't want to tell my friends until the investigation was complete and I had an official answer. My heart held a secret that I wanted to share, but I kept it close to me.

Without being specific, I asked Sgt. Brown, a seasoned airman, to explain to me what a classified background investigation included. When he asked why, I held him off, but I was still able to get him to tell me what I needed to know. As he talked, I realized that investigators would go to both Glen Allen and St. Louis. What a stir this would be for Glen Allen. It was so small that all news traveled fast, and this type of news would travel even faster than most.

25 The investigators would get all the information needed and then some if they happened to run into Miss Doll, our lady who everyone agreed was "tetched" in the head. She always seemed to intercept strangers who came looking for information from the colored side of the town. I had written down the names of my mother, Mary Taulbert, my aunt, Elna Boose, and Rev. McBeth, the colored principal. But if Miss Doll saw a strange car driving slowly, she would walk right up as close as she could and lean in the window. "I'm Louise Morris, pleased to make your acquaintance. New in town, I s'pose." I dreaded to think what she might dream up to tell them in her odd, rambling way. In St. Louis, I had provided the names of Madison Brazier and Oscar Guyton Sr., in whose homes I had stayed during my short time there.

In Glen Allen, the investigators would hear the story of my birth and meet the people who had welcomed me into the world. They would see that I had been among the fortunate ones to have been born in a town where caring had long been a way of life. Despite all hardships, I grew up being loved and learning from those who loved me, people who took their leisure on front porches, where they entertained us, nurtured us, and spoke the secrets of their hearts.

The investigators would learn all of this and more. They would learn about my aptitude as a student, which led to my being named valedictorian of my class. They would learn about my hard work not only in the fields but also in the local hardware store, owned by Mr. Freid, who had me assist him with his yearly inventory, and later in Mr. Hilton's grocery store. And they would learn about the life dreams that brought me to St. Louis and the confectionery at 2629 North Spring Avenue, where Uncle Madison ruled and reigned.

Uncle Madison and Mr. Guyton would tell them about my life in St. Louis, how I took on extra responsibility in my work at the confectionery, and how Jefferson Bank hired me at a time when there were no blacks in meaningful positions. They would learn how the civil rights activists protested the bank's hiring practices and how, after many demonstrations by young black St. Louisians, I was the one who was hired. Both men were proud of that and shared the story as if it were their own.

Dow Air Force Base was a long way from either Glen Allen or St. Louis, but in those two places lived the people who would help determine my chances to get that classified assignment. And now all I had to do was wait.

30 AFTER THE LAST WEEKS OF FALL HAD FADED and the new year had begun, the private wait was over. I held the official letter that said "Congratulations," and now I could tell my friends. I was going to Washington, D.C., to work in the Eighty-ninth Presidential Wing at Andrews Air Force Base. The people at SAC headquarters had called me a "bright boy," which I took to be a compliment. Of course it could also have been military code suggesting that I was a good risk for this new assignment because the investigation into

my past had turned up no evidence of past activities that would have proven to be an embarrassment to the government. But I would never know if their meaning was different from what I took it to be. I had always been told by the old people back home that I had "mother wit," by which they meant the natural ability to make a path for myself, and an old preacher from the colony, the all-black settlement just south of Glen Allen, had once told Poppa that I was marked for good. Thus I assumed that in calling me a "bright boy" the background investigators had made a similar determination about me.

Delighted as I was, I now began to think about the challenges I would face as a new airman. I wanted the job, but because I hadn't thought I'd get it, I had paid very little attention to the skill requirements. I was now apprehensive about my technical ability to do the job. Still, no matter my feelings, I had my orders. They were expecting me at the Eighty-ninth.

While I embraced my new assignment, I also felt a bit of remorse knowing that I'd be leaving Dow. During my last few weeks, as I walked to and from my barracks, a fading green cinderblock two-story building, I fixed in my mind a picture I didn't want to forget. Amid the weekday quiet, I stood at the foot of the fire escape, our entry to the barracks. On weekends in good weather, that fire escape came to life. It was our gathering place, where we yelled at each other, cut hair, and forgot the war. Like the stoops of New York, the verandahs of New Orleans, and even the porches of the Mississippi Delta, it was a small reminder of home, where we were welcomed and visited with friends. There, dates were made and broken, cars were borrowed, and the war was put on hold. In warm weather, we dressed in jeans, cut-offs, and white tee-shirts, our dog tags the only reminders of our military life. As I stood there in the quiet, I pictured all my friends, those of different races and from vastly different social backgrounds, gathering, leaning over the railings, sitting on the steps with the end doors of the barracks propped open wide so that we could all hear the music, our voices mingling in the air like a well-cooked gumbo.

Even though most of us were thankful that we had not been sent to Vietnam, on nights when we sat on the fire escape, we also wished that we were somewhere else, preferably in a city. Getting a good assignment at a base that was close to a city with a great night life was the dream of all the airmen I had come to know, but for most of us, those bases and their cities would always be somewhere else. When the word of my new assignment got around, they were all delighted for me. I was lucky, they said. I had my orders, and they wished me well.

I had only a few weeks left, but for the most part I was gone. My room on the second floor of the barracks would soon house another guy. I hoped that he would appreciate how well I had kept his side. I had put so much wax on the floor that all my replacement would have to do was just hit it softly with a buffer and the barracks sergeant would be pleased. Although our world was focused on the war, we still had to polish those floors, tighten those green blankets, and spit shine everything that didn't move. Often I felt this was a waste of time, but I was assured that obedience to such orders was essential preparation for combat, where commands had to be followed without question if you wanted to stay alive.

35 Excitement and apprehension about my Washington assignment pulled me on. I had never been to the District of Columbia, but the media had brought Washington to me.

I was a little fearful of going there, yet I wanted to experience all it had to offer a young man not long removed from the Delta, where life, it had seemed, would never change. Now, as I readied myself for my new life, I knew that the South was changing as well, as the civil rights movement penetrated ever more deeply the world behind the cotton curtains.

When the day to leave Dow came, I was packed and ready early. Since I didn't have a car, I asked John Palozzi to drive me to the airport. We had become good friends, sharing great conversations and good Italian food. John lived in a barracks close to mine. When he arrived, with a little help from my roommate, we got my duffel bag and suitcases down the hall and down the fire escape.

Although we arrived at the Bangor airport early, the waiting room was full. I knew some of the airmen, and I could tell by their faces and snatches of their conversations that they had not been as lucky as I had been. We didn't talk. There was little to say. During those days, airports were not always the places of pleasure travel that we wanted them to be; they took us to our duty, a duty that we knew could claim our lives. John waited with me until it was time to check in, and seemingly within minutes I found myself on board, buckled in, and flying into my future.

While sitting quietly in the plane, I found myself both looking out and looking back. Much had happened in my life since I left the Mississippi Delta. I was no longer the innocent, dreaming boy who loved his great-grandfather's 1949 Buick, frozen custard ice cream, and hot French bread. The reality of becoming a soldier was maturing me, and my fear of Vietnam made me value the life I had. While stationed at Dow, I had seen scores of airmen shipped off to a war they barely understood, to fight a people they hardly knew. We had been told that they were going to ensure democracy, even though it was not fully realized here at home. As a child, I hadn't had to worry about such issues as democracy denied, because Poppa and my family had protected me as long as they could, but now I was out and on my own.

As my plane approached Washington National Airport, I could see the Potomac shining below. I also caught my first glimpses of monuments I had only read about or seen in pictures. It was as though they were moving up to greet me. The plane moved in closer, and people all around me exclaimed at the sight of the Pentagon and the Washington Monument. Fathers and mothers pointed out the sights to their children, and I eagerly listened and craned my neck to see what they were seeing. I really was in Washington, and I tried desperately to catch sight of the Lincoln Memorial and the reflecting pool, which, after Dr. King's historic 1963 march, had come to symbolize the freedom that my people cherished.

Years earlier, I had left Glen Allen, Mississippi, loaded with dreams, my family's, our friends', and my own. Fueled by those innocent dreams, I went north, where reality led me into the military. Although I had not anticipated taking that path, I accepted the challenges of military life. The small fears that fluttered in my stomach would fade. Tomorrow would be all right. Poppa had always promised me that. In spite of the struggles that Poppa and his friends endured, they always looked forward to the next day. They had experienced more fear and anxiety than I had ever known and still managed to nurture and shield us. They didn't become selfish or cease their dreaming. They embraced the future, and so would I. And if my background had caused me to be classified as a "bright boy," I knew it was because of them.

Exploring Texts and Contexts

For activities with icons, refer to the Guide to Analyzing Readings in Context.

1. Consider the title of this chapter of Taulbert's memoir, "Bright Boy from the Delta." Also consider the title of the memoir as a whole, *Watching Our Crops Come In*. What do these titles tell you about how the author has shaped his memoir? How do they help focus your reading and understanding of the material? If you were to choose different titles, what would they be? Language
2. Taulbert never mentions the raging protests about Vietnam but focuses instead on his personal fear of war and his desire to stay alive. Neither does he say very much about the civil rights movement. Consider how Taulbert defines the contexts that shaped him. How does Taulbert see himself in relation to others? How does he respond to the larger social currents he finds himself in? (For more information about the Vietnam War and the public debate around it and a monument dedicated to the soldiers who lost their lives, see the case study in Chapter 9, "Designing Memorials.") Situation
3. Throughout this chapter of Taulbert's memoir, he moves back and forth between the ever-present possibility of being sent to Vietnam and his memories of his upbringing in Glen Allen. Trace this process and think about how it works to create a picture of the present shaped by the past.

Creating Texts

For activities with icons, refer to the Guides to Analyzing Contexts for Writing and Analyzing Readings in Context. For additional help with these writing projects, read the descriptions of **Essay, Cover Letter/Reflective Essay,** and **Advice Book/Article** in the Genre Glossary.

1. Taulbert's personal story has particular impact and significance because of the background of the civil rights movement and the Vietnam War against which the events of his life took place. Think of an event or set of events from your own life that took place against the background of an important historical event, for example the attack on the World Trade Center and Pentagon or the war in Iraq. Using Taulbert's excerpt as a model, write an essay in which you set a narrative about your own life against the background of larger historical events and discuss how your life reflected or was influenced by them. Situation
2. Taulbert concludes this first chapter of his memoir by looking to the past as well as the future, "Tomorrow would be all right. Poppa had always promised me that. In spite of the struggles that Poppa and his friends endured, they always looked forward to the next day" (203). Taulbert claims that the lessons he learned in Glen Allen offer a key to living in a diverse world. Consider your own experiences and write a section of an advice book in which you tell your audience Genre

what lessons you have learned and how they can be used in today's diverse communities. In addition, write a cover letter about your experience of writing in this genre and what you learned from it.

The Triumph of Burbopolis

Michael Pollan

Michael Pollan writes of his return to the Long Island suburb of his childhood, wistfully taking us down memory lane to find his old house at the intersection of Juneau and Fairbanks Boulevards. He ruefully pokes fun at his younger self—his yearning to be anywhere but in the suburbs, his desire to solo on the Long Island Railroad, and his petty larceny in the pumpkin fields—all the while subtly drawing us into an analysis of how the suburbs have changed over the last 30 years. Lives are no longer centripetal, he explains, drawn to Manhattan's light and energy. But how this energy has changed is not quite clear. Searching for words, Pollan comes up with the attention-getting "Burbopolis" to signal the intermingling of suburb and city, but he only hints at what this will mean for our lifestyles, our jobs, our friends, and our connection with the places we live.

For Pollan, a sense of place is paramount. His recent book, *A Place of My Own: The Education of an Amateur Builder,* published in 1998, chronicles his attempt, having never fixed or built anything in his life, to construct with his own hands a writing hut on the grounds behind his home. Rather than observing residential change from the outside, he contemplates architecture from the inside out with hammer and nails and a first-aid kit at the ready. Pollan has for many years, even before he had a room of his own, written on gardening, nature, and the environment for a wide variety of periodicals including *House and Garden, The New York Times Magazine,* and *Harper's Magazine.*

Connecting with the Conversation

1. If you moved during your childhood and can return to your past residence, visit it and see whether it has changed in any way. Or ask relatives, parents, or older friends about places they've lived before, whether they've been back for any reason, and what they found or would expect to find. Or consider where you might like to live if the usual obstacles to moving did not exist. Write in your journal about these real or imagined changes of residence.
2. Watch reruns of family sitcoms set in the suburban fifties, such as "Leave it to Beaver" or "Father Knows Best" or recent movies, such as *American Beauty,* that use suburbia as a backdrop. What generalizations run through these representations of life in the suburbs? Which seem accurate and which seem exaggerated? Write in your journal about what you have observed.

I grew up in a pretty nice subdivision on Long Island, but try as I might to kindle some spark of nostalgia for "the Gates of Woodbury," the gravitational pull of the place is almost nil. It has been nearly 30 years since I left, and at least until a couple of months ago, I could think of no reason to go back: no people to see (everybody I knew had also left), no curiosity to satisfy. In my imagination Juneau Boulevard is the same as it ever was, except maybe for the cars and the people, which I assume have been regularly updated. Isn't that the way it has always been in the burbs—change without history? More of the same?

A *lot* more of the same, it's true: since I left Long Island in the '70s, resolving henceforth to live somewhere more in the middle of things, more real, the suburbs have quietly and steadily expanded. And then the day came, a few years ago, when I read in the paper that for the first time in history a majority of Americans now lived in the suburbs. America had officially become "a suburban nation"—which sounded to me like one of those utterly weightless demographic truths, empirically verifiable, but without any real echo in experience. For wasn't this really just a change in quantity, not kind? The relative size of middle and fringe may have shifted, but surely not their relative weight.

At least this is what I assumed. It's only recently that I've felt any compulsion to go back to Woodbury to test my assumptions, and that was mostly because I needed a place to set this essay. What I found when I got there was a good bit more than that. What I found looks a lot like a whole new country—or at least a place for which "suburb" is no longer quite the right word.

From the time I was 5 until I got out of high school I lived in the Gates near the corner of Juneau and Fairbanks Boulevards. In all that time, I never really noticed just how goofily dissonant those names are, with their improbable conjunction of Yukon pluck and Old World prissiness. Yet these place names, and the conflicting dreams they embody, tell you just about all you need to know about the place and the time.

5 The development went in on the site of an old North Shore estate that had been subdivided into acre lots during the Suburban Revolution; the developer decided to preserve the wrought-iron entrance gates to give a bit of aristocratic tone to his shiny middle-class development. As for the whole Yukon theme, ground was broken in 1960, soon after Alaska had become a state, and the Gates fashioned itself a forward-looking, even pioneerish kind of place. At the time Woodbury was on the suburban frontier, still mostly farm fields and forest, and the Gates aimed to distinguish itself from the cookie-cutter subdivisions then spreading out across Long Island.

In the same way the suburbs began as a reaction against city life, each new incarnation of suburbia has defined itself in opposition to some earlier, superseded ideal: middle-class utopias keeping one step ahead of history. In the beginning the suburban frontier stood in places like Brooklyn Heights, first made accessible by steam ferry in 1814, but the city quickly followed, folding Brooklyn's row houses into its expanding grid. To prevent that kind of thing from happening again, the next new place (epitomized by Llewellyn Park, built in New Jersey in 1853, and Riverside, built near Chicago in 1868) was carefully planned to keep the city permanently at bay. It would

---

From *The New York Times Magazine,* April 9, 2000, pp. 51–55.

be an ungridded community of free-standing houses in a park, linked to the distant city by trolley or train. Then, beginning in the 1920's, the 19th-century railroad suburb was superseded by more far-flung subdivisions organized around the automobile and, after the war, the mass-production house pioneered by the Levitts.

By 1960, when my parents went house hunting on Long Island, Levittown was passé, and the next new place—the un-Levittown—promised to be the Gates of Woodbury, where the lots were generally a sprawling acre. Instead of identical houses lined up like sparrows on a wire, the developer offered three up-to-date models (ranch, split-level, and colonial), laid out his roads in sweeping, pointless curves and sited the houses so far back on their wooded acres that each appeared lost in a reverie of being a mansion. (Sometimes I think this is what is really meant by a "dream house": the recumbent ranches dreaming of California, the colonnaded white colonials dreaming of Tara.) But if the Alaska angle implied the pastless potential of the next great American place, what was with those prissy "boulevards" and "drives," all those "ways" and "terraces" and, for the cul-de-sacs, "courts"? Understand that in the suburbs a developer will go to heroic lengths not to call a street a street. Street says city, and city is precisely the last thing you want to say. Whereas boulevard said fancy, said *sophisticated,* and if this effeteness jangled alongside muscular Alaska, that evidently didn't bother the developer or his buyers.

Finding your way back to your suburban childhood home is harder than you might think. I didn't know anyone who still lived in the Gates—my folks moved out in 1972, and most of their neighbors had headed down to Florida the minute the kids left for college, there to recreate a grayer, warmer Gates in Boca Raton. (One thing the burbs have done to America is to recast its geography along purely demographic lines.) To find out who lived in my old house, I had to send it a letter, addressed to "current resident." (In quotes, to make sure it didn't get tossed.) "Current resident" turned out to be Stephen and Jena Hall, and they graciously invited me to visit. Since I didn't know anybody to stay with, "going home" to Woodbury meant spending the night in a $79 room in the Executive Inn on Jericho Turnpike, the main commercial strip.

My first impression of Woodbury, after rolling off the expressway onto Jericho Turnpike, was disorientation. Every landmark on my mental map of the area had been stripped and replaced by a big-box retailer, such that it took me the better part of two days to locate my junior high school, its unmarked turn off Jericho having been swallowed up by superstores. I noticed that the brands were all high-end, the kind my mother had had to drive all the way to Manhattan for.

10 Actually the brands should have been my tip-off that this was not the same place I left, that it had a completely different relationship to Manhattan. But I didn't put that together until I turned onto Woodbury Road, passed a bunch of newer developments (including the Woodbury Estates and the almost completely flat Rolling Hills) and made the left onto Froehlich Farm Boulevard. Whenever "farm" (or "forest," or "fairground" or anything venerably rural) is honored in a suburban place name, you can bet the thing is history, and such was emphatically the case with the old Froehlich farm.

The pumpkin field to which Charlie DeSalvo and I used to drag our wagons each fall for the purpose of committing petty larceny had sprouted a half-dozen smoked-glass office buildings, blocky islands in a glittering sea of really nice cars. Gateways Executive Mall, the sign said (I half-expected to see “of Froehlich Farm”), and it listed a phalanx of law firms, insurance companies, medical practices, banks and high-tech firms. Each of those really nice cars represented at least one really good white-collar job, and there must have been a thousand of them right here, smack in the middle of the pumpkin field that backed up against Fairbanks Boulevard.

“THE CITY”: WE LED CENTRIPETAL LIVES IN those days, our heads bent toward Manhattan as if it were the sun. Which in some sense it was, the city being the source not only of all money but also of entertainment and information and—what was especially important to us as teenagers—*authenticity.* The suburbs, we believed, were fake; after all, we had watched them rise like stage sets on the farm fields, seen the instantaneous lawns rolled out over the raw dirt like new linoleum. This creation of a new life ex nihilo was of course exactly what our parents liked about the place, but what was to them a blank canvas was to us an existential void. Nothing was original except, well, except us and these childhoods we were having—a thought disturbing enough to make us wonder if those were somehow fake, too, “sub” to something realer.

Like lots of other dads in the Gates, mine commuted to a job in the real world every day, leaving the house before I woke up and rarely getting home before the dinner dishes had been cleared. Only a few of the moms had jobs, but they'd dress up and drive in a couple of times a month, to shop, catch a matinee, meet the dads for a fancy dinner and a “first run” movie.

Even before kids were old enough to solo on the L.I.R.R., we looked to the city as the source of our styles and shows and news, an all-powerful broadcast antenna to whose frequency we always tried to stay tuned. Tuesday nights Cousin Brucie handed down the Top 40 from Midtown Manhattan, and by Wednesday morning the Sam Goody at the Walt Whitman Mall would have rearranged its shelves accordingly. Later on, the more time you spent in the city, the cooler you were, because you had personally bathed in coolness's headwaters, at the Fillmore East, say, or the Thalia, or the Eighth Street Bookshop.

15 It doesn't seem as though Long Island's cultural and economic antennas point west in quite the same way anymore. Oh, sure, the Long Island Expressway still creeps every morning, but often now it's creeping in both directions, and a lot of those cars are heading to places like the Gateways Executive Mall (Exit 45), rather than to Manhattan. The retail, which once helped light up the city in suburban eyes, is no longer any different: the Walt Whitman shopping area is now basically Lexington Avenue and 59th Street—Gap, Banana Republic, Nine West, Barnes & Noble, J. Crew and Tower Records, all anchored by a Bloomingdale's. But whether this represents the colonization of the suburbs by the city or the opposite is a question.

Radio and network TV still originate in Manhattan, but the newer media have traded broadcasting's radiating waves for centerless webs of wire. Who can say where in the world cable TV comes from? (A lot of it from Long Island, actually: Cablevision's headquarters happen to be in Bethpage.) And the Internet? America Online, perhaps the first great suburban medium, originates somewhere in suburban Virginia, though like the rest of the Web it might as well be anywhere.

One way to tell the story of the American suburbs is as a story of new technologies recasting the relationship of city and countryside. Electric power, trains, automobiles and broadcast television propelled successive waves of decentralization, each along slightly different lines. Until now, however, the pattern those lines formed always resembled the spokes of a wheel, with the city firmly in the center. Radiating highways and radio waves used to reinforce the gravitational pull of cities. But cable and computer networks are forming different patterns now, ones that mirror and speed the emergence of the burbs as free-floating entities with their own overlapping gravitational fields.

TIME HAS BEEN KIND TO MANY OF THE SUBURBS, and Juneau Boulevard is much prettier than I remember it. The conehead evergreens and midget rhododendrons, the paper birches and forsythia—all that dinky nursery stock plunked into backfill by landscapers—have put down roots and grown up to reclaim half-forgotten woodland identities, picturesquely blurring the new developments' blunter edges. By now many of the trees have grown tall enough to cast interesting shadows. The American suburb was conceived in the 19th century by visionary designers like Frederick Law Olmsted, Calvert Vaux and Andrew Jackson Downing to offer Americans a kind of democratically subdivided park, and the nicer ones are actually beginning to look that way.

Modest by comparison to what's built today, the '60s ranches and split-levels in the Gates have mellowed into period pieces: this is the architecture of postwar dreams that, at least from the vantage of a new century, no longer seem grasping or pretentious so much as sweet, even poignant. For this they probably have the newer houses to thank: the fat, bombastic three-story mini-mansions that now dot the Gates, many of them rising from the foundations of tear-downs.

20 Happily, the ranch on Juneau Boulevard hasn't been a tear-down—though I was astonished to find at the far end of the driveway a hulking two-story post-modern building, a design studio perched atop a three-car garage. Jena Hall is a successful home-furnishings designer, and she has employed as many as eight people at a time here. On the exact spot where Binker, my problematic English bulldog, snored her days away in a chain-link dog run, people now come to work.

Jena Hall's home business helped me see that the suburbs have proved to be rather more adaptable to changing lives and times than people once thought. The whole idea behind the suburbs was to draw bright lines and make separations: between city and country, obviously, but also between work and home, public and private. But it turns out we overestimated the power of architectural determinism. The suburbs have proved flexible enough to accommodate working mothers (though not without difficulty: Jena Hall's studio was usually crawling with toddlers, hers and her employees') as well as a great many different kinds of families and lifestyles. Since I left the Gates, its white nuclear families have been joined by singles and gays, Asians and African-Americans, people operating home businesses and empty-nesters. The houses themselves—light, wood-frame—turned out to be as easy to remodel as they had been to build. The world that built the postwar suburbs has passed away, and yet those suburbs still stand, remodeled by the press of history. What they haven't been is reimagined or renamed, at least not yet.

When I was growing up in the Gates, suburban legend had it that one of the big white colonials on Bering Court had served as the model for Ward and June Cleaver's house on TV. They showed the façade at the beginning of every episode, and it certainly looked right. Whether this was true or not (for all I know, every suburb in America nursed the same legend), we all wanted to believe it. Sometimes we regarded Hollywood's notice as flattery, since being on TV made the Gates seem more real and substantial (fiction will do that); other times the fame seemed like the grimmest of jokes, weekly proof of the empty pretensions of the place.

Cleaverism—the sitcom image of suburbia—loomed large in our suburban lives, though its meanings were always complex and unstable. The Cleavers, Ozzie and Harriet, Donna Reed and all the rest proposed an ideal of suburban life that everyone knew was unrealistic and silly; and yet even as we made fun of it, we allowed the stereotype to exert a kind of normative hold on us. Your own family might be hopelessly dysfunctional, but maybe the Grables next door were getting it right. TV was happy to promote the Cleaver ideal because TV (alone among the arts) loved the burbs, and was eager to flatter what was, naturally, its ideal audience. Here were people marooned at home for much of the day, affluent and consumerist by inclination (having already purchased a new lifestyle), and at least at the start, insecure enough about the conduct of their new lifestyles to welcome the guidance of advertisers.

But what's remarkable is how Cleaverism continues to organize so much of our thinking about suburbia. Now, though, it's the lie of Cleaverism—call it Cheeverism—that dominates the popular image, offering writers and moviemakers a cheap way to construct a gothic version of suburbia, to throw its dark side into sharp relief. Now behind every smiling lawn is a dysfunctional family: Donna Reed's sleeping with the woman next door and Eddie Haskell's got a gun.

25 Yet the façade remains the organizing principle; in defiance of everything we know, we can't seem to see the suburbs without it. Without the ghosts of the Cleavers hovering over them, the families in "American Beauty," say, or of any number of recent suburban-gothic productions, just don't make a whole lot of sense.

Before I left the Gates I drove into Bering Court to see if I could find the Beav's old place. If I had the right one, the house has had a complete face lift since the '60s. The stately white faux-colonial now has diagonal siding painted an unfortunate shade of puce, lots of opaque glass bricks and, out front, a berm thickly planted with shrubs to hide the facade. Very '80s, it seemed, but for the life of me I could not name the dream behind this house.

It's hard to spend time driving around Long Island today without a gathering sense of cognitive dissonance. So many of our generalizations about the burbs no longer stick, which almost seems a shame, since generalization was one of the things that we liked best about them. Is it even right to call a place like Woodbury—no longer "sub" to any "urb"—a "suburb" any more? "Urban sprawl" might be a better term. Certainly "sprawl" hints at the centerlessness of it, "urban" at the fact there's nothing in the city you can't find here. And maybe, as some have suggested, that is what I'm looking at but can't quite yet see: a new kind of city, one we still don't have the words or name for. "Edge City" is one proposal, though that still implies a center. "Technoburb," another, hints at the role technology has played in freeing these place from their urban orbits, but it's awfully cold. How about something more floppy-effervescent, like "burbopolis"?

Whatever it ultimately gets called, the horizontal city that is now Nassau County, Long Island, is fast acquiring a city's jangly diversity, though, being horizontal, it takes a car to really see it. Freeport has its African-American neighborhoods and Great Neck a community of Persians, and even in my very white elementary school you see Indian and Asian faces now. Street culture, of all things, has come to certain suburban lanes: in Glen Cove, Central American immigrants collect on corners and in front yards, talking and playing music as if they were still in Guatemala City. (The village issued a flier gently instructing them in suburban custom.) The new city has city problems too: housing shortages, crime waves, pollution; dilapidated "first ring" suburbs are said to be in the throes of a full-fledged "urban crisis."

Though even here the generalizations don't hold. Before I left Long Island I took a long walk through Levittown, where the suburban history of Long Island got its start half a century ago. A first-ring suburb built fast and on the cheap, Levittown by all rights should be crumbling by now. Yet the place I visited appeared to be doing just fine, in defiance of every stereotype that has been thrown at it. Held up as an example of conformity and monotony, Levittown's 17,000 identical capes have mutated into an exuberant architectural Babel: the sparrows on a wire have each grown their own distinctive plumage.

Yet this free-for-all of Home Depot fantasy is held together nicely by the steady setback line of the houses and the mature shade trees marching down the gridded streets. Even more surprising, though, was the sidewalk scene, which even in late winter was about as lively as a New Urbanist could wish for, the young mothers out with their strollers, the kids biking home from school, the gray-haired joggers doing the loop in slo-mo. By the time I got back in my car, I felt completely confused about where, exactly, it was I'd been.

The monolith that was supposed to be suburban America—middle class, homogenous, white—has become just one of a great many neighborhoods in a larger and more complicated mosaic. So why is this new suburbia so hard to see plain, without the filter of suburban cliché? Maybe it's because we've lost our old vantage point.

When my parents moved to the Gates in 1960, one-third of America was suburb, one-third city, one-third rural. Even those of us who lived in the first third tended to look at it from the perspective of the second. The city still held what amounted to a monopoly on descriptions and, for obvious reasons, the city didn't much like what it saw rising up around it.

Forty years later, the suburbs—or whatever they are—have grown up and taken over: more people now live in suburban American than rural and urban America combined. Suburbia *is* America, and not just demographically. Today our politics are ruled by the suburbs; suburbia's agenda—that is, issues bearing on the well-being of families with children, around which the suburbs still revolve—is now America's. (Even the erstwhile party of the city has moved to the burbs, with Bill Clinton doing the driving.) Suburbia's cultural power is harder to see, but that may be because it's everywhere, indistinguishable from the air we breathe.

On the drive back to the country, where I live now, or where at least I *think* I live, I thought about the various ways suburban qualities have seeped beyond the burbs themselves. I thought about the suburbanization of the city, manifest in freshly themed neighborhoods and malled retailing, and I thought about Silicon Valley, which in some ways represents the apotheosis of suburbia: the first time in history an important economic, technological and cultural revolution has its roots in a suburb.

I also thought about manners. Ever since Levittown was built America has become a progressively more informal place, one where social distinctions get played down, where even the rich and famous feel compelled at least to act like normal suburbanites, and where hierarchical distinctions like high- and low-brow—which are fundamentally urban distinctions—come to seem quaint. Suburbia's too horizontal a place for all that.

I thought about clothes too. I usually wear a tie and sport jacket when I'm reporting, but not on this trip. Suburbanites dress up only to go to the city, a place where the presentation of self is far more serious business. That's probably because all you really have to present in the city is yourself in public, dressed this way or that. In the burbs you've got the house and the car and the lawn all working overtime to tell the world who you are, and this leaves you free to dress down. Nowadays everybody dresses down; on Fridays, even the starchiest urban offices go suburban.

I wondered too if what we used to think of as the fakeness of the suburbs hasn't also left its mark on the broader culture. To grow up on a "boulevard" conjured in a field is to be at home with the façade and the themed environment, with the quick-change and the quotation marks, not to mention the willing suspension of disbelief. It may be that ironic detachment is a mental habit we children of the burbs have come by naturally.

Anyway, these were my desultory highway thoughts, entertained on the long drive home from suburbia. The funny thing is, the closer to home I got, the more omnipresent the place I'd been began to feel. Suburbia, I realized, is no longer somewhere you go, or leave. Wherever we live now, it's where we live.

Exploring Texts and Contexts

For activities with icons, refer to the Guide to Analyzing Readings in Context.

1. Pollan places much emphasis on names, for instance of the streets he grew up on, but he is also concerned with finding a name for what the suburbs have become. Reread Pollan's essay and consider how his focus on language helps him develop his essay. Consider, too, how the activity of naming helps Pollan characterize changes in demographics and lifestyle.

2. Pollan describes a stark contrast between the "then" of his childhood and the Gates of Woodbury today. What changes does he see and what does he see as the causes of these changes? Do you think Pollan intended his article to have any impact on the phenomena he describes? What consquences might an article like Pollan's have?

3. Pollan mentions that new technologies have contributed to the changes he sees occurring in the suburbs. Explain what he means, and consider how technological changes might continue to influence the suburbs.

Creating Texts

For activities with icons, refer to the Guides to Analyzing Contexts for Writing and Analyzing Readings in Context. For additional help with these writing projects, read the description of **Essay** in the Genre Glossary.

Situation

1. Pollan remembers the newness, and to some extent the inauthenticity, of the suburbs: "after all, we had watched them rise like stage sets on the farm fields, seen the instantaneous lawns rolled out over the raw dirt like new linoleum" (161). Clifton Taulbert, on the other hand, remembers how his home connected him to both the past and the future: "The Mississippi Delta was my home and I wanted to . . . return to the house built by my great-grandfather Sidney Peter. . . . The front porches became the place where visiting relatives from up north would sit and spin their intoxicating tales of northern life" (151). Write an essay in which you discuss how time-honored traditions on the one hand and change on the other hand contribute to establishing a sense of place.

CHAPTER 7

CASE STUDY

On *Painting* *a* House *Purple*

The Case

In the mid-1990s, Sandra Cisneros, author of the acclaimed and widely read novel *The House on Mango Street* and recipient of a MacArthur Foundation genius grant, bought a house in the King William neighborhood of San Antonio, Texas, a district whose residents must agree to abide by design guidelines developed to preserve the neighborhood's historic look. As one of a number of renovations that she made to the almost 100-year-old house, she decided to paint it a bright purple and, because of a series of miscommunications, thought that she had received approval from the San Antonio Historic and Design Review Commission (HDRC) when in fact she had not. The HDRC subsequently told Cisneros that she must either repaint the house in an approved color or demonstrate that the color she had chosen was historically appropriate.

On August 6, 1997, Cisneros presented her case to the HDRC, arguing that although bright purple might not be a historically documented color for houses in that neighborhood—primarily mansions built by wealthy German Americans at the turn of the century—bright colors like the one she had chosen were commonly used in the nearby Mexican neighborhood where Cisneros's house had originally stood; built in 1903, it had been moved to the King William neighborhood in 1913. But the HDRC did not accept that argument, sticking to their stated guidelines that house colors must be either the original color of the house, a color used on other houses in the neighborhood, or a color available in the period of the home's construction, as documented for example by paint company records of the period. Cisneros responded that the colors of houses in poor neighborhoods, like much else about the lives of the poor and members of minority groups, simply had not been documented in written records, but she also pointed to research supporting her claim that bright colors had long been common in the Mexican-American neighborhoods of San Antonio.

There is some disagreement about who agreed to what at this point, but a final decision was deferred to a later meeting to give the two sides a chance to work out a compromise. In the meantime, the controversy had received extensive local and even some national press coverage and was the subject of much heated discussion in the San Antonio community. People saw it either as a matter of recognizing the historical significance of

Sandra Cisneros's home in the King William neighborhood of San Antonio. To see its controversial color, go to http://www.accd.edu/sac/english/mcquien/htmlfils/kingwill.htm

"undocumented" groups, believing the HDRC had a narrow and biased view of history, or as a matter of everyone equally abiding by established community standards, believing that Cisneros had used her celebrity status to force the board to make an exception in her case. But in the end it was Mother Nature who resolved the stand-off: By the fall of 1998, the vibrant purple of Cisneros's house had faded to more of a lavender, and lavender is listed as one of the fourteen paint colors for sale in the Sears catalogue of 1903. Thus the HDRC agreed that, with a few minor touch-ups, Cisneros's house could stay as it was. This compromise, though in some ways satisfactory to everyone, ironically also managed to avoid taking a stand on either of the principles invoked by the two sides: inclusion of minority experience and values in historic guidelines or the necessity to apply the same rules to all. Thus the matter of Cisneros's purple house is officially settled, but the questions it raised about self-expression, community values, minority inclusion, and fairness to all continue to be hotly debated.

The Issues

Almost everyone who has written about the purple house has noted how Cisneros's fictional themes seem to eerily foreshadow the controversy. In *The House on Mango Street* and *Woman Hollering Creek,* her collection of short stories, Cisneros writes powerfully about the experiences of the poor and about self-determination for women. Two passages in particular from *The House on Mango Street* are often referred to, for example this passage from the section "Bums in the Attic":

> I want a house on a hill like the ones with the gardens where Papa works. . . .
>
> People who live on hills sleep so close to the stars they forget those of us who live too much on earth. They don't look down at all except to be content to live on hills. They have nothing to do with last week's garbage or fear of rats. Night comes. Nothing wakes them but the wind.
>
> One day I'll own my own house, but I won't forget who I am or where I came from.

Or the second-to-last section of the book, "A House of My Own":

> Not a flat. Not an apartment in back. Not a man's house. Not a daddy's. A house all my own. With my porch and my pillow, my pretty purple petunias. My books and my stories. My two shoes waiting beside the bed. Nobody to shake a stick at. Nobody's garbage to pick up after.
>
> Only a house quiet as snow, a place for myself to go, clean as paper before the poem.[1]

These passages have complex meanings within the context of the novel, and for the many participants in and observers of the controversy who had read the novel, these meanings gave resonance to an otherwise rather mundane disagreement over paint colors and historic guidelines.

But historic guidelines, if somewhat mundane, have their own complexities. The creation of historic districts in the United States has long been a popular way of preserving buildings considered to have aesthetic or historical significance, of raising property values in neighborhoods that were often falling into disrepair, and of teaching citizens about the past. But each of these goals, though laudable in itself, raises complicated questions. Who decides which buildings and neighborhoods have historic or aesthetic value, and what are the criteria for making those decisions? And raising property values in a neighborhood, while necessary to ensure that privately owned buildings are kept in good repair, often also means that the people who have been living in the neighborhood are squeezed out to make room for people who can afford to buy and maintain the now more expensive buildings. Finally, whose version of history do we teach in preserving these areas? Many of these difficult and emotional questions came into play in the debates over the purple house. Thus what might have seemed a fairly clear-cut issue—the periwinkle paint color of Cisneros's house did not exist when the house was built and was not currently used on any other houses in the neighborhood: case closed—became much more complicated when Cisneros introduced the issue of minority inclusion in standard histories and historical documents.

Whatever side they might take on these issues, most Americans have a strong belief in the democratic principle that rules must be applied equally and fairly for everyone. Although everyone knows that the world, even the American system, doesn't always work

[1]Sandra Cisneros, *The House on Mango Street.* New York: Vintage Books, 1989, pp. 86–87, 108.

this way, most people believe that it should and are resentful when it doesn't. Thus many people felt that the issue was less a question of whose history was being recognized than a question of a celebrity getting special treatment because her lawyers, fans, press coverage, and savvy enabled her to pressure the HDRC into a stand-off and then into a compromise. One board member was quoted as saying, "It's not about ethnicity. It's about eccentricity."[2] Others wondered whether Cisneros's painting of her house might have been just a publicity stunt to garner attention, or even an effort to generate material, for her next book. Suspicions and resentments over the celebrity issue were exacerbated by a related controversy over Cisneros's demand that, if a powerful local magazine wanted to interview her, they must send a Latina reporter—a demand that ultimately resulted in that magazine's hiring more Hispanic reporters.

This development, in turn, throws a different light on the "special treatment" issue. Is Cisneros a celebrity exploiting her clout to get special personal treatment or an artist using her creative gifts to make social changes? Is she using her art to transform the world or manipulating real people and situations to benefit her art? These questions return us to the broad themes of this unit: the need for individuals to challenge or transcend their environment through self-discovery and self-expression and the need for self-discovery and self-expression to be regulated or contained by community values and practices that protect and benefit everyone. As you read the documents in the case study, consider how they help us think about these different needs.

The Documents

- The **City of San Antonio** distributes a brochure, **"Historic Districts of San Antonio: Neighbors in History,"** with pictures from San Antonio's historic districts and various descriptions and guidelines related to historic preservation. The section "Understanding the Preservation Process" and the description of the King William neighborhood from the section "Neighborhoods Preserving San Antonio's Past" will give you a sense of how San Antonio residents learn about the meaning and process of historic preservation and the historic significance of the King William neighborhood.
- On Saturday, July 26, 1997, on the front page of the Metro Section of the *San Antonio Express-News,* a brief news article describes the controversy and refers readers to a column by **Susan Yerkes, "King William Seeing Red over Purple,"** which tells the story in greater detail. Yerkes's column may have been the first that many San Antonians had read about the issue, and a few days later Yerkes wrote a follow-up column, **"Now We Know Why It's Called Purple Passion,"** in which she describes a variety of emotional responses to her earlier column.
- On August 6, Cisneros made her case before the San Antonio Historic and Design Review Commission, and in the following few days a number of newspapers covered

[2]Sara Rimer, "Novelist's Purple Palette Is Not to Everyone's Taste," *New York Times,* July 13, 1998, section A.

the story, including the *San Antonio Express-News,* in an article headlined **"Purple Debate Reaches Commission—Cisneros Agrees to Work with City Staff on Mutually Acceptable Color Scheme"** by reporter and columnist **Mike Greenberg.**

- In the weeks following the first reports of the controversy, many San Antonio residents wrote **letters to the editor** of the *San Antonio Express-News.* These signed, published letters are in general much more reasonable and temperate in tone than the anonymous voicemail messages that Yerkes quotes in her July 30 column—though some make use of the sarcasm that often characterizes this genre, in which writers must catch an editor's attention and make their point in relatively few words—but they do reveal the strong personal responses that San Antonians were having to this issue.
- Not long after the August 6 hearing, the *San Antonio Express-News* published opinion pieces by Cisneros and a member of the HDRC, which elaborated the positions briefly reported in the news articles on the hearing. In **"Purple Politics—Our Tejano History Has Become Invisible," Cisneros** uses a more personal approach but combines this with references to research on the house colors of Mexican American neighborhoods and also appeals directly to the community for support. In **"Purple Politics: Individuality Surrendered for Preservation,"** HDRC member **Milton Babbitt,** himself a well-known member of the arts community, builds his argument through a series of carefully enumerated points and takes care to establish that he is writing as a commissioner, not a private citizen; the position he takes as a commissioner does not, he says, necessarily reflect his personal opinion. Notice how these two pieces, so different from each other in tone, are similar in scope in ways that distinguish them from the letters to the editor and even Yerkes's opinion columns.
- Although the purple house controversy was covered by some of the larger newspapers in the Southwest, it remained essentially a local story through the summer and early fall of 1997. But in November **Michele Norris** did a story on it for *World News Tonight,* and the following summer, on July 15, 1998, about a year after the story first broke, she did a longer piece for *Good Morning America.* People who have been involved in or closely following a local news story are often startled to see how it is represented to a larger audience: Facts that seem crucial are left out or distorted, aspects that seem peripheral are emphasized as if they are central, and the coverage often seems superficial. Consider that this may be the only coverage of the story that most people outside Texas will be exposed to; how will they understand the issue? What does this piece focus on, what does it add to our understanding of the story, and what does it leave out?

YOUR ROLE

The case of the purple house has been resolved, but the issues it raises about individual expression and community values continue to be sources of conflict. Indeed, as more people choose to live in communities that have guidelines for home design and individual behavior, such issues may be more relevant today and in the future. Thus the writing assignments for this case study ask you first to identify and research a more recent situation in which an individual and a community have come into conflict and write an opinion piece about it; and then to write an essay examining the larger principles and contexts involved in such cases.

1. Identify a recent—ideally ongoing—situation in which an individual has come into conflict with community standards or guidelines. It might be a situation in your hometown or neighborhood or in your college dormitory. If you don't know of any local situations, do some research online or in your library's newspaper and article databases, using keywords such as "homeowner association guidelines" and "conflict" or "controversy." Several recent cases have involved conflicts over flags and flagpoles, so you might try using these as keywords as well. By reading news reports and documents related to the case and, if possible, interviewing people who are part of the situation, find out as much as you can about the facts, rules, principles, and arguments involved. Using as models the opinion pieces by Sandra Cisneros and Milton Babbitt included in the case study, write an opinion piece, for the local newspaper, in which you take a stand on the issue. (See **Opinion Piece/Commentary** in the Genre Glossary.)
2. Drawing on the purple house case study and the cases that you and your classmates researched for assignment 1, write an essay in which you explore how these cases were influenced by the larger social issues that surround them. For example, in the purple house case, the larger social issues included the history of Mexicans and Americans in Texas and the inclusion of minority experiences and perspectives in official community histories. Most of the controversies over flags and flagpoles have happened since 2001, in the context of the renewed feelings of patriotism following September 11. And the overall issue of individual rights and community standards has assumed more importance as more people choose to live in gated communities in which, surrounded by people like themselves, they feel safe. How have these larger social contexts helped to create and/or influenced the debates about conflicts between individuals and communities? (See **Essay** in the Genre Glossary.)

Understanding the Preservation Process

Why Is Preservation Important?

In its City Code, San Antonio recognizes the vital importance of preservation. By ordinance, we maintain the city's unique cultural heritage by preserving our buildings, monuments, missions, acequias, and the San Antonio River. By setting aside historically valuable buildings, landmarks and areas by specific historic designation, the city actively participates in the preservation of cultural and neighborhood identity.

Examples of San Antonio's Historic Districts

Downtown	Alamo Plaza
	Main Plaza
	Military Plaza
Residential	King William
	Dignowity Hill
	Monte Vista
Largest	Mission
Single-use Clusters	Old Ursuline Academy
	(Southwest Craft Center)
	Old Lone Star Brewery
	(S. A. Museum of Art)
Commercial	Cattleman Square
	St. Paul Square
	La Villita

Historic Exceptional Landmarks are those considered most unique in terms of historic, cultural, archaeological, or architectural significance. Demolition would mean an irreplaceable loss to the quality and character of the city.

Examples: *The Alamo, Municipal Auditorium*

Historic Significant Landmarks are those considered to be important and their demolition would mean a serious loss to the character of the city.

Example: *Irish Flats houses neighborhood near Ave. E*

Designation Process

Receiving Historic Designation does not affect the use of a property. Land use is regulated by Zoning. It does, however, affect the aesthetics of any exterior changes made to the landmarks or property within the district.

What Is a Certificate of Appropriateness?

To make any exterior changes to a property with historic designation, you will need a **Certificate of Appropriateness.** *With the exception of painting,* you will also need a building permit. To obtain a permit from the Building Inspection Department, you must first present a Certificate of Appropriateness issued by the Historic Preservation Office. It will show that all proposed changes have met the aesthetic and preservation guidelines and design considerations

How owners (or the City) request designation of property as an Historic District or Landmark:

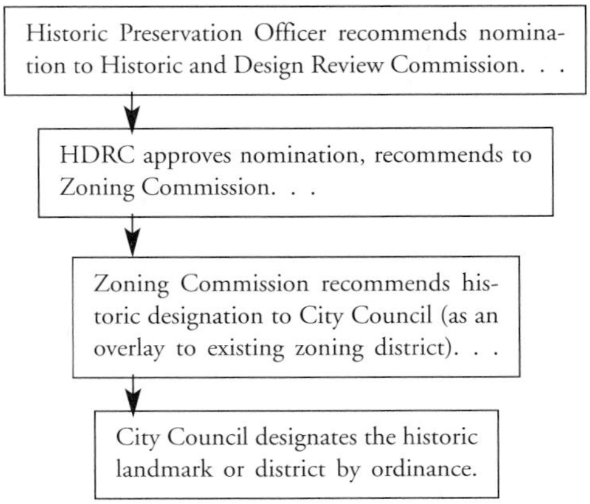

Historic Preservation Officer recommends nomination to Historic and Design Review Commission. . .

↓

HDRC approves nomination, recommends to Zoning Commission. . .

↓

Zoning Commission recommends historic designation to City Council (as an overlay to existing zoning district). . .

↓

City Council designates the historic landmark or district by ordinance.

(continued)

This brochure was funded in part through a Certified Local Government Grant from the National Park Service, U.S. Department of the Interior, as administered by the Texas Historical Commission and the City of San Antonio.

of the Historic and Design Review Commission (HDRC). Changes can be defined as, but are not limited to:

- Additions (construction or reconstruction)
- Rehabilitation and restoration
- Stabilization
- Landscaping
- Signage
- Demolition

The "Short Form" for Ordinary Repair and Maintenance

You may be eligible to complete the Certificate of Appropriateness "Short Form" if your proposed work to a structure of Historic Designation is **ordinary repair and maintenance,** defined as follows:

- Repair using same materials and design as original
- Re-painting with existing colors
- Re-roofing using same type and color of materials
- Repair of sidewalks and driveways using same type and color of materials

The Certificate of Appropriateness is issued by the Historic Preservation Officer and may be available the same day that you submit your application. You will be required to present it to the Building Inspections Department when requesting a permit.

The "Short Form" Application Requires:

- Photos of structure
- Brief written description of proposed work
- Samples of replacement materials or paint chips
- Legal description of property from Building Inspections Department

To Apply for a Certificate of Appropriateness:

Application forms are available through the Historic Preservation Office (HPO) at Municipal Plaza Building, 114 W. Commerce, or by calling 207-7900. Return completed application to the HPO. HPO staff will review it over a two-week period, and will make a recommendation to the HDRC. The Commission holds its public meeting on the first and third Wednesdays of each month. If your project is presented, the HDRC will act to *approve, approve with modifications,* or *deny* your application.

What Information Will You Be Asked to Provide for a Certificate of Appropriateness?

For proposed work which is not considered to be ordinary repair and maintenance, include with your application:

- Detailed, written description of proposed work with square footage, materials list, location, etc.
- Plans, Elevations, Sections and Details of proposed exterior changes
- Photos of existing site and/or structure
- Legal description of property, obtained through the Building Inspections Department / 9th floor 114 W. Commerce / San Antonio, TX 78205
- Samples of materials you want to use (paint swatches, roof shingles)
- Site Plan or Plot Plan that defines the structure's location or landscape on the site.

What If Your Application Is Denied?

The HDRC will make recommendations for changes to your proposed project to bring it into compliance with its guidelines as defined by ordinance. You may then modify your proposed project to incorporate these recommendations and resubmit your application, or you may appeal the HDRC's decision to City Council.

Design Considerations

If you anticipate presenting a project to the HDRC, be prepared to discuss the following design considerations:

Additions

- Should be compatible in size, materials, and style of original
- Should not radically change, obscure, damage, or destroy original or character-defining features

Example: the Fairmount Hotel restoration uses original features of the old building; the addition (behind lighter area of brick) is distinct from *the original building* but relates well *in use of materials, colors, and "rhythm" of elements on the façade.*

New Construction

New construction in a Historic District requires careful consideration to ascertain that the "infill construction" is in harmony with the existing buildings. Fundamental criteria include:

- Height and width in proportion to surrounding buildings
- Set-back from the street consistent with adjacent structures
- Roof shape and form similar to those nearby
- Composition, rhythm, and proportion of façade
- Compatible materials

Colors

- Use no more than three colors to highlight a façade:
  1. **Base Color** (walls)
  2. **Major Trim** (windows, columns, cornice)
  3. **Minor Trim** (doors, bulkheads, window mullions, small details)

Thinking About Working on an Old House?

Some Tips Before You Start

Research

Architecture, History, Previous Owners, Builder, Architect, Neighborhood

Plan Properly and On Paper

- Take "before" photos.
- Inspect structure's original interior and exterior materials and finishes; hire professional help if needed.
- Research local sources for replacement materials.

Set Goals

- Do you plan to *Preserve? Rehabilitate? Restore?*
- Set realistic cost and time goals.

Make Sure You Can Reverse Anything You Do

Examples:

- **Don't** tear out old woodwork and discard it.
- **Don't** install aluminum or perma-stone siding, which can irreparably damage façade.
- **Repair and restore** rather than remove and replace.
- **Save** as much of original structure as possible.

Be In Control of the Project

- Make sure contractors are aware of the sensitive nature of your project, and are qualified to do the work.

From "How to Love An Old House (In 10 Easy Lessons)," *The Old House Journal Catalog, The Old Journal Corporation,* 1984.

(continued)

What Are the Secretary of the Interior's Standards?

1. A property shall be used for its historic purpose or be placed in a new use that requires minimal change to the defining characteristics of the building and its site and environment.
2. The historic character of a property shall be retained and preserved.
3. Each property shall be recognized as a physical record of its time, place, and use.
4. Most properties change over time; the changes have acquired historical significance.
5. Distinctive features, finishes, and construction techniques or examples of craftsmanship unique to a property shall be preserved.
6. Deteriorated historic features shall be repaired rather than replaced.
7. Chemical or physical treatments such as sandblasting shall not be used.
8. Significant archaeological resources affected by a project shall be protected and preserved.
9. New additions or exterior alterations shall not destroy historic materials that characterize the property.
10. Changes shall not permanently alter the essential form and integrity of the historic property.

(*Standards are abbreviated*)

- Use original colors of paint and materials as guidelines for new colors.
- Use paint to minimize problems in façade, if necessary.

Landscaping

- Use a variety of native plants.
- Group plants for a more natural look.
- Determine soil pH and make adjustments.
- Consider plant colors (leaves and blooms) when making selections.
- Consider plant's purpose (ornament, shade, color, wind break).
- Consider maintenance/water required.

Signs

- Effective signs are legible; contain a simple message; are attractive and durable.
- Unobtrusive, yet noticeable signs can be placed within the architectural framework of the building. Signs should not obscure or cover architectural features. They can be attached to a board placed on the upper façade, or painted on the doors, windows, or awnings.
- Color coordination with the building is important.
- Design signage in accordance with the type and quality of merchandise or service offered, as well as the architectural character of the building.

Terms Defined: National Register of Historic Places

District
Geographically definable area, urban or rural, with a significant concentration linkage, or continuity of sites, building, structures, or objects that are related historically or aesthetically.

Site
Past location of a significant event, activity, building, or structure, usually of substantial archaological interest. Example: Black Swan Battle site

Building
House, church, barn, store, or hotel that shelters any form of human activity.

Structure
Man-made construction of interdependent and interrelated parts, organized in a definite pattern. Often a large-scale railroad engineering project. Locally this includes Crockett Street Bridge, the Hayes St. Bridge and the Tower of the Americas.

Object
Material thing of functional, aesthetic, cultural, historic, or scientific value. May be movable by nature or design, yet related to a specific setting or environment. Objects listed in San Antonio include Lady Bird Fountain, (behind the Alamo), and the Madero Bust (100 Block, Concho St.)

Reconstruction
Using new construction to reproduce the form, design, and detail of a structure or object, complete or in part, as it once appeared.

Rehabilitation
(Adaptive Reuse) Repairing or upgrading a structure or property for contemporary use (such as converting a warehouse into an art gallery), while preserving its historical, architectural, and culturally important features.

Renovation
Changing and improving an old or historic structure in a way that should not duplicate its original appearance.

Restoration
Returning a building or property to its former look by removing later additions or replacing earlier features that are now missing.

This brochure was funded in part through a Certified Local Government grant from the National Park Service, U. S. Department of the Interior, as administered by the Texas Historical Commission and the City of San Antonio.

(continued)

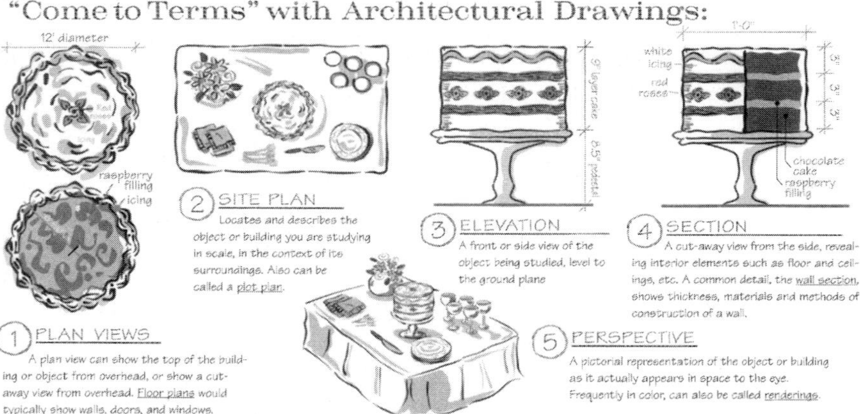

King William

Canals flowing from the San Antonio River and farmland belonging to the 1731 mission of Nuestra Señora de la Purísma Concepción de Acuna originally comprised the King William Historic District. By the beginning of the 19th century, the San Antonio missions were fully secularized, and the land belonging to the Mission Concepción was divided into tracts. Thomas Jefferson Devine, a lawyer and land speculator, bought the tracts in the 1840s and sold them to others who continued to divide and sell the property for residences.

One of the earliest to settle here was Carl Guenther, a German immigrant who had built a mill near Fredericksburg, Texas. Purchasing a tract of land on the lower bend of the San Antonio River in 1859, he constructed a second mill, which became Pioneer Flour Mills, and a stone cottage, which is now part of the present Guenther house at the mills. This served as the southern anchor for the King William neighborhood.

A number of other successful and influential German immigrants also began building residences in the King William area, using Greek Revival, Victorian, and Italianate architectural styles for their mansions. Ernst Altgelt, builder of the first house on King William, is credited with naming his street after King Wilhelm I of Prussia.

When San Antonio's fashionable neighborhoods to the north such as Terrell Hills and Alamo Heights began attracting King William residents in the 1920s, the grand mansions of the "Sauerkraut Bend" neighborhood were sold or turned into apartments. For more than 30 years, the district declined, until a group of creative young professionals took an interest in living and working there. At the same time, the San Antonio Conservation Society acquired the Eduard Steves house at 509 King William, leading the way for a period of revival. In 1967, the neighborhood became the King William Historic District, the first Historic District in Texas. The district was expanded in 1984 to include a more eclectic neighborhood of cottages South of Alamo Street-affectionately known as "Baja King William."

King William Seeing Red over Purple

Susan Yerkes

Purple ribbons tied to gates and trees in King William aren't there to welcome The Artist Formerly Known As Prince, who's coming to the Alamodome Aug. 8.

They're there for nationally acclaimed author and current King William housing cause célèbre Sandra Cisneros, whose home is rousing purple passions in the historic district.

The house is purple. Not a shrinking violet purple. A pulsating, passionate "periwinkle," Cisneros calls it.

And the paint job has some of her neighbors seeing red.

King William, you see, is a microcosm of S.A. life—and strife.

The picturesque area around Kaiser Wilhelm Street, where monied German burghers once built mansions, has been regentrified recently, sending housing prices soaring and creating schisms over issues from zoning to tour buses.

The dynamic King William Association takes some strong stands. But Cisneros' purple home is not one of them, association president Sarida Bradley stresses. At its last meeting, the group voted not to take sides.

"We do not endorse or condemn the color of her house," she says. "We don't want neighbors pitted against neighbors. Personally," she adds, "I don't think color is that important. It's transitory."

Some neighbors, however, do think it's important and have complained to the city's Historic Preservation Office.

Cisneros had her own historic perspective in mind when she chose the purple hue, she says. She wanted to reflect the passionate, colorful spirit of South Texas and Mexico.

"Everything I've done, from changing the concrete walks to limestone to having special wooden porch pillars made, has been to keep the integrity of spirit here."

Cisneros was commuting to Chicago as her father neared death this spring and summer, and the contractor who was painting her house met with the city's design review committee on her behalf.

Although the committee recommended muting the purples after seeing the back of the house painted, the deep shade tints the whole house.

"I started getting calls from King William," says S.A. Historic Preservation Office head Ann McGlone. And they were not pro-purple.

McGlone notified Cisneros that her color scheme violated city historic district requirements.

"It's very appealing," McGlone says. "But it's not appropriate to history. This isn't about taste; it's about historical context."

But Cisneros hasn't given up. And if she can justify the color scheme historically, McGlone says, the purple paint may stay.

Meanwhile, supportive neighbors started the purple-ribbon campaign. And in what some see as a strike against the anti-tour bus residents of the neighborhood, artist Terry Ybanez designed a purple "I (heart) (trolleys)" pictograph plaque for Cisneros' front yard—another flip in the faces of some neighbors.

Architect Ron Bechtol, who chose the more conservative color scheme that Cisneros' house sported before she bought it, has gone to bat for purple, too.

"Though the colors themselves may not be typical of local tradition," he wrote to McGlone, "they are harmonious within their distinctive vocabulary—much more so, in my opinion, than many neighborhood examples pairing yellow and green, green and red, red and yellow."

Cisneros will defend her case at the city committee's Aug. 6 meeting.

"I hope my periwinkle house will encourage baja and Lavaca residents to be even more colorful," she says.

Now We Know Why It's Called Purple Passion

Susan Yerkes

Since Saturday's column about author Sandra Cisneros and her controversial "periwinkle" purple house in S.A.'s historic King William district, the phones and computer modem have been lit up like Fourth of July fireworks.

Some folks say "right on!" to Sandra's quest to keep the deep purple her house was painted, against the behest of the city's historic review board.

A number of others—even Alaskan Dan Flanders, a regular poster on my EN-Connect forum who once worked with architect O'Neil Ford—point out Cisneros chose to live in a historic district with tight architectural rules.

But what makes the flap so interesting is the purple passion Cisneros and her bright berry of a house have generated.

Passion such as the venom of the anonymous women with condescending voices on my ExpressLine.

"The reason we're seeing red over her purple color, honey, is not the color, but because she's such a b——," one said acidly.

"She has a bad attitude, and we've just had enough of her b———. Have a nice day."

The feisty Cisneros, who contends that the deep purple expresses the passionate spiritual palate of Mexico, leaps on personal attacks as proof "how deep-seated, how much more complex this is than simply a capricious color choice."

And indeed, ExpressLine callers provide plenty of insight into attitudes that inflame the story of the purple place on Guenther Street.

"As a U.S. citizen, I'm getting real tired of these people that want to bring Mexico to the United States," a caller typical of this school harumphed.

"If they want to live in Mexico, why in the hell don't they, ah, she, go back where she came from?"

(Cisneros came from Chicago. Who'd go back there from here?)

That kind of response, which Cisneros says she often gets, is part of the city's darkest side.

But many King William folks are flat distressed that the purple-house flap has come to this.

"When you say 'King William is seeing red,' " asks Penny Wiederhold, "who is King William? It's unfair to damn the whole neighborhood because of a few people."

In fact, the King William Association voted not to take a stand on the purple cottage.

"We believe in the process," noted association vice prez Jim Johnson, whose wife is another well-known writer, Paulette Giles.

"It seems like when we get in arguments it's when the process hasn't been fully exercised. I think the historic review board is doing what it's supposed to do—protect the historic district."

On Aug. 6, the city's design review commission will hear Cisneros' appeal to keep her purple house. She's not optimistic.

"This is a part of the world where there's been such a long history of conflict, it's too bad this house issue can't be seen as opportunity for harmony among different cultures," she muses.

Attorney and King William neighbor Nancy Shivers echoes the sentiment, from a slightly different slant: "It's just sad to me to see what little we gain from this," she says. "How is it helping us make a better neighborhood?"

Stay tuned.

Purple Debate Reaches Commission—Cisneros Agrees to Work with City Staff on Mutually Acceptable Color Scheme

Mike Greenberg

Novelist Sandra Cisneros' tale of the purple house is to be continued.

Cisneros appeared Wednesday before the Historic and Design Review Commission, five TV cameras and about 30 supporters—many wearing garments in various shades of purple—to request after-the-fact approval for the predominantly purple palette of her King William Historic District House.

No vote was taken, and the case was continued to a future meeting. Cisneros agreed to work with city staff to seek a mutually acceptable paint scheme for the house on Guenther Street and return to the commission for approval.

But she reserved the right "to defend my colors" if agreement isn't reached.

Decisions by the commission, which is an advisory body, may be appealed to the City Council.

History was pitted against history in Cisneros' exchange with the commission and historic preservation officer Ann McGlone.

McGlone had recommended denial of the color scheme "because there is no evidence or documentation that these colors were ever used in the King William area."

To be deemed acceptable, McGlone said, the color scheme would have to be "appropriate to the house, the neighborhood or the era" in which the house was built.

The house, a folk Victorian cottage, was built in 1903, and according to McGlone the deep purple hue that dominates the house was not manufactured until much later.

Couching the issue as being about "historical inclusion" for the Tejano people, Cisneros countered: "According to my history, purple is a historical color. . . . This was Mexico, and the Mexican color palette isn't being allowed."

Cisneros admitted her error in beginning the paint job last year without seeking commission approval. The rear of the house already had been painted when Cisneros sought approval in October.

The commission's architectural review committee met with her painting contractor and advised muting or eliminating some paint colors and painting a test sample prior to final approval.

But Cisneros said her contractor didn't communicate that advice to her, and the color scheme was continued to the front of the house.

She told the commission she was willing to change the colors if she and staff could find a mutually agreeable scheme.

"But I still think we need to change the vision of the people on this board," she said.

Fourteen residents, including several of Cisneros' immediate neighbors, spoke in support of her color scheme. One, Emily Brace, began by singing, "for purple mountains' majesty. . . ."

Letters to the Editor

Viva el Color!

re: the Purple House of Sandra Cisneros.

The King William area is a beautiful part of our city. I appreciate the entrepreneurial spirit, creativity, and individuality of those who turned a decaying area of San Antonio into a thing of beauty and joy for us all.

Can we not also be grateful for the individuality and creativity of Sandra Cisneros? I went by to see her home for myself after reading the article in Saturday's paper. The workmanship appeared to be of excellent quality, and the finishing touches were added with artistry. I found the whole effect to be aesthetically stimulating and delightful. (Then, who am I to say since I also immediately loved "The Big Enchilada"?)

In a city which benefits immeasurably from its Hispanic roots and the colorful fiesta culture which is San Antonio's trademark, wouldn't a distaste for "periwinkle" be a little on the stuffy side?

Viva el color!

Mary Lil Chappell
August 10, 1997
San Antonio Express-News

Real Issue Behind Purple House Is Tolerance

I find the purple controversy over Sandra Cisneros' house in the King William neighborhood to be shocking and offensive.

So far, I have yet to hear anyone discuss the moral and ethical issue of the city government having the authority to harass and intimidate people about the personal choices they have regarding their own property.

What makes city government think it knows what's best for us?

We pay for our homes, pay taxes, make repairs, maintain our yards and live with all of the problems that go along with living in older, inner-city neighborhoods.

For me, a neighborhood is first and foremost a community of people living and working in harmony and mutual respect.

As a designer and lover of antiques and architecture, I appreciate many of the benefits of having our historic buildings protected, especially against demolition or poor renovation, but legislating color choice is absurd.

I also appreciate the value of color as a form of self-expression and cultural evolution.

The real issue here is tolerance. Most people conform by nature. When one individual attempts to express a different point of view, the city design authorities whip out their big paintbrush and wipe out those poisonous colors before they spread.

Scary, isn't it?

Martha Durke
August 12, 1997
San Antonio Express-News

Cisneros Put Cart before the Horse

I've got to hand it to San Antonio author Sandra Cisneros. She certainly used the media to bring notoriety to herself and her house. However, what is the true agenda?

A search for historical truth or a colorful plotline for her next book?

I have never read Cisneros' work, nor do I live in the King William neighborhood, but I would venture to guess that she is not the only person of Mexican-American origin who works hard and lives well in this wonderful neighborhood.

Perhaps someone should ask the residents of the

neighborhood if they are not annoyed by the unwarranted publicity this gives their community, as well as bothered by someone who doesn't see fit to follow the rules they all abide by.

It's OK to try to change the way others think, but didn't Cisneros put the cart before the horse by painting her house before doing her research? I don't find the color purple at all offensive, but I find Cisneros' behavior less palatable than her palette.

Nancy de Wied
August 23, 1997
San Antonio Express-News

Go Ahead and Name Paper after Purple House

It might be time to consider changing the masthead of the *Express-News* to read "San Antonio Express-Purple House" to more accurately reflect your interests.

Hayden Freeman
August 23, 1997
San Antonio Express-News

Reader Overdosed on 'Cisneros Edition'

Re: the Saturday, Nov. 15, issue of the "Sandra Cisneros Express-News":

Having been inundated in one issue with three articles and two pictures of San Antonio's favorite part-time house painter and full-time self-promoter, it occurs to me that your readership might be better served if you just go ahead and include a separate "Sandra Says" section several times a week. Her adoring fans can more easily access your relentless coverage of her, and those of us who find same to be an annoyance and perhaps just a tad redundant, can remove it easily.

If the "Sandra Says" section is still not enough for you, I certainly wouldn't mind articles about her in the only sections that were Sandra-free in Saturday's issue, i.e., the classified ads, the business section and sports. Indeed, I look forward to seeing her name in an ad under "seeking employment," a business story on how she gets daily free advertising.

Charles Stallcup
November 23, 1997
San Antonio Express-News

Purple Politics—Our Tejano History Has Become Invisible

Sandra Cisneros

Ay que telenovela mi vida! What a telenovela my life! One day I painted my house Tejano colors, and the next day my house is in all the news, cars swarming by, families having their photos taken in front of my purple casita as if it was the Alamo. The neighbors put up an iced tea stand and made $10.

All this happened because I choose to live where I do. I live in San Antonio because I'm not a minority here. I live in the King William neighborhood because I love old houses.

Since my neighborhood is historic, there are certain code restrictions that apply. Any house alteration plans have got to be approved by the Historic Design and Review Committee. This is to preserve the neighborhood's historic character, and that's fine by me.

Because I thought I had permission, I gave the go-ahead to have my house painted colors I considered regional, but, as it turned out, hadn't been approved. However, I was given the chance to prove them historically appropriate. So I did my research, and what I found is this.

We don't exist.

My history is made up of a community whose homes were so poor and unimportant as to be considered unworthy of historic preservation. No famous architect designed the houses of the Tejanos, and there are no books in the San Antonio Conservation Society library about the houses of the working-class community, no photos romanticizing their poverty, no ladies auxiliary working toward preserving their presence. Their homes are gone, their history is invisible.

The few historic homes that have survived have access to them cut off by freeways because city planners did not judge them important (i.e. Casa Ximenes and the Little Chapel of Miracles.) Or they are buildings fenced in by the Plaza Hotel; I wasn't even aware they were part of Tejano history until I began my research into my house colors even though I walk past them almost every day.

Our history is in the neighborhoods like the famous Laredito barrio, heart of the old Tejano community and just a block from City Hall; it proved so "historically valuable" it was demolished and converted into a jail, parking lot and downtown police station with only the casa of Tejano statesman Jos Angel Navarro as evidence Laredito was ever there.

Our past is present only in the churches or missions glorifying a Spanish colonial past. But I'm not talking about the Spaniards here. My question is where is the visual record of the Tejanos?

The issue is bigger than my house. The issue is about historical inclusion. I want to paint my house a traditional color. But I don't think it unreasonable to include the traditions of los Tejanos who had a great deal to do with creating the city of San Antonio we know today.

I wouldn't mind painting my house a historical color, but please give me a broader palette than surrey beige, sevres blue, hawthorne green, frontier days brown, and Plymouth Rock grey.

These colors are fine for some houses, and I think they look handsome on the dignified mansions on King William Street. But look at my casita, it's not a mansion. It's a late Victorian rental cottage, built circa 1903. (My house was originally located on South Saint Mary's, then known as Garden Street, just off Alamo, on the corner where the Babylon Restaurant now sits. In 1913 my house was sawed in two like a Houdini magic act and wheeled to its present location. This accounts for its architectural affinity with the houses in the Baja and Lavaca communities.)

Frankly, I don't understand what all the fuss is about. I thought I painted my house a historic color. Purple is historic to us. It only goes back a thousand years or so to the pyramids. It is present in the Nahua codices, book of the Aztecs, as is turquoise, the color I used for my house trim; the former color signifying royalty, the latter, water and rain. We don't have papers. Our books were burned in the conquest, and ever since then we have learned to keep quiet, to keep our history to ourselves, to keep it alive generation to generation by word of mouth, perhaps because we feared it would be taken away from us again. Too late; it has been taken from us.

In San Antonio when we say historic preservation we don't mean everyone's history, even though the historic review office is paid for by everybody's taxes. When they ask me to prove my colors historically appropriate to King William they don't mean Tejano colors. But I am certain Tejanos lived in this neighborhood too. That's what my neighbors have told me. Mr. Chavana, who lives across the street, says his family has been living in this downtown area since the 1830s, and I know he's not lying; he's not allowed to, he's a reverend.

Color is a language. In essence, I am being asked to translate this language. For some who enter my home, these colors need no translation. However, why am I translating to the historical professionals? If they're not visually bilingual what are they doing holding a historical post in a city with San Antonio's demographics? It shouldn't even be an issue.

Color is a story. It tells the history of a people. We don't have beautiful showcase houses that tell the story of the class of people I come from. But our inheritance is our sense of color. And it's been something that has withstood conquests, plagues, genocide, hatred, defeat. Our colors have survived. That's why you all love fiesta so much, because we know how to have a good time. We know how to laugh, we know a color like bougainvillea pink is important because it will lift your spirits and make your heart pirouette.

We have a tradition of bright colors. Dr. Daniel Arreola, of Texas A&M University, has written that in a survey of 1,065 houses in a Mexican-American district in San Antonio, 50 percent showed evidence of brightly painted exteriors, even if only evidenced in the bright trim. From the Arab influence of elaborate paint exteriors carried over to the Iberian peninsula, as well as to the use of intense pigment in the pre-Colombian structures, our people have always decorated their exterior walls brightly. In some pre-Colombian centers there is not only evidence of a love of color, but a love of vivid visual effects; in Teotihuacan it is the drama of red contrasted with blue. That passion for color is seen even now in our buildings on both sides of the border. Mango yellow, papaya orange, Frida Kahlo cobalt, Rufino Tamayo periwinkle, rosa mexicana and,

(continued)

yes, even enchilada red! King William architecture has been influenced by European, Greek Revival, Victorian, and Neoclassical styles. Why is it so difficult to concede a Mexican influence, especially when so many people of Mexican descent lived in the city?

This issue is not about personal taste, but about historical context. It is about the HDRC serving all of the community, not the personal interests of some. And history belongs not only to the architecturally elite, but also to los Tejanos, as well as the Germans, the African Americans, Poles, Czechs, Italians, Jews, Lebanese, Greeks, Irish, French, Native Americans, and yes, even the poor. History belongs to us all.

My purple house colors are not deemed historically appropriate because "there is no evidence or documentation these colors were ever used in King William." But if the HDRC is true to their word, oral testimonies should count as evidence. I am inviting the community to assist me. I invite Brackenridge High School especially; I'm told they've adopted my purple house because it's their school color, so why not an oral history project they could get credit for? Why not a documentation of our ancestors? It's about time we had our history count on paper.

If you know someone who lived in San Antonio at the turn of the century who remembers the colors of the Tejanos who lived in the King William/La Vaca community, document their story on paper. What block did they live on? What kind of house? What color was the main body? The trim? Do you have an old house that you could scrape to see what layers lie underneath? Would you like to be part of a collection of Tejano oral histories? If so, tell me your story. I would love to collect them and publish them in a book we could gift to the San Antonio Conservation Society, the San Antonio Public Library, the King William Association, the Historic Review Office, the city of San Antonio. After all, maybe someone else will be inspired and follow my example and paint their house a beautiful South Texas color too and nobody would raise a fuss. Now wouldn't that be something!

Purple Politics—Individuality Surrendered for Preservation

Milton Babbitt

There are three important issues to be taken into account in the case of Sandra Cisneros and the color of her house. These are the nature and importance of historic districts, guidelines for development within historic districts and the process for ensuring that these guidelines are respected.

One of the tasks of the Historic and Design Review Commission, or HDRC, working with the staff of the city's Office of Historic Preservation, is to provide oversight of development in the city's historic districts. Presently, there are five primarily residential historic districts and they represent but a tiny fraction of the residential land area in the city.

Why, then, do we have historic districts?

The importance of sustainability in development practices and design is becoming more widely understood. The ultimate in construction recycling is the rehabilitation of existing structures, and historic district designation provides an incentive for stability and neighborhood revitalization. Historic districts protect property values.

Many suburban developments safeguard values and exclude inappropriate development with restrictive covenants and subdivision regulations. These are unavailable to urban dwellers in older neighborhoods and historic designation can offer protection in much the same way.

Historic districts attract tourists—sometimes too many, as parts of the King William district can attest. Our suburban neighborhoods look like their counterparts anywhere, but our historic districts are unique and people enjoy visiting them.

Finally, historic districts educate by giving a very real link to the past, bringing meaning to history.

Historic district designation is initiated by the citizenry, not the city. Fifty-one percent of the property owners in the area must endorse the concept before the legal process of designation begins. As might be expected, some owners will be unhappy with the designation. However, in the public hearings that preceded designation of the newest district, Monticello Park, all of the speakers appearing before the HDRC spoke in support of historic designation.

Once a historic distict is created, exterior alterations to any structure are subject to review by the Office of Historic Preservation and the HDRC. With the benefits provided by district designation comes responsibility as well. A bit of individual freedom is surrendered in that owners are no longer free to do whatever they want to the exterior of their property.

We review landscape development, fencing, driveway design, new construction, building additions and alterations such as re-roofing, window replacement, porch reconstruction and repainting—yes, color. Major color issues are unusual, though color, being highly subjective, is a sensitive issue. It's far easier to deal with a homeowner who somehow feels compelled to pave his or her entire front yard with concrete.

There are no "approved" colors despite what you may have heard or read, even in this newspaper, but there are

(continued)

guidelines which establish a very broad palette of historically acceptable colors. First, a thorough paint analysis can be performed to ascertain what the original colors were. This is rarely done for homes, primarily because of the cost but also because the homeowner might not like what is found, even though they would be under no obligation to replicate the original scheme.

Second, colors which are appropriate to the neighborhood may be sought. Since historical color photographs do not exist, the tools for finding appropriate schemes are limited, consisting of reports on houses where the colors have actually been analyzed and documented or oral neighborhood histories.

Third, colors that were in use in the era of original construction can be sought. The major paint companies have histories extending well back into the 19th century and retain records of available products by time period. For example, the Sears Roebuck catalog of 1902 lists its available colors of house paint - all 16 of them! One of these was lavender. Lavender would be an appropriate color for a house built in the first decade of this century.

There is a process for securing approval and, in the vast majority of situations, the process works well. Some color changes are so minor that they don't make the HDRC agenda; the staff approves them.

Another large group of cases involving color appear on the consent agenda with a recommendation for approval by staff, pulled for individual consideration only when a commission member has a concern about some element of the case.

A third group represents color changes which are substantial or controversial enough to warrant review by the entire commission. Typically, after an initial presentation to the commission, these cases are referred to the architecture committee, generally composed of commission members who are architects. An on-site meeting is held with the owner, committee and staff. The owner's rationale for the proposed selections are heard, suggestions for changes made and common ground sought—and usually found. The committee reports the results of its meeting at the next commission meeting and the commission almost always approves a motion based on the committee recommendation.

In the Cisneros case, the process was followed up to a point. The committee met with the owner's designated representative to review a sample of the color scheme painted on the back of the house. He was informed that the colors applied in the sample were not acceptable in a historic district. Subsequently, the owner painted the remainder of the house in the same colors.

Historic preservation is not anti-color nor is the HDRC the color police. In approving colors, we do not act arbitrarily nor do we make judgments based on personal preference. Our determinations are made using the above-stated guidelines. The results are hardly timid, as the King William district has many houses with vivid color schemes—more than any other local historic district. This is primarily because the exuberant Victorian architecture of the neighborhoods suggests it and because, at least in some documented instances, it is historically accurate. I have said publicly that the color scheme which Cisneros has used is exquisite. I believe it. It is the carefully concocted product of someone who knows a great deal about color. But the fact that I like it can have no effect on my opinion as a commissioner, and my opinion is that it is wrong for the house, wrong for the neighborhood and wrong for the district. The colors chosen by Ms. Cisneros fail when held up to any guideline for historic preservation.

The Purple House
Coat of Paint Causes Cultural War in San Antonio

Michele Norris and Lisa McRee

LISA McREE, Host: The issue of color is once again dividing a community, but not in the way you might think. When noted Mexican-American author Sandra Cisneros chose to paint her historic San Antonio home, it was the color purple that landed her in trouble. ABC's Michele Norris joins us from Washington this morning with the details. Michele?

MICHELE NORRIS, ABC News:
Good morning, Lisa.

LISA McREE:
Good morning.

MICHELE NORRIS:
This is a story about color and culture and history, but the question is, whose history? And it's hard to believe that a simple coat of paint could cause a cultural war, but that's exactly what happened in San Antonio.

SANDRA CISNEROS:
"A house all my own, with my porch and my pillow, my pretty purple petunias."

MICHELE NORRIS:
(voice-over) Sandra Cisneros is the author of "The House on Mango Street," a story about a poor Latina girl who yearns for a house of her own.

SANDRA CISNEROS:
Now I see, I'm living what I wrote.

MICHELE NORRIS:
(voice-over) Cisneros grew up poor. Now she lives in one of the most prestigious neighborhoods in San Antonio, the King William Historic District, a collection of graceful homes built by wealthy German merchants almost 100 years ago.

But the Cisneros house is quite like no other. It's a bright shade of purple, a neon hue called periwinkle, and it's attracting quite a bit of attention.

DAVID NEWBERN:
There aren't any other houses dominantly painted that fluorescent purple in the area.

MICHAEL GREENBERG:
A lot of people have been driving by and looking at it. Everybody had to find out what it really looks like.

MICHELE NORRIS:
(voice-over) Cisneros says the attention-getting color pays tribute to her Mexican-American heritage.

SANDRA CISNEROS:
This is my first home. I was just trying to make it look like my home. And all the things that are in my house are—many things point to my Mexican culture.

MICHELE NORRIS:
(voice-over) But making such a vivid cultural declaration has split this city along color lines. On one side, pro-purple supporters display ribbons in their yards.

ADREN PRYOR:
It adds interest, that's what's neat about this whole neighborhood.

MICHELE NORRIS:
(voice-over) On the other side, this purple house has the Historic Design and Review Board seeing red.

MILTON BABBITT,
Historic Commission: This is more a fashion statement, I think, than it is an architectural statement.

MICHELE NORRIS:
Living in this historic district comes with certain requirements.

(continued)

From *ABC Good Morning America,* July 15, 1998.

When residents want to paint their homes, they must meet at least one of three conditions, that the proposed color was used on the home at least some point in the past, that it was used in the era when the home was built, or that it can now be found on other houses in the neighborhood.

ANN BENSON McGLONE, Historic Preservation Officer:
This is about the process of—and responsibility of—living in a historic district, and how you try to make personal taste mesh with the responsibility in the process of living in a historic district.

MICHELE NORRIS:
You moved into a historic district. You know the rules.

SANDRA CISNEROS:
The rules are very racist. All you have to do is look and see what colors they're espousing, what palettes they're espousing, and look and see how they're defining what's historically accurate.

MICHELE NORRIS:
(voice-over) Supporters argue that purple has its place in Mexican-American history.

MAN IN BLACK T-SHIRT:
It's larger than just the color of paint on a house. Is our aesthetic valid? Is our history valid? Does our history even exist?

MICHELE NORRIS:
(voice-over) San Antonians do celebrate the color and culture of Mexico in festivals like this Day of the Dead procession, in tourist attractions, and in the modern enchilada-red library, a building approved by the same commission that has rejected the purple house.

SANDRA CISNEROS:
And that's supposed to be avocado?

MICHELE NORRIS:
(voice-over) For now, Cisneros is working with the city to find an acceptable paint scheme.

(on camera) Now, what do you think of these colors?

SANDRA CISNEROS:
Pretty sad.

MICHELE NORRIS:
(voice-over) Don't expect this outspoken writer to settle on quiet colors for her home. This is Michele Norris for Good Morning America.

LISA McREE:
So Michele, how—where do the negotiations stand today?

MICHELE NORRIS:
Well, the two sides were supposed to come together and decide on a mutually acceptable palette, something might—a color scheme that might speak of her Mexican heritage without shouting. But so far, the two sides are in limbo. They haven't come together, they've scheduled meetings, they've canceled meetings. And all this means that the purple house is still there.

LISA McREE:
How does it look in person?

MICHELE NORRIS:
One person described it as a California swimsuit color. It literally vibrates. It's got this sort of neon undertone. And the camera doesn't really capture it.

LISA McREE:
All right. Thanks so much, Michele Norris, keep us in touch with what's going on in San Antone.

UNIT IV

Participating in Civic Conversations

This photograph of a sculpture called "Conversation Piece," by Juan Muñoz, taken in the sculpture garden of the Hirshhorn Museum in Washington D.C., illustrates the power and limitations of both sculpture and photography. By choosing the angle from which to take the picture, the photographer controls how we see the sculpture. This is especially significant with this sculpture, for it is about the relationship between the different figures. But the photograph thus fixes that relationship. When we view the sculpture in person, we can see the figures from many different angles and thus see different possible relationships between them. That is why this sculpture appealed to us so powerfully as an illustration for this unit. In a democracy, it is crucial for citizens to talk to each other about important public issues, but in a democracy as large and diverse as ours, it can be difficult to include everyone in these conversations. Because these conversations take place through many different channels, it can be difficult even to know who is participating. It may require a change of perspective to know whose voices have been heard.

CHAPTER 8

Participating in Civic Conversations

Situation: What larger situation do you think this scene is a part of? Use your imagination to speculate, but also use specific clues from the photo to support your speculations.

Genre: Compare this photograph with the one on page 287 and then with the one on page 470. What different stories do these pictures tell on the one hand about civic participation and on the other hand about work?

Language: The amount of detail in this photo can make it confusing at first. What specific details and patterns help you begin to make sense of it?

Consequences: Do you think this photograph was meant to communicate a message of some sort? What impact did it have on you?

Waupun, Wisconsin: small-town rural America. The well-manicured lawns and shaded streets lead you through a downtown lined by a library, churches, and small shops. While the town is too big for everyone to know everyone else, ordinary people take part in governing it; the mayor, for instance, also teaches sixth-grade math. Even small towns like this one experience vandalism, domestic violence, crime, and, perhaps most importantly, the steadily increasing isolation that some say tears at the fabric of our society. Last fall, a group of about thirty students—some quiet, some known as troublemakers, others new to the town—met one evening to decide what projects they would do over the course of the school year. They hit on the idea of a bike path into Pine Street Park, which was accessible only by a fast-moving, two-lane road. This group, Waupun Do Something, assisted only by an adult coach who kept a low profile, worked with the city council to design the path, to obtain grants to fund the project, and to get permission from property owners for the bike path to cross their land.[1]

Newark, New Jersey: Urban and diverse, this city of more than a quarter of a million people is a short drive from New York City. Newark is home to Rutgers and Seton Hall Universities and home as well to Newark Do Something, a chapter of the national youth-led organization that mobilizes students to become local leaders. Hundreds of students met here last fall for a Speak Out meeting to determine their work for the coming year. The previous year they had registered over four hundred people to vote and this year they decided to honor Martin Luther King's birthday by designating a two-week period during which they would commit acts of kindness and justice.

These two locations couldn't be more different, but the challenge is the same. The national organization Do Something recognizes that if youth from all parts of the country don't develop a sense of civic commitment, the social ills that plague us will only become worse. Research tells us that the number of young voters, those below the age of 25, has dropped by about 15 percent since 1972.[2] Do Something aims at young people because its founders, Andrew Shue and Michael Sanchez, who grew up together in New Jersey and who wanted to make a difference, realized that a commitment to community building must start no later than junior high. Do Something leader Anthony Welch worries that, "If people are not involved by fourteen, you've lost them. Twenty-five is too late."[3] Not only has voting decreased, but in many more ways we are becoming a nation of isolated individuals consumed by self-interest. Robert Putnam's 2000 book, *Bowling Alone,* traces how, over the past 60 years, we as a people not only vote less, but talk less to each other, and rarely connect the way we used to by sitting on our front stoop, by seeing each other at the market, or by meeting up to work on community projects. Getting people to become involved in the day-to-day life of a democracy and getting them to participate in sustaining our democracy remains one of our most intractable social problems.

As we see in the readings in this chapter, conversations about becoming actors rather than spectators in our ongoing civic drama are conducted in a variety of contexts: Some look to historical patterns and events for clues about how work can contribute to the public good. Others propose that organizations such as Do Something are building an asset called *social capital,* a term that refers to the networks and connections that are constructed to help communities cohere. Part of our problem in building community lies in the inflammatory talk that pervades our media. Journalists struggle with ways to present the news that will encourage citizens to participate in public life. As you read the selections in this chapter and write about these issues, keep these underlying perspectives in mind.

Notes

1. Robert D. Putnam and Lewis M. Feldstein. *Better Together: Restoring the American Community,* New York: Simon & Schuster, 2003. pp. 142–165.
2. Peter Levine and Mark Hugo Lopez. "Youth Voter Turnout has Declined, by Any Measure" September 2002. *Circle: The Center for Information & Research on Civic Learning and Engagement.* University of Maryland's School of Public Affairs. http://www.civicyouth.org/research/products/fact_sheets_outside.htm
3. *Better Together,* pp. 147–148.

Hate Radio

Why We Need to Tune In to Limbaugh and Stern

Patricia J. Williams

In this article that appeared in *Ms.* magazine, Patricia J. Williams writes about her experiences as an African American woman making her way through her everyday routine: listening to the radio, rushing to an appointment, catching a cab. More and more, the social space she inhabits is becoming hostile and unfriendly. She hears code words like "blafrican" used to insinuate slurs about people of color; she gets out of a cab before her destination to avoid the driver's insulting stare. In an uncivil society, she is a scapegoat for all the problems of society—joblessness, poverty, and unwed mothers. It concerns her that in the wider society, she is not an individual personality but a stand-in for a dangerous and suspect group.

Williams sees a connection between the confrontational style of what she calls hate radio and her lack of a sense of community and well-being. Although the power and influence of Rush Limbaugh and Howard Stern have waned since she first wrote about them in 1995, their brand of divisive, inflammatory rhetoric is a feature of national and local political campaigns, special-interest Web sites, and radio and TV talk shows. It gains its power by appealing to individual self-interest and pitting "us" against "them." Along the way, the facts get blurred or are misrepresented, and the solution to social problems becomes a matter of targeting a specific group for blame. Although best known for her work on race and the law, Williams has turned her keen intellect to the relationship between the way we talk to each other and our ability to solve our problems.

Williams is a professor of law at Columbia University and the author of *The Alchemy of Race and Rights* and, more recently, *Seeing a Color-Blind Future.* Her column, "Diary of a Mad Lawyer," appears in *The Nation.*

Connecting with the Conversation

1. Do you listen to Rush Limbaugh, Bob Grant, or Howard Stern? What about your friends or family? Why do they say they choose these programs in particular? In your journal, speculate on why these talk show hosts have such a large following.
2. Code words are a kind of shorthand to refer to complex concepts and ideas. For example, in the 1994 election "soccer moms" was used to refer to a group of people who were voting for Bill Clinton and also as a way of capturing the political, social, and economic issues that made him their favorite candidate. What code words have emerged from recent events? Make a brief list of any you can think of, and note whether the usage is positive or negative. In a small group, compare your lists. What conclusions can you draw about the use of code words?

Three years ago I stood at my sink, washing the dishes and listening to the radio. I was tuned to rock and roll so I could avoid thinking about the big news from the day before—George Bush had just nominated Clarence Thomas to replace Thurgood Marshall on the Supreme Court. I was squeezing a dot of lemon Joy into each of the wineglasses when I realized that two smoothly radio-cultured voices, a man's and a woman's, had replaced the music.

"I think it's a stroke of genius on the president's part," said the female voice.

"Yeah," said the male voice. "Then those blacks, those African Americans, those Negroes—hey 'Negro' is good enough for Thurgood Marshall—whatever, they can't make up their minds [what] they want to be called. I'm gonna call them Blafricans. Black Africans. Yeah, I like it. Blafricans. Then they can get all upset because now the president appointed a Blafrican."

"Yeah, well, that's the way those liberals think. It's just crazy."

5 "And then after they turn down his nomination the president can say he tried to please 'em, and then he can appoint someone with some intelligence."

Back then, this conversation seemed so horrendously unusual, so singularly hateful, that I picked up a pencil and wrote it down. I was certain that a firestorm of protest was going to engulf the station and purge those foul radio mouths with the good clean soap of social outrage.

I am so naive. When I finally turned on the radio and rolled my dial to where everyone else had been tuned while I was busy watching Cosby reruns, it took me a while to understand that there's a firestorm all right, but not of protest. In the two and a half years since Thomas has assumed his post on the Supreme Court, the underlying assumptions of the conversation I heard as uniquely outrageous have become commonplace, popularly expressed, and louder in volume. I hear the style of that snide polemicism everywhere, among acquaintances, on the street, on television in toned-down

From *Ms.*, March/April 1994, pp. 25–29.

versions. It is a crude demagoguery that makes me heartsick. I feel more and more surrounded by that point of view, the assumptions of being without intelligence, the coded epithets, the "Blafrican"-like stand-ins for "nigger," the mocking angry glee, the endless tirades filled with nonspecific, nonempirically based slurs against "these people" or "those minorities" or "feminazis" or "liberals" or "scumbags" or "pansies" or "jerks" or "sleazeballs" or "loonies" or "animals" or "foreigners."

At the same time I am not so naive as to suppose that this is something new. In clear-headed moments I realize I am not listening to the radio anymore, I am listening to a large segment of white America think aloud in ever louder resurgent thoughts that have generations of historical precedent. It's as though the radio has split open like an egg, Morton Downey, Jr.'s clones and Joe McCarthy's ghost spilling out, broken yolks, a great collective of sometimes clever, sometimes small, but uniformly threatened brains—they have all come gushing out. Just as they were about to pass into oblivion, Jack Benny and his humble black sidekick Rochester get resurrected in the ungainly bodies of Howard Stern and his faithful black henchwoman, Robin Quivers. The culture of Amos and Andy has been revived and reassembled in Bob Grant's radio minstrelry and radio newcomer Daryl Gates's sanctimonious imprecations on behalf of decent white people. And in striking imitation of Jesse Helms's nearly forgotten days as a radio host, the far Right has found its undisputed king in the personage of Rush Limbaugh—a polished demagogue with a weekly radio audience of at least 20 million, a television show that vies for ratings with the likes of Jay Leno, a newsletter with a circulation of 380,000, and two best-selling books whose combined sales are closing in on six million copies.

From Churchill to Hitler to the old Soviet Union, it's clear that radio and television have the power to change the course of history, to proselytize, and to coalesce not merely the good and the noble, but the very worst in human nature as well. Likewise, when Orson Welles made his famous radio broadcast "witnessing" the landing of a spaceship full of hostile Martians, the United States ought to have learned a lesson about the power of radio to appeal to mass instincts and incite mass hysteria. Radio remains a peculiarly powerful medium even today, its visual emptiness in a world of six trillion flashing images allowing one of the few remaining playgrounds for the aural subconscious. Perhaps its power is attributable to our need for an oral tradition after all, some conveying of stories, feelings, myths of ancestors, epics of alienation, and the need to rejoin ancestral roots, even ignorant bigoted roots. Perhaps the visual quiescence of radio is related to the popularity of E-mail or electronic networking. Only the voice is made manifest, unmasking worlds that cannot—or dare not?—be seen. Just yet. Nostalgia crystallizing into a dangerous future. The preconscious voice erupting into the expressed, the prime time.

10 What comes out of the modern radio mouth could be the *Iliad,* the *Rubaiyat,* the griot's song of our times. If indeed radio is a vessel for the American "Song of Songs," then what does it mean that a manic, adolescent Howard Stern is so popular among radio listeners, that Rush Limbaugh's wittily smooth sadism has gone the way of primetime television, and that both vie for the number one slot on all the best-selling book lists? What to make of the stories being told by our modern radio evangelists and their tragic unloved chorus of callers? Is it really just a collapsing economy that spawns this drama of grown people sitting around scaring themselves to death with fantasies of black feminist Mexican able-bodied gay soldiers earning $100,000 a year on welfare

who are so criminally depraved that Hillary Clinton or the Antichrist-of-the-moment had no choice but to invite them onto the government payroll so they can run the country? The panicky exaggeration reminds me of a child's fear. . . . *And then, and then, a huge lion jumped out of the shadows and was about to gobble me up, and I can't ever sleep again for a whole week.*

As I spin the dial on my radio, I can't help thinking that this stuff must be related to that most poignant of fiber-optic phenomena, phone sex. Aural Sex. Radio Racism with a touch of S & M. High-priest hosts with the power and run-amok ego to discipline listeners, to smack with the verbal back of the hand, to smash the button that shuts you up once and for all. "Idiot!" shouts New York City radio demagogue Bob Grant and then the sound of droning telephone emptiness, the voice of dissent dumped out some trapdoor in aural space.

As I listened to a range of such programs what struck me as the most unifying theme was not merely the specific intolerance on such hot topics as race and gender but a much more general contempt for the world, a verbal stoning of anything different. It is like some unusually violent game of "Simon Says," this mockery and shouting down of callers, this roar of incantations, the insistence on agreement.

But, ah, if you *will* but only agree, what sweet and safe reward, what soft enfolding by a stern and angry radio god. And as an added bonus, the invisible shield of an AM community, a family of fans who are Exactly Like You, to whom you can express, in anonymity, all the filthy stuff you imagine "them" doing to you. The comfort and relief of being able to ejaculate, to those who understand, about the dark imagined excess overtaking, robbing, needing to be held down and taught a good lesson, needing to put it in its place before the ravenous demon enervates all that is true and good and pure in this life.

The audience for this genre of radio flagellation is mostly young, white, and male. Two thirds of Rush Limbaugh's audience is male. According to *Time* magazine, 75 percent of Howard Stern's listeners are white men. Most of the callers have spent their lives walling themselves off from any real experience with blacks, feminists, lesbians, or gays. In this regard, it is probably true, as former Secretary of Education William Bennett says, that Rush Limbaugh "tells his audience that what you believe inside, you can talk about in the marketplace." Unfortunately, what's "inside" is then mistaken for what's outside, treated as empirical and political reality. The *National Review* extols Limbaugh's conservative leadership as no less than that of Ronald Reagan, and the Republican party provides Limbaugh with books to discuss, stories, angles, and public support. "People were afraid of censure by gay activists, feminists, environmentalists—now they are not because Rush takes them on," says Bennett.

15 U.S. history has been marked by cycles in which brands of this or that hatred come into fashion and go out, are unleashed and then restrained. If racism, homophobia, jingoism, and woman-hating have been features of national life in pretty much all of modern history, it rather begs the question to spend a lot of time wondering if right-wing radio is a symptom or a cause. For at least 400 years, prevailing attitudes in the West have considered African Americans less intelligent. Recent statistics show that 53 percent of people in the U.S. agree that blacks and Latinos are less intelligent than whites, and a majority believe that blacks are lazy, violent, welfare-dependent, and unpatriotic.

I think that what has made life more or less tolerable for "out" groups have been those moments in history when those "inside" feelings were relatively restrained. In fact, if I could believe that right-wing radio were only about idiosyncratic, singular, rough-hewn individuals thinking those inside thoughts, I'd be much more inclined to agree with Columbia University media expert Everette Dennis, who says that Stern's and Limbaugh's popularity represents the "triumph of the individual" or with *Time* magazine's bottom line that "the fact that either is seriously considered a threat . . . is more worrisome than Stern or Limbaugh will ever be." If what I were hearing had even a tad more to do with real oppressions, with real white *and* black levels of joblessness and homelessness, or with the real problems of real white men, then I wouldn't have bothered to slog my way through hours of Howard Stern's miserable obsessions.

Yet at the heart of my anxiety is the worry that Stern, Limbaugh, Grant, et al. represent the very antithesis of individualism's triumph. As the *National Review* said of Limbaugh's ascent, "It was a feat not only of the loudest voice but also of a keen political brain to round up, as Rush did, the media herd and drive them into the conservative corral." When asked about his political aspirations, Bob Grant gloated to the *Washington Post,* "I think I would make rather a good dictator."

The polemics of right-wing radio are putting nothing less than hate onto the airwaves, into the marketplace, electing it to office, teaching it in schools, and exalting it as freedom. What worries me is the increasing-to-constant commerce of retribution, control, and lashing out, fed not by fact but fantasy. What worries me is the reemergence, more powerfully than at any time since the institution of Jim Crow, of a sociocentered self that excludes "the likes of," well, me for example, from the civic circle, and that would rob me of my worth and claim and identity as a citizen. As the *Economist* rightly observes, "Mr. Limbaugh takes a mass market—white, mainly male, middle-class, ordinary America—and talks to it as an endangered minority."

I worry about this identity whose external reference is a set of beliefs, ethics, and practices that excludes, restricts, and acts in the world on me, or mine, as the perceived if not real enemy. I am acutely aware of losing *my* mythic individualism to the surface shapes of my mythic group fearsomeness as black, as female, as left wing. "I" merge not fluidly but irretrievably into a category of "them." I become a suspect self, a moving target of loathsome properties, not merely different but dangerous. And that worries me a lot.

20 What happens in my life with all this translated license, this permission to be uncivil? What happens to the social space that was supposedly at the sweet mountaintop of the civil rights movement's trail? Can I get a seat on the bus without having to be reminded that I *should* be standing? Did the civil rights movement guarantee us nothing more than to use public accommodations while surrounded by raving lunatic bigots? "They didn't beat this idiot [Rodney King] enough," says Howard Stern.

Not long ago I had the misfortune to hail a taxicab in which the driver was listening to Howard Stern undress some woman. After some blocks, I had to get out. I was, frankly, afraid to ask the driver to turn it off—not because I was afraid of "censoring" him, which seems to be the only thing people will talk about anymore, but because the driver was stripping me too, as he leered through the rearview mirror. "Something the matter?" he demanded, as I asked him to pull over and let me out well short of my destination. (I'll spare you the full story of what happened from there—trying to get another cab, as the cabbies stopped for all the white businessmen who so much as scratched their heads near the curb; a nice young white man, seeing my plight, giving me his cab, having to thank him, he hero, me saved-but-humiliated, cabdriver pissed and surly. I fight my way to my destination, finally arriving in bad mood, militant black woman, cranky feminazi.)

When Yeltsin blared rock music at his opponents holed up in the parliament building in Moscow, in imitation of the U.S. Marines trying to torture Manuel Noriega in Panama, all I could think of was that it must be like being trapped in a crowded subway car when all the portable stereos are tuned to Bob Grant or Howard Stern. With Howard Stern's voice a tinny, screeching backdrop, with all the faces growing dreamily mean as though some soporifically evil hallucinogen were gushing into their bloodstreams, I'd start begging to surrender.

Surrender to what? Surrender to the laissez-faire resegregation that is the metaphoric significance of the hundreds of "Rush rooms" that have cropped up in restaurants around the country; rooms broadcasting Limbaugh's words, rooms for your listening pleasure, rooms where bigots can capture the purity of a Rush-only lunch counter, rooms where all those unpleasant others just "choose" not to eat? Surrender to the naughty luxury of a room in which a Ku Klux Klan meeting could take place in orderly, First Amendment fashion? Everyone's "free" to come in (and a few of you outsiders do), but mostly the undesirable nonconformists are gently repulsed away. It's a high-tech world of enhanced choice. Whites choose mostly to sit in the Rush room. Feminists, blacks, lesbians, and gays "choose" to sit elsewhere. No need to buy black votes, you just pay them not to vote; no need to insist on white-only schools, you just sell the desirability of black-only schools. Just sit back and watch it work, like those invisible shock shields that keep dogs cowering in their own backyards.

How real is the driving perception behind all the Sturm und Drang of this genre of radio-harangue—the perception that white men are an oppressed minority, with no power and no opportunity in the land that they made great? While it is true that power and opportunity are shrinking for all but the very wealthy in this country (and would that Limbaugh would take that issue on), the fact remains that white men are still this country's most privileged citizens and market actors. To give just a small example, according to the *Wall Street Journal,* blacks were the only racial group to suffer a net job loss during the 1990–91 economic downturn at the companies reporting to the Equal Employment Opportunity Commission. Whites, Latinos, and Asians, meanwhile, gained thousands of jobs. While whites gained 71,144 jobs at these companies, Latinos gained 60,040, Asians gained 55,104, and blacks lost 59,479. If every black were hired in the United States tomorrow, the numbers would not be sufficient to account for white men's expanding balloon of fear that they have been specifically dispossessed by African Americans.

25 Given deep patterns of social segregation and general ignorance of history, particularly racial history, media remain the principal source of most Americans' knowledge of each other. Media can provoke violence or induce passivity. In San Francisco, for example, a radio show on KMEL called "Street Soldiers" has taken this power as a responsibility with great consequence: "Unquestionably," writes Ken Auletta in the *New Yorker,* "the

show has helped avert violence. When a Samoan teenager was slain, apparently by Filipino gang members, in a drive-by shooting, the phones lit up with calls from Samoans wanting to tell [the hosts] they would not rest until they had exacted revenge. Threats filled the air for a couple of weeks. Then the dead Samoan's father called in, and, in a poignant exchange, the father said he couldn't tolerate the thought of more young men senselessly slaughtered. There would be no retaliation, he vowed. And there was none." In contrast, we must wonder at the phenomenon of the very powerful leadership of the Republican party, from Ronald Reagan to Robert Dole to William Bennett, giving advice, counsel, and friendship to Rush Limbaugh's passionate divisiveness.

The outright denial of the material crisis at every level of U.S. society, most urgently in black inner-city neighborhoods but facing us all, is a kind of political circus, dissembling as it feeds the frustrations of the moment. We as a nation can no longer afford to deal with such crises by *imagining* an excess of bodies, of babies, of job-stealers, of welfare mothers, of overreaching immigrants, of too-powerful (Jewish, in whispers) liberal Hollywood, of lesbians and gays, of gang members ("gangsters" remain white, and no matter what the atrocity, less vilified than "gang members," who are black), of Arab terrorists, and uppity women. The reality of our social poverty far exceeds these scapegoats. This right-wing backlash resembles, in form if not substance, phenomena like anti-Semitism in Poland: there aren't but a handful of Jews left in that whole country, but the giant balloon of heated anti-Semitism flourishes apace, Jews blamed for the world's evils.

The overwhelming response to right-wing excesses in the United States has been to seek an odd sort of comfort in the fact that the First Amendment is working so well that you can't suppress this sort of thing. Look what's happened in Eastern Europe. Granted. So let's not talk about censorship or the First Amendment for the next ten minutes. But in Western Europe, where fascism is rising at an appalling rate, suppression is hardly the problem. In Eastern and Western Europe as well as the United States, we must begin to think just a little bit about the fiercely coalescing power of media to spark mistrust, to fan it into forest fires of fear and revenge. We must begin to think about the levels of national and social complacence in the face of such resolute ignorance. We must ask ourselves what the expected result is, not of censorship or suppression, but of so much encouragement, so much support, so much investment in the fashionability of hate. What future is it that we are designing with the devotion of such tremendous resources to the disgraceful propaganda of bigotry?

Exploring Texts and Contexts

For activities with icons, refer to the Guide to Analyzing Readings in Context.

1. Now that you have read Williams's article, try to answer her implied question: "Why do we need to tune in to Limbaugh and Stern?" What does she say are the consequences of ignoring these talk show hosts? 

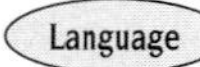

2. Williams's article critiques the polemics of right-wing radio and its argumentative style. Search through her article for all the words that she uses to describe this kind of language. Based on your review, compose a definition for this style of argument.
3. According to Williams we can no longer afford to deal with our social poverty by using scapegoats, that is, by blaming our problems on "welfare mothers" or "overreaching immigrants." What does she mean by this? What does she feel will be the social consequences? Point to specific ideas in her writing that help you understand her position.

Creating Texts

For activities with icons, refer to the Guides to Analyzing Contexts for Writing and Analzing Readings in Context. For additional help with these writing projects, read the description of **Comics** in the Genre Glossary.

1. Comics, in particular the political cartoons found in the editorial section of the paper, are a particularly useful medium to characterize the way we talk to each other in highly politicized or charged situations. Sketch an interaction between identifiable characters that uses humor to capture a particular moment in the communication process.

Symposium on Minority Journalists and the Media

Ray Suarez, Ellis Cose, Joie Chen, George de Lama, and Mark Trahant

Among the ancient Greeks, a symposium was a lively party fueled by drink, talk, and intellectual entertainment. Today's symposia keep the conversation but not the drink; their purpose is to get a group of people together to talk about a particular topic, as in this symposium on minority journalists and the media. This symposium focuses on the role of minority journalists in providing balanced coverage and diverse perspectives in the media. It aired on "Talk of the Nation," a popular call-in radio show produced by National Public Radio (NPR) and hosted by Ray Suarez for many years.

A national meeting of minority journalists, Unity '99, allowed Suarez to bring his professional interests as a journalist of color to his own radio call-in show. Suarez aired the symposium from Unity '99, at which journalists met from four organizations: the Asian American Journalists Association, the National Association of Hispanic Journalists, the National Association of Black Journalists, and the Native American Journalist Association. These organizations have recently emerged to offer support for media professionals who find themselves either the only person or one of a very few people of color in a news organization. For example, in 1978 newspapers had fewer than 4 percent people of color on their staff, but now have about 12 percent. Still, as many as 40 percent of newsrooms have no people of color.

Throughout the transcript of this live radio symposium, we can follow the participants as they respond to each other and answer questions from callers. The question posed initially by Suarez gets to the heart of civic participation: How does our shifting sense of self—say, from African American to managing editor—influence the way we do our job and the way we represent the news to our audience? As you read the transcript of the symposium, notice how the respondents bring their own experiences and perspectives to the table.

Connecting with the Conversation

1. Listen to a radio or television symposium; check the listings for C-SPAN or your local National Public Radio station. Take notes on the questions asked by the audience and how the symposium participants respond. How would you characterize the interaction between the symposium participants and the audience? In your opinion, was the topic explored fully? If not, why not? Write up your responses to these questions, and bring your notes to class.
2. For the next few days as you watch television, listen to the radio, or read the newspaper make note of minority journalists and the sorts of stories they cover. Bring your notes to class for a discussion of whether minority journalists contribute a particular perspective.

RAY SUAREZ, *host:* This is TALK OF THE NATION. I'm Ray Suarez.

We're coming to you this hour from the Seattle Convention Center where the largest-ever meeting of American journalists is under way, Unity '99. It's a meeting of the big four national minority journalists organizations, held for the first time in five years. We're back together and still arguing with our business about some of the same fundamental questions we faced back in Atlanta in 1994.

So what are we saying to the American news business? That we're as good as anyone else, but different? That we can cover our own communities better than anyone else, but cover any other community as well as anyone else? Are we somehow signaling to the people who hire that we are ethnically, personally, culturally authentic and imposing on ourselves a requirement that our newsroom colleagues have no need to bother with? And as our business becomes increasingly middle-class, increasingly well-educated, professionally secure, does this obligation to authenticity involve a kind of subterfuge that we, white-collar and increasingly mainstream, can explain a complex American experience that is, in fact, increasingly remote from our own lives, to a largely white audience? Are we trying to straddle a double life, neither one thing or the other?

Authenticity, ethnic presentation and the life of the newsroom this hour on the program. All my guests are with me here at Unity '99 in Seattle. Ellis Cose is a

From "Talk of the Nation," July 8, 1999, National Public Radio.

columnist and contributing editor for *Newsweek* and the author of "Colorblind: Seeing Beyond Race in a Race-Obsessed World." Welcome to the program.

Mr. ELLIS COSE (*Newsweek*): Thank you, Ray. Glad to be here.

5 SUAREZ: Joie Chen is an anchor and correspondent for "The World Today" at CNN. Welcome.

Ms. JOIE CHEN (CNN): Thank you, Ray.

SUAREZ: George de Lama is associate managing editor for foreign and national news at the *Chicago Tribune.* Good to have you with us.

Mr. GEORGE de LAMA (*Chicago Tribune*): Thank you, Ray.

SUAREZ: And Mark Trahant is a columnist for *The Seattle Times.*

10 Mr. MARK TRAHANT: Thank you, Ray.

SUAREZ: As always, we'll take your calls from around the country, and we'll also hear from our Unity '99 conventioneers here in the studio audience.

Ellis Cose, I wanted to start with you, since the half a million or so of our close, personal friends that are listening in other places and aren't going to be here won't make it for your panel "Is It Race or Is It Me?" What are you going to tell people who are looking for an answer to that question?

Mr. COSE: Well, I think basically—and this goes to the first point—or the first question you were asking, Ray: What are we trying to say to people? What are we trying to say to the editors? I think what we're trying to say to editors and publishers is that we are all part of the American family, that the various communities that we come from are part of either their readership or their audience, which they ought to be concerned about.

I think, though, that we as organizations—and I don't speak for an organization, but we as members of organizations—have too often focused too much on just numbers, and we've had the sort of assumption that if you hire enough of us, everything's going to somehow work out and be better. And I think that's just not enough. It's just not far enough. And it really comes from the historical reasons why this movement started. I mean, it actually started because of the riots in the '60s and the Kerner Commission, which said, in effect, 'Hey, we had no clue of what was going to be happening to our country. We need some people who do.' And if we look at who populates newspapers and television stations, there are virtually no blacks, firstly, no people of color. That has to change, and it has changed, to some extent. But the next step is, OK, once it begins to change, what does all this change mean?

15 SUAREZ: I wonder if there's a trap, though, waiting in that assumption. You mentioned the pitfalls of saying, 'If you hire enough of us, things will take care of themselves.' But America, for all its remaining problems, is still a very different place for—let's take the example for black Americans—than it was in 1966. And when we say that there has to be some presence in the newsroom, and indeed, a lot of major American news organizations hired their first black editorial staff after those riots. . . .

Mr. COSE: Right.

SUAREZ: Are we presenting a uniform self to the news business as Exhibit A, in the same way that we would have in 1966? Do you have to be a representative of black culture, a representative of black America, when all you want to do is be a metro editor or a photog or just a working stiff?

Mr. COSE: Well, I mean, certainly it's a key question. And I think if we're smart, the answer to that is no, we don't say that we represent anybody but ourselves. But I think that we also recognize that, in representing ourselves, we represent all kinds of things. And let me just use a brief example. Several years ago, when I was first starting in the business, I went to *Esquire* magazine to try to get an assignment there as a free-lance writer. And I remember having this bizarre conversation with a senior editor there who looked at me sort of incredulously, at one point, and said to me, 'Well, Ellis, you know, I'm not sure how many black readers we have. I'm not sure we need someone like you writing for us.' And I, of course, was extremely angry and a bit baffled and confused because, clearly, what he was saying was that he could only see me as someone who would address a black audience.

But the larger point, you know, is that we come to this business, we as people, with all kinds of baggage and with all kinds of experiences. And it would be naive to assume that some of those experiences aren't rooted in the different treatment that we've had as different ethnic groups and as different racial groups. So inevitably, we're going to bring something different to a newsroom than someone who hasn't had those experiences. We also, as a profession, are in the knowledge business, which means that we're in the business of trying to find out as much about as many things, as many people, as many cultures, as we can. And to the extent that we increase the number of people who represent something different, whatever that difference is, we're a bit ahead. But I think you're absolutely right; no, I mean, we shouldn't be in the trap of saying, you know, 'I represent this group' or 'Someone else represents the other group.' In the final analysis, I just represent me.

SUAREZ: But, Joie Chen, the physical presence that television provides sort of forces being a symbol on some people, whether they signed up for the symbol business or not. The camera does not blink, and there you are.

Ms. CHEN: I think that those of us who are minorities and journalists can test that question constantly in our own lives. When I walk into a room, am I a journalist first? Am I Asian first? When I come into the room in a professional capacity, I think I'm certainly a reporter before I'm an Asian, but I don't think you could fail to notice what I look like. I think that these questions are always going to be with you, in a way.

Recently, for example, in the Chinese Embassy bombing in Belgrade, I had someone who's actually very close to me in the newsroom say, 'Well, I saw your reporting. Were you angry about the Chinese Embassy being bombed?' And I thought, 'Was I angry about the Chinese Embassy being bombed?' Well, yeah, I mean, I do think, certainly, that it was a bad thing to accidentally bomb an embassy. Was I particularly, personally angry because I'm half ethnically Chinese? No. But apparently, there was some perception, some misperception, some understanding that perhaps I was receiving it in a way differently than a white colleague or a black colleague would.

SUAREZ: So for the record, you would have been upset if it was the Latvian Embassy that . . .

Ms. CHEN: Sure. Well, I mean, I think from a political standpoint it was a particularly bad idea for that mistake to be made. But, you know, was I personally more offended by this? No, of course not.

SUAREZ: George, the American Society of Newspaper Editors has recently and famously had to back away from a commitment it made to newsroom diversity, and has had to take a lot of heat for that. And while you might admire the honesty that comes with saying, 'Hey, we're not going to make it. Let's figure out what we can do and by when we can do it,' it is still seen as a large disappointment that it didn't happen. And you're sort of in this funny inside-outside position.

25 Mr. de LAMA: Well, I think justifiably so that there was a lot of heat. That's—you know, I personally was very disappointed. I think that's not good enough. I'll tell you, as an editor, one of the phrases I hate the most is, particularly when we're recruiting for a senior-level position, the phrase, 'Well, there aren't many minority candidates out there' or 'There aren't any,' I hear sometimes. And excuse me; sure, there are. You just need to know where to look. You know, this place right here in these few days is a good example. There's a lot of talent here. But I think they're well-meaning people in most of the—certainly the larger newspapers, and they mean well and the intentions are good. I personally have to admit I get very frustrated sometimes.

SUAREZ: Is the *Tribune* a different product because its staff is a different animal than it was 20 years ago? There wouldn't have been a George de Lama, a Cuban guy, being an associate managing editor 20 years ago.

Mr. de LAMA: No. As a matter of fact, I think last Saturday made 21 years for me there, and I was the second Hispanic reporter in the history of the *Tribune.* This is a 150-year-old organization. We have a couple associate managing editors, Latinos, now, and others of color as well. I like to think we're a much better newspaper in that we have many more people of different backgrounds. I agree with Ellis. We bring different things to the table as individuals. So does somebody who speaks Russian or somebody who's well-traveled or somebody who's an expert in science.

It's funny; we're all the sum of our experiences. We're the products of what we know. The thing about news is that news is what we don't know. And I think when you have more people, it's good common sense to—diversity—the question earlier, is diversity good? It's good common sense. It makes for better journalism. And that, in turn, is good business. And the last one, that's the one that gets the attention of all the nice people who run newspapers and news organizations these days.

SUAREZ: Mark Trahant, the Native American journalists, away from more formal programs like this one, can be heard to complain loudly or privately that they are sometimes the afterthoughts, even at an organizational meeting like this one, where they should be central to our thoughts. And I wonder if that's just—after a while you take that as part of the given of the territory, or whether there is a real expectation that it has to change and some anger that it hasn't quite.

30 Mr. TRAHANT: Sure. I think part of that is a phenomenon of numbers; just the sheer numbers of Native American populations in general is so much smaller that it takes it a while to catch up. I do have a specific example, though, that I was thinking about, building on the previous point on examples of how newsroom coverage could be different and improved. When the hantavirus crisis broke out in the Southwest, I was in management at *The Salt Lake Tribune,*

And two interesting things happened. One, we happen to have Navajo-speaking reporters and correspondents, interestingly enough, one of whom was co-opted by National Public Radio during the process. And the second thing was, in preparing for our coverage, I had decided that I didn't want us to cover funerals, because Navajos felt that was offensive. And to prepare my argument for the news meetings, I went and researched all the coverage of the Legionnaires' disease in Philadelphia, and could find no funeral coverage. I went into the news meeting with all of that material, saying, 'Look, here's how it was covered before.' And it was funny; I didn't even get to present it. Once I said I didn't think we should be at funerals, everyone agreed with me. So I think in a real quiet, effective way, you can change how the business covers these stories.

SUAREZ: Is it less remarkable having you around than it was when you were just starting out?

Mr. TRAHANT: Absolutely. My first mainstream—I went back and forth between tribal newspapers and mainstream papers my whole career, and my first mainstream newspaper was the *Arizona Republic.* And I think the first two years everyone thought I was going to leave. And so anytime something would happen, there would be rumors about that more than what I was doing.

SUAREZ: If you want to join the conversation, our number is (*800*) 989-8255; that's (*800*) 989-TALK.

We'll go first to Pasadena, California. Richard, welcome to the program.

RICHARD (*Caller*): Thank you very much. I just wanted to comment on what a racist question you're discussing here: How do journalists of a particular ethnic background influence the news? And, you know, I'm tired of Americans being split up and pitted against each other racially by programs like this and others. And I'd comment to your Asian journalist, Joie Chen, when she's deciding whether to report as an Asian or a journalist, how about being an American? It's really—you know, for myself, I'm getting really tired of it. The—if you look at the programs that are on television, if you would substitute the word 'white' in place of things like 'Miss Black College beauty contest' or 'Hispanic music awards' or 'Ebony Awards'—if you put 'white' in there, everyone would be up in arms.

And then when you get a guy like Clinton doing what he's doing and the black community is supporting him, on the Monica Lewinsky thing—Clinton is the guy that gave us NAFTA, that took the jobs away from a lot—all Americans—minorities, whites, everyone, and everybody keeps supporting him. It's time to get down to the real truth of this thing, that we're all Americans, and let's act like it.

SUAREZ: Well, Richard, I understand the point you're trying to make, but I'm wondering, when in a place where all kinds of people live and live in large numbers, if you were to walk into the newsroom of a large media organization in that metropolitan area and basically see a sea of white faces, should that be taken as a coincidence, unremarkable and not worth being remarked upon? Or is that something that—a question we shouldn't even concern ourselves with?

RICHARD: Well, I don't know where you're looking, but when I turn television on, here in the Los Angeles area, I'd say that 80 percent of the reporters on television are not white. They're other ethnic backgrounds. Connie Chung was here in LA, Tritia Toyota, etc., etc., etc. And so as far as being represented, it appears to me that they have a very high representation, and I have no prejudice. In my business, I deal with the Chinese-Americans, I deal with Korean-Americans, I deal with black Americans; I deal with people of all ethnic backgrounds. And I look at them not as minorities;

I look at them as Americans. And that's how I deal with them. And can't we get back to that? Can't we do that?

40 SUAREZ: Yeah. I—'Can't we do that,' I think, is a better, more rational question than 'Can't we get back to that,' because back then, we didn't do that. So yeah, I. . .

RICHARD: Well, that. . .

SUAREZ: But I take your point.

RICHARD: That isn't necessarily true. When there was full employment in the United States, when the jobs were here in the United States, there was much—there was discrimination. But there was much less problems with the amount of money people were making, fighting over jobs of inequality—of quality, not inequality, but jobs of quality. And everyone got along much better. Now the jobs are gone from the country. No cars are manufactured in the United States. You look at every product you see and it's manufactured in some other country by slave labor. Incidentally, if they want a global economy, let's have a global minimum-wage law. And that's why the races are really fighting against each other, but nobody wants to address that problem.

SUAREZ: Well, I think, Richard. . .

45 Mr. COSE: Well, I'm not quite sure I understand all the points. I mean, at present, we have the fullest—excuse me—fullest employment economy since the 1960s. So I'm not quite clear what he's trying to say about the employment stats. But I think that what Richard has articulated, you know, is a wonderful and fantastic dream. I think the problem is grappling with the reality. If we, in fact, could all just be Americans, we wouldn't have segregated communities. We wouldn't be even able to talk about a black neighborhood or an Italian-American neighborhood or a Chinatown or any of these things, because they wouldn't exist. There would just be one community where everybody sort of lived among each other. We wouldn't be actually even able to talk about racial groups because everybody would be getting married to one another, and there wouldn't be this whole division that we have here. I think what we're sort of grappling with is, how do you deal with the reality where there are racial distinctions that are made and racial categories that exist and racialized thinking as a consequence of that?

I think that's the issue that we're talking about here, you know, not how can we just sort of close our eyes, forget that these differences exist and pretend that we're all Americans, starting from the fact that we're not sort of all at that same point and that same place.

SUAREZ: Well, Richard's comments gorgeously illustrate what, in more narrow senses, we've been saying to managements and saying to bosses and saying to owners for 40 years. But it's very hard to see it when you look back at a world and say, 'Once it was better. We shouldn't label people,' and that, in fact, a lot of the dragons are already slain. There is no problem.

Mr. COSE: Well, see—well, once, it was better, because the only world that mattered to a lot of people who were in a position to say anything was the white world.

Mr. de LAMA: I want to build on that. I think one of America's unresolved questions—and I think it's critical that we come to a conclusion on it for the next century—is the idea that I would call cultural manifest destiny, or assimilation. Can this country allow and respect cultures to be different in the next generation, and to somehow fuse that as an American value?

50 SUAREZ: So you are optimistic?

Mr. TRAHANT: Yeah. I mean, it's a slow process. I guess I look at it with a very long view. One of the ways I think this conversation started—and I mentioned it in my column today—is that in 1947, a group of all white scholars came together, the Hutchins committee, chaired by Robert Maynard Hutchins, and they talked about the notion that if America couldn't understand its constituent groups—they didn't even call it race—constituent groups, that American democracy would be fragile. And I think that's still true.

Mr. de LAMA: I agree with Ellis very much. I think there's one other point, though, as the—you've been talking about here, Ray, as minorities, increasingly, not just in newsrooms, become more the majority, the mainstream—the demographics say minorities will be the majority in this country—I think it's also incumbent on us to present other images and to erase some of the stereotypes or try to combat some of the stereotypes. For instance, in coverage of poverty, we really, when we write welfare stories, we need to seek out welfare recipients who are not African-American.

I think it's interesting, as President Clinton, in his anti-poverty swing, the White House was very conscious of symbolically having the different faces, ethnically also, and racially, of poverty over the last few days as he's gone around the country. I think by the same token, when we write about black doctors, it shouldn't only be in stories about black middle-class or black professionals. It should be quoting black doctors about osteoporosis. And I—that's something that we've heard a lot from our readers. And I think that's a good point—I mean, from our minority readers.

SUAREZ: But how do you change the habits, though, because even the minority reporters that you have in your newsroom fall into those same habits, going back to the same profs at the local universities to get a quote on science, going back to the same authorities in various fields to get a quote. I mean, we all do that, even though, supposedly, we're supposed to be more conscious about these questions.

55 Ms. CHEN: I think one of the great failures of all of the news media today is that pack mentality, I think, Ray, that you're sort of referring to, that we tend to fall on the same experts, the same voices of whatever community we think we're talking to, you know? I grew up in Chicago and I remember a time when we actually were convinced that Jesse Jackson spoke for all black people in the country, you know, that he was the voice. And if you had an issue that somehow involved African-Americans, then Jesse Jackson was the only voice. But clearly, we know today. And that is—that advancement goes back to what Richard was saying. There—what we have learned—and, I think, ultimately, that is the best of what journalism is. It is about education and what we learn and what we provide as journalists is new information, new things to learn for the communities. I think that's something that we have done, and I think that it is most effectively done when you have a lot of different voices.

It wouldn't matter if we were talking about division that were not by race. Say they were by gender, say they were by understanding of sports or of medicine or of space or whatever. Whatever our expertise is, we bring that to the table. Whatever our understanding, whatever our interests are, we bring that to the table and we broaden understanding by doing that.

SUAREZ: Yes, let's go to the floor.

Mr. HARRISON CHESTING(*ph*): Hi, Ray. My name is Harrison Chesting. I'm with KPOO Radio in San Francisco. And there's going to be a panel tomorrow, called "The Color of Film," talking about the problems people of color, particularly Asians and Latins, are having being represented—and Native Americans—in television and on the movies. And issues concerning African-Americans and other people of color in the movie business often get first reported in the ethnic media and then they get picked up by the mainstream press. In the newsrooms, do you find that there's a dilemma of: 'I know the story's out there, but if myself, as a person of color, if I don't bring it to the editors or write it up or report it myself, it won't get covered.' Or on the flip side, do you have a situation where you, as a person of color, feel, 'I don't want to be the reporter that is constantly reporting on the issues concerning people of color.' And conversely, should newspapers and media outlets do their own research and coverage of issues, rather than depending on the ethnic media to find out about these stories and just more or less rewrite it or rebroadcast it from the ethnic press?

SUAREZ: Great question.

Mr. COSE: Want me to take a crack at it?

SUAREZ: Sure.

Mr. COSE: The answer to the second part of it first, I think there's always going to be a function for the ethnic press. I think there's always going to be a function for specialized press. And there are, to some extent, going to be tip sheets for the so-called mainstream media, which are going to look at them and get information from them for things they don't cover as well or as consistently. And I think that function will always exist.

The more interesting question, though, I think, is the one you asked as your first question. And I just want to share, again, a brief anecdote. Several years ago, when I was in Chicago with the *Chicago Sun-Times,* which is where I began my career, for a brief time, I was asked by the editor, then a fellow named Jim Hoge, to head up a team of reporters. I was in charge of a task force of reporters who were charged with covering what—with what he considered the minority community, which meant Asian-Americans, Latinos and blacks in Chicago. And I had a small group of reporters, four reporters, to do this with. And I was given responsibility or at least the charge to do stories about everything in all sections of the paper.

I did that exercise for about six months, and we got a hell of a lot more coverage of all of those communities in the newspaper, in all sections, than we had before that. And yet, at the end of the six months, I found myself going back to Jim Hoge and saying, 'This is a bad idea,' because part of what I found was that the city editor, for instance—and these were in the days talking about Jesse Jackson and Jesse Jackson and Operation Breadbasket, dating myself a bit—you know, and he used to have this Saturday morning meeting every morning. The city editor would come to me and say, 'Well, I'm not gonna staff that, Ellis, because you're sending one of your people, right?' You know, and it became a ghettoization of the news function. What happened was that all of these other editors who otherwise you would have expected to have been responsible for this coverage sort of decided, well, they really didn't have to think about this anymore because this special minority team or team dealing with the minority community was going to think about that.

65 I mean, I offer that anecdote because I think that it illustrates sort of the paradox that a lot of journalists of color sometimes face and that the question are raised, which is the one, 'Yes, if you do take responsibility, personal responsibility, to make sure things get covered in your community, you probably are going to get a lot more coverage than there would otherwise. The problem with that is that it also encourages other people to think they don't have to do that.' And ideally, what you should do is be able to force other people to accept that as part of their mandate.

SUAREZ: But there, there's the trap that I began the program talking about because if journalists who belong to these organizations say, 'One of the reasons you need us in your newsrooms is because of what we bring,' then we jump salty when the editor says, 'OK, I brought you in here to bring this. Bring it.' That seems like a little bit of bait-and-switch. I sold myself as a certain bill of goods, but now I don't want to be the go-to guy on everything Latino, everything American Indian.

Mr. TRAHANT: You know, and being a columnist, you have a lot of freedom, but one of the things I try to bring to my task is to be an eagle bird, to fly as high as I can and look at the region. And part of that is bringing that experience, but it—also, an understanding of the other experiences and then trying to show how the fabric is working together or not. And that is not really—it's not an either/or. You can do both. You can—I think you learn to change the face of what you're going to cover pretty easily.

SUAREZ: Either of you want to jump in on that?

Mr. de LAMA: Well, I think, Ellis—I had a very similar experience at *The Tribune* covering Latino affairs in Chicago when I was a young reporter, but that said, I remember talking to my editors and I didn't want to be just perceived as that, as almost being professionally minority. And I think it's incumbent on minority reporters, you have to balance that. These communities need to be covered. It helps to have people who understand them, can penetrate them, can provide us with some context and insight. At the same time, you want to balance that and have the same expanded opportunities to grow up to be Carol Simpson or Ray Suarez and to be thought of as a White House correspondent or a foreign correspondent. Those are the same opportunities our colleagues have always had, so it's incumbent on reporters and editors to be able to visualize themselves and visualize your staff in these positions, to be able to project them there and provide those opportunities.

70 Ms. CHEN: And visualize how that helps your organization.

Mr. de LAMA: Absolutely. And you have to go get it because nobody's going to hand it to you, which is probably fair enough.

SUAREZ: Yeah, but how does that square with us saying, 'We have to be there because of what we bring'?

Mr. COSE: Well, I think it squares very simply, Ray. And the answer is, 'Yes, we're there because of what we're bring, but we're also there for many other reasons' and deal with complexity because that's reality.

SUAREZ: We'll go back to the floor. Yes.

75 Ms. ENUPE SINGLA(*ph*): Hi. I'm Enupe Singla. I'm a reporter with Bloomberg News and I'm a member of Asian American Journalists Association as well as the South

Asian Journalists Association. And it really struck me that we're here at Unity and the presidents of all four minority organizations this year are women.

And, Joie, I'd just like you to talk about the struggles you possibly went through being a woman of color in journalism, as well as where you see the future for women in the newsroom.

Ms. CHEN: You know, actually, this is going to sound a little backward, but I'm a little bit concerned that the future of television journalism actually becomes too dominated by women. And the reason I feel this way is that I've been in a number of journalism schools recently where the population is about 80 percent female.

And my concern about this is that I suspect that this is becoming something of a girl job in the most pejorative sense, the kind of job that a pretty girl gets for a few years until she finds a wealthy husband and does this. I don't see it as of much of a commitment to journalism as I would like to, as much as I see a number of young women who are committed to being on television. That concerns me greatly.

I think that I will admit that I've come from a generation that probably had great advantage coming as a woman and a minority. I'm in recognition that that is probably the case. Certainly, I had the sense of certain discrimination. I was hired by my first news director in Charleston, South Carolina, and I remember thinking, 'Why would Charleston, South Carolina's, television stations need to have an Asian-American woman on there for their audience? What possible use would I be in their audience?' And I went to interview with him and he said—talked a lot about issues, about the news and a number of skills. And he said to me, 'You know, I was stationed in Korea and you look just like a girl I used to date.' And I recognized then and there that that was the reason I was sitting in the room. I had an advantage. It was not an advantage I particularly wanted to have. But it is the advantage that I had.

SUAREZ: And in a burst of self-righteous rage, you told him he could take his job and his station . . .

Ms. CHEN: No, I took the job. I took the job and made the most of it because, let me tell you what, for every disadvantage you get, there may be an advantage in it. And I'm willing to understand that there are trade-offs and some I have taken. And that happened to be one of them.

SUAREZ: Ian writes from Minneapolis, 'With the media becoming increasingly corporate, does the individual journalist or their ethnicity matter anymore? If a newscast wants a mainstream anchor, does it matter if that anchor happens to be black? I see black anchors who are only distinguishable from their peers by their skin color, not their accent, their clothing or the news they read. On the radio, everyone at the Unity meeting sounds white. Is this stealth tactics or have they sold out?' Well, Ian, I don't think you give us much choice there: Is it stealth tactics or have we sold out? I don't know if I want to choose from either of those choices, but fair enough question.

Mr. COSE: Well, let me start with a very idiosyncratic definition of news. News is what an editor finds interesting. And what you find interesting has a lot to do with who you are and where you come from. So even in this age where a few corporations seem to own most of the major communications outlets of the countries, ultimately, a lot of decisions get left up to the personal idiosyncratic proclivities of editors. And those editors—there's no way to automate that, there's no way to put that on any sort of other than individual basis. Certainly, you can allocate a certain number of—certain types of stories that you want more of and certain types you don't. But ultimately, it comes down to people and the individuals making the decisions, even in this corporate age.

I mean, this question of everyone sounding white, I'm not quite sure what sounding white is. So I won't even dare address that.

85 SUAREZ: Well, maybe you should get a tape of this show afterwards. But, Ian, by making his point in that way, I mean, he brings up the question: Can you be an unreconstructed race man? Can you be some sort of—some urban primitive, every bit of what you were and what your family has been and not learn the well-modulated tones and careful accents of the radio performer. There, I said it, performer (*pronounced PAH-former*). Excuse me—performer and hope to have a career? And/or do you submit a certain part of yourself or what you see as yourself to the needs of a wider organization that—and the needs of making a living?

Mr. TRAHANT: I think you pay attention to craft. And if your craft is radio, you learn some simple techniques to help you be better at it. The same if you're a writer, you learn things that pass on ways of telling stories that are better. It's no different than if you're a tremendous storyteller learning what works with a group in front of you.

Ms. CHEN: I think there's a really—to go after what Ian wrote about—I think that there's a really practical side to all this. I live in Atlanta, where all of the evening television newscasts, local evening television newscasts, are anchored by a white man with a black woman, all the way across the board. Now you could argue—it makes a difference, it doesn't make a difference. Well, apparently, it makes a difference (*technical difficulties*) make decisions in those four television stations, the only four television stations in that city. They made the decision that that was going to have the greatest appeal to their audience. And they all made the same decision, so maybe they're basing it on the same research. I don't know. But they've all made the same decision. They're doing it over and over again. And I think that they have the perception that that's the best thing for their business. And maybe it's the most simplistic and awful way to view it, but maybe it's the best business decision and that's how they made it.

SUAREZ: Are any of the four a younger white man paired with an older black woman?

Ms. CHEN: Well, I haven't checked their driver's license for their ages . . .

90 SUAREZ: Ah, come on, Joie.

Ms. CHEN: . . . but, no, I mean, I think that they're actually fairly balanced in age for the most part. I think in one case, the woman may be older than the man. I'm not quite sure. But none of the women are significantly younger than the man.

SUAREZ: Because that's been a very common entry ramp in television, to be Tonto to an aging Lone Ranger. And . . .

Mr. COSE: But I think part of the question in that is how much power do these respective anchors have? I mean, you know, Joie, a lot more about television than I do. But it seems there are some anchors who actually make decisions about what gets on the air, and there are other anchors who are basically faces, who read what they're given. And if you're asking whether it makes a heck of a lot of difference if the person is merely a reader, what complexion they are, it probably makes relatively little, except for the audience, if you ask . . .

Ms. CHEN: Except for the marketing question.

95 Mr. COSE: Except for the marketing question. Yeah, if you're asking something about who determines what is news, it may make a bit more of a difference. But I think it depends upon how much power that anchor has.

Mr. TRAHANT: So many of our judgments about news also are what's in the front of the book or the lead on television. I think part of where both the authenticity and how we make a difference is what's in the back of the book. I think of stuff that gets clipped out and put on refrigerators. And if that's the stuff where we can contribute so young kids can look and see, 'Hey, I'm in this newspaper, too,' that may be far more significant than anything we put on the front page over time.

Mr. de LAMA: I think the bottom line of a lot of what we've been talking about and about diversity in our coverage and so forth is if you just hold up to people images, stories, coverage of themselves and people like themselves, really, you run the risk of just—we're holding up a mirror to people. And that just reinforces preconceptions and existing values, when we're really in the business of when we're at our best of holding up a window to the world to try to bring about a little better understanding. And the world is beyond somebody's self. It's what's out there beyond them. And that's the challenge for us. And all of this diversity, we talk about it as an end, but it's not an end, it's a means also to really do our job better. And the way that people and corporations take that and instill that as a value in the corporations is, bottom line, frankly, if they think that will be better for their businesses. And that's what they'll decide it on.

Ms. CHEN: And underlying everything that we've said here is, I think, what you were saying earlier, Ellis, if the presenters, the front men, are the people of color, but the decision-making isn't, then, no, you really haven't solved any sort of issue at all. You haven't done any sort of service to your viewer or to your reader or anything else. If you're only doing it cosmetically, no, you don't change the picture at all. It really doesn't matter who it is. But I think that's one of the underlying issues of this conference and of the thinking of a number of these organizations: How do you get more people in positions of power who change coverage in not necessarily pro or con ways but diversify it, where diversity does not represent a positive or a negative, just a reality?

SUAREZ: Scott is with us now from New Castle, Indiana. Sorry I made you wait so long, Scott, but thanks for hanging on.

100 SCOTT (*Caller*): That's OK, Ray. It was worth the wait. Yeah, I'd like to address some of the—you answered a question, actually, a rebuttal from a question from the floor, Mr. Ellis answered. I think you did hit the nail right on the head there, Ray. It just seems it's never enough. You know, affirmative action is nothing more than reverse discrimination and it's not a perfect world. It's never going to be a perfect world. And it seems to me some of these people like to just form these organizations for one purpose: to find something to complain about. I think they ought to be grateful for what they have, count their blessings and say, 'Hey, you know, I've made it this far. Hey, this is great.' And let time—let fate take its course. You know, it's just—it's a cry baby country, and I'm just flooded with tears here and I have no sympathy for anyone.

SUAREZ: Well, had we just let nature take its course 20 or 30 years ago, when there was zero hiring of various ethnic minorities in many newsrooms, are you convinced that without groups to advocate for this kind of change, that it would have just (*technical difficulties*) organically?

SCOTT: I—no, I am completely for the diversification that's there. I see diversification everywhere, on all news channels. And I don't understand why there are—what the big deal is. I mean, they want more power. That seems to me—they want to be in control. Hey, I think there are a lot of people of color are CEOs in this country, of color, you know, quite a few, as a matter of fact.

SUAREZ: No, but I'm suggesting to you that one of the ways they got there for you to see them was from the cry baby culture that you were just talking about.

SCOTT: Perhaps. Perhaps it was just somebody finally waking up and saying, 'Hey, these people are equal. They're just as good as we are.' And I think that's where it's at right now. I think they're equal. Everyone is equal. And I think that's where it's at now. And I want it to stay that way, and it just seems to me they want more and more and more and more. And I think they should count their blessings and say, 'Hey, we've done a great job,' and not be so negative.

SUAREZ: Fair enough, Scott in New Castle, Indiana, thanks for your call. That's all the time we have for today. I want to thank everyone who called and wrote and spoke to us from the floor, and especially my guests.

Exploring Texts and Contexts

For activities with icons, refer to the Guide to Analyzing Readings in Context.

1. How is the transcript of a symposium like this one different from an essay? How does the situation in which participants talk to each other and answer questions change the way information is expressed to an audience? Characterize the differences. What are the benefits and difficulties of using a symposium to explore this topic versus using an essay? **Genre**

2. During this symposium, Cose makes the following statement: **Situation**

   > . . . we come to this business, we as people, with all kinds of baggage and with all kinds of experiences. And it would be naïve to assume that some of those experiences aren't rooted in the different treatment that we've had as different ethnic groups and as different racial groups. . . . We also, as a profession, are in the knowledge business, which means that we're in the business of trying to find out as much about as many things, as many people, as many cultures, as we can. (205)

   Perhaps you are in school preparing to join a particular profession or perhaps you are already working and have come back to school. To what extent and in what ways does Cose's statement apply to you? Write an essay in which you explore the relationship between your "baggage" and experiences and your professional orientation.

Creating Texts

For activities with icons, refer to the Guides to Analyzing Contexts for Writing and Analyzing Readings in Context. For additional help with these writing projects, read the description of **Dialogue/Symposium/Debate** and **Essay** in the Genre Glossary.

Situation

1. As a class, organize a symposium on a topic related to civic participation. Your topic might be, for example, how to get college students more actively engaged in public deliberations about issues that concern them. The class should decide collectively who will be participants—for example, a journalist or talk show host, a politician, a college administrator, a student activist, a couple of typical students, and a moderator. The class should then divide into groups, with each group responsible for researching and discussing what one of the participants would say. Typically in a symposium, after an introduction from the moderator, the participants begin by making a statement of their position, sometimes in response to a specific question from the moderator. Then, with encouragement from the moderator, the participants respond to each other's statements, which ideally should lead them into the spontaneous back-and-forth of a conversation. Ideally, too, at least some of the participants will learn something from some of the others. Each group might want to write a general description of the person it is representing and that person's views; the person's opening statement; two or three other prepared comments on different aspects of the issue; and ideas for how the person might respond to the other participants. Then each group should choose a member to actually play that person's role, and the symposium can begin. The rest of the class can be the audience, which at some point will be invited to ask questions and make comments.
2. Drawing on the discussion in Connecting with the Conversation 2, write an essay in which you make an argument about whether minority journalists contribute a particular perspective and whether or not they should.

The FDR Memorial

Who Speaks from the Wheelchair?

Rosemarie Garland-Thomson

Throughout the 1990s, as the Americans with Disabilities Act was changing many aspects of the public sphere and becoming part of our public discourse about disability, the disability rights movement continued to work on other issues related to disability. During the discussion about the design of the national memorial to President Franklin Delano Roosevelt, disability rights activists argued that Roosevelt should be represented in his wheelchair. Roosevelt lost the use of his legs to polio when he was 39, making it

necessary for him to use a wheelchair. He learned to stand with assistance so that, as president, he was rarely seen by the public in his chair. As the memorial was being planned and designed, the prevailing view was that it should represent Roosevelt as he preferred to be seen during his lifetime. But after the memorial was dedicated in 1997, disability rights activists, arguing that this was an opportunity to change our national "story" about disability, persuaded President Clinton to support an addition to the memorial including a life-size bronze statue showing Roosevelt in his wheelchair.

As the addition was being completed, disability rights activists and disability studies scholars were asked to propose quotations to be carved into the stone near the new statue. In this article from the *Chronicle of Higher Education,* disability studies scholar and professor of English Rosemarie Garland-Thomson discusses the controversy over this inscription. The story of this controversy gives us a glimpse into how new ideas about disability might change the way we see and represent ourselves as a people.

Connecting with the Conversation

1. Have you visited public memorials in Washington, D.C., or other places? How do they "tell a story" about the person or event memorialized?
2. What do you know about our thirty-second president, Franklin Delano Roosevelt? What mental images do you have of him?

As public spaces transformed into collective stories, memorials are inherently controversial. Didactic narratives about who we are and what we believe, they span generations and vast differences in human perceptions, bringing to light all sorts of divisions in the national "we." One of those divides has occurred between a group of scholars in disability studies and the designers of the Franklin Delano Roosevelt Memorial in Washington. The five-year struggle over the collective story told by the F.D.R. memorial ended only this month, when President Clinton dedicated an addition to the memorial. The controversy—and, unfortunately, its not entirely satisfactory conclusion—tells us much about disability in American culture, about disability studies, and about ourselves.

Even before its dedication, on May 2, 1997, the memorial had splintered the national "we." The original monument consisted of four granite-walled outdoor "rooms," which narrated F.D.R.'s presidency with inscriptions of his own words and with nine bronze bas-reliefs and statues, representing scenes of his presidency, all intermingled with pools, waterfalls, and greenery.

The segment of the American "we" representing disability-rights activists and scholars in disability studies had wanted to avoid repeating the persistent stereotypes of disability—the ones that tell us that disability is a shameful personal problem relegated to the private realm of charity and medicine, but inappropriate in the public sphere.

We had wanted the memorial to tell the story of a man who was both disabled by polio and president of the United States for 12 years; to claim F.D.R. as a disabled public figure who represented not just the 15 percent of the U.S. population who have disabilities, but everyone, since we will all become disabled if we live long enough. The memorial's present and future audiences, we had argued, would consist of people whose consciousness had been transformed by civil-rights movements that included the disability-rights movement, and by legislation like the Americans with Disabilities Act, the landmark law that mandates full integration of people with disabilities into American society.

5 But the only statue that even remotely referred to F.D.R.'s disability showed him seated, covered by a cape, on a chair with small wheels barely peeking out. The threat of protests by disability activists at the memorial's dedication convinced President Clinton to seek an addition, and the designers agreed—the first time that an existing national memorial was to be changed. Maya Lin's controversial Vietnam Veterans Memorial was augmented with representational figures of soldiers, but those traditionally heroic statues only flank, rather than fundamentally change, the somber black-granite slab and the space of meditation and mourning it creates.

The bold mandate to reimagine F.D.R. as at once heroic and disabled has now been realized. A new "room" at the entrance to the present memorial contains a simple, life-size bronze statue depicting Roosevelt seated in his wheelchair, wearing his trademark rumpled suit, pince-nez, and fedora. It differs from the regal, robed, larger-than-life figure represented in the third room, where the ample cloak erases and denies the

From *The Chronicle of Higher Education,* January 26, 2001. pp. B11–B12.

mark of his disability. The new statue witnesses the simple humanity of the great leader and registers it as the universality of disability. It also marks today's historical moment, when disability defined as a civil-rights issue is superseding disability as a medical or charitable issue.

YET THE CONTROVERSY CONTINUES, because the story that the new "room" of the F.D.R. memorial tells is still fraught with contradiction. At issue is the phrasing of the words inscribed on the granite wall behind the new statue of F.D.R. A group of us from the field of disability studies had been invited to recommend potential quotations, from which the designers were to choose an inscription. As historians and literary critics who traffic in words, we relished the chance to influence the way that people present and future would understand disability. The memorial's other inscriptions are illustrious words that enrich the story told by the spaces and the statues. F.D.R.'s eloquent verbal commitments to equality are literally set in stone, shaping the story of his presidency and of the nation itself. One powerful quotation reads, "We must scrupulously guard the civil rights and civil liberties of all citizens, whatever their background. We must remember that any oppression, any injustice, any hatred, is a wedge designed to attack our civilization." We wanted the new addition to continue the theme of equal rights that is the hallmark of both the disability-rights movement and the F.D.R. memorial.

We had a story about disability that we wanted the new room to tell. We sought to offer a quotation as crisp, powerful, and unambiguous as the bold "I hate war" chiseled into the wall above the tumbled stones that suggest the blasted buildings of World War II while creating a majestic waterfall that implies transcendence.

F.D.R.'s strategy in the Depression had been to alter the environment to meet the needs of the people. That was parallel, we reasoned, to the idea that people with disabilities need a material situation that accommodates the differences of their bodies or minds. So we looked for a quotation to convey the idea that political equality and access to the workplace for people with disabilities requires a leveling of the playing field—both literally, in the case of wheelchair users like F.D.R., and metaphorically, for those of us who need other accommodations to be fully integrated into the public sphere.

10 We also wanted to tell the story of a determined man who used a wheelchair, and whose use of it influenced the world around him. As scholars in disability studies, we examine disability as a cultural concept that shapes history, belief, art, literature, and other aspects of culture. We saw F.D.R. as someone whose disability shaped him and who, in turn, shaped his own world and the world that has come after. We looked for a quotation telling that story about disability while eschewing stereotypical stories about courageous people who overcame their disabilities or found serenity through suffering.

Enough of those oppressive narratives dominate public thought and circulate in telethons, fiction, and sentimental tracts. The F.D.R. memorial should offer up an accomplished leader, not a cheerful or chastened cripple.

To provide criteria for selecting the inscription in the new room, we suggested three themes that should be emphasized, and three that should be avoided. We sought a quotation, first of all, that would advance the idea that disability is integral to a person's character and life experience, rather than a defect to be eliminated. Second, we wanted a quotation suggesting that the experience of disability can enrich a life, foster leadership, and create a sense of community. Third, in keeping with the human scale of the statue, we searched for words hinting that F.D.R.'s disability made him an accessible—rather than a lofty—hero. In other words, we recommended that any new inscription present disability as a common, yet influential, human experience, one that can be integrated into a meaningful and full life.

CONVERSELY, WE ARGUED that the quotation should avoid the stereotypical narrative that disability is a tragic experience to be overcome. Discrimination, more than impairment, is what people with disabilities have to surmount. Our second caveat was more complex: In keeping with our conviction that disability should be viewed as a political issue of rights and access, we intended to circumvent the idea that disability is simply a matter of having an individual impairment to contend with. Recasting social attitudes and removing environmental barriers are more important for improving the lives of people with disabilities than are their own spunk, saintliness, iron will, or the generosity of others. Third—the most subtle point to convey—we strove to dispel the pervasive attitude that disabled people warrant attention only to provide lessons or inspirations to others. We wanted to focus on how F.D.R. himself experienced disability, rather than turn him into a homily for the nondisabled that inspires pity and admiration—or gratitude that they are not themselves disabled.

Gracing the humble but commanding statue of a disabled F.D.R. with a quotation that could do all of that political and cultural work was challenging. After reviewing more than 100 possibilities, consulting with other scholars and disability activists, and, at times, disagreeing among ourselves, we offered a unanimous recommendation to the designers, trusting that they would understand and support our criteria: "We know that equality of individual ability has never existed and never will, but we do insist that equality of opportunity still must be sought." Combined with the image of a U.S. president using a wheelchair, those words sent the unequivocal message that disability is an issue of equal opportunity.

15 To our dismay, however, the designers and the other people advising them selected an inscription for the new room of the F.D.R. memorial that has exactly the effect we'd hoped to avoid. Disregarding our recommendation, they instead used a quotation from Eleanor Roosevelt: "Franklin's illness gave him strength and courage he had not had before. He had to think out the fundamentals of living and learn the greatest of all lessons—infinite patience and never-ending persistence." That quotation is compelling, and it even fulfills some of our criteria, because it interprets F.D.R.'s disability as a positive influence on his life. Indeed, we had offered it along with several others as a possible addition that might augment our recommended choice. But we did not want it to be the only story of disability that the memorial would tell.

Alone, Eleanor Roosevelt's words undermine disability-rights goals. To begin with, we believe that F.D.R. should speak for himself. Too often, others have spoken for and about people with disabilities. In the old way of understanding disability, people with disabilities were silenced while the authority to define them and to narrate their experience was appropriated by medical experts, service providers, or family members. Having another person speak for F.D.R. repeats the humiliating experience of being ignored that people with disabilities often endure. A quotation from his wife also reinforces the myth that F.D.R. denied his disability—especially since nowhere else in the memorial do quotations from anyone but him appear.

Even more important, to have the first two words a visitor encounters at the memorial be "Franklin's illness" presents disability in a way that doubly violates the spirit of equality. "Illness" is a synonym for impairment, a term that disability scholars and activists use to denote functional limitation. "Disability," on the other hand, is a term we use to describe the system of representation that produces discriminatory attitudes and barriers to full integration. In essence, "impairment" and "illness" are about bodily differences, whereas "disability" is about the social and political context in which our bodies operate. The distinction is much the same as the one that scholars often draw between "sex" and "gender." "Illness" locates the story of disability in hospitals and rehabilitation centers. We want the story of disability to be placed in independent-living centers. To object to "illness" is not to fault Eleanor Roosevelt for being politically incorrect; rather, it is to suggest that the way we view disability in 2001 and beyond has changed from the way it was imagined in 1949. After all, a memorial should not simply replicate the past, but use history to create a future vision.

"Franklin's illness" also personalizes rather than politicizes disability. While the quotation the designers propose is certainly moving, it tells the stereotypical, apolitical story of disability as an individual catastrophe, psychological adjustment, and moral chastening. Impairment is a private problem that an individual must overcome, not a public problem of environmental and attitudinal barriers that can be removed through legislation, policy, and education. Moreover, opening with this quotation places the F.D.R. memorial in the genre of public works intended for collective grieving—like war memorials, the AIDS Memorial Quilt, the Oklahoma City National Memorial, or plaques for sailors lost at sea.

In our debate with the designers, they asserted that their quotation would make F.D.R. "very personal, very accessible." But they confused their intent to humanize F.D.R. with personalizing his disability. The inscription that now flanks the statue encourages visitors to respond with sympathy, admiration, and charity rather than with support for equal access and integration. A more effective way to humanize F.D.R. would be to suggest that his impairment reinforced his commitment to the universal mandate for "equality of opportunity," a point to which our recommended quotation alludes.

20 The designers also mistakenly justified the choice of their text on aesthetic grounds. The story of "Franklin's illness" as well as of his "strength," "courage," "patience," and "persistence" would create an aesthetically differentiated and inspirational space, they argued in commenting on our recommendation. The new room was to be a "prologue." In reality, that suggests separating the personal story of disability from the political content of the memorial's other rooms. The quotation clings to the stubborn stereotypes of disability that still feel comfortable to many Americans, simply because those ideas are so easily recognizable. A wheelchair-using F.D.R., spoken about by others, is segregated within his own memorial. That denies the political work of disability-rights activists and scholars, who have sought to eliminate precisely such segregation.

Many of us in disability studies wish to register our dissent from the choice of the inscription for the new room of the F.D.R. memorial. Pleased as we are with the statue itself, we worry that this memorial to our first markedly disabled president ultimately replicates the segregation and privatization of disability. The inscription undermines the work of disability-rights advocates who worked so hard to make the new room a reality. It tells the story that disability is separate from politics—a personal problem rather than a public political struggle.

In the year 2001, we are on the cultural cusp of a new way to understand disability. The memorial's figures, spaces, and, particularly, its words implicitly instruct visitors in how they should imagine disability. In the controversy over the F.D.R. memorial, our evolving national narrative of disability was played out as a quarrel between aesthetics and politics. But underneath, the disagreement was a struggle between familiar old stories and bold new ones, between moving stories about personal suffering and empowering ones about social equality. While the designers of the F.D.R. memorial have laudably affirmed disability with the depiction of the president using a wheelchair, they did not succeed in rewriting the story of disability in terms that will resonate for future generations.

The addition to the F.D.R. memorial suggests two conflicting stories: yesterday's story of disability as a personal failing overcome by individual effort, and today's and tomorrow's story of disability as an issue of civil rights, integration, and diversity. Our national disability politics has come a long way since the 1930s. Shouldn't our national aesthetics now take up the challenge to transform the meaning of disability?

Creating Texts

For assignments with icons, refer to the Guides to Analyzing Contexts for Writing and Analyzing Readings in Context. For additional help with these writing projects, refer to the descriptions of **Address/Speech** and **Essay** in the Genre Glossary.

1. Imagine that you have a sibling, cousin, or neighbor in eighth grade. This young person's class is planning a graduation visit to Washington, D.C., and they have invited a series of speakers to talk with the class about the various places they plan to visit. Knowing that you have been writing about disability, they invite you to speak about the FDR Memorial, which has become one of the most popular sites in the capital. Prepare a talk in which you give some background on Roosevelt himself, explain the controversy over the memorial, and put this controversy into the wider context of the disability rights movement. Using the Internet or your school library, find pictures that you can use to illustrate your talk.
2. The controversy over the FDR Memorial centers on the relationship between art, reality, and representation. Write an essay in which you explore the relationship between artistic freedom and integrity and the responsibilities of representation. You might want to use actual or hypothetical situations to illustrate the relationship you support. For example, you might imagine a meeting between a disability rights group and an artist commissioned to paint a mural for a new playground.

CHAPTER 9

CASE STUDY
Designing Memorials

The Case

This case study focuses on two different sets of events: the public conversations surrounding the design and construction of the Vietnam Veterans Memorial in the early 1980s and the design of the World Trade Center Memorial that began in 2003.

In 1979, a group of Vietnam veterans formed a commission to design and dedicate a memorial that came to be known as the Vietnam Veterans Memorial. The enormously positive public response to the completed memorial almost completely obscures the intense civic debate that dogged its planners for the entire length of the project. The choice of Maya Lin's V-shaped wall of polished black granite inscribed with names of the soldiers sparked a public debate that became so contentious it threatened to derail the project. The memorial was eventually funded and built but not officially dedicated until two statues were added to the site. The memorial has since become one of the most loved public sites in the country.

On September 11, 2001, Americans stood transfixed in horror and disbelief as terrorists flew airplanes into the Pentagon and the twin towers of the World Trade Center. Since that moment, and through our long, painful recovery, the conversation about how to memorialize those who died has continued. In the first edition of this book, this case study focused on the Vietnam Veterans Memorial and we also made mention of the memorial that was built to commemorate the bombing of the Alfred P. Murrah Federal Building in Oklahoma City. As we've used this case study in our classes we naturally followed the discussion about the design of the memorial to those who died in the collapse of the World Trade Center. And, indeed, much of the ongoing conversation has commented on what the public has learned from the design of the Vietnam Veterans Memorial. Thus, this case study focuses on the two memorials and the design issues they share.

The Issues

Public memorials have come to represent many things in our culture: a way to pay tribute to the victims of a tragedy, a way to create some meaning in an otherwise senseless act of violence, and a form of therapy for a bereaved community and nation. In an era when public

apathy is reflected in low voter turnout and declining participation in community groups, the intensity of civic engagement with public memorials is noteworthy. Both the Vietnam Veterans Memorial and the World Trade Center Memorial make a good case for thinking about the issues involved in public art controversies and the significance of these deliberations in a democratic culture. Although the issues surrounding both designs are varied and complex, they might be organized into those having to do with history, politics, art, and religion or spirituality.

History and Politics. The Vietnam War was the longest engagement in our nation's history, and it ended in defeat. An infamous photo of U.S. military and South Vietnamese government officials crowding aboard a helicopter on the roof of the U.S. Embassy to flee the advancing North Vietnamese soldiers captures the ignominy of the withdrawal. The strong feelings that Americans had about the war were reignited in the national debate about the memorial.

Although the national political debates have been intense, the politics around the design of the new World Trade Center have been more local than national. The land on which the World Trade Center was built is extremely valuable real estate and at the same time it is just a New York City neighborhood; since September 11, it has become the burial ground for those who died in the attack. None of these complications were present in the planning and design of the Vietnam Veterans Memorial, which was built on public land designated for that purpose. The design of the two memorials is influenced in different ways by the history and politics of the events being memorialized.

Art and Spirituality. Memorials must serve as a place to help visitors make peace with a loved one's death. With this single aim in mind, Maya Lin designed a simple, abstract memorial that would allow individuals to connect with their memory of someone they had lost. Her vision for the memorial grew from personal experiences but emerged as a form only after seeing the potential site. Lin's decisions to include the names of the dead in the chronological order of their deaths and to use shiny, mirror-like black granite for the monument contributed to the impact of the monument on the individuals who visited it.

In the case of the Vietnam Veterans Memorial, the history of the war influenced the political debate about the monument, just as the politics of the debate influenced the discussion of artistic issues. The abstract design, the black granite V-shaped wall, was seen by some as a critique of the war rather than an honoring of those who died. Some insisted that a realistic representation of soldiers was the best way to focus on the human lives rather than on the concept of the war. Maya Lin herself insisted that she had not intended any political comment on the war, but instead had thought about how each visitor would respond to the memorial. Lin has been proven right by the millions who have visited since the memorial opened. Every aspect of its design has had a powerful impact on its visitors. Perhaps the memorial is so well loved because Maya Lin focused on the spiritual aspects of the design. In writing her proposal, she focused on the way in which the memorial would help individuals come to terms with death itself rather than with any specifics of the war.

Our acceptance of the abstract design of the Vietnam Veterans Memorial might have made it easier for the American public to accept and appreciate this sort of abstract or highly symbolic design. And yet the question of realism—whether or not to include a realistic statue of soldiers as part of the design—has not disappeared from the debate. At least one of the design proposals for the World Trade Center Memorial included a plan for projecting changing photographs of the victims. Thus the artistic issues seem simpler and less rancorous; on the other hand the spiritual aspects seem more difficult to resolve. Because the site is not simply a memorial to the dead but is actually the burial site for many victims, the victims' families feel strongly that this fact should be recognized in the design. In addition, discussions note that the attacks themselves had a religious dimension and yet people of many religious faiths died in the attack. This circumstance has, in fact, promoted agreement that while the site should have a powerful spiritual dimension, this memorial should not include any specific religious symbols.

The following documents will help you explore in more depth these and other issues involved in the design and building of these two memorials so important to American history, civic life, and culture.

The Documents

- In early November 1980, the competition for the Vietnam Veterans Memorial Design was announced to the public. Given out as a press release, this **statement of purpose** written by **Robert Doubek,** the executive director of the Vietnam Veterans Memorial Fund, was intended to explain what the veterans hoped to accomplish by building a memorial. The founders conceived of the memorial as a way to reconcile a nation still reeling from the bitter controversy caused by the war. By building a memorial that honored their comrades but didn't make judgments about the war itself, the founders believed they could achieve a measure of public healing. As you read Doubek's explanation of the project, notice how he tries to influence the memorial's design.
- In May 1981 **Maya Lin,** then a 20-year-old undergraduate at Yale University, submitted her design for the competition as part of a project for her class in funerary art. The proposal accompanying her pastel sketch of the memorial describes her design. Presented as part of the competition submission, the **proposal** needed to account for the major criteria set out by the VVMF: The memorial must have a contemplative character and be in harmony with its surroundings; the names of all who died or remained missing must appear; and it should make no political statements about the war. Her design was chosen unanimously from 1,421 entries. Since Lin included only a sketchy illustration with her proposal, her writing must have played an important role in persuading the jury. What aspects of her writing do you think were most effective?
- As the memorial was being completed in 1982, **Maya Lin** began writing her own personal account of how the memorial was designed and constructed. But it wasn't until she published her memoir, ***Boundaries,*** in 2000 that she was able to finish writing her account of those events. As she says in the memoir, for years after the memorial was built she wanted to put the events behind her and move on with her life. Indeed, it wasn't until she saw a documentary about herself, *Maya Lin: A Strong Clear Vision,* by Frieda Lee Mock, that she was able to write again about these events. In this chapter from her memoir, she describes from her own perspective the complex series of events that unfolded throughout the early 1980s as the memorial design was being debated

and the memorial constructed. This chapter will give you a good insight into the historical, political, artistic, and spiritual issues that surrounded the design and construction of the memorial. A little over a year after Lin published her memoir, she became involved in the design of another memorial: She was asked to be one of the judges in the contest to design a memorial for the World Trade Center. As we see in the next three documents, the similarities and differences between the situations surrounding the two memorials became an important part of the conversation about the design of the memorial for the World Trade Center.

- Just days after the attacks on the World Trade Center and Pentagon, a public conversation began about how to rebuild the sites, especially the World Trade Center site, and how to memorialize these terrible events. Almost any extended discussion of how to design a memorial for the World Trade Center site eventually turns to how this situation is both similar to and different from the situation surrounding the Vietnam Veterans Memorial, as well as how we can learn from that experience. This document is an article from the July 2002 issue of the magazine *Architectural Record,* "**Memorials, Monuments, and Meaning,**" by architect **Robert Ivy**. This cover story from a magazine addressed primarily to other architects focuses on a wide range of historical, philosophical, artistic, and religious aspects of memorial design. Ivy addresses very broad questions about human nature, attitudes toward death, and spiritual beliefs, and he discusses how these questions have been played out in the discussions about both the Vietnam Veterans Memorial and the proposed World Trade Center Memorial.
- The next document was published in the *New York Times* on August 31, 2003. In **"The New Ground Zero: Finding Comfort in the Safety of Names," Michael Kimmelman** discusses the significance of including names of the dead on memorials even when, as with the Vietnam Veterans Memorial, the numbers are in the thousands. The chronological listing of names on the Vietnam Veterans memorial has become one of its most powerful features, and Kimmelman asks what we can learn from that as we contemplate possible designs for the World Trade Center Memorial.
- Throughout 2002 and 2003, as we can see in the previous two documents, discussions about the World Trade Center site and memorial took place in many different forums. In the spring of 2003, while tentative plans were being made for rebuilding on the site of the World Trade Center, a contest was announced for the design of the memorial that would be included in the site. In some ways this contest was similar to the one for the Vietnam Veterans Memorial: It was open to the public and it included the stipulation that all victims of the attacks on September 11 be recognized in the design. But in other ways it was quite different: Although anyone over 18 could potentially enter, all entrants had to pay a fee and had to enter in conjunction with a professional design team, among other fairly complicated restrictions. But what the contests had in common was the often heated discussions that the memorial design stimulated, often led by the families of those who had died. In the fall of 2003, eight finalists were announced, and pictures and descriptions of their designs began to be widely discussed around the country, but especially in New York. This document is a **transcript of a news story** that aired on **NPR's Tavis Smiley Show on December 5, 2003,** soon after the finalists were announced, and it gives a glimpse into the public debate about the emotional topic of the memorial design.

- On January 14, 2004, designers Michael Arad and Peter Walker presented their revised design, *Reflecting Absence,* in a press release. The choice of the design launched the process of bringing the memorial to reality. The final document in the case study is a **photograph of the model of the design.** We include for comparison photographs of the Vietnam Veterans Memorial (224) and the Oklahoma Murrah Building Memorial (225).

YOUR ROLE

The Vietnam Veterans Memorial and the World Trade Center Memorial make good cases for thinking about the role of memorials in our national life and culture and about the role of public discussion and debate in making important public decisions. In the first of the writing projects, we ask you to reflect on the impact of one of these memorials and to design a brochure for students planning to visit one of the memorials. In the second writing project, we ask you to write an essay in which you analyze the public discussions surrounding the building of these memorials.

1. Imagine that your school sponsors an annual trip by an interdisciplinary group of students to various important national sites. This year the group will visit either the Vietnam Veterans Memorial or the World Trade Center Memorial (you decide). You are part of a group that's been chosen to produce a brochure for the students who will be going on the trip this year. Design a brochure that gives general information and background about the memorial as well as information that would be of specific interest to students from several different disciplines, including for example history, political science, art/architecture, and philosophy/theology/religious studies. Your brochure should be visually appealing, reader friendly, and useful for this particular audience. (See **Brochure** in the Genre Glossary.)
2. Write an essay in which you discuss what U.S. society can learn about the possibilities and pitfalls of public debate from the processes surrounding the design and building of the Vietnam Veterans Memorial and the World Trade Center Memorial. What was done right and what went wrong in the public debates surrounding the design and construction of these memorials, and what can we learn from these processes for future debates about other issues of public importance? (See **Essay** in the Genre Glossary.)

FOR IMMEDIATE RELEASE

Vietnam Veterans Memorial Statement of Purpose

While debate and demonstrations raged at home, these servicemen and women underwent challenges equal to or greater than those faced in earlier wars. They experienced confusion, horror, bitterness, boredom, fear, exhaustion, and death.

In facing these ordeals, they showed the same courage, sacrifice, and devotion to duty for which Americans traditionally have honored the nation's war veterans in the past.

The unique nature of the war—with no definite fronts, with vague objectives, with unclear distinctions between ally and enemy, and with strict rules of engagement—subjected the Vietnam soldier to unimaginable pressures.

Because of inequities in the draft system, the brunt of dangerous service fell upon the young, often the socially and economically disadvantaged.

While experiences in combat areas were brutal enough in themselves, their adverse effects were multiplied by the maltreatment received by veterans upon their return home. . . .

The purpose of the Vietnam Veterans Memorial is to recognize and honor those who served and died. It will provide a symbol of acknowledgment of the courage, sacrifice, and devotion to duty of those who were among the nation's finest youth.

The Memorial will make no political statement regarding the war or its conduct. It will transcend those issues. The hope is that the creation of the Memorial will begin a healing process.

Excerpted From Jan C. Scruggs and Joel L. Swerdlow, *To Heal a Nation: The Vietnam Veterans Memorial.* New York: Harper and Row, 1985, p. 53.

Statement by Maya Ying Lin, March 1981, Presented as Part of Her Competition Submission

Walking through this park-like area, the memorial appears as a rift in the earth, a long, polished, black stone wall, emerging from and receding into the earth. Approaching the memorial, the ground slopes gently downward and the low walls merging on either side, growing out of the earth, extend and converge at a point below and ahead. Walking into this grassy site contained by the walls of the memorial we can barely make out the carved names upon the memorial's walls. These names, seemingly infinite in number, convey the sense of overwhelming numbers, while unifying these individuals into a whole.

The memorial is composed not as an unchanging monument, but as a moving composition to be understood as we move into and out of it. The passage itself is gradual; the descent to the origin slow, but it is at the origin that the memorial is to be fully understood. At the intersection of these walls, on the right side, is carved the date of the first death. It is followed by the names of those who died in the war, in chronological order. These names continue on this wall appearing to recede into the earth at the wall's end. The names resume on the left wall as the wall emerges from the earth, continuing back to the origin where the date of the last death is carved at the bottom of this wall. Thus the war's beginning and end meet; the war is 'complete,' coming full-circle, yet broken by the earth that bounds the angle's open side, and continued within the earth itself. As we turn to leave, we see these walls stretching into the distance, directing us to the Washington Monument, to the left, and the Lincoln Memorial, to the right, thus bringing the Vietnam Memorial into an historical context. We the living are brought to a concrete realization of these deaths.

Brought to a sharp awareness of such a loss, it is up to each individual to resolve or come to terms with this loss. For death is in the end a personal and private matter, and the area contained with this memorial is a quiet place, meant for personal reflection and private reckoning. The black granite walls, each two hundred feet long, and ten feet

From competition submission for the Vietnam Veterans Memorial, March, 1981.

below ground at their lowest point (gradually ascending toward ground level) effectively act as a sound barrier, yet are of such a height and length so as not to appear threatening or enclosing. The actual area is wide and shallow, allowing for a sense of privacy, and the sunlight from the memorial's southern exposure along with the grassy park surrounding and within its walls, contribute to the serenity of the area. Thus this memorial is for those who have died, and for us to remember them.

The memorial's origin is located approximately at the center of the site; its legs each extending two hundred feet towards the Washington Monument and the Lincoln Memorial. The walls, contained on one side by the earth, are ten feet below ground at their point of origin, gradually lessening in height, until they finally recede totally into the earth, at their ends. The walls are to be made of a hard, polished black granite, with the names to be carved in a simple Trajan letter. The memorial's construction involves recontouring the area within the wall's boundaries, so as to provide for an easily accessible descent, but as much of the site as possible should be left untouched. The area should remain as a park, for all to enjoy.

Vietnam Veterans Memorial

It's taken me years to be able to discuss the making of the Vietnam Veterans Memorial, partly because I needed to move past it and partly because I had forgotten the process of getting it built. I would not discuss the controversy surrounding its construction and it wasn't until I saw the documentary, *Maya Lin: A Strong Clear Vision,* that I was able to remember that time in my life. But I wrote the body of this essay just as the memorial was being completed—in the fall of 1982. Then I put it away . . . until now.

I think the most important aspect of the design of the Vietnam Veterans Memorial was that I had originally designed it for a class I was taking at Yale and not for the competition. In that sense, I had designed it for me—or, more exactly, for what I believed it should be. I never tried to second-guess a jury. And it wasn't until after I had completed the design that I decided to enter it in the competition.

The design emerged from an architectural seminar I was taking during my senior year. The initial idea of a memorial had come from a notice posted at the school announcing a competition for a Vietnam Veterans Memorial. The class, which was on funereal architecture, had spent the semester studying how people, through the built form, express their attitudes on death. As a class, we thought the memorial was an appropriate design idea for our program, so we adopted it as our final design project.

At that point, not much was known about the actual competition, so for the first half of the assignment we were left without concrete directions as to what "they" were looking for or even who "they" were. Instead, we had to determine for ourselves what a Vietnam memorial should be. Since a previous project had been to design a memorial for World War III, I had already begun to ask the simple questions: What exactly is a memorial? What should it do?

My design for a World War III memorial was a tomblike underground structure that I deliberately made to be a very futile and frustrating experience. I remember the professor of the class, Andrus Burr, coming up to me afterward, saying quite angrily, "If I had a brother who died in that war, I would never want to visit this memorial." I was somewhat puzzled that he didn't quite understand that World War III would be of such devastation that none of us

From *Boundaries* by Maya Lin. New York: Simon and Schuster, 2000.

would be around to visit any memorial, and that my design was instead a prewar commentary. In asking myself what a memorial to a third world war would be, I came up with a political statement that was meant as a deterrent.

I had studied earlier monuments and memorials while designing that memorial and I continued this research for the design of the Vietnam memorial. As I did more research on monuments, I realized most carried larger, more general messages about a leader's victory or accomplishments rather than the lives lost. In fact, at the national level, individual lives were very seldom dealt with, until you arrived at the memorials for World War I. Many of these memorials included the names of those killed. Partly it was a practical need to list those whose bodies could not be identified—since dog tags as identification had not yet been adopted and, due to the nature of the warfare, many killed were not identifiable—but I think as well the listing of names reflected a response by these designers to the horrors of World War I, to the immense loss of life.

The images of these monuments were extremely moving. They captured emotionally what I felt memorials should be: honest about the reality of war, about the loss of life in war, and about remembering those who served and especially those who died.

I made a conscious decision not to do any specific research on the Vietnam War and the political turmoil surrounding it. I felt that the politics had eclipsed the veterans, their service and their lives. I wanted to create a memorial that everyone would be able to respond to, regardless of whether one thought our country should or should not have participated in the war. The power of a name was very much with me at the time, partly because of the Memorial Rotunda at Yale. In Woolsey Hall, the walls are inscribed with the names of all the Yale alumni who have been killed in wars. I had never been able to resist touching the names cut into these marble walls, and no matter how busy or crowded the place is, a sense of quiet, a reverence, always surrounds those names. Throughout my freshman and sophomore years, the stonecutters were carving in by hand the names of those killed in the Vietnam War, and I think it left a lasting impression on me . . . the sense of the power of a name.

One memorial I came across also made a strong impression on me. It was a monument to the missing soldiers of the World War I battle of the Somme by Sir Edwin Lutyens in Thiepval, France. The monument includes more than 100,000 names of people

(continued)

who were listed as missing because, without ID tags, it was impossible to identify the dead. (The cemetery contains the bodies of 70,000 dead.) To walk past those names and realize those lost lives—the effect of that is the strength of the design. This memorial acknowledged those lives without focusing on the war or on creating a political statement of victory or loss. This apolitical approach became the essential aim of my design; I did not want to civilize war by glorifying it or by forgetting the sacrifices involved. The price of human life in war should always be clearly remembered.

But on a personal level, I wanted to focus on the nature of accepting and coming to terms with a loved one's death. Simple as it may seem, I remember feeling that accepting a person's death is the first step in being able to overcome that loss.

I felt that as a culture we were extremely youth-oriented and not willing or able to accept death or dying as a part of life. The rites of mourning, which in more primitive and older cultures were very much a part of life, have been suppressed in our modern times. In the design of the memorial, a fundamental goal was to be honest about death, since we must accept that loss in order to begin to overcome it. The pain of the loss will always be there, it will always hurt, but we must acknowledge the death in order to move on.

What then would bring back the memory of a person? A specific object or image would be limiting. A realistic sculpture would be only one interpretation of that time. I wanted something that all people could relate to on a personal level. At this time I had as yet no form, no specific artistic image.

The use of names was a way to bring back everything someone could remember about a person. The strength in a name is something that has always made me wonder at the "abstraction" of the design; the ability of a name to bring back every single memory you have of that person is far more realistic and specific and much more comprehensive than a still photograph, which captures a specific moment in time or a single event or a generalized image that may or may not be moving for all who have connections to that time.

Then someone in the class received the design program, which stated the basic philosophy of the memorial's design and also its requirements: all the names of those missing and killed (57,000) must be a part of the memorial; the design must be apolitical, harmonious with the site, and conciliatory.

These were all the thoughts that were in my mind before I went to see the site.

Without having seen it, I couldn't design the memorial, so a few of us traveled to Washington, D.C., and it was at the site that the idea for the design took shape. The site was a beautiful park surrounded by trees, with traffic and noise coming from one side—Constitution Avenue.

I had a simple impulse to cut into the earth.

I imagined taking a knife and cutting into the earth, opening it up, an initial violence and pain that in time would heal. The grass would grow back, but the initial cut would remain a pure flat surface in the earth with a polished, mirrored surface, much like the surface on a geode when you cut it and polish the edge. The need for the names to be on the memorial would become the memorial; there was no need to embellish the design further. The people and their names would allow everyone to respond and remember.

It would be an interface, between our world and the quieter, darker, more peaceful world beyond. I chose black granite in order to make the surface reflective and peaceful. I never looked at the memorial as a wall, an object, but as an edge to the earth, an opened side. The mirrored effect would double the size of the park, creating two worlds, one we are a part of and one we cannot enter. The two walls were positioned so that one pointed to the Lincoln Memorial and the other pointed to the Washington Monument. By linking these two strong symbols for the country, I wanted to create a unity between the nation's past and present.

The idea of destroying the park to create something that by its very nature should commemorate life seemed hypocritical, nor was it in my nature. I wanted my design to work with the land, to make something with the site, not to fight it or dominate it. I see my works and their relationship to the landscape as being an additive rather than a combative process.

On our return to Yale, I quickly sketched my idea up, and it almost seemed too simple, too little. I toyed with adding some large flat slabs that would appear to lead into the memorial, but they didn't belong. The image was so simple that anything added to it began to detract from it.

I always wanted the names to be chronological, to make it so that those who served and returned from the war could find their place in the memorial. I initially had the names beginning on the left side and ending on the right. In a preliminary critique, a (continued) professor asked what importance that left for the apex, and I, too, thought it was a weak point, so I changed the design for the final critique. Now the chronological sequence began and ended at the apex so that the time line would circle back to itself and close the sequence. A progression in time is memorialized. The design is not just a list of the dead. To find one name, chances are you will see the others close by, and you will see yourself reflected through them.

The memorial was designed before I decided to enter the competition. I didn't even consider that it might win. When I submitted the project, I had the greatest difficulty trying to describe it in just one page. It took longer, in fact, to write the statement that I felt was needed to accompany the required drawings than to design the memorial. The description was critical to understanding the design since the memorial worked more on an emotional level than a formal level.

Coincidentally, at the time, I was taking a course with Professor Vincent Scully, in which he just happened to focus on the same memorial I had been so moved by—the Lutyens memorial to the missing. Professor Scully described one's experience of that piece as a passage or journey through a yawning archway. As he described it, it resembled a gaping scream, which after you passed through, you were left looking out on a simple graveyard with the crosses and tombstones of the French and the English. It was a journey to an awareness of immeasurable loss, with the names of the missing carved on every surface of this immense archway.

I started writing furiously in Scully's class. I think he has always been puzzled by my connection to the Lutyens memorial. Formally the two memorials could not be more different. But for me, the experiences of these two memorials describe a similar passage to an awareness about loss.

The competition required drawings, along with the option to include a written description. As the deadline for submission approached, I created a series of simple drawings. The only thing left was to complete the essay, which I instinctively knew was the only way to get anyone to understand the design, the form of which was deceptively simple. I kept reworking and reediting the final description. I actually never quite finished it. I ended up at the last minute writing freehand directly onto the presentation boards (you can see a few misprints on the actual page), and then I sent the project in, never expecting to hear about it again.

The drawings were in soft pastels, very mysterious, very painterly, and not at all typical of architectural drawings. One of the comments made by a juror was "*He* must really know what he is doing to dare to do something so naive" (italics mine). But ultimately, I think it was the written description that convinced the jurors to select my design.

On my last day of classes my roommate, Liz Perry, came to retrieve me from one of my classes, telling me a call from Washington had come in and that it was from the *Vietnam Veterans Memorial* Fund; they needed to talk to me and would call back with a few questions about the design. When they called back, they merely said they needed to ask me a few questions and wanted to fly up to New Haven to talk to me. I was convinced that I was number 100 and they were only going to question me about drainage and other technical issues. It never occurred to me that I might have won the competition. It was still, in my mind, an exercise—as competitions customarily are for architecture students.

And even after three officers of the fund were seated in my college dorm room, explaining to me that it was the largest competition of its kind, with more than fourteen hundred entries, and Colonel Schaet, who was talking, without missing a beat calmly added that I had won (I think my roommate's face showed more emotion than mine did at the time), it still hadn't registered. I don't think it did for almost a year. Having studied the nature of competitions, especially in Washington (for instance, the FDR Memorial, still unbuilt in 1981, nearly forty years after it was first proposed, or the artwork Robert Venturi and Richard Serra collaborated on for L'Enfant Plaza, which was completely modified as it went through the required Washington design process of approvals), my attitude about unusual projects getting built in Washington was not optimistic. Partly it's my nature—I never get my hopes up—and partly I assumed the simplicity of the design, and its atypical form and color, would afford it a difficult time through the various governmental-approval agencies.

After the design had been chosen, it was subject to approval by various governmental agencies at both the conceptual and design development phases. I moved to Washington and stayed there throughout these phases. I expected the design to be debated within the design-approval agencies; I never expected the politics that constantly surrounded its development and fabrication.

(continued)

I was driven down to D.C. the day of my college graduation, and I immediately became part of an internal struggle for control of the design. I think my age made it seem apparent to some that I was too young to understand what I had done or to see it through to completion. To bring the design into reality would require that I associate with an architect of record, a qualified firm that would work with me to realize the design. I had a very difficult time convincing the fund in charge of the memorial, the VVMF, of the importance of selecting a qualified firm that had experience both in architecture and landscape-integrated solutions, and that would be sympathetic to the design.

I had gone to Cesar Pelli, then dean of Yale's School of Architecture, for the names of some firms that could handle the job. A firm by the name of Cooper-Lecky was the one he recommended, and I presented its name to the fund, unaware that the competition's adviser was the fund's choice as architect of record. I was told by the fund that this person was the architect of record, and that was that.

After a few weeks of tense and hostile negotiations (in which at one point I was warned that I would regret these actions, and that I would "come crawling back on my hands and knees"), I was finally able to convince the fund to go through a legitimate process of selecting a firm to become the architect of record. The then architecture critic for the *Washington Post,* Wolf Von Eckardt, was instrumental in pressing the fund to listen to me. But the struggle left a considerable amount of ill will and mistrust between the veterans and myself.

Through the remaining phases of the project I worked with the Cooper-Lecky architectural firm. We worked on the practical details of the design, from the addition of a safety curb to a sidewalk to the problems in inscribing the names. Many of the issues we dealt with were connected to the text and my decision to list the names chronologically. People felt it would be an inconvenience to have to search out a name in a book and then find its panel location and thought that an alphabetical listing would be more convenient—until a tally of how many Smiths had died made it clear that an alphabetical listing wouldn't be feasible. The MIA groups wanted their list of the missing separated out and listed alphabetically. I knew this would break the strength of the time line, interrupting the real-time experience of the piece, so

I fought hard to maintain the chronological listing. I ended up convincing the groups that the time in which an individual was noted as missing was the emotionally compelling time for family members. A system of noting these names with a symbol* that could be modified to signify if the veteran was later found alive or officially declared dead would appease the concerns of the MIA groups without breaking the time line. I knew the time line was key to the experience of the memorial: a returning veteran would be able to find his or her time of service when finding a friend's name.

The text of the memorial and the fact that I had left out everything except the names led to a fight as to what else needed to be said about the war. The apex is the memorial's strongest point; I argued against the addition of text at that point for fear that a politically charged statement, one that would force a specific reading, would destroy the apolitical nature of the design. Throughout this time I was very careful not to discuss my beliefs in terms of politics; I played it extremely naive about politics, instead turning the issue into a strictly aesthetic one. Text could be added, but whatever was said needed to fit in three lines—to match the height of the dates "1959" and "1975" that it would be adjacent to. The veterans approved this graphic parameter, and the statements became a simple prologue and epilogue.

The memorial is analogous to a book in many ways. Note that on the right-hand panels the pages are set ragged right and on the left they are set ragged left, creating a spine at the apex as in a book. Another issue was scale; the text type is the smallest that we had come across, less than half an inch, which is unheard of in monument type sizing. What it does is create a very intimate reading in a very public space, the difference in intimacy between reading a billboard and reading a book.

The only other issue was the polished black granite and how it should be detailed, over which I remember having a few arguments with the architects of record. The architects could not understand my choice of a reflective, highly polished black granite. One of them felt I was making a mistake and the polished surface would be "too *feminine.*" Also puzzling to

---

*Each name is preceded (on the west wall) or followed (on the east wall) by one of two symbols: a diamond or a cross. The diamond denotes that the serviceman's or servicewoman's death was confirmed. The cross symbolizes those who were missing in action or prisoners at the end of the war. When a serviceperson's remains were returned, the diamond symbol is superimposed over the cross. If a serviceman or woman returns alive, a circle will be inscribed around the cross.

(continued)

them was my choice of detailing the monument as a thin veneer with barely any thickness at its top edge. They wanted to make the monument's walls read as a massive, thick stone wall, which was not my intention at all. I always saw the wall as pure surface, an interface between light and dark, where I cut the earth and polished its open edge. The wall dematerializes as a form and allows the names to become the object, a pure and reflective surface that would allow visitors the chance to see themselves with the names. I do not think I thought of the color black as a color, more as the idea of a dark mirror into a shadowed mirrored image of the space, a space we cannot enter and from which the names separate us, an interface between the world of the living and the world of the dead.

One aspect that made the project unusual was its politicized building process. For instance, the granite could not come from Canada or Sweden. Though those countries had beautiful black granites, draft evaders went to both countries, so the veterans felt that we could not consider their granites as options. (The stone finally selected came from India.) The actual building process went smoothly for the most part, and the memorial was built very close to my original intentions.

As far as all of the controversy, I really never wanted to go into it too much. The memorial's starkness, its being below grade, being black, and how much my age, gender, and race played a part in the controversy, we'll never quite know. I think it is actually a miracle that the piece ever got built. From the very beginning I often wondered, if it had not been an anonymous entry 1026 but rather an entry by Maya Lin, would I have been selected?

I remember at the very first press conference a reporter asking me if I did not find it ironic that the memorial was for the Vietnam War and that I was of Asian descent. I was so righteous in my response that my race was completely irrelevant. It took me almost nine months to ask the VVMF, in charge of building the memorial, if my race was at all an issue. It had never occurred to me that it would be, and I think they had taken all the measures they could to shield me from such comments about a "gook" designing the memorial.

I remember reading the article that appeared in the *Washington Post* referring to "An Asian Memorial for an Asian War" and I knew we were in trouble. The controversy exploded in Washington after that article. Ironically, one side attacked the design for being "too Asian," while others saw its simplicity and understatement, not as an intention to create a more

Eastern, meditative space, but as a minimalist statement which they interpreted as being non-referential and disconnected from human experience.

This left the opinion in many that the piece emanated from a series of intellectualized aesthetic decisions, which automatically pitted artist against veterans. The fact that I was from an Ivy League college, had hair down to my knees, further fueled this distrust of the design and suspicions of a hippie college liberal or aesthetic elitist forcing her art and commentary upon them.

Perhaps it was an empathetic response to the idea about war that had led me to cut open the earth—an initial violence that heals in time but leaves a memory, like a scar. But this imagery, which some detractors would later describe as "a black gash of shame and sorrow" in which the color black was called the "universal color of shame and dishonor," would prove incredibly difficult to defend. The misreading of the design as a negative political statement that in some way was meant to reflect upon the service of the veterans was in part fueled by a cultural prejudice against the color black as well as by the misreading or misinformation that led some veterans to imagine the design as a ditch or a hole. It took a prominent four-star general, Brigadier General George Price, who happened to be black, testifying before one of the countless subcommittee hearings and defending the color black, before the design could move forward.

But the distrust, the fact that no veterans had been on the jury, the unconventionality of the design and the designer, and a very radical requirement made by the Vietnam veterans to include all the names of those killed made it inevitable that the project would become controversial. I think ultimately that much of the negative response goes back to the very natural response to cover up or not acknowledge that which is painful or unpleasant. The very fact that the veterans themselves had required the listing and therefore the acknowledgment of the more than 57,000 casualties, which is a landmark in our country in terms of seeing a war via the individual lives lost, was very hard for many to face. I remember Ross Perot when he was trying to persuade the veterans that it was an inappropriate design, asking me if I truly didn't feel that the veterans would prefer a parade instead, something happy or uplifting, and I can

(continued)

remember thinking that a parade would not in the long term help them overcome the enormous trauma of the politics of that war.

I do not think I fully realized until the dedication and homecoming parade that the veterans needed both. In effect the veterans gave themselves their own homecoming. In November 1982, I was in tears watching these men welcoming themselves home after almost ten years of not being acknowledged by their country for their service, their sacrifice.

But until the memorial was built I don't think they realized that the design was experiential and cathartic, and, most importantly, designed not for me, but for them. They didn't see that the chronology of the names allowed a returning veteran the ability to find his or her own time frame on the wall and created a psychological space for them that directly focused on human response and feeling. I remember one of the veterans asking me before the wall was built what I thought people's reaction would be to it. I realized then that these veterans were willing to defend a design they really didn't quite understand. I was too afraid to tell him what I was thinking, that I knew a returning veteran would cry.

An architect once told me to look always at what was originally envisioned and try to keep it. I left Washington before ground breaking. I had to. The fund and I knew that we had to accept a compromise. The closer you watch something grow, the less able you are to notice changes in it. When I saw the site again, the granite panels were being put up and the place was frighteningly close to what I thought it should be. It terrified me. It was a strange feeling, to have had an idea that was solely yours be no longer a part of your mind but totally public, no longer yours.

Memorials, Monuments, and Meaning

Two vast and trunkless legs of stone
Stand in the desert. Near them, on the sand,
Half sunk, a shattered visage lies
And on the pedestal, these words appear:
"My name is Ozymandias, king of kings:
Look on my works, ye Mighty, and despair!"

Ozymandias
Percy Bysshe Shelley

How do we, the living, recall the dead? How do we signal the people or places that altered history? How do we institutionalize pain? How do we signify what matters to our civilization? The questions sound abstract, yet in this fractious, dangerous world, the issues confront and confound us with urgency, and architects find themselves at the center of the debate. Not all solutions are architectural, however.

Society knows that we will remember what we are reminded of; history, whether oral or written, is a structured narrative that reforms the past, interweaving memory and experience into a singular tale, says Craig Barton in his book, *Sites of Memory.* When we build for remembrance's sake, we recast history—from objects to whole cities. Barton refers to the process as "the codification of memory," an idea apparent in symbols as obvious as the great St. Louis Gateway Arch, which leaps toward Manifest Destiny and the opening of the American West. Our traditions, our prejudices, and our beliefs flow from such constructions.

Historically, remembrance has been central to architecture. For more than five thousand years, architects have made monuments to the dead, to glorious battles, and to ideas. Ironically, the earliest and grandest abide. Despite ancient social upheavals, shifts in pharaonic power, unification and dispersal of Upper and Lower Kingdoms, Hellenism, Rome, Islam, and the birth of the modern state, Khufu's monumental pyramid (ca. 2500 b.c.) still stands, a memorial to the god-king and a monument to ancient Egypt's collective genius. In death, Khufu traveled to other realms; in life, only the stones remain.

Jump to the 20th century. Spoleto Festival, 1997, outside Charleston, South Carolina. At McLeod Plantation, the landscape architect and artist Martha Schwartz hung multiple cotton sheets arrayed near the houses of former slaves. As the day progressed, the fabric scrim altered with changing light; morning and evening breezes animated each piece and changed its form. Animate, poetic, Schwartz's art installation stirred emotions within the viewer and provoked speculation in an unexpected way about slavery—both about the system itself and the contributions of slaves to material culture.

The two illustrations underscore the differentiation between two apparently similar words, monument and memorial. While linguists might debate the distinctions, fundamentally a monument comprises a designed and constructed physical object intended as a commemoration. Memorials that celebrate or grieve may take a more ephemeral form—including the strewing of flowers in memory of the deceased, such as occurred during the Memorial Day/Decoration Day movement of the 19th century or the free-form floral outpouring at the gates of Kensington Palace following the death of Princess Diana. Both involve the physical world, both involve remembrance.

While structures may house ideas, it is people who actually do the remembering, and people

(continued)

From "Memorials, Monuments, and Meaning" by Robert Ivy. *Architectural Record 190,* Issue 7 (July 2002), p. 84.

vary. The vastly differing populations comprising the early Egyptians and 20th-century museum-goers each carry the baggage of time; location; political, social, and cultural history; and religion that author James Young in *The Texture of Memory* calls "collected memory." Each person brings to the memorial experience a personal set of expectations—not a reflection of zeitgeist so much as a composite of emotion and recollected thought—that the effective memorial recalls. Those memories shift over time, much like the light at McLeod Plantation.

Evolution of meaning. Memorials shift in meaning as generations change. Time alters understanding and blurs memory; architecture remains. According to James Young (and Shelley), "Monuments that resist transformation risk losing their significance to future generations." Following the immediacy of loss, when grief has thinned or disappeared, we inevitably begin to appreciate the monument or the memorial for its more abstract qualities. Ultimately, time may blur our collective vision and we may entirely forget the events that generated the memorial, so removed from our lives or so potent has the architecture or the symbol grown. Although few persons might know the historical roots of the Arc de Triomphe as a representation of Napoleonic victories, today everyone identifies the arch with the city of Paris.

Fixed power. Monuments may be fixed or temporary. In writing about the blues (in *Blues Ideology and Afro-American Literature—A Vernacular Theory*), Houston Baker addresses stability. According to Baker, "Fixity is a function of power." He states that those who "maintain place, who decide what takes place and dictate what has taken place, are power brokers of the traditional." The rootless, the "placeless," by contrast, find other, more "fluid" ways of memorializing. To Maya Angelou, as she says in her novel *I Know Why the Caged Bird Sings,* rather than any buildings or monuments, the poetry of preachers and the blues epitomizes African-American memorial making. To Baker, the crossroads becomes the symbol where art and memory conjoin.

Thus, the Vietnam Memorial on the Mall in Washington, a fixed, evocative monument, represents the tragic consequences of war by the nation-state. By contrast, the AIDS quilt, "nomadic, portable, constantly being added to," formed a temporary installation that was spread on the same Washington soil occupied by the Vietnam Memorial. Both affected the American conscience and consciousness, through two different means. Both resonate today, although only one remains in place.

The resolution of a memorial depends on who tells the story. Monument building, like museum design, can be construed as a political act, controlling the narrative of actual events, determining the sequence of experiences, and interpreting them for subsequent generations. Digital guides and video-speak round out the story, much as guides or interpreters at historic sites like Chartres Cathedral tell us their history and thereby frame our understanding of events. Their narratives reflect controlled authorship and ownership of ideas.

In a democracy like our own, split wide open by the Internet, everyone has a say. Architecture's role becomes a "repository of our collective and individual cultural history and memory," says author Craig Barton. Reductivist in nature, architecture compresses and contains history in a single place at one time, while democratizing forces that surround us in cyberspace may call for dispersal across time and space. James Young encourages the search for the "art of public memory," a process that engages audiences in the making and the viewing, creating a dialogue that transcends the mere appearance of any memorial.

Some sites blend media to probe authenticity. In Amsterdam, at the Anne Frank House, the visitor passes by an orchestrated pathway through the actual chambers inhabited by the Frank family from 1942–1944. According to careful design, space after space reveals the mundane artifacts of daily life—toys, games, a sink—for a particular Jewish family hidden from German authorities in a high attic. By clustering around strategically placed monitors, gaggles of people from all over the world can hear Anne's own words from her diary and view the video testimony of her childhood friend or of Miep Gies, the secretary who helped keep the Frank family alive. Anne's house museum memorializes a family's struggles, and for a brief moment, brings them vividly to life.

Abstractions. How abstract should a memorial be? The response varies with the proximity to the event. Survivors of a tragedy often raise potent arguments for realistic monuments that appropriately memorialize their lost loved ones. They belong to the camp that views the memorial as a "witness and reminder," says Young. A review of recent monument making in Washington, D.C., however, raises questions about the literal. The Korean Monument, for example, depicts a squad of soldiers in bronze, but their representation, unfortunately, makes them appear lost, and the meaning of the war becomes compromised as we confront the limitations of the objects themselves. The words and spaces and elementary materials at Washington's FDR Memorial seem more potent than the sculptural figures meant to recall Depression hardship. Imagination trumps the literal.

Touch and feelings. Memory and the locus of emotions can be unlocked by the senses. Tactility, for example. How many of us have reached the Vietnam Memorial Wall to rub the names of lost friends with our own hands? Water, in particular, represents the mythic veil between the real and spiritual realms. Fire, such as the eternal flame at John Kennedy's simple grave on the Arlington hillside, or present in Hindu cremation, conjures up transformation. Moving water moves the hearing, which affects the mind: calming in a fountain, or churning as it falls with a cavernous, preternatural force in Tadao Ando's work at the Sayamaike Historical Museum near Osaka.

From Ground Zero. Since September 11, the process of memorial making has already shifted from the individual to the institution. While countless little altars, handmade signs, poems mounted to fences, and photographs once sprang up across the city—at Union Square, at Brooklyn's Promenade, at Grand Central—the fire from a thousand candles is beginning to be extinguished. Even the number of poignant obituaries of the deceased in the *New York Times* is diminishing with each week.

With the removal of the last structural column from the devastated site, we are entering a new phase, searching for an appropriate memorial for a cataclysmic event that tore at the heart of a city, took almost 3,000 lives, and wrenched New York's optimistic spirit. How will the city respond? With monument or memorial? With literal interpretation of events? With knowledge of and accommodation to change?

Victor Iannuzi, an interpersonal psychoanalyst, warns that whatever happens, we must reconcile with the meaning of the event. If not, "those meanings go underground—they go into our unconscious, where they wreak havoc." The answer will depend on who tells the story, and how responsive those in power prove to an event larger than themselves.

The New Ground Zero
Finding Comfort in the Safety of Names

Michael Kimmelman

The capitalized words printed just above these, which you may have read or maybe your eye skipped over them, are my first and last names. In the cafeteria of the building where I work, a similar name—Jay M. Kimmelsman—appears on a plaque commemorating *New York Times* employees killed during World War II. Jay M. Kimmelsman worked in the department of outgoing mail. When I pass the plaque, I think of him. I feel a connection.

What is it about a name? Its power is palpable but mysterious. Without thinking, we say we know someone when we know his name. "Do you know who that is?" "Yes, that's Jay from outgoing mail." But how much do we know? We react to names that resemble ours, or resemble the names of people we know, in the same vague way that we scour other people's family snapshots. We hunt for clues to what they tell us, often idly. We look for something of ourselves.

But names, like photographs, unless they are ours or those of our friends and family, say much less than we expect.

The competition guidelines for the memorial at ground zero require that the design "recognize each individual who was a victim" on Sept. 11, 2001, and on Feb. 26, 1993, when the World Trade Center was first attacked. It's a safe bet that many of the 5,200 submissions interpret that as some kind of list of names. By aesthetic and social consensus, names are today a kind of reflexive memorial impulse, lists of names having come almost automatically to connote "memorial," just as minimalism has come to be the presumptive sculptural style for memorial design, the monumental blank slate onto which the names can be inscribed.

During the past week the news broke that the remains of more than 1,000 of the 2,792 people who are missing from the Sept. 11 attack will be buried at the memorial. Investigators cannot identify more than 12,000 body parts—the DNA is too badly damaged—and so the remains will be dried and vacuum sealed, preserved, like ancient mummies, in white opaque pouches, in the hope that technologies of the future can decode who is who. The Lower Manhattan Development Corporation, in addition to requiring recognition of each victim, instructed entrants in the competition to include space to store remains, just in case.

So now the memorial becomes a literal cemetery, with the oldest form of human identification, names, most likely testifying to victims the newest science can't distinguish. The ethos will be different from that of the Vietnam Veterans Memorial. There are no bodies buried at the Vietnam memorial, nor any unaccounted-for remains. That memorial is a list of names, a neutral place to meditate abstractly on the war and on the dead and missing, who are elsewhere.

By the afternoon of Sept. 11, people were already taping photocopied fliers with the names and pictures of their dead or missing friends and relatives at makeshift shrines around the city: instant, homegrown demonstrations against the anonymity of mass killing.

From "The New Ground Zero: Finding Comfort in the Safety of Names" by Michael Kimmelman. *The New York Times,* Arts and Leisure, August 31, 2003. p. 1, 22.

The fliers, which were at first missing-persons posters, quickly became private memorials, reminding everybody that the people who died at the World Trade Center were not numbers but someone's husband or sister or son.

This isn't new. The impulse to name names already became commonplace with World War I. Partly, it democratized war. Foot soldiers were recognized not as nameless peons but as individuals, like the generals who sent them to die. The war had made many people cynical about everything except the doughboys in the trenches. These men emerged as the everyday heroes, if there still were any heroes, instead of the military leaders or lone Paul Revere types who had traditionally been singled out for memorials. The listing of their names reduced the distance between the recruit and the officer but also represented a tacit protest against the anonymity of modern warfare. Names both stood for the individual soldier and, correlatively, pleaded for a more humane approach to battle, which is to say they gained both literal and symbolic value.

World War I also inspired tombs of the unknown soldier. The tomb tried to reconcile two conflicting ideologies about war: the dehumanizing anonymity of death and the nobility of personal sacrifice. The unknown soldier symbolized both the masses of anonymous dead and each missing soldier, whose name we were implicitly meant to attach to the tomb.

To this morbid history, World War II contributed lists of innocent victims. Fifty years after its founding, Israel's Holocaust memorial, Yad Vashem, which in Hebrew means "a monument and a name," is still recovering the names of the Jews who died during the Holocaust, a vain and fruitful enterprise in that all the names will never be accounted for, so that the process of trying to remember cannot end.

By the time of Maya Lin's Vietnam memorial in 1982, the idea of names, engraved simply and identically—a visual equivalent to the monotone roll-call of the dead, which has also become a standard memorial ritual—achieved Platonic form, more moving for being so spare. Minimalism proved itself there as the sculptural language of the memorial sublime, combining the abstraction of the memorial's physical form with the absolute specificity of the names of every dead and missing soldier. It was the inverse of the tomb to the unknown soldier, which had become nearly obsolete, thanks to improved forensic science and record keeping, or so it seemed until Sept. 11.

Ms. Lin's memorial, which carefully took no side in the debate about Vietnam, was made out of polished black granite so that people would literally see themselves reflected in the names on the wall, a mirror of perception. The Vietnam War was an unresolved issue, but the dead and missing from that war could be listed. Names seemed morally neutral. They were a compromise in a society that could not decide where it stood. Today, it is too early to know the historical lessons of the attacks on the World Trade Towers, but the casualty list can be drawn up. A world that does not seem to agree about anything can settle on the names of the dead. Lists of names promise closure, a conflict-averse path to catharsis in an age of instant gratification and short attention spans.

But written words, as Shimon Attie, an artist of memorials, has said, are images, and images have an aesthetic component and a political one. A long list of names is, first of all, an incantatory sight, the length of the list implying the scale of the event memorialized. Seeing 57,000 names is

(continued)

not the same as seeing 168 (the number of people killed in the 1995 bombing of the Alfred P. Murrah Federal Building in Oklahoma City) or 2,792 or 6 million, by which point a list becomes almost unreadable. Numbers suggest the enormity of loss but are a dubious measure of history. Not many people died at Lexington and Concord, but what happened there changed the fate of the nation.

And names only seem morally neutral. Ms. Lin's Vietnam memorial made names the basic irreducible fact of this episode in history. Names were all that was left after the pomp and flourish of old-fashioned memorial design were stripped away. In hundreds of years, when the historical debates Ms. Lin studiously sidestepped may be forgotten, the names of the men will be what remain written in stone. Picture, for a second, that memorial without the names: a plain black tombstone, an open wound on the Washington Mall, which was how Ms. Lin imagined the design sculpturally. The message about the war would be very different.

Names animate space. They are like ghosts. We read into them. The ethnic variety of names on the Vietnam memorial summons up an image of a diverse population, a model democracy, a political portrait that belies the rifts of the culture. One nation. One family.

The Vietnam memorial is also shaped like a book. Ms. Lin purposely chose a small typeface, unheard of in monumental design, so that reading the names would seem more intimate, like scanning a printed page. The memorial is supposed to be our national story. She also listed the 57,000 names not alphabetically but chronologically according to when the soldiers died or went missing, an artistic device. Imagine all the John Smiths who died in Vietnam listed alphabetically. Now imagine that your father or son or brother or husband were one of them. Which John Smith on the wall would you touch or pin a photograph beside or leave flowers underneath?

The engraved style of these names, sans pomp and serif, is now standard. The names on the 168 chairs that, like headstones in rows, represent the dead in Oklahoma City are graphic descendants of the names on the Vietnam memorial. But names are fickle signifiers, containers for information that can be filled differently by different people, depending on what they know or think or hear about the person named. In Oklahoma City, some parents, unhappy with their sons-in-law, wanted their dead daughters' maiden names on the memorial, not their daughters' married names. Names are loaded. A list of the dead SS officers buried at Kolmeshohe cemetery in Bitburg, Germany, would have a different effect on their relatives than on Jews.

We engrave the names of donors on walls of museums and other public buildings. Your money or your life. Lists democratize veterans in battle, but they are also signs of difference. At Oklahoma City, a committee needed to be formed to decide who qualified for a list of survivors. If you were injured and went to a hospital, you would be eligible; if you went to a doctor's office, you might not be. If you lost friends and colleagues and your life was turned upside down but you had left the Murrah building for a dentist's appointment before the explosion or had stayed home sick that day, you were not a survivor, although of course you were. Just not in name.

Edward Linenthal, who wrote a book about the memorial in Oklahoma City, has described memorial hierarchies. Resolving them—who gets named and how—is, he argues, part of the process of setting history right, a service to the dead, the essence of what memorials are for. In Oklahoma City, there are the names of the dead on the chairs but also a museum, in which anyone can tell his or her story.

Ground zero may consider something similar: the museum as egalitarian bulletin board, a repository of consolations to survivors, who can decide how they want to remember their dead. Families of the firefighters who died in the World Trade Center, for example, have pleaded publicly that their dead relatives be identified as firefighters in the memorial. The families said the men lived and died as firefighters. Their ladder units were their other families. It isn't that they were greater human beings than the stockbrokers and restaurant workers who died, only that the dead men would want to be remembered as firefighters. They belonged to a community. Their names should be accompanied by F.D.N.Y., maybe even grouped separately. But then how does a list not rank the dead?

The memorial at ground zero, with its unidentified remains, will be a special kind of memorial. It is partly a tomb of the unknown victim, with the abstract language of memorial design, if it ends up being abstract, that much more in tension with the literal: in this case not just literally lists of names but parts of bodies, the corporeal and the symbolic. Many people may think about these bodies when they stand there reading the names: about their own inability to connect the remains to names, about the insufficiency of names to conjure up and stand in for the people who are lost.

What's in a name? Memorials are ultimately local, as the historian James Young has said. They are above all for the families and for a community, common ground to grieve. There are many ways to enshrine and recall the dead. Memorials can be places of contention, which keep alive history through debate. Names, foreclosing political conflicts that may be the real unhealed wounds of the event memorialized, provide instead the possibility of solace for the relatives of the victims. Strangers show up and may be overwhelmed by the sight of long lists of people they did not know, with whom they can only try to identify, just as we all greet unfamiliar names, whose meanings remain elusive.

Finally, only the families and friends of the dead can really know what those names mean.

Continuing Controversy over Construction of a Memorial at the World Trade Center Site

TONY COX, host:
In New York, a spirited dialogue is raging over what will be built on the 16 acres once occupied by the World Trade Center. Eight finalists were recently selected in a competition to design a memorial on the site. But disagreements over what ultimately should be constructed there are far from over. Our reporter Allison Keyes sorts out the controversy and its effect on some who lost loved ones.

ALLISON KEYES:
Linda McGee sits in the living room of her Bronx, New York, house and shakes her head as she talks about her twin sister, Brenda Conway, who was killed in the attacks on September 11th, 2001. She worked on the 97th floor of Tower One and vanished after the planes hit.

Ms. LINDA McGEE:
We just never really heard from her since she left for work that morning. We spent a lot of time searching and looking but nothing was ever found of her.

ALLISON KEYES:
McGee, an African-American third-grade teacher and mother of two, is still trying to come to terms with the loss of the woman she shared everything with.

Ms. McGEE:
It's very difficult and I'm still really having a very difficult time adjusting to life without her because I'm so used to doing everything with her.

KEYES:
McGee says she's been paying only scant attention to the debate raging over what will eventually be constructed on the 16-acre site, but she does have some ideas about the elements that should be included in the memorial. She's glad it will include a sacred space where families can get away from the tourists that flock to the site every day. McGee thinks there should also be a way for people to see the faces of the near 3,000 people who died.

Ms. McGEE:
I think the ones with the pictures would be great, especially—like we have a couple of nephews or even people as small children that may not, say, as they get older, really remember. At least they'll be able to see the picture.

Unidentified Woman #1:
We thought about how this is set in an urban setting and all of the buildings—a lot of the buildings that surround the site are going to be high-rises and they're going to be tall. That's how we set up our landscape.

KEYES:
Just before Thanksgiving, the eight finalists in the design competition for the World Trade Center memorial were announced with much fanfare. One, called Dual Memory, features the photos of the victims McGee and many other family members say they'd like to see at the site. The pictures would be projected onto glass panels along with a short history of each person. Another design, Suspending Memory, turns the so-called footprints where the twin towers stood into two islands in the midst of a vast tree-covered pool separated by a single bridge. But competing interests have made it difficult to decide on the final configuration of the site. For example, many firefighters, police officers and emergency workers want their names to be listed apart from the civilians who died.

From National Public Radio's Tavis Smiley Show, December 5, 2003.

Lieutenant MICHAEL MARSHALL (Vice President, Vulcan Society):
Not that our lives were worth any more than anybody else's lives, but just the fact that we were there as rescuers. People were going out; we were going in to save lives.

KEYES:
Lieutenant Michael Marshall is vice president of the Vulcan Society, an advocacy group for New York's black firefighters.

Lt. MARSHALL:
One guy that came out, survived, told me that the look on the chiefs' faces like they were sending us to our deaths, and guys still went in. And, you know, I mean, this is what we do and we know that there's—every time we go out the door there's a life risk, but, you know, I just think that we need to be listed separately.

KEYES:
Also, another advocacy organization, the Coalition for 9/11 Families, issued a report card giving the designs an F. Many in the coalition want the footprints to extend down to the original foundation, where the remains of many victims were found. Some family members, like Monica Iken, who lost her husband, Michael, in the attacks, thinks the design selection jury did a great job whittling 5,201 submissions from 63 nations down to eight.

Ms. MONICA IKEN:
All of them were significant. They reflected the key things that I was looking for: spirituality, a sense of peace, a sense of hope.

KEYES:
But other people don't think the design plans tell the real story of what happened on September 11th. That was the reaction of Ann Van Heim, who attended a recent workshop where members of the public were discussing the memorial plans.

Ms. ANN VAN HEIM (Workshop Attendee):
Some of these—I mean, they are beautiful and very innovative and all that, but if you went there and you knew nothing of what happened that day, you would learn nothing of what happened that day. You would not know that a plane hit into the towers and they collapsed.

KEYES:
Rick Bell, executive director of the New York chapter of the American Association of Architects, agrees. He's part of a coalition of designers and planners who've sent a letter to the design jury criticizing the finalists. Bell thinks there's room in the memorial for some of the steel left standing when the towers collapsed.

Mr. RICK BELL:
People who did that clearance were able to save those fragments, and the expectation was that those fragments would come back in some manner.

KEYES:
Most of that steel was recycled but the Port Authority of New York and New Jersey, which owns the site, still has a few pieces of it. Some say the spirit of the memorial designs continues a trend which began in 1981 with the Vietnam Veterans Memorial for Washington's National Mall. Max Page is an associate professor of architecture at the University of Massachusetts.

Professor MAX PAGE:
What we see here is actually a continuation, I think, of the abstract design of memorials that Maya Lin pioneered. In other words, it is an effort to not try to picture the single hero but rather to make a space that will be open to a lot of different people's viewpoints and will be evocative to a lot of different people.

KEYES:
Kevin Rampe, president of the Lower Manhattan Development Corporation, says the bottom line is that the final

(continued)

design for the memorial will likely be different from any of the finalists' proposals.

Mr. KEVIN RAMPE:
There's probably a high chance that the ultimately selected memorial will be different from any of the eight that we see out there right now because of the changes that will occur in response to the jury's concerns, the jury's consideration.

KEYES:
The LMDC is overseeing the site's redevelopment. Rampe says the design guidelines for the master plan for the 16-acre site, which will determine the size and look of the office buildings that will surround the memorial, are also being revised. But Linda McGee says she's less worried about what the finished site should look like than she is about getting through the holidays without her twin sister, Brenda Conway.

Ms. McGEE:
But a lot of my emphasis really isn't on the design as far as it is trying to get on with my life, you know, just trying to find what is normal now without her.

KEYES:
For the TAVIS SMILEY show, I'm Allison Keyes in New York.

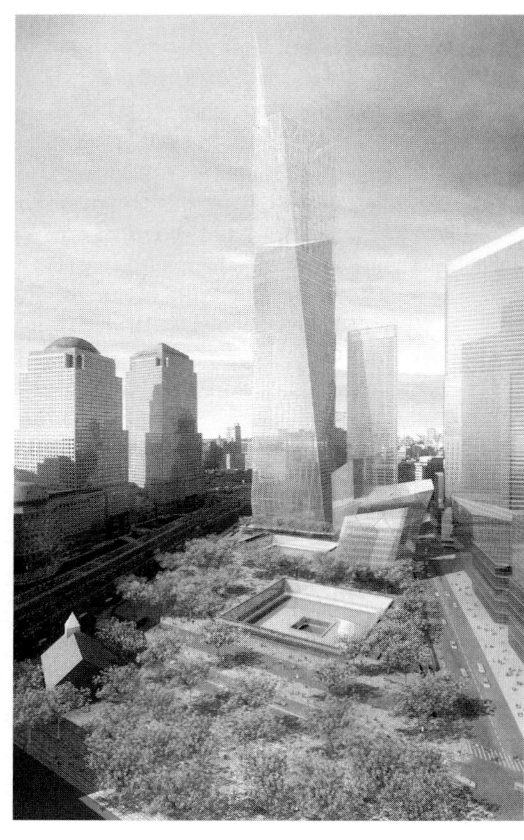

UNIT V

Adapting to the Changing Economy

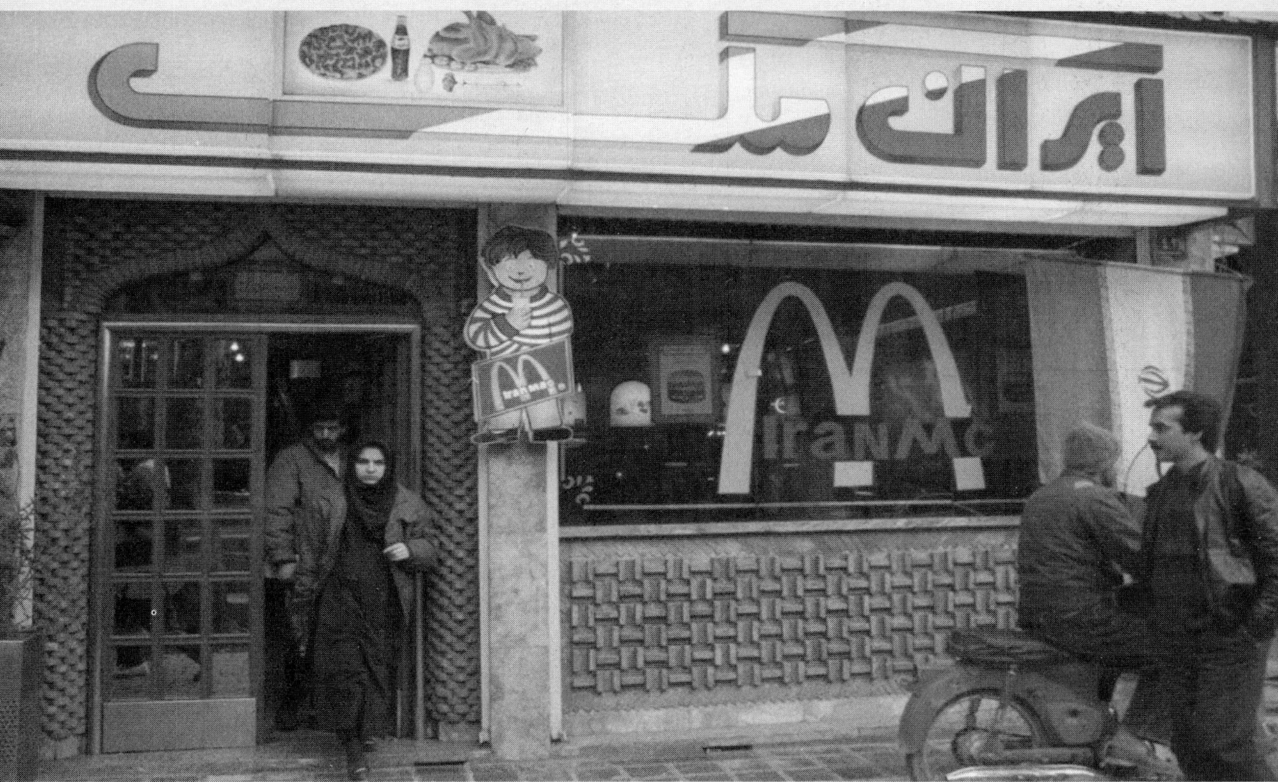

If one thing unites our conversations about the global economy and the changing workplace, it is McDonald's. Vying with Disney as the most visible and despised symbol of American consumer culture, McDonald's is the target of protests whenever it opens a restaurant overseas. For many Americans, though, the most damning argument against McDonald's comes from the American workplace. Even in the economic optimism of the late 1990s, many worried that too many jobs were only "McJobs": low skill, low wage, low benefits jobs that kept people employed but outside the American dream. Yet McDonald's continues to be the restaurant of choice for millions here and abroad. The appeal of McDonald's may go beyond the satisfaction of individual consumer cravings. Journalist Thomas Friedman pointed out in 1999 that no two countries with McDonald's franchises had gone to war with each other since their McDonald's opened. Though he has since modified this claim, his larger point is that participation in the global economy promotes international cooperation. The way we feel about McDonald's—and about globalization—may have much to do with how we see ourselves in the American workplace, the American economy, the global economy, and global culture. What is your reaction to this photograph?

CHAPTER 10

Adapting to the Changing Workplace

Situation: What is the person in this photo doing? In what context do you think the photo was taken? What other kinds of photos might be grouped with this one?

Genre: In what situations might a photo like this be used?

Language: How does the photographer's position determine what you see in the photo?

Consequences: If the purpose of this photo is to convince you of something, what might that be?

What could be more important to a college student than knowing what jobs will be available in five or ten years? But such projections are notoriously difficult to make. Just within the last ten years, for example, the number of jobs requiring computer skills has fluctuated tremendously.

Guidance counselors, curriculum planners, business training specialists, and academics interested in long-range employment trends often turn to the Bureau of Labor Statistics to help them make projections. In their 2000–2001 *Occupational Outlook Handbook,* the Bureau reports that the largest increase in occupational growth is in the service-oriented job categories and that projections for the ten fastest-growing job categories reflect the needs of a service-oriented information economy.

One common reaction to changing workplace expectations is demand for new education and training programs. But these demands come at a time when the relationship between education and jobs is not all that clear. When measured by amount of educational preparation needed, the jobs are clustered around opposite ends of a continuum. According to information published by the Bureau, four of the job categories on the fastest-growing list require a four-year degree: computer engineer, systems analyst, database administrator, and physician's assistant. The remaining jobs require an associate's degree or on-the-job training only. A surprising number of the jobs on the list are auxiliary in nature, defined in terms of the support, assistance, or aid they provide.

The uncertainty about the relationship of jobs to education is compounded by the uncertainty of workforce predictions in general. Although most forecasts emphasize high-tech jobs, a statistic frequently reported is that Microsoft, the most high-profile company in the new, technological economy, employs only 23,000 people, whereas General Motors, the giant of the old, industrial economy, still employs 250,000. Although at one time it was the old-economy, industrial jobs that were most likely to move overseas, today it is the high-tech jobs that are the most likely to be moved to countries where there are well-educated workers willing to work for lower wages.

The changing nature of the workplace is accelerating the uneven distribution of income. Robert Reich, a public intellectual and one of the writers in this unit, observes in the foreword to his book *The Work of Nations,* "Each nation's primary political task will be to cope with the centrifugal forces of the global economy which tear at the ties binding citizens together—bestowing ever greater wealth on the most skilled and insightful, while

The 10 Fastest-growing Occupations, 1998–2008
(Numbers in thousands of jobs)

	Employment		Change	
Occupation	**1998**	**2008**	**Number**	**Percentage**
Computer engineers	299	622	323	108
Computer-support specialists	429	869	439	102
Systems analysts	617	1194	577	94
Database administrators	87	155	67	77
Desktop-publishing specialists	26	44	19	73
Paralegals and legal assistants	136	220	84	62
Personal-care and home-health aides	746	1179	433	58
Medical assistants	252	398	146	58
Social and human-services assistants	268	410	141	53
Physician's assistants	66	98	32	48

Source: Bureau of Labor Statistics News Release, Nov. 30, 1999.

consigning the less skilled to a declining standard of living" (3). How widening economic inequality will affect social relations is of particular concern in a democratic society. The promise of upward social mobility has always been a fundamental tenet of our national identity. Because an unregulated free-market economy is not working for some Americans, they are becoming increasingly disillusioned as they work harder, retrain, and follow migrating jobs with relatively few gains in income, while another segment of society is growing fabulously wealthy. Diminishing expectations for future generations may disrupt the way many Americans have come to define themselves.

And it seems that for both the "winners" and the "losers" in this economy, the competitive nature of the new workplace requires longer hours on the job and more time spent away from family and community. Experts from a wide range of fields including economists, psychologists, and sociologists are beginning to wonder whether evidence of increasingly maladjusted and needy children is a sign that the changing nature of work is having a detrimental effect on family life and community institutions. As increasing numbers of women enter the workforce and the number of two-job families grows, we will continue to grapple with the relationship between workplace commitments and the needs of our families and communities.

Adapting to the changing workplace isn't something that applies only to recent college grads and people in the process of reevaluating their careers. For all of us, the changing economy will require imaginative transformations in the way we educate ourselves, work, raise our families, and relate to neighbors in our communities. These changes can be exciting as well as frightening, but they require us, as individuals and as a nation, to think carefully about the kind of world we want for ourselves, our children, and our grandchildren.

For This We Sent You To College?

Robyn Meredith

After paying $10,000 a year or more for college, you are washing cars as part of your job, and your parents are understandably upset. Through a series of profiles, Robyn Meredith introduces us to several recent college graduates, some entering high-tech industries with excellent salaries and some who feel they are underemployed. Even in a growing economy, labor-market analysts tell us that service jobs are on the rise and that high-end jobs are moving to other parts of the world. Others argue that young people finishing college are more likely to find temporary work or work at lower salaries than they'd hoped.

However, talk about jobs is not the only focus in this ongoing conversation about adapting to the changing workplace. Meredith's article assumes that college is about work, and one of the two letters to the editors written in response to the article questions that assumption, asking what we mean by work. Broader questions of what college and work mean are hardly hinted at in this feature story that appeared on graduation weekend in the Money and Business section of the *New York Times.* Some argue that the broader purpose of a college education is to prepare students to contribute to a vital civic life and that work, too, should be thought of as contributing to one's civic responsibilities. These enduring questions, however, are sometimes placed in the background at graduation time when families celebrate this momentous transition.

Connecting with the Conversation

1. Visit your college's career center and talk to its staff. Ask about how students with a general liberal arts education develop a career focus. Report to the class on what you find.
2. Search your library's online resources for articles in the popular press on a liberal education. Consider what constitutes a good undergraduate education.

As sure as the promise of a spring day, millions of proud parents have been descending lately on the nation's campuses, snapping pictures of their daughters and sons collecting college diplomas.

Parents and students alike have been preparing for this moment for decades, before many parents took out second mortgages and the typical graduate piled up $12,300 in debt to help cover bills for tuition, room and board that average $10,000 a year. Now it is time for that steep investment, as much as $130,000 in the case of some elite private schools, to return dividends.

There is plenty of good news for those receiving undergraduate degrees this year, but with just enough caveats to keep some people on edge.

Over all, the job market for the 1.2 million graduates this year is the strongest in memory, partly because companies, in their aggressive downsizing drives of recent years, may have laid off too many workers of their parents' generation.

5 Many Ivy League graduates and those with degrees in highly marketable areas like business administration and computer science can expect plenty of job offers at high pay. And the nation's highest-profile student, Chelsea Clinton, is unlikely to find herself behind a counter waiting on customers when she graduates from Stanford, where she will be a freshman this fall. In contrast, those with weak grades and little patience for job searches may struggle to find work, as they always do.

But just how good is it for the rest of the army that is resolutely marching out of the classrooms and into the real world?

It turns out to be pretty good indeed for a broad swath of the newly minted grads. Many had the luxury of choosing among several job offers months before commencement exercises began. And starting salaries are, for the most part, higher than they were last year.

But even in such upbeat times, the jobs can be far from glamorous. For instance, Rachel D. Gunderson is busy making sure there is enough dirt on the shelves of Target

---

From the *New York Times,* June 8, 1997, Money and Business section pp. 10–11. Also two letters to the editor, which appeared in subsequent issues, by Peter A. Benoliel and Peter Vergano.

A. William D. Lucy, *Southwest Missouri State University, rents out vehicles for* Enterprise Rent-a-Car (5,000 *graduates hired; starting pay from* $22,000 *to* $30,000). **B.** Linda C. Roman, University *of* Florida, *develops packaging for* Kraft *cottage cheese and dips* (85 *graduates hired; starting pay from* $21,000 *to* $42,000). **C.** *Rachel* D. Gunderson, *University of* Wisconsin, *orders potting soil for* Target *stores* (1,150 *hired by* Target's *parent,* Dayton Hudson; *starting pay from* $30,000 *to* $34,000). **D.** Malane Rogers, University *of* Arkansas, *creates reports for clients of* Andersen Consulting (4,200 *hired; starting pay from* $31,000 *to* $45,000).

stores. After graduating from the University of Wisconsin, she landed a job ordering potting soil for the chain. Linda C. Roman, of the University of Florida, has signed on at Kraft Foods to improve the packaging for cottage cheese and sour cream.

In fact, many new graduates are fast learning a lesson that their predecessors have had to accept over the decades: they have landed at the bottom of the workaday ladder, with plenty of dues to pay before they step up to the next rung.

Rebecca E. Johnson, a University of Michigan graduate and merchant trainee for Dayton's in Minneapolis, helps select the ties sold by the department store chain.

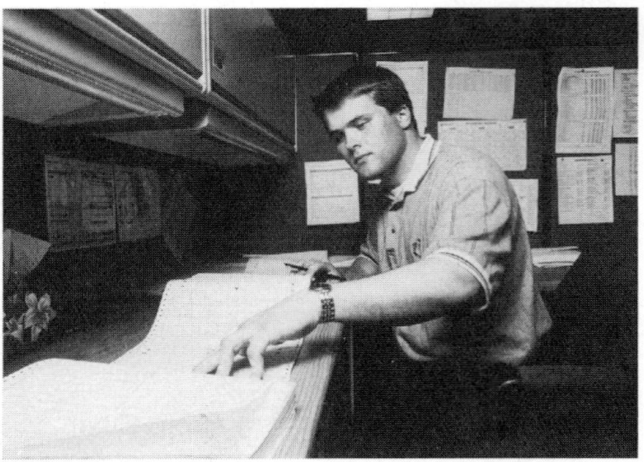

After Douglas M. Fischer left the University of Minnesota, he was put in charge of buying stationery for Target Stores. His orders on one recent day came to $350,000.

10 And for a growing number of graduates, that ladder isn't even the one that they—or their long-suffering parents—originally had in mind. For them, it is not always clear why an expensive education was needed.

"None of my friends ever told me about the carwashing part," said Julie A. Schenk, 22, who turned down two other offers to work as a management trainee at Enterprise Rent-a-Car after graduating in December from the University of Dayton.

Ms. Schenk, whose major was communications management, isn't the only one washing cars—5,000 members of the Class of 1997 are expected to sign up with Enterprise, where cleaning is just one of the dues-paying chores.

Others have taken similar training jobs at department store chains, where they wait on customers.

That can leave some parents horrified that their children don't have more to show for all the financial sacrifices.

15 "It is like sticker shock," said Kevin J. Nutter, the career services director at the University of Minnesota in Minneapolis. The problem for people in this group isn't that they won't find work, "but that they may not find what they think is good work," Mr. Nutter said.

That is because the number of service-sector jobs has grown as the number of management positions has shrunk, he said. At the same time, so many people are now graduating from college that a degree no longer carries the cachet that it did even a generation ago.

If the experience of recent graduating classes is any guide, many in this year's crop will quickly grow dissatisfied. Members of the Class of 1994 at the University of Illinois at Urbana-Champaign, for example, were asked a year after they graduated whether their college training was being put to good use.

"Almost 40 percent considered themselves underemployed," nearly double the percentage of recent years, said David S. Bechtel, director of the university's career services center.

But there is little complaining so far from the new graduates.

20 "I had a lot of friends who were working for Enterprise, and they all spoke highly of it," said Ms. Schenk, who said she was not disappointed in her job, despite being surprised by some of her duties.

Others who have crossed over to the working world in recent months are also making do or even flourishing.

Following are four tales from the trenches that offer hope and guidance to those just now trading in their diplomas, caps and gowns for briefcases and business suits.

Rental Clerks

Joining a Fraternity with 12-Hour Days

Few parents who squirrel away money for years to pay college bills picture their children hanging up a hard-won diploma behind a rental car counter, but about 10,000 moms and dads will watch it happen this year.

Indeed, Enterprise Rent-a-Car is probably hiring more members of this year's graduating class than any other company. The 5,000 graduates scheduled to join Enterprise will be paid $22,000 to $30,000, depending on where they live, and all will start out behind the counters of the company's 3,000 branches around the country.

25 Most graduates who join Enterprise—along with their parents—must first get over the idea of working for a car rental company.

"Recruiting is tough," said Andrew C. Taylor, president and chief executive of Enterprise, based in St. Louis. Some of those who accept jobs have a hard time breaking the news to their families. "What do you think their parents' reaction might be?" Mr. Taylor asked.

Still, satisfied Enterprise hires said they found the jobs refreshing because the company is so entrepreneurial, offering responsibility and a chance to move up quickly.

Mr. Taylor's company tends to hire men and women who are a lot like him—friendly, clean-cut and active at college in fraternities or sororities or team sports. Oh, and they must not be too proud to clean cars from time to time, either.

"The management of this business started behind a rent-a-car counter," Mr. Taylor said, telling how he recently pitched in to vacuum a car during a visit to a busy Enterprise branch.

30 Consider William D. Lucy, 25, who was a member of Delta Chi and played intramural volleyball and flag football at Southwest Missouri State University in Springfield. He graduated last year with a 3.2 grade-point average, with a major in marketing and a minor in management.

"I did not go to college thinking I wanted to rent cars," Mr. Lucy acknowledged. Instead, "I saw myself going into business."

The affable Mr. Lucy, who likes to grasp your shoulder when he shakes your hand, had several sales jobs to choose from, but Enterprise looked the best to him. Since starting in March in St. Louis, Mr. Lucy has been working 12-hour days, what passes for normal at Enterprise, starting at 7:15 each morning. He pins a gold name tag—just plain "Bill"—on his gray suit and greets customers as they walk in the door.

He rents cars during the morning and evening rushes—including driving to pick up customers at their homes or offices, Enterprise's trademark service touch. In between, he calls body shops on behalf of renters whose cars were crumpled in accidents. When the mechanics take longer than promised, he calls the renters' insurance companies to arrange for extensions of Enterprise rentals. Once a week, Mr. Lucy spends part of the day delivering pizza or doughnuts to mechanics at nearby repair shops and secretaries at local offices, trying to win business for Enterprise with his company's equivalent of taking a client to lunch.

Now, Mr. Lucy sees himself as the businessman he always wanted to be. "I'm wearing a suit every day," he said with a proud smile.

35 About 25 percent of Enterprise's trainees will grow dissatisfied and leave the company within six months. Most of those who remain will have a chance to apply for a promotion within a year. Those who make the grade get raises, are named assistant managers and have their salaries tied to the performance of their branches.

If Mr. Lucy does well, he could turn out like Cory A. Phillips, 26, a 1992 graduate of Columbia College in Columbia, Mo., who joined Enterprise 14 months ago and has already been promoted twice.

"If you prove yourself, you don't have to worry about spending two years before you become a manager," said Mr. Phillips, now a branch manager in St. Louis. The training means that all managers learn the business from the bottom up and have a financial interest in seeing it succeed, he said.

Mr. Taylor, the chief executive, said he thought of his company "as a confederation of small businesses run by entrepreneurs."

The strategy seems to have worked: Enterprise now has 31,200 domestic employees but just 1,000 at its corporate headquarters, with 700 of those responsible for keeping the company's computer network up and running. The privately held company has grown 25 percent a year for 11 years, and now has the largest fleet in the rental car business. It avoids airport business, concentrating instead on the so-called replacement niche, providing rentals for customers whose cars are being repaired or who just need an extra set of wheels for a while.

40 Mr. Taylor, a business major who graduated from the University of Denver, was social chairman of his fraternity, Tau Kappa Epsilon. Things haven't changed all that much he said with a smile, in the three decades since he graduated.

"You see," he said, "I'm the social chairman of a very large company."

Packaging Developer

Trading the Stage for Live Culture

Linda C. Roman started her college career as a theater major who made ends meet by working as a waitress. "Every once in a while I see someone on TV I waited tables with," she said.

But Ms. Roman, too, has left waitressing behind for a full-time job in culture—in "live cultures," that is, the kind that produce sour cream, cottage cheese and chip dips.

After changing her major to chemical engineering, Ms. Roman was offered a job in Glenview, Ill., at Kraft Foods, which is owned by Philip Morris and is the country's largest packaged-food company. She helps develop the packaging for 126 varieties of Kraft products, chief among them Breakstone's sour cream, Light 'n Lively cottage cheese and Kraft creamy onion dip.

45 Kraft plans to hire 85 new graduates like Ms. Roman this year to help sell more Jell-O, Stove Top Stuffing, Maxwell House coffee, Kool-Aid, Toblerone chocolate bars and Cheez Whiz spread, paying salaries of $21,000 to $42,000. Thousands of similar entry-level jobs will be filled at companies like General Mills, Nabisco and Frito-Lay; Procter & Gamble will hire more than 700.

When Ms. Roman, 31, graduated last August from the University of Florida in Gainesville with a grade-point average of 3.75, she had long since sewn up the job at Kraft; its offer was one of five that came her way. So in the weeks after graduation, she took the time to portray the Wicked Witch in a children's play before moving to the Chicago suburbs last September to begin at Kraft.

There, she works in her cubicle or in a lab, and has so far visited five of the six factories where her sour creams, dips and cottage cheeses are made, making sure the plastic tubs and boxes work properly and helping to develop better packaging for future products. In the lab, she measures and tests the packages, checking, for instance, that when a customer opens a lid, it peels off smoothly and doesn't tear. "I love the consumer end," she said.

She didn't expect to. Ms. Roman recalls her negative reaction when she came upon Kraft at a college recruiting fair. "When I first saw Kraft, I didn't want to work for them," she said. She thought that serious chemical engineers worked for oil and chemical corporations, she said, not a company best known for macaroni and cheese.

Kraft's competitors face similar hurdles. A glossy brochure distributed by Procter & Gamble at recruitment fairs shows young employees standing proudly next to their wares: Metamucil, Sure deodorant and Charmin toilet paper.

50 Still, one irresistible force lured plenty of candidates to the Kraft recruiting booth on campus. "They had free food," Ms. Roman said with a shrug. After a summer internship in which she helped develop apple-cinammon-flavored cream cheese, she discovered that she liked applying what she learned in the classroom to the real world of supermarket shelves.

Being an actress might be more glamorous, but her father, Kenneth Roman, said he used to worry about her plans to make a living on stage. "Two out of a thousand make it," he said.

Now, Mr. Roman says he feels his daughter has a secure future. "I really had no idea that she would go into engineering," Mr. Roman said. "I feel very proud."

Indeed, his daughter is among those that Kraft found through its college recruitment program. Kraft focuses its recruiting efforts on a short list of large colleges and universities where it previously had success: Ohio State, Wisconsin, Penn State, Purdue, Howard, Florida and Michigan State, along with Illinois and Northwestern—schools that are relatively near its headquarters in Northfield, Ill.

Kraft weeds out some students in short, on-campus interviews, then brings the rest to Chicago for further screening. Students check into a hotel the night before their interview to find duffel bags full of—what else?—Kraft food. With the economy booming, recruiters try to decide quickly whom to hire.

55 "If you wait to make an offer," said Karen Y. Vaughn, a senior human resources manager at Kraft, "the good students are gone."

New Blood

Number of 1997 college graduates each company is planning to hire this year.

Enterprise Rent-a-Car	5,000
Andersen Consulting	4,200
Lockheed	2,040
Price Waterhouse	1,500
General Electric	1,300
*Dayton Hudson**	1,150
Motorola	1,000
Procter & Gamble	700
Osco Drugs (American Stores)	600
Caterpillar	400
Amoco	200
Ameritech	150
Chrysler	160
Hyatt	150
Kraft†	65

*Owns Target Stores.
†Owned by Philip Morris.
Source: Listed companies

Merchandise Analysts

From Shirt Buying to Dirt Buying

Deep inside a building in downtown Minneapolis, past the rows of cubicles watched over by a giant Winnie the Pooh and dozens of other stuffed animals, beyond the spot where the furry animals give way to plants lining the offices, is the desk of Rachel D. Gunderson, 22.

Ms. Gunderson, a graduate of the University of Wisconsin at Madison, is one of the newest merchandise analysts at the headquarters of Target, the discount-store chain.

"I'm in charge of soil," Ms. Gunderson said. As in potting soil. Target sells about 20 different bags, and it falls on Ms. Gunderson to make sure there is enough on the shelves of the chain's 750 stores nationwide.

Buying dirt for Target is typical of the entry-level responsibilities that thousands of this year's graduates will soon assume. The Dayton Hudson Corporation, based in Minneapolis, owns Target, Mervyn's and three department store chains: Dayton's, Hudson's and Marshall Field's. The company plans to hire 1,150 graduates this year at starting pay of $30,000 to $34,000. Dayton Hudson's competitors—including the May Department Stores, Neiman Marcus, J.C. Penney, Kmart and Federated Department Stores—together hire thousands more.

Ms. Gunderson, who graduated with a 3.0 grade-point average in December, started her job in mid-April. A journalism major who specialized in marketing and had a minor in business, she turned down an offer from Andersen Consulting and instead took this 8-to-5 job, which came with 12 weeks of training.

Ms. Gunderson inherited the potting-soil responsibilities from her designated mentor. She is learning how to send electronic orders to Target's suppliers, how to use spreadsheets to show soil sales histories and how to project how many bags of dirt Target will need on hand when an ad for potting soil appears.

Jacqueline T. Punch, central human resources director for Dayton Hudson, said competition for high-quality graduates was fierce. "There is definitely a sense that they can be very selective," Ms. Punch said. "The last two years it has really become more difficult."

Still, Dayton Hudson hires only 5 to 7 percent of the students it talks to, so the competition goes both ways.

The entry-level merchandising jobs go fast. "This job is like the most sought-after position" at the Carlson School of Management of the University of Minnesota, said another new Target merchandise analyst, Douglas M. Fischer, 23.

After graduating in March with an accounting major and a 3.0 grade-point average, Mr. Fischer was put in charge of buying stationery at Target. His best day so far came when he pushed a button on his computer to order $350,000 worth of paper and envelopes.

Across the street, Rebecca E. Johnson, 23, who graduated from the University of Michigan with an art history degree and a 3.4 grade-point average, is a merchant trainee for Dayton's. Her job is to help select the men's shirts and ties for the department store chain.

By the time Ms. Johnson, Ms. Gunderson and Mr. Fischer hand their shirt buying, dirt-buying and stationery-buying responsibilities to the graduates of 1998, they could be well on their way to solid futures at Dayton Hudson. Within five years, successful new hires earn $45,000 to $70,000 as full-fledged buyers, Ms. Punch said.

Technical Assistants

Helping Hands for Various Clients

Andersen Consulting is a ubiquitous name at college career fairs. More than 150,000 seniors—about 13 percent of the nation's graduating class—sent their résumés to the company this year. About 4,200 will be hired by Andersen Consulting, the management and technical consulting arm of Andersen Worldwide.

So what do all those new hires do? Think of Andersen Consulting as a giant temporary firm, only with far better pay (starting salaries are $31,000 to $45,000) and more challenging assignments than those of, say, Kelly Services or Manpower Inc.

Many Fortune 500 companies depend on Andersen Consulting to send teams of energetic, well-educated workers to complete short-term tasks or complicated grunt work—like making various computer systems talk to one another—for which they don't want to hire their own staff.

Companies also use Andersen for more traditional management consulting jobs—to guide strategic planning, for instance—but Andersen hires mostly M.B.A.'s for those spots.

The Dallas office is one of 23 nationwide for Andersen Consulting, but only a small percentage of its employees in the region work in the tidy offices on the 54th floor of a glass skyscraper downtown. Most report to the offices of Andersen clients in the area for a few weeks or months, then move to another project at a different client.

Malane Rogers, 23, is a good example. She graduated from the University of Arkansas in December with a degree in industrial engineering and a 2.9 grade-point average. She started at Andersen in February, and travels each morning to the Dallas office of Texas Instruments.

Her task is to pull detailed financial data from Texas Instruments' huge mainframe computers and fashion them into easy-to-read reports for company executives. When a vice president wants to check quarterly revenues in a certain region, Ms. Rogers finds the needles in the data haystack.

College on the Up and Up - and Up

DESPITE CLIMBING COSTS...

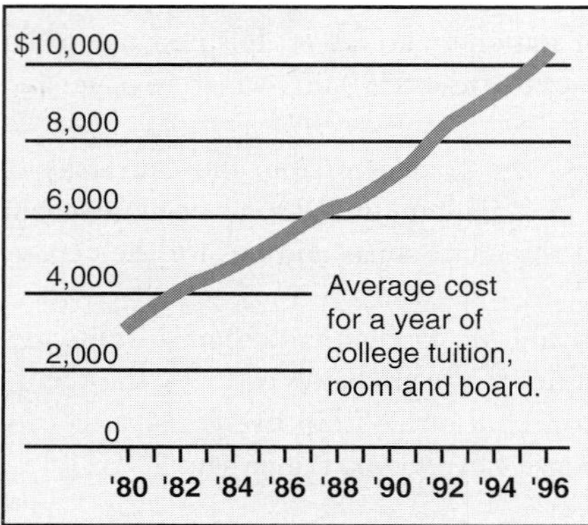

...GRADUATING CLASSES GROW...

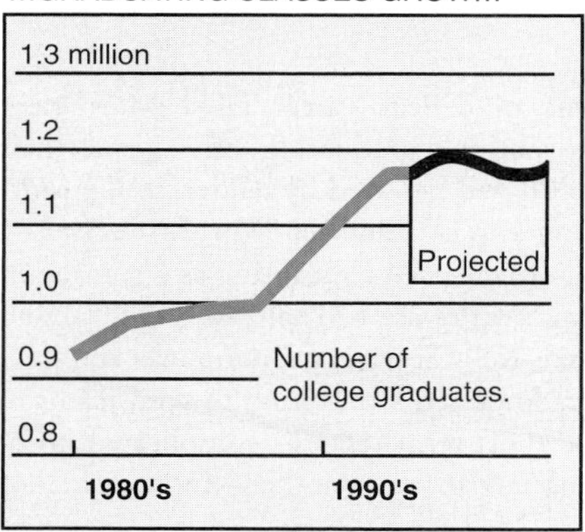

...AND STUDENTS ACQUIRE MORE DEBT

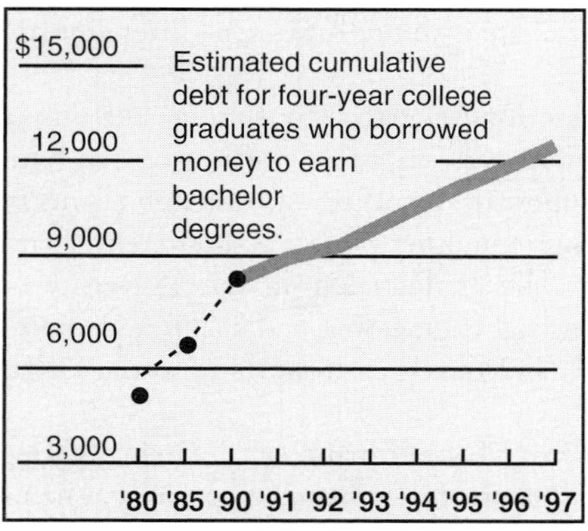

Well before she graduated, Ms. Rogers had four other job offers, and would have had more had she not tightly limited her interviewing to companies in which she was keenly interested.

Thousands of graduates like Ms. Rogers are hired by Andersen and its brethren in the consulting field—Price Waterhouse and Ernst & Young's consulting arms, as well as computer consulting firms like Electronic Data Systems. The Big Six accounting firms—including Andersen Consulting's sister company, Andersen Accounting—hire still more thousands for traditional accounting jobs.

Kim K. Dodson, 23, turned down 11 other offers to sign on at Andersen Consulting. She graduated from Texas A & M with a 3.4 grade-point average, having majored in business analysis, and started work in February. She wears a gold Aggie ring—a popular accessory in Andersen's Dallas office—with her business suit. For the last six weeks, she has been driving to the Fort Worth offices of Burlington Resources, an oil and gas company, to help program its computers.

Also working on Burlington's new computer codes is Nichole A. Inloes, 22, a December graduate of Texas A & M with a major in marketing. She programs Burlington's computers to cut checks automatically for energy royalties.

She is glad she chose Andersen over the other company that offered her a job: Enterprise Rent-a-Car.

Her father, Gerald T. Inloes of San Antonio, said he was looking forward, now that the college expenses were past, to resuming the family's trips to the beach at Corpus Christi and an annual vacation in Las Vegas, luxuries the Inloes had been doing without.

Still, the financial sacrifice was worth it. "I don't regret it for a second," Mr. Inloes said. "I am just so proud of her."

Exploring Texts and Contexts

For activities with icons, refer to the Guide to Analyzing Readings in Context.

1. Read the two letters to the editor that respond to Meredith's article, and consider who wrote them and how their experience might have contributed to their point of view. Show this article to several people you know: an older person, perhaps a parent; someone from work; or a friend, and ask them what they make of it. From what other perspectives do people respond to this article? Consider, too, that this article appeared in 1997. Has the situation for workers changed since then? 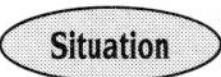

2. Examine the photos, captions, tables, and the general layout of this article. How does the visual arrangement contribute to its message? What other kinds of data might you have included? 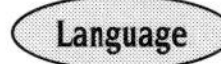

Creating Texts

For activities with icons, refer to the Guides to Analyzing Contexts for Writing and Analyzing Readings in Context. For additional help with these writing projects, read the descriptions of **Feature Story/Profile** and **Letter to the Editor** in the Genre Glossary.

1. Write a feature story or profile of several recent college graduates. You will want to tell a compelling story as well as offer some insightful analysis. The point you make could be quite different from Meredith's and will depend, in part, on how you choose your subjects and what lessons can be learned from their experiences.
2. Write a letter to the editor in response to this article. Remember to state Meredith's position before you elaborate on your own response. You may want to focus on your own experience or those of friends and acquaintances.

Nickel-and-Dimed

On (Not) Getting by in America

Barbara Ehrenreich

There is a long history in journalism of investigative stories in which the reporter goes "undercover" in order to enter and report on an unfamiliar world. Reporters have used this method to write stories about mental hospitals, prisons, street gangs, homeless communities, and other institutions or aspects of life that are usually hidden from or somehow strange to most readers of the stories and to the reporters themselves. This is essentially what Barbara Ehrenreich does in this piece, though with one important difference. The world she enters and writes about—low-wage service work—is not really hidden from Ehrenreich's audience, the readers of *Harper's* magazine; they probably see such workers all the time.

But Ehrenreich is most interested in revealing something that she assumes *is* hidden to her readers: how these workers support themselves and their families on such jobs, where they live, how they get to and from work, whether they have health insurance, and how they feel about their work and lives. And she wants to reveal this for a reason: She is concerned about the long-term impact of welfare reform, the changes to the welfare system passed in 1995 that set limits on the length of time single women with dependent children can receive welfare benefits, encouraging these women to find jobs to support themselves and their children. Ehrenreich is concerned that although this may sound good—who could object to the idea of people taking responsibility for the support of themselves and their children?—the reality of the American workplace and economy makes it very difficult for people with dependent children and few skills to make an income that they can live on.

Over the past 30 years, Ehrenreich has developed into a writer who often makes her readers uncomfortable and sometimes impatient. When she began writing in the early 1970s, her typical audience was young baby boomers who shared her liberal-to-radical leftwing perspective. But as her audience aged, settled down, and started to earn money, and as the country in general seemed to grow more prosperous, the issues that Ehrenreich continued to write about—the growing gap between rich and poor, the anxieties of the middle class, the conditions of life for those left behind by the nation's general prosperity—were often issues that her well-educated and generally well-off readers might prefer not to think about. But Ehrenreich's witty style and the rich detail with which she describes the worlds she enters keep her readers engaged. Thus, though Ehrenreich presents this piece as an argument against welfare reform, the funny and gripping stories she tells stand on their own. This piece was published in *Harper's* magazine, but later appeared in her book of the same name, published in May 2001 by Metropolitan Books.

Connecting with the Conversation

1. Many of us have had some experience working in low-wage service jobs—including waiting tables, working in fast-food restaurants, and doing housekeeping, maintenance, and many retail jobs—but often, especially when we are young, we don't think of these jobs as lifetime occupations. Have you ever had a job like this? How did you feel about it? How would you have felt if you had thought of it as a lifelong occupation? Write about your experiences and perceptions.

2. With the class divided into groups, each group should search a section of the Sunday want ads, looking at job ads in waiting tables, fast food, and housekeeping. Make note of the average hourly wages, benefits, and hours. Do any of the ads mention drug testing as a condition of employment? Each group should report its findings to the class, and then discuss with the class as a whole the implications of the overall findings.
3. Search your library's article database for articles by Ehrenreich. What kinds of topics does she write about, and in what kinds of periodicals does she publish? Given where she usually publishes, how would you characterize her target audience, and do you consider yourself a member of this audience?

At the beginning of June 1998 I leave behind everything that normally soothes the ego and sustains the body—home, career, companion, reputation, ATM card—for a plunge into the low-wage workforce. There, I become another, occupationally much diminished "Barbara Ehrenreich"—depicted on job-application forms as a divorced homemaker whose sole work experience consists of housekeeping in a few private homes. I am terrified, at the beginning, of being unmasked for what I am: a middle-class journalist setting out to explore the world that welfare mothers are entering, at the rate of approximately 50,000 a month, as welfare reform kicks in. Happily, though, my fears turn out to be entirely unwarranted: during a month of poverty and toil, my name goes unnoticed and for the most part unuttered. In this parallel universe where my father never got out of the mines and I never got through college, I am "baby," "honey," "blondie," and, most commonly, "girl."

My first task is to find a place to live. I figure that if I can earn $7 an hour—which, from the want ads, seems doable—I can afford to spend $500 on rent, or maybe, with severe economies, $600. In the Key West area, where I live, this pretty much confines me to flophouses and trailer homes—like the one, a pleasing fifteen-minute drive from town, that has no air-conditioning, no screens, no fans, no television, and, by way of diversion, only the challenge of evading the landlord's Doberman pinscher. The big problem with this place, though, is the rent, which at $675 a month is well beyond my reach. All right, Key West is expensive. But so is New York City, or the Bay Area, or Jackson Hole, or Telluride, or Boston, or any other place where tourists and the wealthy compete for living space with the people who clean their toilets and fry their hash browns.[1] Still, it is a shock to realize that "trailer trash" has become, for me, a demographic category to aspire to.

So I decide to make the common trade-off between affordability and convenience, and go for a $500-a-month efficiency thirty miles up a two-lane highway from the employment opportunities of Key West, meaning forty-five minutes if there's no road construction and I don't get caught behind some sun-dazed Canadian tourists. I hate the drive, along a roadside studded with white crosses commemorating the more effective head-on collisions, but it's a sweet little place—a cabin, more or less, set in the

From *Harper's Magazine,* January 1999, pp. 37–49, excerpted.

swampy back yard of the converted mobile home where my landlord, an affable TV repairman, lives with his bartender girlfriend. Anthropologically speaking, a bustling trailer park would be preferable, but here I have a gleaming white floor and a firm mattress, and the few resident bugs are easily vanquished.

Besides, I am not doing this for the anthropology. My aim is nothing so mistily subjective as to "experience poverty" or find out how it "really feels" to be a long-term low-wage worker. I've had enough unchosen encounters with poverty and the world of low-wage work to know it's not a place you want to visit for touristic purposes; it just smells too much like fear. And with all my real-life assets—bank account, IRA, health insurance, multiroom home—waiting indulgently in the background, I am, of course, thoroughly insulated from the terrors that afflict the genuinely poor.

5 No, this is a purely objective, scientific sort of mission. The humanitarian rationale for welfare reform—as opposed to the more punitive and stingy impulses that may actually have motivated it—is that work will lift poor women out of poverty while simultaneously inflating their self-esteem and hence their future value in the labor market. Thus, whatever the hassles involved in finding child care, transportation, etc., the transition from welfare to work will end happily, in greater prosperity for all. Now there are many problems with this comforting prediction, such as the fact that the economy will inevitably undergo a downturn, eliminating many jobs. Even without a downturn, the influx of a million former welfare recipients into the low-wage labor market could depress wages by as much as 11.9 percent, according to the Economic Policy Institute (EPI) in Washington, D.C.

But is it really possible to make a living on the kinds of jobs currently available to unskilled people? Mathematically, the answer is no, as can be shown by taking $6 to $7 an hour, perhaps subtracting a dollar or two an hour for child care, multiplying by 160 hours a month, and comparing the result to the prevailing rents. According to the National Coalition for the Homeless, for example, in 1998 it took, on average nationwide, an hourly wage of $8.89 to afford a one-bedroom apartment, and the Preamble Center for Public Policy estimates that the odds against a typical welfare recipient's landing a job at such a "living wage" are about 97 to 1. If these numbers are right, low-wage work is not a solution to poverty and possibly not even to homelessness.

It may seem excessive to put this proposition to an experimental test. As certain family members keep unhelpfully reminding me, the viability of low-wage work could be tested, after a fashion, without ever leaving my study. I could just pay myself $7 an hour for eight hours a day, charge myself for room and board, and total up the numbers after a month. Why leave the people and work that I love? But I am an experimental scientist by training. In that business, you don't just sit at a desk and theorize; you plunge into the everyday chaos of nature, where surprises lurk in the most mundane measurements. Maybe, when I got into it, I would discover some hidden economies in the world of the low-wage worker. After all, if 30 percent of the workforce toils for less than $8 an hour, according to the EPI, they may have found some tricks as yet unknown to me. Maybe—who knows?—I would even be able to detect in myself the bracing psychological effects of getting out of the house, as promised by the welfare wonks at places like the Heritage Foundation. Or, on the other hand, maybe there would be unexpected costs—physical, mental, or financial—to throw off all my calculations. Ideally, I should do this with two small children in tow, that being the welfare average, but mine are grown and no one is willing to lend me theirs for a month-long vacation in penury. So this is not the perfect experiment, just a test of the best possible case: an unencumbered woman, smart and even strong, attempting to live more or less off the land.

ON THE MORNING of my first full day of job searching, I take a red pen to the want ads, which are auspiciously numerous. Everyone in Key West's booming "hospitality industry" seems to be looking for someone like me—trainable, flexible, and with suitably humble expectations as to pay. I know I possess certain traits that might be advantageous—I'm white and, I like to think, well-spoken and poised—but I decide on two rules: One, I cannot use any skills derived from my education or usual work—not that there are a lot of want ads for satirical essayists anyway. Two, I have to take the best-paid job that is offered me and of course do my best to hold it; no Marxist rants or sneaking off to read novels in the ladies' room. In addition, I rule out various occupations for one reason or another: Hotel front-desk clerk, for example, which to my surprise is regarded as unskilled and pays around $7 an hour, gets eliminated because it involves standing in one spot for eight hours a day. Waitressing is similarly something I'd like to avoid, because I remember it leaving me bone tired when I was eighteen, and I'm decades of varicosities and back pain beyond that now. Telemarketing, one of the first refuges of the suddenly indigent, can be dismissed on grounds of personality. This leaves certain supermarket jobs, such as deli clerk, or housekeeping in Key West's thousands of hotel and guest rooms. Housekeeping is especially appealing, for reasons both atavistic and practical: it's what my mother did before I came along, and it can't be too different from what I've been doing part-time, in my own home, all my life.

So I put on what I take to be a respectful-looking outfit of ironed Bermuda shorts and scooped-neck T-shirt and set out for a tour of the local hotels and supermarkets. Best Western, Econo Lodge, and HoJo's all let me fill out application forms, and these are, to my relief, interested in little more than whether I am a legal resident of the United States and have committed any felonies. My next stop is Winn-Dixie, the supermarket, which turns out to have a particularly onerous application process, featuring a fifteen-minute "interview" by computer since, apparently, no human on the premises is deemed capable of representing the corporate point of view. I am conducted to a large room decorated with posters illustrating how to look "professional" (it helps to be white and, if female, permed) and warning of the slick promises that union organizers might try to tempt me with. The interview is multiple choice: Do I have anything, such as child-care problems, that might make it hard for me to get to work on time? Do I think safety on the job is the responsibility of management? Then, popping up cunningly out of the blue: How many dollars' worth of stolen goods have I purchased in the last year? Would I turn in a fellow employee if I caught him stealing? Finally, "Are you an honest person?"

10 Apparently, I ace the interview, because I am told that all I have to do is show up in some doctor's office tomorrow for a urine test. This seems to be a fairly general rule: if you want to stack Cheerio boxes or vacuum hotel rooms in chemically fascist America, you have to be willing to squat down and pee in front of some health worker (who has no doubt had to do the same thing herself). The wages Winn-Dixie is offering—$6 and a couple of dimes to start with—are not enough, I decide, to compensate for this indignity.[2]

I lunch at Wendy's, where $4.99 gets you unlimited refills at the Mexican part of the Superbar, a comforting surfeit of refried beans and "cheese sauce." A teenage employee, seeing me studying the want ads, kindly offers me an application form, which I fill out, though here, too, the pay is just $6 and change an hour. Then it's off for a round of the locally owned inns and guest-houses. At "The Palms," let's call it, a bouncy manager actually takes me around to see the rooms and meet the existing housekeepers, who, I note with satisfaction, look pretty much like me—faded ex-hippie types in shorts with long hair pulled back in braids. Mostly, though, no one speaks to me or even looks at me except to proffer an application form. At my last stop, a palatial B&B, I wait twenty minutes to meet "Max," only to be told that there are no jobs now but there should be one soon, since "nobody lasts more than a couple weeks." (Because none of the people I talked to knew I was a reporter, I have changed their names to protect their privacy and, in some cases perhaps, their jobs.)

Three days go by like this, and, to my chagrin, no one out of the approximately twenty places I've applied calls me for an interview. I had been vain enough to worry about coming across as too educated for the jobs I sought, but no one even seems interested in finding out how overqualified I am. Only later will I realize that the want ads are not a reliable measure of the actual jobs available at any particular time. They are, as I should have guessed from Max's comment, the employers' insurance policy against the relentless turnover of the low-wage workforce. Most of the big hotels run ads almost continually, just to build a supply of applicants to replace the current workers as they drift away or are fired, so finding a job is just a matter of being at the right place at the right time and flexible enough to take whatever is being offered that day. This finally happens to me at one of the big discount hotel chains, where I go, as usual, for housekeeping and am sent, instead, to try out as a waitress at the attached "family restaurant," a dismal spot with a counter and about thirty tables that looks out on a parking garage and features such tempting fare as "Pollish [sic] sausage and BBQ sauce" on 95-degree days. Phillip, the dapper young West Indian who introduces himself as the manager, interviews me with about as much enthusiasm as if he were a clerk processing me for Medicare, the principal questions being what shifts can I work and when can I start. I mutter something about being woefully out of practice as a waitress, but he's already on to the uniform: I'm to show up tomorrow wearing black slacks and black shoes; he'll provide the rust-colored polo shirt with HEARTHSIDE embroidered on it, though I might want to wear my own shirt to get to work, ha ha. At the word "tomorrow," something between fear and indignation rises in my chest. I want to say, "Thank you for your time, sir, but this is just an experiment, you know, not my actual life."

SO BEGINS MY CAREER at the Hearthside, I shall call it, one small profit center within a global discount hotel chain, where for two weeks I work from 2:00 till 10:00 P.M. for $2.43 an hour plus tips.[3] In some futile bid for gentility, the management has barred employees from using the front door, so my first day I enter through the kitchen, where a red-faced man with shoulder-length blond hair is throwing frozen steaks against the wall and yelling, "Fuck this shit!" "That's just Jack," explains Gail, the wiry middle-aged waitress who is assigned to train me. "He's on the rag again"—a condition occasioned, in this instance, by the fact that the cook on the morning shift had forgotten to thaw out the steaks. For the next eight hours, I run after the agile Gail, absorbing bits of instruction along with fragments of personal tragedy. All food must be trayed, and the reason she's so tired today is that she woke up in a cold sweat thinking of her boyfriend, who killed himself recently in an upstate prison. No refills on lemonade. And the reason he was in prison is that a few DUIs caught up with him, that's all, could have happened to anyone. Carry the creamers to the table in a monkey bowl, never in your hand. And after he was gone she spent several months living in her truck, peeing in a plastic pee bottle and reading by candlelight at night, but you can't live in a truck in the summer, since you need to have the windows down, which means anything can get in, from mosquitoes on up.

At least Gail puts to rest any fears I had of appearing overqualified. From the first day on, I find that of all the things I have left behind, such as home and identity, what I miss the most is competence. Not that I have ever felt utterly competent in the writing business, in which one day's success augurs nothing at all for the next. But in my writing life, I at least have some notion of procedure: do the research, make the outline, rough out a draft, etc. As a server, though, I am beset by requests like bees: more iced tea here, ketchup over there, a to-go box for table fourteen, and where are the high chairs, anyway? Of the twenty-seven tables, up to six are usually mine at any time, though on slow afternoons or if Gail is off, I sometimes have the whole place to myself. There is the touch-screen computer-ordering system to master, which is, I suppose, meant to minimize server-cook contact, but in practice requires constant verbal fine-tuning: "That's gravy on the mashed, okay? None on the meatloaf," and so forth—while the cook scowls as if I were inventing these refinements just to torment him. Plus, something I had forgotten in the years since I was eighteen: about a third of a server's job is "side work" that's invisible to customers—sweeping, scrubbing, slicing, refilling, and restocking. If it isn't all done, every little bit of it, you're going to face the 6:00 P.M. dinner rush defenseless and probably go down in flames. I screw up dozens of times at the beginning, sustained in my shame entirely by Gail's support—"It's okay, baby, everyone does that sometime"—because, to my total surprise and despite the scientific detachment I am doing my best to maintain, I care.

15 The whole thing would be a lot easier if I could just skate through it as Lily Tomlin in one of her waitress skits, but I was raised by the absurd Booker T. Washingtonian precept that says: If you're going to do something, do it well. In fact, "well" isn't good enough by half. Do it better than anyone has ever done it before. Or so said my father, who must have known what he was talking about because he managed to pull himself, and us with him, up from the mile-deep copper mines of Butte to the leafy suburbs of the Northeast, ascending from boilermakers to martinis before booze beat out ambition. As in most endeavors I have encountered in my life, doing it "better than anyone" is not a reasonable goal. Still, when I wake up at 4:00 A.M. in my own cold sweat, I am not thinking about the writing deadlines I'm neglecting; I'm thinking about the table whose order I screwed up so that one of the boys didn't get his kiddie meal until the rest of the family had moved on to their Key Lime pies. That's the other powerful motivation I hadn't expected—the customers, or "patients," as I can't help thinking of them on account of the mysterious vulnerability that seems to have left them temporarily unable to feed themselves. After a few days at the Hearthside, I feel the service ethic kick in like a shot of oxytocin, the nurturance hormone. The plurality of my customers are hard-working locals—truck drivers, construction workers, even housekeepers from the attached hotel—and I want them to have the closest

to a "fine dining" experience that the grubby circumstances will allow. No "you guys" for me; everyone over twelve is "sir" or "ma'am." I ply them with iced tea and coffee refills; I return, mid-meal, to inquire how everything is; I doll up their salads with chopped raw mushrooms, summer squash slices, or whatever bits of produce I can find that have survived their sojourn in the cold-storage room mold-free.

There is Benny, for example, a short, tight-muscled sewer repairman, who cannot even think of eating until he has absorbed a half hour of air-conditioning and ice water. We chat about hyperthermia and electrolytes until he is ready to order some finicky combination like soup of the day, garden salad, and a side of grits. There are the German tourists who are so touched by my pidgin "Willkommen" and "Ist alles gut?" that they actually tip. (Europeans, spoiled by their trade-union-ridden, high-wage welfare states, generally do not know that they are supposed to tip. Some restaurants, the Hearthside included, allow servers to "grat" their foreign customers, or add a tip to the bill. Since this amount is added before the customers have a chance to tip or not tip, the practice amounts to an automatic penalty for imperfect English.) There are the two dirt-smudged lesbians, just off their construction shift, who are impressed enough by my suave handling of the fly in the piña colada that they take the time to praise me to Stu, the assistant manager. There's Sam, the kindly retired cop, who has to plug up his tracheotomy hole with one finger in order to force the cigarette smoke into his lungs.

Sometimes I play with the fantasy that I am a princess who, in penance for some tiny transgression, has undertaken to feed each of her subjects by hand. But the non-princesses working with me are just as indulgent, even when this means flouting management rules—concerning, for example, the number of croutons that can go on a salad (six). "Put on all you want," Gail whispers, "as long as Stu isn't looking." She dips into her own tip money to buy biscuits and gravy for an out-of-work mechanic who's used up all his money on dental surgery, inspiring me to pick up the tab for his milk and pie. Maybe the same high levels of agape can be found throughout the "hospitality industry." I remember the poster decorating one of the apartments I looked at, which said "If you seek happiness for yourself you will never find it. Only when you seek happiness for others will it come to you," or words to that effect—an odd sentiment, it seemed to me at the time, to find in the dank one-room basement apartment of a bellhop at the Best Western. At the Hearthside, we utilize whatever bits of autonomy we have to ply our customers with the illicit calories that signal our love. It is our job as servers to assemble the salads and desserts, pouring the dressings and squirting the whipped cream. We also control the number of butter patties our customers get and the amount of sour cream on their baked potatoes. So if you wonder why Americans are so obese, consider the fact that waitresses both express their humanity and earn their tips through the covert distribution of fats.

Ten days into it, this is beginning to look like a livable lifestyle. I like Gail, who is "looking at fifty" but moves so fast she can alight in one place and then another without apparently being anywhere between them. I clown around with Lionel, the teenage Haitian busboy, and catch a few fragments of conversation with Joan, the svelte fortyish hostess and militant feminist who is the only one of us who dares to tell Jack to shut the fuck up. I even warm up to Jack when, on a slow night and to make up for a particularly unwarranted attack on my abilities, or so I imagine, he tells me about his glory days as a young man at "coronary school"—or do you say "culinary"?—in Brooklyn, where he dated a knock-out Puerto Rican chick and learned everything there is to know about food. I finish up at 10:00 or 10:30, depending on how much side work I've been able to get done during the shift, and cruise home to the tapes I snatched up at random when I left my real home—Marianne Faithfull, Tracy Chapman, Enigma, King Sunny Ade, the Violent Femmes—just drained enough for the music to set my cranium resonating but hardly dead. Midnight snack is Wheat Thins and Monterey Jack, accompanied by cheap white wine on ice and whatever AMC has to offer. To bed by 1:30 or 2:00, up at 9:00 or 10:00, read for an hour while my uniform whirls around in the landlord's washing machine, and then it's another eight hours spent following Mao's central instruction, as laid out in the Little Red Book, which was: Serve the people.

I COULD DRIFT ALONG like this, in some dreamy proletarian idyll, except for two things. One is management. If I have kept this subject on the margins thus far it is because I still flinch to think that I spent all those weeks under the surveillance of men (and later women) whose job it was to monitor my behavior for signs of sloth, theft, drug abuse, or worse. Not that managers and especially "assistant managers" in low-wage settings like this are exactly the class enemy. In the restaurant business, they are mostly former cooks or servers, still capable of pinch-hitting in the kitchen or on the floor, just as in hotels they are likely to be former clerks, and paid a salary of only about $400 a week. But everyone knows they have crossed over to the other side, which is, crudely put, corporate as opposed to human. Cooks want to prepare tasty meals; servers want to serve them graciously; but managers are there for only one reason—to make sure that money is made for some theoretical entity that exists far away in Chicago or New York, if a corporation can be said to have a physical existence at all. Reflecting on her career, Gail tells me ruefully that she had sworn, years ago, never to work for a corporation again. "They don't cut you no slack. You give and you give, and they take."

20 Managers can sit—for hours at a time if they want—but it's their job to see that no one else ever does, even when there's nothing to do, and this is why, for servers, slow times can be as exhausting as rushes. You start dragging out each little chore, because if the manager on duty catches you in an idle moment, he will give you something far nastier to do. So I wipe, I clean, I consolidate ketchup bottles and recheck the cheesecake supply, even tour the tables to make sure the customer evaluation forms are all standing perkily in their places—wondering all the time how many calories I burn in these strictly theatrical exercises. When, on a particularly dead afternoon, Stu finds me glancing at a *USA Today* a customer has left behind, he assigns me to vacuum the entire floor with the broken vacuum cleaner that has a handle only two feet long, and the only way to do that without incurring orthopedic damage is to proceed from spot to spot on your knees.

On my first Friday at the Hearthside there is a "mandatory meeting for all restaurant employees," which I attend, eager for insight into our overall marketing strategy and the niche (your basic Ohio cuisine with a tropical twist?) we aim to inhabit. But there is no "we" at this meeting. Phillip, our top manager except for an occasional "consultant" sent out by corporate headquarters, opens it with a sneer: "The break room—it's disgusting. Butts in the ashtrays, newspapers lying around, crumbs." This windowless little room, which also houses the time clock for the entire hotel, is where we stash our bags and civilian clothes and take our half-hour meal breaks. But a break room is not a right, he tells us. It can be taken away. We should also know that the lockers in the break room and whatever is in them can be searched at any time. Then comes gossip; there has been gossip; gossip (which seems to mean employees talking among themselves) must stop. Off-duty employees are henceforth barred from eating at the restaurant, because "other servers gather around them and gossip." When Phillip has exhausted his agenda of rebukes, Joan complains about the condition of the ladies' room and I throw in my two bits about the vacuum cleaner. But I don't see any backup coming from my fellow servers, each of whom has subsided into her own personal funk; Gail, my role model, stares sorrowfully at a point six inches from her nose. The meeting ends when Andy, one of the cooks, gets up, muttering about breaking up his day off for this almighty bullshit.

Just four days later we are suddenly summoned into the kitchen at 3:30 P.M., even though there are live tables on the floor. We all—about ten of us—stand around Phillip, who announces grimly that there has been a report of some "drug activity" on the night shift and that, as a result, we are now to be a "drug-free" workplace, meaning that all new hires will be tested, as will possibly current employees on a random basis. I am glad that this part of the kitchen is so dark, because I find myself blushing as hard as if I had been caught toking up in the ladies' room myself: I haven't been treated this way—lined up in the corridor, threatened with locker searches, peppered with carelessly aimed accusations—since junior high school. Back on the floor, Joan cracks, "Next they'll be telling us we can't have sex on the job." When I ask Stu what happened to inspire the crackdown, he just mutters about "management decisions" and takes the opportunity to upbraid Gail and me for being too generous with the rolls. From now on there's to be only one per customer, and it goes out with the dinner, not with the salad. He's also been riding the cooks, prompting Andy to come out of the kitchen and observe—with the serenity of a man whose customary implement is a butcher knife—that "Stu has a death wish today."

Later in the evening, the gossip crystallizes around the theory that Stu is himself the drug culprit, that he uses the restaurant phone to order up marijuana and sends one of the late servers out to fetch it for him. The server was caught, and she may have ratted Stu out or at least said enough to cast some suspicion on him, thus accounting for his pissy behavior. Who knows? Lionel, the busboy, entertains us for the rest of the shift by standing just behind Stu's back and sucking deliriously on an imaginary joint.

The other problem, in addition to the less-than-nurturing management style, is that this job shows no sign of being financially viable. You might imagine, from a comfortable distance, that people who live, year in and year out, on $6 to $10 an hour have discovered some survival stratagems unknown to the middle class. But no. It's not hard to get my coworkers to talk about their living situations, because housing, in almost every case, is the principal source of disruption in their lives, the first thing they fill you in on when they arrive for their shifts. After a week, I have compiled the following survey:

25 • Gail is sharing a room in a well-known downtown flophouse for which she and a roommate pay about $250 a week. Her roommate, a male friend, has begun hitting on her, driving her nuts, but the rent would be impossible alone.

• Claude, the Haitian cook, is desperate to get out of the two-room apartment he shares with his girlfriend and two other, unrelated, people. As far as I can determine, the other Haitian men (most of whom only speak Creole) live in similarly crowded situations.

- Annette, a twenty-year-old server who is six months pregnant and has been abandoned by her boyfriend, lives with her mother, a postal clerk.
- Marianne and her boyfriend are paying $170 a week for a one-person trailer.
- Jack, who is, at $10 an hour, the wealthiest of us, lives in the trailer he owns, paying only the $400-a-month lot fee.

30
- The other white cook, Andy, lives on his dry-docked boat, which, as far as I can tell from his loving descriptions, can't be more than twenty feet long. He offers to take me out on it, once it's repaired, but the offer comes with inquiries as to my marital status, so I do not follow up on it.
- Tina and her husband are paying $60 a night for a double room in a Days Inn. This is because they have no car and the Days Inn is within walking distance of the Hearthside. When Marianne, one of the breakfast servers, is tossed out of her trailer for subletting (which is against the trailer-park rules), she leaves her boyfriend and moves in with Tina and her husband.
- Joan, who had fooled me with her numerous and tasteful outfits (hostesses wear their own clothes), lives in a van she parks behind a shopping center at night and showers in Tina's motel room. The clothes are from thrift shops.[4]

IT STRIKES ME, IN my middle-class solipsism, that there is gross improvidence in some of these arrangements. When Gail and I are wrapping silverware in napkins—the only task for which we are permitted to sit—she tells me she is thinking of escaping from her roommate by moving into the Days Inn herself. I am astounded: How can she even think of paying between $40 and $60 a day? But if I was afraid of sounding like a social worker, I come out just sounding like a fool. She squints at me in disbelief, "And where am I supposed to get a month's rent and a month's deposit for an apartment?" I'd been feeling pretty smug about my $500 efficiency, but of course it was made possible only by the $1,300 I had allotted myself for start-up costs when I began my low-wage life: $1,000 for the first month's rent and deposit, $100 for initial groceries and cash in my pocket, $200 stuffed away for emergencies. In poverty, as in certain propositions in physics, starting conditions are everything.

There are no secret economies that nourish the poor; on the contrary, there are a host of special costs. If you can't put up the two months' rent you need to secure an apartment, you end up paying through the nose for a room by the week. If you have only a room, with a hot plate at best, you can't save by cooking up huge lentil stews that can be frozen for the week ahead. You eat fast food, or the hot dogs and styrofoam cups of soup that can be microwaved in a convenience store. If you have no money for health insurance—and the Hearthside's niggardly plan kicks in only after three months—you go without routine care or prescription drugs and end up paying the price. Gail, for example, was fine until she ran out of money for estrogen pills. She is supposed to be on the company plan by now, but they claim to have lost her application form and need to begin the paperwork all over again. So she spends $9 per migraine pill to control the headaches she wouldn't have, she insists, if her estrogen supplements were covered. Similarly, Marianne's boyfriend lost his job as a roofer because he missed so much time after getting a cut on his foot for which he couldn't afford the prescribed antibiotic.

35 My own situation, when I sit down to assess it after two weeks of work, would not be much better if this were my actual life. The seductive thing about waitressing is that you don't have to wait for payday to feel a few bills in your pocket, and my tips usually cover meals and gas, plus something left over to stuff into the kitchen drawer I use as a bank. But as the tourist business slows in the summer heat, I sometimes leave work with only $20 in tips (the gross is higher, but servers share about 15 percent of their tips with the bus-boys and bartenders). With wages included, this amounts to about the minimum wage of $5.15 an hour. Although the sum in the drawer is piling up, at the present rate of accumulation it will be more than a hundred dollars short of my rent when the end of the month comes around. Nor can I see any expenses to cut. True, I haven't gone the lentil-stew route yet, but that's because I don't have a large cooking pot, pot holders, or a ladle to stir with (which cost about $30 at Kmart, less at thrift stores), not to mention onions, carrots, and the indispensable bay leaf. I do make my lunch almost every day—usually some slow-burning, high-protein combo like frozen chicken patties with melted cheese on top and canned pinto beans on the side. Dinner is at the Hearthside, which offers its employees a choice of BLT, fish sandwich, or hamburger for only $2. The burger lasts longest, especially if it's heaped with gut-puckering jalapeños, but by midnight my stomach is growling again.

So unless I want to start using my car as a residence, I have to find a second, or alternative, job. I call all the hotels where I filled out housekeeping applications weeks ago—the Hyatt, Holiday Inn, Econo Lodge, HoJo's, Best Western, plus a half dozen or so locally run guesthouses. Nothing. Then I start making the rounds again, wasting whole mornings waiting for some assistant manager to show up, even dipping into places so creepy that the front-desk clerk greets you from behind bulletproof glass and sells pints of liquor over the counter. But either someone has exposed my real-life housekeeping habits—which are, shall we say, mellow—or I am at the wrong end of some infallible ethnic equation: most, but by no means all, of the working housekeepers I see on my job searches are African Americans, Spanish-speaking, or immigrants from the Central European post-Communist world, whereas servers are almost invariably white and monolingually English-speaking. When I finally get a positive response, I have been identified once again as server material. Jerry's, which is part of a well-known national family restaurant chain and physically attached here to another budget hotel chain, is ready to use me at once. The prospect is both exciting and terrifying, because, with about the same number of tables and counter seats, Jerry's attracts three or four times the volume of customers as the gloomy old Hearthside.

I START OUT WITH the beautiful, heroic idea of handling the two jobs at once, and for two days I almost do it: the breakfast/lunch shift at Jerry's, which goes till 2:00, arriving at the Hearthside at 2:10, and attempting to hold out until 10:00. In the ten minutes between jobs, I pick up a spicy chicken sandwich at the Wendy's drive-through window, gobble it down in the car, and change from khaki slacks to black, from Hawaiian to rust polo. There is a problem, though. When during the 3:00 to 4:00 P.M. dead time I finally sit down to wrap silver, my flesh seems to bond to the seat. I try to refuel with a purloined cup of soup, as I've seen Gail and Joan do dozens of times, but a manager catches me and hisses "No eating!" though there's not a customer around to be offended by the sight of food making contact with a server's lips. So I tell Gail I'm going to quit, and she hugs me and says she might just follow me to Jerry's herself.

But the chances of this are minuscule. She has left the flophouse and her annoying roommate and is back to living in her beat-up old truck. But guess what? she reports to me excitedly later that evening: Phillip has given her permission to park overnight in the hotel parking lot, as long as she keeps out of sight, and the parking lot should be totally safe, since it's patrolled by a hotel security guard! With the Hearthside offering benefits like that, how could anyone think of leaving?

True, I take occasional breaks from this life, going home now and then to catch up on e-mail and for conjugal visits (though I am careful to "pay" for anything I eat there), seeing *The Truman Show* with friends and letting them buy my ticket. And I still have those what-am-I-doing-here moments at work, when I get so homesick for the printed word that I obsessively reread the six-page menu. But as the days go by, my old life is beginning to look exceedingly strange. The e-mails and phone messages addressed to my former self come from a distant race of people with exotic concerns and far too much time on their hands. The neighborly market I used to cruise for produce now looks forbiddingly like a Manhattan yuppie emporium. And when I sit down one morning in my real home to pay bills from my past life, I am dazzled at the two- and three-figure sums owed to outfits like Club BodyTech and Amazon.com.

40 MANAGEMENT AT JERRY'S is generally calmer and more "professional" than at the Hearthside, with two exceptions. One is Joy, a plump, blowsy woman in her early thirties, who once kindly devoted several minutes to instructing me in the correct one-handed method of carrying trays but whose moods change disconcertingly from shift to shift and even within one. Then there's B.J., a.k.a. B.J.-the-bitch, whose contribution is to stand by the kitchen counter and yell, "Nita, your order's up, move it!" or, "Barbara, didn't you see you've got another table out there? Come on, girl!" Among other things, she is hated for having replaced the whipped-cream squirt cans with big plastic whipped-cream-filled baggies that have to be squeezed with both hands—because, reportedly, she saw or thought she saw employees trying to inhale the propellant gas from the squirt cans, in the hope that it might be nitrous oxide. On my third night, she pulls me aside abruptly and brings her face so close that it looks as if she's planning to butt me with her forehead. But instead of saying, "You're fired," she says, "You're doing fine." The only trouble is I'm spending time chatting with customers: "That's how they're getting you." Furthermore I am letting them "run me," which means harassment by sequential demands: you bring the ketchup and they decide they want extra Thousand Island; you bring that and they announce they now need a side of fries; and so on into distraction. Finally she tells me not to take her wrong. She tries to say things in a nice way, but you get into a mode, you know, because everything has to move so fast.[5]

I mumble thanks for the advice, feeling like I've just been stripped naked by the crazed enforcer of some ancient sumptuary law: No chatting for you, girl. No fancy service ethic allowed for the serfs. Chatting with customers is for the beautiful young college-educated servers in the downtown carpaccio joints, the kids who can make $70 to $100 a night.

What had I been thinking? My job is to move orders from tables to kitchen and then trays from kitchen to tables. Customers are, in fact, the major obstacle to the smooth transformation of information into food and food into money—they are, in short, the enemy. And the painful thing is that I'm beginning to see it this way myself. There are the traditional asshole types—frat boys who down multiple Buds and then make a fuss because the steaks are so emaciated and the fries so sparse—as well as the variously impaired—due to age, diabetes, or literacy issues—who require patient nutritional counseling.

I make friends, over time, with the other "girls" who work my shift: Nita, the tattooed twenty-something who taunts us by going around saying brightly, "Have we started making money yet?" Ellen, whose teenage son cooks on the graveyard shift and who once managed a restaurant in Massachusetts but won't try out for management here because she prefers being a "common worker" and not "ordering people around." Easy-going fiftyish Lucy, with the raucous laugh, who limps toward the end of the shift because of something that has gone wrong with her leg, the exact nature of which cannot be determined without health insurance. We talk about the usual girl things—men, children, and the sinister allure of Jerry's chocolate peanut-butter cream pie—though no one, I notice, ever brings up anything potentially expensive, like shopping or movies. As at the Hearthside, the only recreation ever referred to is partying, which requires little more than some beer, a joint, and a few close friends. Still, no one here is homeless, or cops to it anyway, thanks usually to a working husband or boyfriend. All in all, we form a reliable mutual-support group: If one of us is feeling sick or overwhelmed, another one will "bev" a table or even carry trays for her. If one of us is off sneaking a cigarette or a pee,[6] the others will do their best to conceal her absence from the enforcers of corporate rationality.

But my saving human connection—my oxytocin receptor, as it were—George, the nineteen-year-old, fresh-off-the-boat Czech dishwasher. We get to talking when he asks me, tortuously, how much cigarettes cost at Jerry's. I do my best to explain that they cost over a dollar more here than at a regular store and suggest that he just take one from the half-filled packs that are always lying around on the break table. But that would be unthinkable. Except for the one tiny earring signaling his allegiance to some vaguely alternative point of view, George is a perfect straight arrow—crew-cut, hard-working, and hungry for eye contact. "Czech Republic," I ask, "or Slovakia?" and he seems delighted that I know the difference. "Václav Havel," I try. "Velvet Revolution, Frank Zappa?" "Yes, yes, 1989," he says, and I realize we are talking about history.

My project is to teach George English. "How are you today, George?" I say at the start of each shift. "I am good, and how are you today, Barbara?" I learn that he is not paid by Jerry's but by the "agent" who shipped him over—$5 an hour, with the agent getting the dollar or so difference between that and what Jerry's pays dishwashers. I learn also that he shares an apartment with a crowd of other Czech "dishers," as he calls them, and that he cannot sleep until one of them goes off for his shift, leaving a vacant bed. We are having one of our ESL sessions late one afternoon when B.J. catches us at it and orders "Joseph" to take up the rubber mats on the floor near the dishwashing sinks and mop underneath. "I thought your name was George," I say loud enough for B.J. to hear as she strides off back to the counter. Is she embarrassed? Maybe a little, because she greets me back at the counter with "George, Joseph—there are so many of them!" I say nothing, neither nodding nor smiling, and for this I am punished later when I think I am ready to go and she announces that I need to roll fifty more sets of silverware and isn't it time I mixed up a fresh four-gallon batch of blue-cheese dressing? May you grow old in this place, B.J., is the curse I beam out at her when I am finally permitted to leave. May the syrup spills glue your feet to the floor.

45 I make the decision to move closer to Key West. First, because of the drive. Second and third, also because of the drive: gas is eating up $4 to $5 a day, and although Jerry's is as high-volume as you can get, the tips average only 10 percent, and not just for a newbie like me. Between the base pay of $2.15 an hour and the obligation to share tips with the busboys and dishwashers, we're averaging only about $7.50 an hour. Then there is the $30 I had to spend on the regulation tan slacks worn by Jerry's servers—a setback it could take weeks to absorb. (I had combed the town's two downscale department stores hoping for something cheaper but decided in the end that these marked-down Dockers, originally $49, were more likely to survive a daily washing.) Of my fellow servers, everyone who lacks a working husband or boyfriend seems to have a second job: Nita does something at a computer eight hours a day; another welds. Without the forty-five-minute commute, I can picture myself working two jobs and having the time to shower between them.

So I take the $500 deposit I have coming from my landlord, the $400 I have earned toward the next month's rent, plus the $200 reserved for emergencies, and use the $1,100 to pay the rent and deposit on trailer number 46 in the Overseas Trailer Park, a mile from the cluster of budget hotels that constitute Key West's version of an industrial park. Number 46 is about eight feet in width and shaped like a barbell inside, with a narrow region—because of the sink and the stove—separating the bedroom from what might optimistically be called the "living" area, with its two-person table and half-sized couch. The bathroom is so small my knees rub against the shower stall when I sit on the toilet, and you can't just leap out of the bed, you have to climb down to the foot of it in order to find a patch of floor space to stand on. Outside, I am within a few yards of a liquor store, a bar that advertises "free beer tomorrow," a convenience store, and a Burger King—but no supermarket or, alas, laundromat. By reputation, the Overseas park is a nest of crime and crack, and I am hoping at least for some vibrant, multicultural street life. But desolation rules night and day, except for a thin stream of pedestrian traffic heading for their jobs at the Sheraton or 7-Eleven. There are not exactly people here but what amounts to canned labor, being preserved from the heat between shifts.

In line with my reduced living conditions, a new form of ugliness arises at Jerry's. First we are confronted—via an announcement on the computers through which we input orders—with the new rule that the hotel bar is henceforth off-limits to restaurant employees. The culprit, I learn through the grapevine, is the ultra-efficient gal who trained me—another trailer-home dweller and a mother of three. Something had set her off one morning, so she slipped out for a nip and returned to the floor impaired. This mostly hurts Ellen, whose habit it is to free her hair from its rubber band and drop by the bar for a couple of Zins before heading home at the end of the shift, but all of us feel the chill. Then the next day, when I go for straws, for the first time I find the dry-storage room locked. Ted, the portly assistant manager who opens it for me, explains that he caught one of the dishwashers attempting to steal something, and, unfortunately, the miscreant will be with us until a replacement can be found—hence the locked door. I neglect to ask what he had been trying to steal, but Ted tells me who he is—the kid with the buzz cut and the earring. You know, he's back there right now.

I wish I could say I rushed back and confronted George to get his side of the story. I wish I could say I stood up to Ted and insisted that George be given a translator and allowed to defend himself, or announced that I'd find a lawyer who'd handle the case pro bono. The mystery to me is that there's not much worth stealing in the dry-storage room, at least not in any fenceable quantity: "Is Gyorgi here, and am having 200—maybe 250—ketchup packets. What do you say?" My guess is that he had taken—if he had taken anything at all—some Saltines or a can of cherry-pie mix, and that the motive for taking it was hunger.

So why didn't I intervene? Certainly not because I was held back by the kind of moral paralysis that can pass as journalistic objectivity. On the contrary, something new—something loathsome and servile—had infected me, along with the kitchen odors that I could still sniff on my bra when I finally undressed at night. In real life I am moderately brave, but plenty of brave people shed their courage in concentration camps, and maybe something similar goes on in the infinitely more congenial milieu of the low-wage American workplace. Maybe, in a month or two more at Jerry's, I might have regained my crusading spirit. Then again, in a month or two I might have turned into a different person altogether—say, the kind of person who would have turned George in. But this is not something I am slated to find out.

50 I can do this two-job thing, is my theory, if I can drink enough caffeine and avoid getting distracted by George's ever more obvious suffering.[7] The first few days after being caught he seemed not to understand the trouble he was in, and our chirpy little conversations had continued. But the last couple of shifts he's been listless and unshaven, and tonight he looks like the ghost we all know him to be, with dark half-moons hanging from his eyes. At one point, when I am briefly immobilized by the task of filling little paper cups with sour cream for baked potatoes, he comes over and looks as if he'd like to explore the limits of our shared vocabulary, but I am called to the floor for a table. I resolve to give him all my tips that night and to hell with the experiment in low-wage money management. At eight, Ellen and I grab a snack together standing at the mephitic end of the kitchen counter, but I can only manage two or three mozzarella sticks and lunch had been a mere handful of McNuggets. I am not tired at all, I assure myself, though it may be that there is simply no more "I" left to do the tiredness monitoring. What I would see, if I were more alert to the situation, is that the forces of destruction are already massing against me. There is only one cook on duty, a young man named Jesus ("Hay-Sue," that is) and he is new to the job. And there is Joy, who shows up to take over in the middle of the shift, wearing high heels and a long, clingy white dress and fuming as if she'd just been stood up in some cocktail bar.

Then it comes, the perfect storm. Four of my tables fill up at once. Four tables is nothing for me now, but only so long as they are obligingly staggered. As I bev table 27, tables 25, 28, and 24 are watching enviously. As I bev 25, 24 glowers because their bevs haven't even been ordered. Twenty-eight is four yuppyish types, meaning everything on the side and agonizing instructions as to the chicken Caesars. Twenty-five is a middle-aged black couple, who complain, with some justice, that the iced tea isn't fresh and the tabletop is sticky. But table 24 is the meteorological event of the century: ten British tourists who seem to have made the decision to absorb the American experience entirely by mouth. Here everyone has at least two drinks—iced tea and milk shake, Michelob and water (with lemon slice, please)—and a huge promiscuous orgy of breakfast specials, mozz sticks, chicken strips, quesadillas; burgers with cheese and without, sides of hash browns with cheddar, with onions, with gravy, seasoned fries, plain fries, banana splits. Poor Jesus! Poor me! Because when I arrive with their first tray of food—after three prior trips just to refill bevs—Princess Di refuses to eat her chicken strips with her pancake-and-sausage special, since, as she now reveals, the strips were meant to be an appetizer. Maybe the others would have accepted their meals, but Di, who is deep into her third Michelob, insists that everything else go back while they work on their "starters." Meanwhile, the yuppies are waving me down for more decaf and the black couple looks ready to summon the NAACP.

Much of what happened next is lost in the fog of war. Jesus starts going under. The little printer on the counter in front of him is spewing out orders faster than he can rip them off, much less produce the meals. Even the invincible Ellen is ashen from stress. I bring table 24 their reheated main courses, which they immediately reject as either too cold or fossilized by the microwave. When I return to the kitchen with their trays (three trays in three trips), Joy confronts me with arms akimbo: "What is this?" She means the food—the plates of rejected pancakes, hash browns in assorted flavors, toasts, burgers, sausages, eggs. "Uh, scrambled with cheddar," I try, "and that's . . ." "NO," she screams in my face. "Is it a traditional, a super-scramble, an eye-opener?" I pretend to study my check for a clue, but entropy has been up to its tricks, not only on the plates but in my head, and I have to admit that the original order is beyond reconstruction. "You don't know an eye-opener from a traditional?" she demands in outrage. All I know, in fact, is that my legs have lost interest in the current venture and have announced their intention to fold. I am saved by a yuppie (mercifully not one of mine) who chooses this moment to charge into the kitchen to bellow that his food is twenty-five minutes late. Joy screams at him to get the hell out of her kitchen, please, and then turns on Jesus in a fury, hurling an empty tray across the room for emphasis.

I leave. I don't walk out, I just leave. I don't finish my side work or pick up my credit-card tips, if any, at the cash register or, of course, ask Joy's permission to go. And the surprising thing is that you *can* walk out without permission, that the door opens, that the thick tropical night air parts to let me pass, that my car is still parked where I left it. There is no vindication in this exit, no fuck-you surge of relief, just an overwhelming, dank sense of failure pressing down on me and the entire parking lot. I had gone into this venture in the spirit of science, to test a mathematical proposition, but somewhere along the line, in the tunnel vision imposed by long shifts and relentless concentration, it became a test of myself, and clearly I have failed. Not only had I flamed out as a housekeeper/server, I had even forgotten to give George my tips, and, for reasons perhaps best known to hardworking, generous people like Gail and Ellen, this hurts. I don't cry, but I am in a position to realize, for the first time in many years, that the tear ducts are still there, and still capable of doing their job.

When I moved out of the trailer park, I gave the key to number 46 to Gail and arranged for my deposit to be transferred to her. She told me that Joan is still living in her van and that Stu had been fired from the Hearthside. I never found out what happened to George.

55 In one month, I had earned approximately $1,040 and spent $517 on food, gas, toiletries, laundry, phone, and utilities. If I had remained in my $500 efficiency, I would have been able to pay the rent and have $22 left over (which is $78 less than the cash I had in my pocket at the start of the month). During this time I bought no clothing except for the required slacks and no prescription drugs or medical care (I did finally buy some vitamin B to compensate for the lack of vegetables in my diet). Perhaps I could have saved a little on food if I had gotten to a supermarket more often, instead of convenience stores, but it should be noted that I lost almost four pounds in four weeks, on a diet weighted heavily toward burgers and fries.

How former welfare recipients and single mothers will (and do) survive in the low-wage workforce, I cannot imagine. Maybe they will figure out how to condense their lives—including child-raising, laundry, romance, and meals—into the couple of hours between full-time jobs. Maybe they will take up residence in their vehicles, if they have one. All I know is that I couldn't hold two jobs and I couldn't make enough money to live on with one. And I had advantages unthinkable to many of the long-term poor—health, stamina, a working car, and no children to care for and support. Certainly nothing in my experience contradicts the conclusion of Kathryn Edin and Laura Lein, in their recent book *Making Ends Meet: How Single Mothers Survive Welfare and Low-Wage Work,* that low-wage work actually involves more hardship and deprivation than life at the mercy of the welfare state. In the coming months and years, economic conditions for the working poor are bound to worsen, even without the almost inevitable recession. As mentioned earlier, the influx of former welfare recipients into the low-skilled workforce will have a depressing effect on both wages and the number of jobs available. A general economic downturn will only enhance these effects, and the working poor will of course be facing it without the slight, but nonetheless often saving, protection of welfare as a backup.

The thinking behind welfare reform was that even the humblest jobs are morally uplifting and psychologically buoying. In reality they are likely to be fraught with insult and stress. But I did discover one redeeming feature of the most abject low-wage work—the camaraderie of people who are, in almost all cases, far too smart and funny and caring for the work they do and the wages they're paid. The hope, of course, is that someday these people will come to know what they're worth, and take appropriate action.

Notes

1. According to the Department of Housing and Urban Development, the "fair-market rent" for an efficiency is $551 here in Monroe County, Florida. A comparable rent in the five boroughs of New York City is $704; in San Francisco, $713; and in the heart of Silicon Valley, $808. The fair-market rent for an area is defined as the amount that would be needed to pay rent plus utilities for "privately owned, decent, safe, and sanitary rental housing of a modest (non-luxury) nature with suitable amenities."
2. According to the *Monthly Labor Review* (November 1996), 28 percent of work sites surveyed in the service industry conduct drug tests (corporate workplaces have much higher rates), and the incidence of testing has risen markedly since the Eighties. The rate of testing is

highest in the South (56 percent of work sites polled), with the Midwest in second place (50 percent). The drug most likely to be detected—marijuana, which can be detected in urine for weeks—is also the most innocuous, while heroin and cocaine are generally undetectable three days after use. Prospective employees sometimes try to cheat the tests by consuming excessive amounts of liquids and taking diuretics and even masking substances available through the Internet.

3. According to the Fair Labor Standards Act, employers are not required to pay "tipped employees," such as restaurant servers, more than $2.13 an hour in direct wages. However, if the sum of tips plus $2.13 an hour falls below the minimum wage, or $5.15 an hour, the employer is required to make up the difference. This fact was not mentioned by managers or otherwise publicized at either of the restaurants where I worked.

4. I could find no statistics on the number of employed people living in cars or vans, but according to the National Coalition for the Homeless's 1997 report "Myths and Facts About Homelessness," nearly one in five homeless people (in twenty-nine cities across the nation) is employed in a full- or part-time job.

5. In *Workers in a Lean World: Unions in the International Economy* (Verso, 1997), Kim Moody cites studies finding an increase in stress-related workplace injuries and illness between the mid-1980s and the early 1990s. He argues that rising stress levels reflect a new system of "management by stress," in which workers in a variety of industries are being squeezed to extract maximum productivity, to the detriment of their health.

6. Until April 1998, there was no federally mandated right to bathroom breaks. According to Marc Linder and Ingrid Nygaard, authors of *Void Where Prohibited: Rest Breaks and the Right to Urinate on Company Time* (Cornell University Press, 1997), "The right to rest and void at work is not high on the list of social or political causes supported by professional or executive employees, who enjoy personal workplace liberties that millions of factory workers can only daydream about. . . . While we were dismayed to discover that workers lacked an acknowledged legal right to void at work, (the workers) were amazed by outsiders' naive belief that their employers would permit them to perform this basic bodily function when necessary. . . . A factory worker, not allowed a break for six-hour stretches, voided into pads worn inside her uniform; and a kindergarten teacher in a school without aides had to take all twenty children with her to the bathroom and line them up outside the stall door when she voided."

7. In 1996, the number of persons holding two or more jobs averaged 7.8 million, or 6.2 percent of the workforce. It was about the same rate for men and for women (6.1 versus 6.2), though the kinds of jobs differ by gender. About two thirds of multiple jobholders work one job full-time and the other part-time. Only a heroic minority—4 percent of men and 2 percent of women—work two full-time jobs simultaneously. (From John F. Stinson Jr., "New Data on Multiple Jobholding Available from the CPS," in the *Monthly Labor Review,* March 1997.)

Exploring Texts and Contexts

For activities with icons, refer to the Guide to Analyzing Readings in Context.

1. In Connecting with the Conversation Activity 3, what did you conclude about Ehrenreich's target audience? Do you think the people she describes in this piece are members of that audience? How do you think audience considerations influenced the way Ehrenreich wrote this piece? Situation

Creating Texts

For assignments with icons, refer to the Guides to Analyzing Contexts for Writing and Analyzing Readings in Context. For additional help with these writing projects, read the descriptions of **Essay** and **Academic Article/Research Paper** in the Genre Glossary.

Consequences

1. Write an essay in which you describe a good or bad experience you've had in the workplace. Ehrenreich's piece is in many ways like a personal essay, but she makes it clear that it is more than a description of a personal experience; her larger goal is to get people to think about the lives and working conditions of the working poor and in particular the long-term consequences of welfare reform. Ehrenreich hopes that her piece will show people that it's not as easy as policy-makers would like us to believe for single mothers with few job skills to support themselves. Think of your essay in terms of the kinds of consequences you would like it to have; what larger point about work, the economy, employers, and employees would you like to make?

Situation

2. Although Ehrenreich's piece is structured primarily like a personal essay, with narrative, dialogue, and description intertwined with commentary, she also includes footnotes with additional facts and information about sources. Choose one of the issues that Ehrenreich raises—for example, the effects of welfare reform on former welfare recipients, homelessness among the working poor, drug testing in the workplace, the rights of workers to breaks and amenities, the numbers of workers working more than one job, or other issues that you identify—and write a short research paper on this topic. You might use Ehrenreich's footnotes as hints to get you started, but you should also use your online and library research skills to find other relevant and up-to-date sources. Discuss with your teacher whether the paper should be a report or a research-based argument. Include a brief note at the end about the new perspective your research adds to Ehrenreich's story and argument.

A Man's Place

Victoria de Grazia, Claudia Goldin, Jacqueline Jones, Juliet B. Schor, Marta Tienda, William Julius Wilson, and moderator Michael Weinstein

This panel discussion which appeared in the *New York Times Magazine,* examines the transformations in women's lives that took place during the course of the twentieth century. In "A Man's Place," experts from a variety of academic fields including economics, sociology, and history assess the changing economic circumstances of women during the last hundred years.

One way of measuring women's economic gains of the last hundred years is by looking at the numbers. In the United States, the proportion of women in the workforce has been increasing steadily since the 1920s; by 2008 women are projected to make up 48 percent of the workforce. Although statistics differ on the issue of wage equity, almost no one disagrees that the wage gap is narrowing and according to some statistics the pay for men and women of equal education and experience is virtually equal.

Yet the workplace that the women's rights movement envisioned is far from a reality. Technological innovation and increased productivity once promised a 20-hour workweek and the possibility of job sharing. However, the fast pace and competition of the global economy have actually increased the number of hours in the workweek for both men and women. Although men are spending more time rearing children and participating in the housework, women still put in twice as many hours caring for the family and doing household chores. In the discussion that follows, the panelists examine present-day work issues and family concerns in light of women's role in the economy.

Connecting with the Conversation

1. Write about the difference in economic circumstances between your mother and her mother. If you are female, write about the way your situation differs from either your mother's or your grandmother's. If you are male, describe any differences you see between male and female economic circumstances in your family.
2. Review several newspapers for articles and editorials on work, women, and the economy. What sorts of issues are being discussed? Discuss your impressions in your class or online.

When the subject is women's economic progress, it's easy to get lost in the controversies of the moment. So the *New York Times Magazine* convened six experts to consider how that progress has played out over a longer stretch of history. They began by examining the transformation in the lives of working women, then looked at the power of women as consumers and finally appraised how well (or poorly) the economy has adapted to women's needs and desires.

The conversation was moderated by Michael Weinstein, an economist who writes the Economic Scene column in the *Times.* The panelists:

Victoria de Grazia, professor of history at Columbia University and author of "The Sex of Things: Gender and Consumption in Historical Perspective."

Claudia Goldin, professor of economics at Harvard University and author of "Understanding the Gender Gap: An Economic History of American Women."

From the *New York Times Magazine,* May 16, 1999, pp. 48, 64–68, 73–74.

5 *Jacqueline Jones,* Truman professor of history at Brandeis University and author of "American Work: Four Centuries of Black and White Labor."

Juliet B. Schor, economics lecturer at Harvard and author of "The Overspent American: Why We Want What We Don't Need."

Marta Tienda, professor of sociology and public affairs at Princeton University and author of "The Hispanic Population of the United States."

William Julius Wilson, Geyser University professor at Harvard and author of "The Bridge Over the Racial Divide: Rising Inequality and Coalition Politics."

A Woman's Place Is in the Workplace

MICHAEL WEINSTEIN: How far have women come over the past century or so? How would the economic circumstances of, say, a 20-year-old woman living in the United States 100 years ago be different from her counterpart's today?

10 CLAUDIA GOLDIN: Typically, she would have spent a lot of time working alongside and learning from her mother. One of the profound changes in the 20th century was the movement of young women from being "at home" to being "at school." I'm referring to the large movement of young women first to high school and then to college. In terms of working outside the home, if you were a young woman in rural America and had gone to school beyond eighth grade, you would probably have become a teacher for a while. In cities, we would find the women described by the Progressives as the pitiable young factory women—those of O. Henry's New York stories—about half of whom worked for piece rates. By the 1920's, young women would be working in retail sales and in offices.

VICTORIA DE GRAZIA: One of the biggest changes in women's lives is their capacity to control their fertility. Efficient contraception was almost unimaginable 100 years ago. The risk of pregnancy, not to mention the hardship of childbearing, enormously determined how women lived.

MARTA TIENDA: There is also the issue of how family arrangements constrained women. Even as recently as 15 or 20 years ago in the Southwest, the idea of women moving out of the parental household and living alone was unacceptable.

GOLDIN: But women did move out of the parental household, and their stories gave rise to the literature of Dreiser and O. Henry. They wrote about the young women who moved off the farm into the boarding houses that filled New York City and Chicago. Carroll Wright, the great early-20th-century labor statistician, studied the young women who lived alone and worked in manufacturing and who, to him, faced an increased risk of becoming prostitutes.

JACQUELINE JONES: One of the dramatic changes in the last 100 years is that most white women—I'm uncomfortable limiting this discussion to white women—today believe, and rightly so, that they'll probably work for wages after marriage.

15 WILLIAM JULIUS WILSON: Let me shift the focus to black women. Noncollege black women had very little chance during the first half of this century to take a job other than as a domestic servant. After 1960, demand increased for clerical and service workers. Black women were able to take those positions, so much so that by 1980, only

a small percentage of black women were domestic household servants. But, ironically, just as blacks and Hispanics started to move into those clerical positions, changing demand began to reduce opportunities as bank tellers, typists and so on. Now, folks who don't have college degrees face a new challenge because the areas that were opening up are starting to close. Yet it's far better than it was.

GOLDIN: Let's talk about occupations 100 years ago. You could hardly find an occupation in which both men and women did the same job. Many industries excluded women, perhaps because they were unionized or because they involved work in dirty and hot places like iron foundries and steel mills, or in disgusting places like slaughterhouses. Being part of the labor force was not considered progress for much of our history. Progress was having enough money to liberate your wife from the dirty, disgusting work of the factory, so she didn't have to be at risk of sexual advances and injury. The aim was not to preserve a patriarchal system but to create a better family life, a kinder life for women.

WEINSTEIN: Victoria, did you want to say more about family structure?

DE GRAZIA: A century ago, the role of women's unpaid household labor in maintaining the family was simply huge. Take into account the primitive equipment. Consider the difficulties of carrying provisions from the market. Think of the time involved in cooking, which meant getting coal or hauling wood. But even with new equipment, there has still been more "work for mother," as standards of hygiene and nutrition and the quality of caring for children have been raised. That suggests the question: has there been real progress or only a change in how women work in the household?

JONES: Can I add a couple of points about changes? One is that 100 years ago, women played very small roles in labor leadership and in fact, there were very few unions composed of women. Today, obviously, women are in the forefront of union organizing because of the shift in the economy and the importance of the service sector in particular. Another point is that 100 years ago, modern jobs went only to whites. The conventional wisdom said African-Americans should not work machines.

20 TIENDA: If you just compare white and minority women between 1960 and the early 1970's, the occupational distribution of black and white women converged. But since 1980, the trend has reversed. Asian women, with their higher college-completion rates, have benefited from the increased demand for skilled labor, but black and Hispanic women have fallen back.

GOLDIN: Many people think that the late 1960's, with the revival of feminism, was also the beginning of women's increase in labor-force participation. That is not the case. Among married women, labor-force participation rates rose 10 percentage points per decade for each 10-year period from 1940 to 1990. So today, the rates are over 70 percent for all women age 25 to 64, and a little over 80 percent for women who have bachelor's degrees, rates that are rapidly approaching those of men.

JULIET SCHOR: That's misleading. You don't want to give people the impression that 100 years ago women weren't working. They were not *officially* in the labor force.

GOLDIN: Let's go beyond labor-force participation rates and look at what has happened to earnings. The mantra in the 60's was 59 cents on the dollar—that was the button many of us wore then, meaning that for every dollar the average man earned, a woman earned 59 cents. It stayed that way through the 1970's. Then, suddenly, it began to zoom so that now, women are earning more like 70 to 75 cents to the male dollar, even 80 to 85 cents when corrected. For young people with college degrees, there's virtual parity. Meanwhile, who's doing the work at home? Here you won't find numbers that make us feel good. In a 1968 survey, husbands claimed to work on average 125 hours a year in housework, not including various child-care tasks. That amounts to a little more than two hours a week. By 1991, husbands claimed to do more than three times that amount—about seven hours a week. But wives in 1968 did nearly 39 hours per week and in 1991 did about 25 hours. In other words, there has been some narrowing, but only some.

The question is: Have women come a long way in the 20th century? The answer is unequivocally yes. They have enormously narrowed the gap in labor-force participation rates and in earnings. Occupational segregation has also decreased and so have hours of housework, enhancing the ability of college-graduate women, for example, to do the ultimate—combine career with family. Of course, there are lots of qualifications. Few women actually achieve both career and family. Women now become doctors at nearly the same rate as men, but they become family physicians, not surgeons.

25 TIENDA: The progress cited by Claudia has been uneven. Labor-force participation of Puerto Ricans has actually declined over a 20-year period. Participation of black women has not kept pace with whites.

GOLDIN: Yet despite the qualifications, women have come a long way. They have gained independence, dignity, respect, greater bargaining power at home, freedom, ability to socialize and have a life apart from family—I think that's extraordinarily important—and of course, the ability to divorce.

Women's Consumption: Might or Myth?

WEINSTEIN: We've been talking exclusively about women at work or home. But how about their role as consumers?

GOLDIN: A role we love.

WEINSTEIN: Is it not true that the more women earn in their own right, the more discretionary income they control, the more the economy will bend toward their needs and tastes? And is consumerism a trap or a route toward further liberation?

30 SCHOR: Much of what women used to do was buy for their family. Mrs. Consumer felt that she, in effect, brought income into the household by saving money through smart purchasing.

DE GRAZIA: The identification of women with consumption has been, as in the 19th century, in part metaphoric. Anything fickle was identified with women, and consumption habits were fickle; therefore, women were consumers. Then, as families' disposable income rose, advertising and other media exaggerated the sexual division of roles: men were producers, women consumers. The image that consumption is natural to women has, rightly, been very much contested by feminists.

JONES: I think all this talk about women as consumers loses sight of the fact that about 14 percent of households are poor. In Boston, the self-sufficiency index for a single head of household and two kids is nearly $40,000 a year, about three times the official poverty level. Yes, she has enough money to buy cosmetics, but not enough to fit the stereotype of women who wield a great deal of economic power. She's buying the necessities for her family.

DE GRAZIA: The question comes down to whether massively increased private consumption gives women choices, whether it empowers women in particular. That would be to say that consumption is a mainly female activity, that the more women consume, the more they make choices, the more power they have to make the economic world go round. This argument has to be unpacked. Consumption means many things. There is social consumption, meaning the significant public expenditure on goods such as Social Security, education, health care and other goods that we need to be effective private consumers. Women have not been able to play a very organized role in shaping the allocations of government budgets on these kinds of consumption. Indeed, with the recent attacks on social programs, one can speak of a lessening of women's role in shaping consumption. As for private consumption, the realm of discretionary spending of women in families is really very small. The media highlight the spending habits of the young, the beautiful and the very rich. The important point is that there is no sign, statistically, that women have significant powers when viewed against this entire range of consumption.

JONES: I find the idea of consumer as an agent of social change to be oxymoronic. The way consumption is practiced in this country is a deeply conservative force. I look at mass advertising, the engine that drives consumption, and the message that comes across is divisive and mean-spirited: You will look young, you will look pretty, you will attract a man, you will outdo your neighbor. These impulses will not lead to radical change, but in fact will keep people stuck in a past that's based on the power of physical appearance and the power of gender.

Detours on the Mommy Track

35 WEINSTEIN: Let's move on to our third question: How has the economic system accommodated women who want to pursue a career as they rear their children?

GOLDIN: By my calculations, less than 20 percent of college-graduate women born between 1944 and 1954 actually achieved both career and family by their early 40's.

SCHOR: We are at an unusual moment in history, in which the idea of a nonpatriarchal society—the idea of equality—has made tremendous inroads. The idea that men and women should have egalitarian marriages and share parenting and housework is a vast departure. That we are asking these questions indicates a tremendous revolution in the last 30 years.

WEINSTEIN: Are there groups that the revolution has skipped?

TIENDA: Many immigrant groups. The Latino and Asian populations are two of the most traditional groups, where the women's movement still lags behind.

40 JONES: Here's a good example of the unevenness of development. Take an upper-middle-class suburban couple, where both the husband and wife have high levels of education. We find these women worked when they first got their degrees, and when the kids started to come, they decided to stay home. The husband becomes the sole breadwinner. She's taking care of the house and the kids and she's dependent on him for the money to run the household, and I think with that economic dependence comes the real vulnerability. The household might be at the vanguard in socioeconomic status, but I think in certain respects, it's very traditional.

WEINSTEIN: Is there a barrier society needs to dismantle, or are these decisions worked out well within the family?

SCHOR: The major barrier is the structure of jobs. We have not been able to make good jobs compatible with child-rearing roles. The labor market is inflexible.

TIENDA: Because we rely on other women to take care of our children, two women can enter the labor force for every one that takes on a new job. When women go to work, we buy child-care services, more takeout food and other services, all of which are driving economic growth in a profound way. It also means that we are fueling stratification. But there are real costs, studied by psychologists, to children who have limited exposure to their parents.

WILSON: You know, Marta, I was thinking not only about the cost to children along the lines you're pointing out, but when you look at the low-income families we are now pushing into labor markets, there's no basic support. Employers are just waiting to fire them if they don't show up for work consistently on time. We don't realize how difficult it is for mothers who do not have basic child-care support. When their child gets sick and the mother stays at home to care for the child, the next thing you know, her job is in jeopardy. This increases stress on the mothers, threatening their interaction with their kids.

DE GRAZIA: Either our criteria for judging progress are too narrow or we are too focused on our own culture. If the convergence of male/female labor-participation rates is the standard, then we would have to recognize the achievement in the former Soviet bloc, where women were medical doctors and engineers, not to mention tractor drivers. Juliet has written amply on the lack of leisure in the U.S. If leisure is regarded as a kind of restoration, of community life and family life, rather than the opportunity to work or spend more, then we would have to look at European social-democratic experiences as models. What does it mean to society when child care is inadequate, as it is in ours? Insofar as we have decent services, they are privatized and discriminate against women in lower income classes.

WEINSTEIN: Roll the tape forward 20 to 40 years. Can you imagine these gender differences disappearing?

JONES: You start in the home where things have not changed that much. There is still "women's work." And until that whole notion disappears, until child care and the drudge work are shared equally by men, all else is secondary. What happens in the home conditions what women do in the workplace and the constraints they face. We're not sitting around talking about whether *men* can combine work and family.

GOLDIN: The playing field is most unlevel inside the home. Let me throw this back another generation. It's the young son who should be taught to wash the dishes and to make his bed and his sister's bed. He needs to be taught to work in the home and to treat that work as respectful, dignified and communal. Until that's done, we will continue to reproduce generations of good men and women who attempt to go on the same path as equals in the labor market, yet who diverge when they enter the front door.

WILSON: It seems to me that we should try to talk about generating ongoing national dialogues. This should become a major public issue that would be discussed in the media, taken up by the President and other leaders. That way we can increase our consciousness as well as our conscience about these things. If we just lay back and hope some evolutionary process will work itself out, we could be in the 22nd century before significant changes take place.

DE GRAZIA: I am skeptical that single families have the power to socialize their offspring to do away with gender inequality in the home, much less the workplace. Too many social trends undermine them.

SCHOR: A big part of women's problem is they entered a male economy, a male work culture, an economy structured to meet the situations of men. Until the workplace changes to accommodate the fact that we are now a society in which men and women participate full time, we will not achieve the goal of equality.

WILSON: I fight pessimism all the time. But I'm going to be a little bit optimistic here. I have in mind a coalition: whites, African-Americans, Hispanics, Asians, Native Americans who will start to demand a serious national debate on the need for social and family supports to mute or cushion the effects of economic changes. We're beginning to see some of that already with increasing talk of child care. And there's research to suggest that if you can reduce child-care costs, it can increase women's labor-force participation, improve the types of jobs they could get and could ultimately result in a reduction in gender inequality. So I'm going to put on my optimistic hat and say I think that the eventual development of this progressive coalition will have many positive effects, including reduction of gender inequality.

Exploring Texts and Contexts

For activities with icons, refer to the Guides to Analyzing Contexts for Writing and Analyzing Readings in Context.

1. The panel brings together people who have a variety of perspectives on women's issues. What is the moderator's role in a panel discussion? Chart the interactions the moderator has with members of the panel. Does the moderator shape and influence the discussion? From the comments made by the moderator, what can you infer about his ideas and beliefs? Explain. Genre
2. In the dialogue, William Julius Wilson calls for a national dialogue to address work and family issues. How does his idea of change differ from that of fellow panel member Claudia Goldin? According to each, what change is needed and how will it be effected?
3. This piece is a transcript of a face-to-face conversation. Does it sound like a conversation? What might the editors have changed to prepare it for publication? Language

Creating Texts

For activities with icons, refer to the Guides to Analyzing Contexts for Writing and Analyzing Readings in Context. For additional help with these writing projects, read the descriptions of **Dialogue/Symposium/Debate** and **Academic Article/Research Paper** in the Genre Glossary.

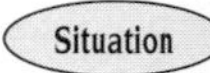

1. This panel discussion ranges over several topics, the changing economic circumstances of women, the power of women as consumers, and how well the economy meets the needs and desires of women. What areas could you add to the discussion? Drawing on both your own experience and the ideas you developed from working with the texts in this unit, choose another issue to add to the discussion. What do you think each panelist would say about this issue? Create a dialogue in which each panelist contributes at least once to the conversation. Create a part for yourself or make yourself the moderator.
2. Panel member de Grazia suggests we might learn something about solving the economic problems facing women and families today by finding out what other countries and societies are doing to support their families. Choose one of the issues raised in the discussion, for example child-care services, the structure of jobs, the lack of leisure time, or another issue, and write a short research paper on how another country or culture approaches that problem. Investigate online as well as print sources, making sure your research is up-to-date. In your paper explore how American society might be affected by seeing the issue from another perspective.

A Genre Glossary

The following glossary describes key features of the genres you will find in this book. The concept of *genre* refers to the way a text's content and form are shaped by the situation in which it occurs. When you watch television, you know whether a particular show aims to be comic or dramatic or even a comic takeoff on a dramatic genre. When you read an epic poem, a lease, or anything else, you know—from common sense and experience—what to expect. Genres provide a kind of social agreement between writers and readers.

Each Genre Glossary entry briefly describes the situations, purposes, forms, content, and language and design choices typically associated with that genre. These descriptions can help you in two ways. As you read, they can help you figure out what genre a reading belongs to and how the reading follows or breaks the conventions of that genre. As you write, they can help you think about what genres you might use in a given situation and what readers typically expect from those genres. Then it is up to you to decide which genre to use and to what extent you will meet those expectations.

Academic Article/Research Paper

(Also referred to as academic essay, paper, study, or research report)

Situation/Purpose This entry describes two genres different in many ways but with much in common: articles written by professors and other professionals and published in disciplinary or professional journals or as chapters in books, and research papers written by students as course assignments.

Academic articles are written by professors and other professionals in order to contribute new ideas, arguments, or research findings to their field. Typically they write about a topic that they have specialized in and may have written about before. Some academics and other professionals, especially in the sciences and social sciences, collaborate with others in research or writing or both. But even scholars who work alone are always working within a complex context that includes their own previous work and that of others both past and present. In fact, a hallmark of academic writing is that it is part of an ongoing conversation in which people interested in the same ideas or problems share information and ideas, argue with each other, and try to work together to solve problems and make progress.

Research papers usually have a double purpose: to learn about a topic and to learn about the values and conventions of academic research and writing. Thus, although students are usually writing about a topic that is new to them, teachers often try to create a situation like the ones in which academic articles are written, providing readings and preparatory assignments that give students a context in which to research and make a claim about a topic. Academic articles are usually written to an audience of peers. Students' research paper topics, especially in upper-level courses, may develop into professional interests.

Teachers may sometimes encourage students to publish their papers—with the Internet there are many more opportunities—or deliver them at student conferences, in which case they cross a genre boundary and become academic articles. But in most cases teachers and students see research papers as apprentice work in which students learn the subject matter, ideas, and methods of a discipline and have an opportunity to share their ideas at least with their teachers and sometimes with others as well.

Content/Form Despite these differences in situation and purpose, academic articles and research papers have much in common in terms of content and form. Academic articles are often longer, are usually read in their published form, and often begin with an abstract followed by a series of key words to help readers search related topics. Beyond this, there are many similarities.

Both academic articles and research papers conduct an inquiry, and in doing so they make a claim about a problem or issue. This claim is sometimes directly stated in a sentence or two in the introduction, usually after some kind of contextualizing discussion. This direct statement of the claim is often called the thesis statement, especially if the article or paper presents an original argument as opposed to a report of research findings. As part of the introduction or immediately after it, the writer often shows how the claim relates to what others have said; if this is done in an extended or formal way, it is sometimes referred to as a review of the literature. Whether or not the claim is stated directly in the introduction, it is developed and supported in the body of the paper with various kinds of analysis, arguments, and evidence. The analysis and argument are the writer's original interpretations of the evidence or positions on the issue. Evidence might include, depending on the field, research data, descriptions of observations or case studies, quotations from analyzed texts, and references to various authorities in the form of quotations, paraphrases, and summaries. There usually is some kind of conclusion, in which the writer draws together different strands of the discussion to make a synthesizing observation, sums up the main points, reiterates the thesis statement, or makes suggestions about future research. In most of these characteristics, the academic article and research paper overlap with the essay as a genre; see the description of **Essay** in this glossary.

What distinguishes academic articles and research papers from other kinds of essays is the use of formalized documentation conventions to indicate the sources of the evidence presented. The most common conventions for documentation involve the use of parenthetical references and lists of works cited; some fields still use footnotes or endnotes and a bibliography. These conventions are more than just formalities to avoid plagiarism; they are an important way of expressing that academic writing is an ongoing, collaborative effort in which one writer builds on or challenges the work of earlier writers.

The format of articles and papers may differ according to the field. In the sciences, writers may make heavy use of headings to mark sections, which may be organized according to a predetermined structure, and they often include charts and other kinds of graphics. Articles and papers in the humanities may be much more loosely organized and may include no graphics or section markers of any kind, although headings are becoming common even in the humanities. Both professional academics and students sometimes publish their papers on the Internet, and in that case they may use hypertext, allowing readers to follow a particular thread of argument or information through related links.

Language/Design Both academic articles and research papers usually use formal, impersonal language intended to convey unbiased judgment, though in some fields and courses a more informal, personal style is acceptable. Academic articles and research papers may also use specialized language related to the field or issue. This specialized language is an important aspect of academic writing but can cause difficulties.

Academic articles usually use special terminology related to the issue or to disciplinary methods; references to people and ideas familiar to those in the discipline; and quotations, paraphrases, and summaries from sources related to the issue. Some readers see this specialized language as an attempt to make the writers sound important or to confuse outsiders, but writers who use specialized language argue that it captures particular meanings important to the discipline or to the writer's particular argument. Some academic writers, especially if they are writing books aimed at a wider audience, might use a less-specialized language; others, especially if they are publishing in journals likely to be read only by other people in the field, use the highly specialized language that they know their readers expect, understand, and respect.

Research papers, often assigned in college classes, draw ideas and information from academic articles, and students are often encouraged to see themselves as engaging in conversation with the writers of these articles. Students may thus adopt in their research papers the specialized language of these academic articles but may feel awkward putting their own ideas into this language; they may also feel awkward putting new and complex ideas into their own words. Using direct quotations, paraphrases, and summaries from sources is particularly challenging because their use depends on fully understanding the material and being able to integrate the language into the discussion. This struggle, however, is a necessary stage in the process through which a practicing writer develops a language that expresses his or her own thinking but also allows the writer to engage in conversation with experts in the field.

(For an example of this genre, see page 60.)

Address/Speech

Situation/Purpose Speeches, also called addresses, are used in a variety of public and private ceremonial occasions including political rallies, dedication and awards ceremonies, religious services, business and educational situations, and weddings, funerals, and graduations. Depending on the situation, the purpose may be to persuade, motivate, celebrate, commemorate, entertain, or instruct.

Content/Form A speech often opens with comments about the specific occasion, remarks to focus the audience's attention and set the tone of the speech, and a statement or foreshadowing of the main idea to be developed. The body of the speech develops this idea with arguments, facts and statistics, and various kinds of examples, including personal anecdotes, depending on the situation and purpose. Speakers must consider how illustrations, pertinent stories, examples, and epigrams can add interest. For example, in commencement addresses, speakers often include personal anecdotes about their education and subsequent use of things they learned in school. Most speeches close with a statement meant to leave the audience reflecting on the topic and the occasion.

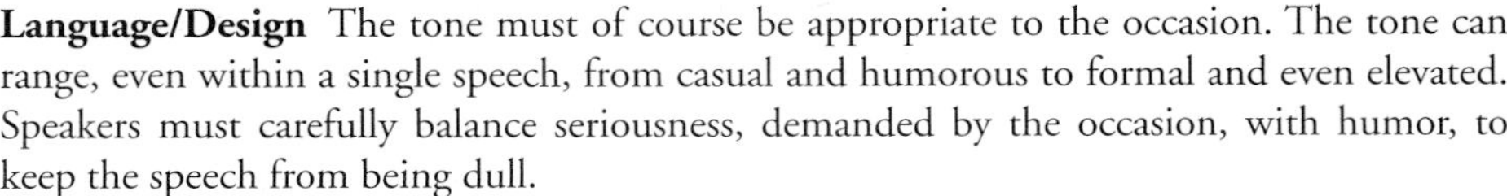

Language/Design The tone must of course be appropriate to the occasion. The tone can range, even within a single speech, from casual and humorous to formal and even elevated. Speakers must carefully balance seriousness, demanded by the occasion, with humor, to keep the speech from being dull.

Advice Book/Article

Situation/Purpose Books and articles giving advice are generally written to help people solve problems that are perceived to be widespread. They usually offer solutions that individuals can implement on their own without other outside assistance. More generally, they respond to a desire for self-improvement and for specific and easy-to-follow guidelines on how to achieve it. They cover a wide range of topics including diet, fitness and health, finding a mate, marital success, child rearing, business and financial success, ways to write well, and ways to stop procrastinating. Advice books are often marketed along with, or through, audio- and videotapes, seminars, and even TV specials. Advice articles usually appear in women's magazines, teen magazines, increasingly in men's magazines, and magazines related to health, fitness, and parenting.

Content/Form Writers of advice books and articles often present a philosophy or analysis related to the problem, but the heart of the book is usually the specific advice. The advice is usually broken into short, very readable sections of prose, usually with liberal use of headings, lists, and other formatting devices, and often with pictures or graphs. The writer usually enumerates aspects and consequences of the relevant problem, qualities to be cultivated, goals to be reached, and steps that must be taken. These lists are usually long enough to be useful but short enough to be manageable. Writers often present themselves as mavericks, going against the standard beliefs about the problem and how to solve it. Advice books and articles often include personal anecdotes and testimony from the writer and others who have succeeded by following the advice.

Language/Design The tone of the language is positive and upbeat. The diction and sentence structures are meant to be accessible to most readers. Sometimes the usage is colloquial.

Brochure

Situation/Purpose A brochure's purpose is to promote an idea, distribute information, or market a product. Although we often think of a brochure as a triple-folded sheet of paper. There are as many approaches to designing brochures as you can imagine. For instance, when you purchase a cell phone, the pocket guide describing its use is a brochure. The glossy sales inserts from department stores that accompany your Sunday newspaper are also brochures. A brochure offers an opportunity to illustrate something, explain how a product works, argue that some action be taken, detail a company's accomplishments, or describe an organization and its services. Sometimes it is the only representation of that product and service because readers may not be able to obtain further information. Often, to develop a brochure, a designer is called in to assist. A brochure may dazzle you with its color and design, but these elements must work with the writing to create a document that is meant to persuade or inform an audience.

Content/Form The content and form of a brochure are extremely flexible, but the key is to communicate through a synthesis of visual and textual information. A brochure uses imaginative techniques to express its message, techniques that combine language, color, shape, texture, and form. For example, a corporation might develop an annual report using a form very much like a children's book: bright colors, bold graphic images, a glossy cover, and text arranged like a story, all designed to suggest a particular reality. Or a low-budget brochure for a school might make creative use of a variety of typefaces to illustrate visually a contrast between the chaotic thoughts of students studying a poorly conceptualized curriculum versus the clear, sharp, interwoven thoughts of students attending the school described in the brochure. These brochures are designed to offer a clear and coherent representation of the service or product, usually through a strong visual argument.

Language/Design The rule in designing brochures is "Show, don't tell." Sometimes this is done through examples but can also be achieved through the brochure's physical design, through shapes, size, and use of color, and even through pop-up or pull-tab additions. The particular type or quality of paper also influences decisions about design. Brochures can be designed and produced with a simple word processor, but most often a designer will rely on software such as QuarkXPress, Adobe Photoshop, or Adobe Illustrator.

(For an example of this genre, see page 173.)

Business Letter/Memo

Situation/Purpose Although much workplace communication takes place on the phone, through e-mail, or face to face, a great deal of it still takes the form of letters and memos. There are many purposes for business letters and memos, but most fall into one of four categories, according to whether the basic purpose is to inform or to request and according to whether the reader will perceive the message as routine or nonroutine, positive/neutral or negative. Thus the four categories might be labeled routine announcements, routine requests, nonroutine requests (often called persuasive messages), and negative announcements, (often called bad-news messages). But keep in mind that some kinds of messages (for example, thank-you notes or notes of congratulation) do not fit into any of these categories; that most messages have some elements of both informing and requesting; and that the line between routine and nonroutine can be fuzzy. Letters are generally used for external correspondence, though they might also be used for very nonroutine internal correspondence. Memos are generally used for internal correspondence, though they might be used for very routine external correspondence.

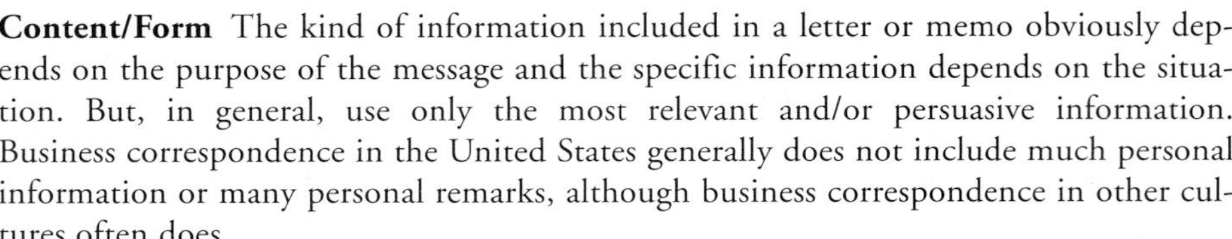

Content/Form The kind of information included in a letter or memo obviously depends on the purpose of the message and the specific information depends on the situation. But, in general, use only the most relevant and/or persuasive information. Business correspondence in the United States generally does not include much personal information or many personal remarks, although business correspondence in other cultures often does.

Although letters and memos have different formats (memos do not include internal addresses; letters usually do not include a subject line, though occasionally they do), the overall structure of the message can be the same for letters and memos. In general, the first paragraph should be fairly brief; it either provides a lead-in to the main point or states the main point. The middle paragraphs develop the different points or aspects of the message in some sort of logical order and are generally of medium length. The last paragraph is generally fairly brief, indicates what, if anything, will or should happen next, and includes a polite closing. Although both letters and memos can be of any length, we generally think of memos as shorter and letters as longer. In general, both should be kept to one page if possible.

Language/Design Letters are generally personal (addressed to a single person) but are also usually formal in tone; memos are usually impersonal (addressed to many people) and can be more informal in tone. But the language of both generally follows these principles:

clarity: specific and precise but simple; formal but not pretentious or jargony

conciseness: as brief as possible

coherence: hangs together and flows smoothly

courtesy: reader-focus, positive emphasis, good manners

correctness: no errors in sentence structure, grammar, or punctuation

Business letters and memos should be carefully revised, edited, and proofread, using spelling and grammar checkers.

Codes/Guidelines

Situation/Purpose Codes of conduct, sometimes also called guidelines, are increasingly common in the workplace because they set the standard for employee conduct by establishing guidelines. These codes both protect the employer from unacceptable employee behavior and inform the employee of employer expectations. Some businesses allow employees to contribute to the development of the codes, thus creating a forum for communication between employees and management. These codes are different from procedural manuals such as employee handbooks; they will not tell you how to do a specific job but will help you make general workplace decisions. These codes also serve a public-relations function by announcing the company's principles and standards to its clients and customers. A code of conduct can play a role in inducting new employees into the company's philosophy and can offer guidance to employees when they are confronted with difficult choices while performing their duties. If the code is to play a role in the day-to-day life of the business, it should reflect the particular circumstances and characteristics of the organization and must be adaptable enough to remain relevant as the economic climate changes.

Content/Form Codes are usually divided into numbered sections. They usually begin with a brief description of the company and a statement of its mission and values, setting the context for the guidelines that follow. Middle sections may cover general principles of behavior such as honesty, loyalty, and commitment to excellence, as well as more specific rules relevant to the particular environment of the company. Codes should spell out the kinds of behavior rewarded in the workplace and the kinds of behavior not accepted, and ideally both reasons and consequences should be explained. A good code will strike a balance between spelling out specific rules and advocating employees' use of sound judgment and ethics.

Language/Design The tone of a code of conduct is usually formal, even stern, in order to convey the seriousness of the guidelines. Beyond that, the language follows rules for writing in the workplace with its demands for brevity and standard edited English usage and mechanics.

Comics

Situation/Purpose Comics are a form of visual communication that include everything from the comic strips and books that young people collect to the increasingly popular graphic novels aimed at adult audiences. In addition, as more and more people become accustomed to learning visually, comics have become another way to present complex and technical information such as that found in instruction manuals for loading a digital camera or scanning images into a computer. In this respect, comics can be instructional as well as entertaining. Comics depend on the particular arrangement of the pictures and words to communicate the stories and ideas and are meant to be read in a sequence.

Content/Form Although comics are often thought of as a simple form of communication, they are really quite complex and require a literate audience. The narrative action proceeds in segments called panels or frames that draw on the reading conventions of the Western world and are meant to be read from left to right and top to bottom. Since space is limited, the artist/writer has to make a series of judgments about what to include and depends on the reader to fill in the gaps. For example, the shape of a human head might be used to indicate a human figure, or the profile of a person with her hands on a steering wheel to create the impression of driving a car. The space between the frames also serves a purpose; it requires the reader to supply the transitions between the frames. In this way, comics require a high level of interaction on the part of the reader. Artists introduce comics in a variety of ways; however, one common way is to include a full-page scene—called a splash page—to set the stage. The writer/artist can impact the reading process to some extent by experimenting with framing devices to achieve different effects. Notice the framing devices in the comics in your favorite newspaper or comic book. The size and shape of the frame may convey important information about narrative action or atmosphere. For example, a series of progressively smaller frames conveys a quickening pace of action, while lengthening the shape of a frame can indicate slowly passing time. Sharp lines around the frame can imply a sense of urgency or horror.

Language/Design In comics, the writer and artist are often the same person. Comics are a highly visual medium; the artistry of the images is often the first thing that captures the reader's attention. Many comics rely on images alone. But more often there is a balance between pictures and words. Often the words support the pictures, but at other times the effect is created by the contrast between word and image. Because comics are a static print medium, conveying things such as mood, sound, and motion presents a particular challenge. Visual clues such as speed lines or even footprints create the effect of motion. The characters' facial expressions and exaggerated gestures help create the mood and depict emotions. Sound can be implied through word balloons. The lines around the balloons indicate the words the characters are saying as well as those they are only thinking. Comics appear in both black-and-white and color. Often the colors are the primary colors, which are easily printed in newspapers.

Cover Letter/Reflective Essay

Situation/Purpose A cover letter is any letter that accompanies and explains another document or artifact. The most common use of cover letters is to accompany and introduce a résumé as part of a job application; for a description of this type of cover letter, see **Resume/Cover Letter** in this glossary. But cover letters may accompany a wide range of other kinds of documents. Teachers may ask students to write a cover letter, note, or reflective essay to accompany an assignment or set of assignments, explaining how the assignment(s) was completed, why certain choices were made, and what was learned. For example, an assignment that asks you to reshape material from one genre into another might ask you to include a cover letter in which you discuss what you learned about the nature of and differences between the two genres. The goal is to have you think about how you work as a writer and how the text works as a piece of writing.

Content/Form Cover letters and reflective essays of this type are typically fairly short. The necessary content is usually specified in the assignment and typically includes a discussion of what was written, a description of the writing process, a discussion of the situation that surrounded the writing, and reflection on insights gained from the assignment. They can be formatted as an informal note or a formal letter, with date, greeting ("Dear . . ."), body, closing ("Yours truly," etc.), and signature, and optionally the writer's address and that of the receiver. Typically they are about one or two pages in length, including a paragraph for each topic that the assignment asks you to address, with optional introductory and concluding paragraphs. The teacher will be looking for a frank, thoughtful discussion that refers to specific aspects of the text, its context, or the writing process. Students should use cover letters as an opportunity to gain insight into their own writing and writing in general.

Language/Design The language might be more personal than in the assignment itself since you might be discussing habits, perceptions, and insights related to your own writing. But it should still follow the principles of academic style in terms of diction and the correctness of sentence structure, grammar, and mechanics.

Dialogue/Symposium/Debate

(This description is adapted from William A. Covino's *Forms of Wondering*.)

Situation/Purpose Symposia and debates often occur in public contexts. You may have seen a roundtable discussion on television or heard one on a radio show. Political candidates often defend their platforms through a process of public debates: A symposium offers an opportunity for conversations that explore different perspectives. A debate, on the other hand, highlights the opposing viewpoints of two or more participants who argue through persuasive technique and through the presentation of evidence. The term *dialogue* can mean many different things, but as we use it here, a dialogue is an intellectual exercise in which a writer creates a hypothetical conversation in order to explore different perspectives on an issue; the Platonic dialogues are probably the best-known examples.

In writing classes, teachers often use dialogues to encourage students to explore different points of view, perhaps the points of view of different readings in the course. A related genre is the symposium, which may be either the transcript of a conversation or a set of written exchanges. In both real symposia and imagined dialogues, different points of views are expressed, but in an imagined dialogue the writer has intentionally created these different points of view in order to explore an issue. Ideally, each perspective should be fairly represented.

Content/Form An imagined dialogue resembles a transcript of a real conversation, but it is in fact more carefully constructed. There may be about four or five characters, representing different points of view, usually specific real or imaginary people. Ideally, each character speaks about the same number of times and in mainly paragraph-length comments, though these may be interspersed with shorter comments. Each comment is carefully planned to express the character's views and to respond to the other characters' comments. If the characters are real people, the comments should accurately reflect their actual opinions and attitudes. It is acceptable but not necessary to use exact quotes from writings by these people. When exact words are used, they should be enclosed in quotation marks. When the characters are imaginary, their comments should express consistent opinions and attitudes. Characters should make compelling arguments supported by convincing evidence. They should be consistent but show a willingness to change their views, if that is what the character would do. Comments should demonstrate an understanding of the participants positions. The responses as a whole should make interesting connections among the perspectives.

Language/Design Each response should be written in the persona of the real or imaginary person. They should be written in the first person and should use the words and sentence structures that the character would use.

(For an example of a symposium, see page 286.)

Essay

Situation/Purpose There are many kinds of essays, from personal narrative or reflective essays that are similar to fiction and even poetry, to impersonal expository essays that are similar to reports and proposals. You may write many kinds of essays in your life, and each might seem very different. But all essays develop a main idea by making connections between related ideas and experiences, whether it is a five-paragraph essay with three examples supporting a stated thesis or a many-page essay interweaving complex ideas and references to develop an implied thesis.

The most common, broadly defined purpose of an essay is for the writer to explore, and allow the reader to explore, ideas and the relationships between ideas. But this broadly defined purpose can be embodied in a variety of situations, each of which will shape the writer's purpose in a particular way. For example, a student might write an essay to analyze the ideas covered in the course or to make connections between the course ideas and the student's personal experience. A public figure might write an essay for a magazine or newspaper in order to persuade an audience about an issue of public concern. In fact, when a persuasive essay is used in this way, we might call it an **Opinion Piece, Column,** or **Commentary** (see page 312). A novelist or a journalist might write an essay to explore and share with the reader a personal experience and give the reader insight into similar experiences. A professional in any field might write an essay to inform other members of the profession of ideas or discoveries important to the field. In all of these cases, the writing might be called an essay, but in each case the content, form, and language will be different.

Content/Form While literary writing usually involves description and narration, and professional, scientific, or workplace writing usually involves the exposition of facts and ideas, essays tend to include a combination of description, narration, and exposition, with the emphasis depending on the particular purpose and situation. What we often call the personal, informal, or literary essay might be mostly narrative, description, and even dialogue, interspersed or framed with expository comments. Such essays are often written by students or by professional writers in literary magazines. What we often call formal, academic, analytic, argumentative, or persuasive essays give more space to exposition—presentation of information or explanation of ideas—but allow for some narrative or description that illustrates or illuminates the exposition. Such essays might be written about public, professional, or academic issues, by students as well as professionals. At the extremes, an essay might be all narrative/description or all impersonal exposition, but for most essays the essential feature is the combination, which allows the reader and the writer to share an experience and contemplate ideas related to it.

Thus there is no single template for essays, which might have almost any overall shape. But typically the first paragraphs draw the reader into the topic of the essay in a way that is appropriate to the situation and subject. Students often begin an essay as if they are directly addressing the teacher in response to a question. But a convention of essays is that any reader should feel invited into and addressed by the essay, which is why the introduction usually does not begin with a thesis statement but rather with something designed to interest the reader in the topic and lead into a statement of the thesis or otherwise point toward the thesis. The middle paragraphs—which can be of almost any number, from one to dozens, and of varying lengths, averaging about five to ten sentences—develop the topic in a logical or associative way, using transitions to clarify connections; these paragraphs may interweave narration/description and exposition. The final paragraphs reiterate important connections between ideas and point these ideas to the world outside the essay. All essays should have a thesis, which simply means that all essays should have a point that the writer wants to convey to the reader. The thesis, whether simple or complex, may be stated outright in the essay—often toward the end of the introduction or toward the beginning of the conclusion—or implied. But if the thesis is not stated outright, it must be implied strongly and clearly enough that the reader could state it.

Language/Design Depending on the type of essay, the language may be poetic, intimate, concrete, and informal, or highly formal, abstract, objective, or anywhere in between. But wherever the essay is on this spectrum, the language must be clear. It can be informal but should not be imprecise; it can be formal but should not be obscure or full of jargon.

Personal, informal, and literary essays are often written throughout in the first person; the writer's personal and individual voice is absolutely essential to the experience of the essay. Academic, journalistic, and other kinds of persuasive essays may intersperse first-person and third-person discussions; the effect is often to move in and out between close, personal perspectives and wider, more impersonal perspectives. The most formal, objective, and scientific essays typically do not use the first person at all; the writer aims to efface him- or herself and give the impression that the subject matter is simply presenting itself without the medium of a particular writer.

As this description suggests, there are many different kinds of essays, and the boundaries between them are not always clear. For essays specifically characterized by the documented use of sources and usually written in an academic context, see the Academic Article/Research Paper (p. 295). For brief, reflective essays that—typically in school situations—accompany an assignment or set of assignments, see the Cover Letter/Reflective Essay (p. 302). For argumentative or persuasive essays on current issues published in newspapers and magazines, see Opinion Piece/Commentary (p. 312).

In the following section we describe some of the key features of two broadly defined and different kinds of essays, the personal, informal, or literary essay, and the argumentative, analytical, or persuasive essay.

Personal/Informal/Literary Essay

Situation/Purpose The key characteristic of personal, informal, or literary essays is that the focus or emphasis is on the writer's experience or perspective. While analytical, argumentative, or persuasive essays may take their authority from evidence, logic, or methodology, personal essays take their authority from a combination of the significance of the personal experience and the power of the essay's language, and they are usually written to offer a personal perspective or testimony about some phenomenon or situation. Personal essays often appear in the front or back pages of magazines or journals or the "op-ed," page of newspapers, kept separate from more academic, professional, or journalistic writing, but the writers of such essays may include experts writing from a personal rather than an "expert" perspective; professional writers using the power of their language skills to evoke a situation or frame a concept; and ordinary people who want to offer a personal perspective on an issue. These ordinary people may be very skilled writers, but even if they are not, if they have a relevant, interesting experience or perspective to share, their essay may have a strong impact. This may be why teachers often ask students to write personal essays, typically asking them to describe a personal experience and draw some kind of conclusion from it or to comment on a situation or phenomenon, drawing on their personal experience to do so. But although such assignments recognize that anyone has the potential to write a good personal essay, they may not recognize that such essays are more complex and more difficult to write than they may seem at first, for reasons we will see below.

Content/Form Personal essays almost always contain some kind of first-person narrative—a story told from the perspective of the writer and in which the writer usually has a part—and some essays may be almost all narrative and thus may seem to many readers to be almost indistinguishable from short (fictional) stories. But what characterizes most personal essays is an interweaving of narrative and descriptive passages with what we might call expository or discussion passages. An essay might simply begin with a personal anecdote and then go on to make connections between this experience and some larger issues, or it might be a complex interweaving of narrative and commentary in which the narrative gives rise to discussion, the discussion gives rise to further narratives, and so on. But in any case almost all personal essays draw on personal experiences to illuminate, comment on, or testify about larger issues or phenomena, and almost all use some combination of literary techniques and expository strategies to create texts that allow readers to both share an experience and understand its larger significance.

Language/Design The language of personal essays is usually somewhat informal and intimate rather than formal or "professional," and it is often highly descriptive, vivid, and idiosyncratic, often making use of figurative language—images and metaphors, for example—and sometimes using dialogue or otherwise incorporating other voices. But the writer's own individual and recognizable voice is the strongest presence in the essay, determining the overall tone of the essay and synthesizing the other voices that might be incorporated.

(For an example of this genre, see page 36.)

Argumentative/Analytical/Persuasive Essay

Situation/Purpose While the emphasis in a personal essay is on the writer's experiences and perspective, the emphasis in an argumentative, analytical, or persuasive essay is on the subject matter and the audience. In a personal essay, the writer reaches inside and draws upon personal experiences in order to share insights with readers; while some personal essays are written in response to ongoing conversations, many personal essays might be said to start new conversations and even to create new audiences. In an argumentative, analytical, or persuasive essay, the writer joins an ongoing conversation in order to state a claim to a targeted audience or persuade that audience to take some action. Such essays are used by academics and other professionals to share ideas and make arguments about issues of professional or disciplinary concern, as well as by public figures or even private citizens to make arguments about issues of public concern. The assumption in a personal or literary essay is often that the writer can speak to anyone, either because the topic is of broad human interest or because the writer's style gives the text an esthetic value apart from its topic and arguments. The premise of an argumentative, analytical, or persuasive essay is that the writer is addressing a particular audience for a particular purpose, and the essay is framed by the expectations of this audience and driven by this purpose.

Content/Form An argumentative, analytical, or persuasive essay usually adheres to generic essay form in a somewhat more disciplined way than the typical personal essay. The introductory section is more likely to state the thesis explicitly, often toward the end of the section. The body paragraphs are more likely to be organized according to some identifiable logic rather than associatively, and the essay is more likely to make use of clear transitional devices. The conclusion is more likely to clearly reiterate the thesis and perhaps to call for further discussion, investigation, or specific action. But perhaps what most distinguishes this type of essay in terms of content and form is the way that it presents its claims or makes its arguments. While a personal essay may make a claim obliquely, indirectly, or by inference, an argumentative, analytical, or persuasive essay usually develops its claims or arguments in very explicit ways, and these all have to do with the important role of the audience in such essays. Because the argument is directed to a specific audience for a specific and fairly immediate purpose, the audience plays an active part in the essay itself. First, as we've already seen, the thesis is usually stated or at least strongly implied in the introduction. Then the body of the essay is developed with the concerns and needs of the audience in mind. The audience might include both those who agree and those who disagree with the claim or argument of the essay, but the disagreers play a more defining role in the essay. Thus, such essays often proceed by first taking into account the arguments or objections to the essay's claims; the paragraphs immediately following the introduction often include a discussion of the issue or question from the perspective of the "other side." Bringing the other side into the essay is a way of both acknowledging the other side and taking control of it by framing and defining it in one's own terms. This is usually followed by, in some cases, an acknowledgment of the legitimacy or force of some aspects of the other side's arguments or view of the situation, then, in most cases, by some kind of rebuttal of the other side's arguments or claims. The rebuttal can take the form of both showing what is wrong or weak in the argument or claim of the other side and presenting arguments and evidence for one's own side. The issue of arguments and evidence is crucial and complex because the arguments and evidence must be defined and presented with a particular audience and situation in mind; what is convincing and even acceptable as an argument and evidence for one audience in one situation may not be acceptable in another. Thus, whereas the content and form of a personal essay may be shaped primarily by the writer's experiences and perceptions, the content and organization of an argumentative, analytical, or persuasive essay are shaped largely by the expectations of a particular audience in a particular situation.

Language/Design At one end of the spectrum, in some literary or personal essays, the writer's individual "voice" is the most forceful source of authority in the essay; and at the other end of the spectrum the writer might try to efface his or her voice so that the argument or evidence seems to present itself directly to the audience without the intervention of a writer. In most argumentative, analytical, or persuasive essays, the voice of the writer is crucial but not in the same ways as in a personal or literary essay. In personal essays, the writer's experience or the esthetic appeal of the writing is crucial; what's crucial in argumentative, analytical, or persuasive essays is the writer's professional, disciplinary, or other kind of expert authority, and of course this must be communicated in a particular situation and to a particular audience. Thus the language of such essays must be not simply generically formal but authoritative to a particular audience. This may involve using a specialized vocabulary, sometimes called *jargon,* though in most situations clarity is valued more than specialized precision.

(For an example of this genre, see page 216.)

Feature Story/Profile

Situation/Purpose Feature stories are a regular part of newspapers and magazines, sometimes placed near a related news story or in a special "features" section. Feature stories are a cross between a news story and a work of literature. They usually relate events in the news but do not so much report facts as try to share with the reader an experience related to the news event. Profiles can be either a special kind of feature story or part of a longer feature story. While a feature may present a situation in a broad focus, a profile usually focuses narrowly on a specific person, place, or thing, describing it in evocative detail or telling a compelling story about it. Writers might use a profile of a specific person or group of people in order to characterize a social, economic, or political trend.

Content/Form Feature writers must tell a good story as well as provide an insightful analysis. The organization can be more complex than a news story, for example, which is typically organized as an inverted pyramid. Profiles include information from interviews, personal stories, and quotes from the people interviewed. Writers interweave these elements with narration about and description of the subject. The stories of the people profiled are arranged to support the writer's particular analysis. But, because the main purpose of a profile is to characterize a phenomenon rather than to simply tell a good story, a keen interpretation of the situation is necessary. Charts, tables, and graphs may be included to document the validity of the writer's analysis. Special layouts, often photographs, provide another dimension to the story.

Language/Design Word choice and quotations help evoke an image. Profiles are often characterized by the use of the third person, although the profile is primarily a subjective account of a societal, cultural, or economic phenomenon.

(For an example of this genre, see page 257.)

Interview

Situation/Purpose People conduct interviews in order to find out information or different perspectives on a topic and to make the information and perspectives known to others. Common interview subjects are politicians, experts of various kinds, athletes, authors, musicians, artists, and other celebrities. In this textbook you will conduct interviews with others to find out information or learn their perspectives on the issues you're exploring. For example, if you want to learn about marketing strategies in the fashion industry, you might interview someone who works in the industry. If you want to learn different perspectives on the question of whether graffiti is art or vandalism, you might interview a museum curator, a graffiti artist, other kinds of artists, a city official, and someone whose garage door has been tagged.

Content/Form The content of an interview consists of the writer's questions about the topic, the subject's responses, and sometimes other discussion by the writer, for example introductory background or additional information. Interviews usually take the form of questions from the interviewer followed by the subject's response, which may be very brief or quite long. Sometimes interviews take the form of an article in which the subject's responses are woven into the writer's discussion of the topic; sometimes an interview may be only a small part of a longer piece of writing. But keep in mind that the final written version is rarely just a transcript of the interview; rather, the writer has selected and shaped the material to focus on the topic and achieve the desired effect.

The interviewer must carefully plan the questions ahead of time in order to cover all the necessary ground but must also be flexible enough to follow the subject's train of thought and ask good follow-up questions. Interviewers develop strategies for establishing a rapport with their subjects—putting them at ease and getting them to open up—for example by beginning with easy questions or sharing their own views on the topic. Some interviewers like to use tape recorders—with the subject's permission—in order to preserve the subject's exact words; others prefer to take notes. Interviewers typically avoid yes or no questions such as "Do you agree that all graffiti is art?" Rather, they try to draw the subject out by using open-ended questions beginning with phrases like "Tell me about . . . " or "Describe for me. . . . " For example, interviewers will often ask the subject to describe a typical day or specific event.

Language/Design One of the reasons people love to read interviews is that they can hear the subject speak in his or her own voice. Rather than reading someone else's summary or

paraphrase, they can read the subject's exact words, which help provide a mental picture of what the subject is like. Thus, in writing up an interview, it is important to use as many of the subject's own words as possible, making sure that the subject is quoted exactly. At the same time, it is important to present the subject's words in such a way that they are not taken out of context and do not misrepresent the subject's intentions.

Letter to the Editor

Situation/Purpose Most newspapers and magazines publish letters from readers, which are usually written in response to an article, column, editorial, or another letter that has appeared in that newspaper or magazine or to issues and events in the news. Letters are usually published on a special page near the beginning of a magazine or on the editorial page of a newspaper. Although they are usually called *letters to the editor,* they are actually aimed more at other readers or the author of an article. Letters to the editor are the most traditional way for ordinary people to communicate their ideas to the public. And although talk radio and the Internet now provide other ways for people to communicate ideas, letters to the editor are still popular. People write letters to the editor when they feel strongly about something or when they feel an issue has not been addressed in the forum they are writing to. The purpose is usually to disagree or agree with a previously published position, to correct a statement of fact, or to add supporting information or ideas to an ongoing discussion.

Content/Form Letters to the editor are subject to screening and editing. This means that a letter is more likely to get published if it meets expectations about form and content. Letters are usually about recently published articles or events and topics currently in the news. They should be as brief as possible while still developing a position convincingly. They usually begin by identifying the topic and/or the article being responded to and briefly stating the writer's position. The position is then developed as concisely but persuasively as possible, making reference to opposing positions when necessary. The ending should be pithy or thought-provoking. Most large newspapers and magazines get more letters than they can publish, so they look for letters that contain very well-argued positions, perspectives that have not been presented before, new information, interesting anecdotes, or humor. Editors usually want to confirm that the letter is authentic and accurate. Most editors will not publish anonymous letters or letters whose authorship has not been confirmed.

Language/Design There is a range of acceptable tones in letters to the editor, from serious, formal, and polite through lightly humorous to angry and sarcastic. But whatever the tone, the language must be clear enough for the average reader of that publication and not offensive or profane, at least not in mainstream publications. The tone and language should follow that used in other letters to that publication but should also express the writer's individuality. Usually letters are edited, but editors might avoid letters that have too many errors; if errors slip by, the writer may feel embarrassed when the letter is published.

(For an example of this genre, see page 182.)

Manifesto

Situation/Purpose A manifesto is a public declaration aimed at changing a social situation. Closely tied to a current, often political situation, the manifesto presents an argument that distinguishes itself as a call to action. Writers compose a manifesto to instigate an immediate and often consequential response. A manifesto is intended to change the course of history, shining a light on previously ignored or misunderstood situations. Not only does a manifesto attempt to explain the past or justify future actions, it also attempts to redefine the situation in which these actions occur. The root of the word, *manifest,* suggests that it makes obvious the previously submerged aspects of the situation. Originally, manifestos were proclamations issued, or at least sanctioned, by a head of state, but they have evolved into a genre that anyone can take up. Most often manifestos represent the concerns of a group rather than the thinking of an individual. The best known manifesto, The Communist Manifesto, by Marx and Engels, was written not only to convince workers of the viability of socialism but also to suggest that revolution was a possible consequence of this new understanding. More recently you may have heard of the years-long hunt for the criminal known as the Unabomber, Theodore Kaczynski, whose essay, "Industrial Society and Its Future," was labeled a manifesto by the press. An even more recent and quite different example can be found in a recent book titled *The Cluetrain Manifesto: The End of Business as Usual,* which proclaims that the Internet is turning business upside down and offers a new way to look at business in the information age.

Content/Form The manifesto is an excellent example of how a genre evolves. Having begun as a proclamation by heads of state, it has been adapted for use in a variety of situations, changing its form in each of these new contexts. Overall, though, manifestos typically begin with an introduction offering a general statement about the problem or situation and proceed through a series of short paragraphs or questions and answers that convince readers of the initial proposition's truth. All of the various possibilities for persuasion exist: emotional appeals, a carefully developed series of logical propositions, a series of definitions or even an extended metaphor that tells a story in a new way. Whatever form the manifesto takes, it aims to bring the reader to a new vision and a readiness to act.

Language/Design The language of a manifesto is formal and carefully crafted but incisive, using strong language to startle or shock its readers with a newly unveiled revelation. For example, the Communist Manifesto begins as follows: "A spectre is haunting Europe—the spectre of communism. All the powers of old Europe have entered into a holy alliance to exorcise this spectre" (Marx and Engels, 1848). Marx used an evocative choice of words to set the stage with an "old" Europe that sees communism as a strange and unholy apparition that must be banished. From this beginning he continued to develop his argument for his particular explanation of capitalism and how it should change.

Online Posts

Situation/Purpose Many teachers now use electronic communication in the classroom to allow students to carry on discussions online, just as people outside the classroom use blogs, listservs, bulletin boards, and MOOs or MUDs. Most of the electronic writing assignments in this textbook involve listservs or online threaded discussions. Listservs allow people to send a message simultaneously to all members of a group. Chatrooms, bulletin boards, and threaded discussion forums allow for the development of a conversation online, which all participants can read as it develops. Unlike other electronic discussion groups, online discussions in a classroom are limited to the students in the class, although discussions can be continued outside the class period.

Content/Form Although students are often tempted to use online discussions to chat about personal matters, teachers generally want them to be reserved for discussion of ideas and issues that come up in class, just as in a face-to-face class discussion. It is important to remember that everyone on the listserv, including the teacher, will read the message. The interaction proceeds at a different pace than a face-to-face discussion; there is time for reflection before you respond. Online posts usually conform to the standards of other informal writing activities in this book, for example, a journal entry. If you have kept a journal for a class, you have an idea of the requirements of such informal writing. Generally, the quality of the ideas takes precedence over demands for correctness. Depending on the assignment, you may be asked to reply to a specific question or raise a question relating to the class. You may use your online posts to respond to a specific text or be asked to participate in the discussion of a broader issue.

Language/Design Although online posts are considered an informal type of writing, they should be well crafted and thoughtful. Although the tone can be informal, as in a face-to-face discussion, writers should attempt to use the terminology of the texts being discussed. Online discussions give students a chance to practice using course- or issue-related terminology before they write more formal papers on the topic. Since many people read online posts, the language should not be offensive, personal, or embarrassing. It's a good idea to reread a comment before you post it.

Opinion Piece/Commentary

Situation/Purpose Opinion pieces and commentaries are an important part of a democratic society. They allow ordinary citizens and public figures to exchange ideas about important public issues. Thus most newspapers and other periodicals devote regular space to these commentaries in a section known as the opinion page or op-ed page. Some of these pieces are regular columns written by local or syndicated columnists while others are written by guest contributors; writers may be private individuals but are usually professional journalists or public figures. Local newspapers, campus newspapers, 'zines, and some online publications might publish the opinions of writers with fewer credentials than are customarily required by national publications. This kind of commentary can address a range of topics. Opinion pieces are meant to be persuasive; the writer wants to convince others to adopt a particular position or, at the very least, consider the issue from a new perspective. Opinion pieces allow the writer to develop a position more extensively than does a related form, the **Letter to the Editor,** which is another form for expressing personal views.

Content/Form An opinion piece is essentially a short argumentative essay. (See **Argumentative Essay** for description.) Usually an opinion piece begins by referring to the context of an ongoing debate or some specific recent event, which leads the reader into the argument.

Many systems have been developed for writing arguments. A commonly used one involves making a claim and supporting the claim with evidence. An important step that writers often leave out is establishing the connection between the claim and the evidence; this connection is called the *warrant.* For example, if a writer wants to argue in support of a civic project for youth, the writer's claim is that getting youth interested in a community project like painting a graffiti mural will increase their commitment to the community and reduce the chances that they will vandalize public property. The writer would offer as evidence the fact that similar projects have had these results in other communities. The writer's warrant for using this evidence, which may or may not be stated in the argument, is that using data from similar projects is a reasonable way to make decisions about a present project. But effective arguments do not simply present one side; readers who disagree may simply say, "Well, that sounds good, but the writer hasn't considered this." An argument is more effective when it takes this opposing position into account and responds to it in some way: the *rebuttal.* For example, a writer might acknowledge that the project will cost a lot of money or that such a project will simply encourage more graffiti. After fairly presenting these perspectives, the writer might respond that the money for the project is a fraction of the cost of removing graffiti from city property and that similar projects have in fact resulted in a reduction of graffiti. But developing a logical appeal may not be enough. The writer can also use emotional appeals, for example appealing to the readers' sympathy for the community's youth or invoking the esthetic value of the mural.

An opinion piece may conclude in many different ways—summaries, restatements of the thesis—but however it ends, it should leave the feeling that the writer has considered both sides fairly and chosen the most reasonable position.

Language/Design Opinion columns usually use the first person. The overall tone and specific word choice reflect the writer's own style as well as the nature of the publication. In this textbook you will find examples of opinion pieces that use a wide variety of writing styles.

(For an example of this genre, see page 246.)

Proposal

Situation/Purpose In business, the professions, and other areas of public life, people are constantly exchanging goods, services, and money. This exchange is regulated partly by the complex mechanisms of supply and demand. But a special mechanism for the distribution of scarce resources or scarce opportunities is the proposal. When people in the workplace need to persuade an outside agency to give them money or other resources, or if they want to be chosen to provide a product or service, they write a proposal. Sometimes proposals are written in response to Requests for Proposal, or RFPs, which are circulated by agencies with resources to distribute and by companies or agencies who need a product or service. Sometimes proposals are used within a company to persuade someone to do something, usually to make a change or solve a problem of some sort, although in this situation they may be called recommendation reports.

Content/Form Proposals are basically organized as a problem/solution discussion. The problem section usually includes detailed descriptions, sets of facts, and statistics. The solution section includes analyses and recommendations. Since the proposal is used to make important decisions and will become part of a permanent record, the information should be as accurate as possible, based on reliable sources or research methods. When outside sources are used, they should be documented, using a standard documentation system, such as the MLA or APA system. When original research is involved, the research process should be carefully described.

Proposals can vary in length from a single page to hundreds of pages. The form of a typical proposal usually moves from description of a problem to presentation of a solution. A typical proposal will have most of the following elements in roughly this order:

Explain the purpose and scope of the proposal.

Describe and give some background on the situation or problem.

Suggest why the reader needs what you are proposing.

Present and analyze possible alternative solutions.

Explain why your proposal is the best solution.

Describe how your proposal would be implemented, including itemizing the costs.

Ask the reader to take some specific action.

Because proposals are meant to be as reader-friendly as possible, they usually include more elaborate formatting than other kinds of writing: headings, often accompanied by a numbering system; bullets; typographical and spacing variations; graphics are typical.

Language/Design The language is generally formal, impersonal, objective, or even scientific. It may include many technical terms, if necessary, but otherwise should be as clear, concise, and jargon-free as possible. As with other workplace or academic writing, it should avoid errors in sentence structure, grammar, and mechanics.

(For an example of this genre, see page 230.)

Report

Situation/Purpose The report is a common, varied, and flexible genre used in all kinds of situations—school, workplace, and other kinds of organizations—in which information must be recorded and communicated. Reports are usually written either to record information for bureaucratic, legal, medical, or scientific reasons or to give decision makers the information they need to make decisions. A student might use a report to record an activity or research findings.

Content/Form Since their purpose is usually to record or present information, reports usually include detailed descriptions, sets of facts, and statistics. They often also include analyses of this information and sometimes recommendations based on the information. Since the report may become part of a permanent record or may influence decisions, the information should be as accurate as possible, based on reliable sources or research methods. When outside sources are used, they should be documented, using a standard documentation system, such as the MLA or APA system. When original research is involved, the research process should be carefully described. Information that is relevant to the report but too extensive to fit smoothly into the body of the report can be included in appendices attached to the end of the report.

Reports vary in form and length. A report usually follows some variation on the following pattern:

> Introductory section that might include the purpose of the report, possibly a brief statement of the overall conclusion or recommendation, or background information.
>
> Body section that might include additional background, a detailed description of a situation or problem, a discussion of research parameters and methods, an analysis of alternatives, arguments to support a recommendation, a description of procedures or implementation steps, or a discussion of benefits and drawbacks; it might also include graphics.
>
> Concluding section that might include a summary, a recommendation, or some other kind of concluding statement.

Because reports are meant to be as reader-friendly as possible and because they convey a lot of information, they usually include more elaborate formatting than other kinds of writing: headings, often accompanied by a numbering system; bullets; typographical and spacing variations; graphics are typical.

Language/Design The language is generally formal, impersonal, objective, or even scientific. It may include many technical terms, if necessary, but otherwise should be as clear, concise, and jargon-free as possible. As with other workplace or academic writing, it should avoid errors in sentence structure, grammar, and mechanics.

Resume/Cover Letter

Situation/Purpose At some point in their lives, most people will apply for a job and for most jobs this will include submitting a resume and cover letter. A resume is a document that includes information about a person's education, job history, job-related skills and credentials, and contact information. Usually when people submit a resume as part of a job application, they submit it with a cover letter—a letter focused specifically on one particular job.

Content/Form Resumes usually follow a fairly standard template, with name, address, phone number, and e-mail address at the top, followed by headed sections for Objectives (the kind of job being sought), Education, Job Experience or Employment History, and Skills and/or Credentials. Many also include names and contact information for people that can give references, though some resumes simply say "References available upon request." Some resumes include personal information about age and marital status, though many do not. Most people's resumes are one page, but people with long and complex careers and qualifications may have multiple-page resumes. The section on Job Experience or Employment is usually the longest and includes a list of jobs that the person has had, usually in chronological order beginning with the most recent, and specific details about responsibilities and accomplishments for each job.

Cover letters are also usually a page long and rarely more than two pages, even for people with long and complex careers, and they typically follow some variation on this format: The first paragraph identifies the job being applied for and usually how the applicant knows about the job, for example from a newspaper ad, a school placement office, or a personal contact. This paragraph may end with a brief overall statement about the applicant's interest in and/or suitability for the job. The content and order of the middle two or three paragraphs depends on the type of job and the applicant's background, but typical arrangements include a paragraph on education, training, and credentials; a paragraph on relevant job experiences; and a paragraph on accomplishments, other qualifications, and interests; or one paragraph on education and job experiences and one paragraph on why the applicant is particularly suited for this job or company. The final paragraph usually includes information on how the applicant can be contacted and a strong statement of interest in discussing the job further.

Sample resumes and cover letters can be found in many books or online sites, and word processing programs often include a variety of templates for both resumes and cover letters. These are very useful in helping you understand the reader's expectations, but avoid following these models and templates too closely, especially in terms of specific wording; remember that since many other people applying for the same job may also use these models and templates, employers may see the exact same sentence dozens or hundreds of time. The key to a successful resume and cover letter is to find the delicate balance between meeting the reader's expectations, which may be fairly narrow and even rigid, and creating a picture of yourself as a uniquely qualified individual.

Language/Design The language of a cover letter should have the characteristics of any business letter: sentences should be clear and concise; word choice should be precise and relatively formal; there should be no errors in grammar, punctuation, or mechanics; and connections between sentences and paragraphs should be clear. The layout on the page should be simple and clean, and the formatting should be fairly simple; for example, use the same type face and font size throughout. It's acceptable to put some information—for example, a list of accomplishments or skills—in the form of a bulleted list rather than a traditional paragraph, but don't rely too heavily on bulleted lists in your cover letter; the majority of the letter should be in the form of connected prose.

The formatting for a resume can be more complex and creative, with headings for categories of information like education, employment history, and skills, and bulleted lists for individual items within these categories. But, again, keep the overall layout as simple and clean as possible. Published samples and templates are generally good models for formatting. The language of a resume should also be clear, correct, and relatively formal, though resumes can make more use of phrases in bulleted lists rather than complete sentences in connected prose.

For both resumes and cover letters, use spell check and grammar check, proofread carefully, have someone else proofread carefully, and then proofread again yourself.

(For an example of a resume and cover letter, see pages 49–50.)

Review

Situation/Purpose Reviews are written in response to books, films, plays, restaurants, musical and dance performances, art exhibits, and architecture. Perhaps it is more useful to distinguish reviews by purpose, for example, scholarly reviews written for professional journals, media reviews written by professional writers, and unsolicited reviews written by the general public and published on the Internet. In the first instance, practitioners in specific disciplines assess the contribution of a text or performance to the field as a whole; media reviewers—often writing on short deadlines—give their readers the first public response to new entertainment; and customer reviews give people a forum to share their opinions about a particular book or exhibit. Part of a professional reviewer's responsibility is to discover fresh talent and original work as well as to cover work by prominent artists. It is worth nothing that a review brings a certain amount of notoriety and attention to a subject. Lack of critical attention often prevents less well-established writers or artists from getting the kind of public notice that would give them an audience. A reviewer has a certain amount of power in determining who and what gets the exposure so crucial to finding an audience.

Content/Form Reviews take much of their interest from the works they describe, but reviews are themselves written texts and, as such, should be able to stand on their own as well-organized, interesting pieces of writing. Reviews differ from reports in that they provide a critical analysis. Even an informal review submitted to an Internet bookseller will not be published online if it does not include some discussion of how and why the opinion is formed. Generally, reviews include a description of the text, exhibit, or performance; an analysis of how well it accomplishes its purpose; and an evaluation of the contribution of the work. Within that framework is much room for variation. Reviewers must include enough information for their readers to understand what they are talking about, but the

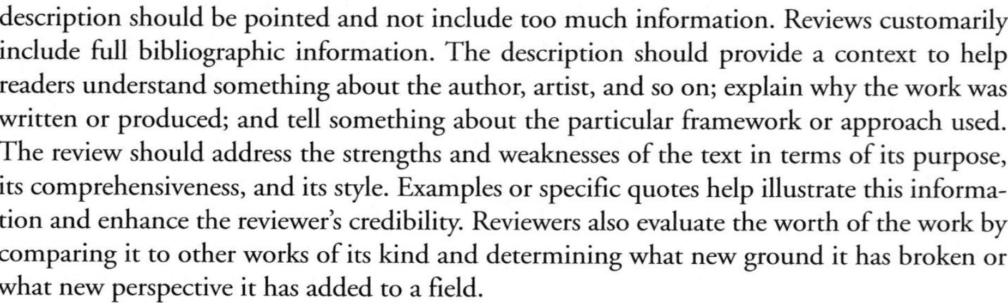

description should be pointed and not include too much information. Reviews customarily include full bibliographic information. The description should provide a context to help readers understand something about the author, artist, and so on; explain why the work was written or produced; and tell something about the particular framework or approach used. The review should address the strengths and weaknesses of the text in terms of its purpose, its comprehensiveness, and its style. Examples or specific quotes help illustrate this information and enhance the reviewer's credibility. Reviewers also evaluate the worth of the work by comparing it to other works of its kind and determining what new ground it has broken or what new perspective it has added to a field.

Language/Design Language may vary depending on who is reviewing, what is being reviewed, and where the review will be published. The overall tone and specific word choice reflect the writer's individual style as well as the nature of the publication. Language may range from casual and hip to formal and academic. Consider whether or not to use the first person. Since the entire review is your opinion, it is not necessary to preface your observations with "I think" or "I believe." Most commonly the first person is reserved to describe the experience of reading or viewing rather than introducing an opinion. For example, "I sat in stunned silence with the rest of the audience after the 20-minute soliloquy." Reviewers usually use the present tense when writing about the text or the author and the past tense when discussing the subject of the book, for example, "This documentary focuses mainly on the alternative rock scene of the 1980s but pays scant attention to rap music, although rap actually contributed more to the reshaping of popular culture while alternative music mainly influenced other musicians."

(For an example of this genre, see page 83.)

Web Page

Situation/Purpose Anyone from a kid to a corporation can have a Web page, and it's likely that in the future more people and institutions will use Web pages to communicate in a variety of ways for a variety of purposes. Students at all levels make Web pages as class projects; business people and professionals have work-related Web pages; and ordinary people have Web pages to express opinions, circulate information, and find others who share their interests. Businesses and other institutions of all sizes use Web pages to sell or otherwise promote their products and services. Individuals might have one Web page that they keep updated throughout their life, they might have several for different aspects of their life, or they might create short-term ones for specific purposes. If you are creating a Web page for a class, the purpose may be just to learn how to do it, and in that case your page may simply be an introduction to yourself. Inside or outside of class, Web pages may also have a variety of specific purposes—to make connections around interests, communicate ideas, promote causes, and publicize events. Part of the purpose of a Web page is to attract people to visit and then read the page, but the primary purpose is to inform, persuade, entertain, surprise, and/or challenge those who visit and stay.

Content/Form The content includes background and current information that may be personal, institutional, or issue oriented, depending on the purpose. A Web "page" is usually in fact multiple pages, and hypertext allows readers to move quickly from one page to another in order to follow a thread of information. Hyperlinks allow readers to follow a thread of information to other sites on the Web. Often Web pages include a place for interaction between the owner and the reader or between readers. A great attraction of Web pages is that they combine words, color graphics, and even sound; and the graphics may include designs, drawings, photos, and even animated elements. The choice and arrangement of the elements should be appropriate to the purpose and intended audience. The text and graphics should interact in interesting ways, but the purpose of each element and the relationships between the elements should be clear.

Language/Design Sometimes the language is very plain and straightforward. even formal; often it is playful, casual, and personal; occasionally it is in-your-face, even offensive. As with the elements of content and form, the language should thoughtfully reflect purpose and audience.

(For an example of this genre, see page 45.)

Credits

Text Credits

Adams, Adrian and Paul McKibben, "Sampling Without Permission Is Theft" as appeared in *Billboard* (Commentary), March 5, 1994. Reprinted by permission of Billboard and its authors.

Babbitt, Milton, "Purple Politics—Individuality Surrendered for Preservation," from Insight Section, *San Antonio Express-News*, August 17, 1997. Copyright © 1997 San Antonio Express-News. Reprinted by permission.

Bernstein, Nell, "Goin Gangsta, Choosin' Cholita" *San Jose Mercury News*, November 13, 1994. Reprinted by permission of Nell Bernstein.

Boyd, Todd, from *Am I Black Enough for You? Popular Culture from the 'Hood and Beyond*. Indiana University Press, 1997. Reprinted by permission of the publisher.

Chappell, Mary Lil, "FOCUS: Viva el Color!" from Editorial Section, *San Antonio Express-News*, August 10, 1997. Copyright © 1997 San Antonio Express-News. Reprinted by permission.

Chiem, Phat X., "Taggers Spray Over Vandal Image," *Chicago Tribune*, September 12, 1996. Copyright © 1996 Chicago Tribune. Reprinted by permission of The Chicago Tribune.

Cisneros, Sandra, "Purple Politics—Our Tejano History Has Become Invisible," Copyright © 1997 by Sandra Cisneros. First published in *San Antonio Express-News*, August 17, 1997. Copyright © 1997 San Antonio Express-News. Reprinted by permission of Susan Bergholz Literary Services, NY. All rights reserved.

City of San Antonio, "Historic Districts of San Antonio: Neighbors in History." From a brochure funded in part by the National Park Service, U.S. Department of the Interior, as administered by the Texas Historical Commission and the City of San Antonio.

Cox, Tony. From Tavis Smiley Show "Continuing Controversy Over Construction of a Memorial at the World Trade Center Site" by Tony Cox, National Public Radio, December 5, 2003. Copyright © NPR 2003. Any unauthorized duplication is strictly prohibited.

Crawford, Margaret, "Mi Casa Es Su Casa" in *Assemblage* 24 August, 1994, pp. 12–19. Reprinted by permission of Margaret Crawford.

Durke, Martha, "Real Issue Behind Purple House Is Tolerance," *San Antonio Express-News*, August 12, 1997. Copyright © 1997 San Antonio Express-News. Reprinted by permission.

Ehrenreich, Barbara, "Nickel and Dimed: On (Not) Getting By in America" as appeared in *Harper's Magazine*, January 1999. Copyright © 1999 by Barbara Ehrenreich. Reprinted by permission of International Creative Management, Inc.

Freeman, Hayden, "Your Turn" ("Cisneros Put Your Cart Before the Horse") from Editorial Section, *San Antonio Express-News*, August 23, 1997. Copyright © 1997 San Antonio Express-News. Reprinted by permission.

Garland-Thomson, Rosemarie, "The FDR Memorial: Who Speaks from the Wheelchair?" as appeared in *The Chronicle of Higher Education*. Reprinted by permission of Rosemarie Garland-Thomson.

Greenberg, Mike, "Purple Debate Reaches Commission, "*San Antonio Express-News*, August 7, 1997. Copyright © 1997 San Antonio Express-News. Reprinted by permission.

Harrington, Richard. "On the Beat: U2's Double Trouble" by Richard Harrington, *Washington Post*, December 18, 1991. Copyright © 1991 by the Washington Post, reprinted with permission.

Island Records Ltd. et al. vs. SST Records et al., United States District Court, Central District of California, Case No. CV 91-4735AAH, September 1991.

Ivy, Robert, "Memorials, Monuments, and Meaning" by Robert Ivy, *Architectural Record*, July 2002, Vol. 190 Issue 7, p. 84. Reprinted by permission.

Kimmelman, Michael. "The New Ground Zero: Finding Comfort in the Safety of Names" by Michael Kimmelman from *The New York Times*, Sunday, August 31, 2003. Copyright © 2003 by The New York Times Co. Reprinted by permission.

Lin, Maya Ying. "Statement by Maya Ying Lin" from the competition submission for the Vietnam Veterans Memorial, March, 1981. Reprinted by permission of Maya Lin.

Lin, Maya Ying. "Vietnam Veterans Memorial." Reprinted with the permission of Simon & Schuster Adult Publishing Group, from *Boundaries* by Maya Lin. Copyright © 2000 by Maya Lin. All rights reserved.

Madden, Shane, "A Portfolio of Self Representations" by Shane Madden. Reprinted by permission of the author.

McDowell, Edwin, "A Noted 'Hispanic' Novelist Proves to be Someone Else" in *The New York Times*, July 22, 1984. Copyright © 1984 by The New York Times Co. Reprinted by permission.

Meredith, Robyn, "For This We Sent You to College?" in *The New York Times*, June 9, 1997. Copyright © 1997 by The New York Times Co. Reprinted by permission.

Negativland, "U2 Negativland: The Case from Our Side" Press Release, November 10, 1991. Reprinted by permission of Negativland, P.O. Box 7218, Olympia, Washington 98502, http://www.negativland.com.

Negativland, "In Fair Use Debate, Art Must Come First," *Billboard* (Commentary), December 25, 1993. Reprinted by permission of Billboard and Negativland, P.O. Box 7218, Olympia, Washington 98502, www.negativland.com.

Norris, Michele and Lisa McRee, "The Purple House," transcript from *ABC Good Morning America*, July 15, 1998. Copyright © 1998 American Broadcasting Companies, Inc. All rights reserved. Reprinted with permission and courtesy of ABC News.

Pollan, Michael, "The Triumph of Burbopolis" as appeared in *The New York Times Magazine*, April 9, 2000. Reprinted by permission of Michael Pollan.

Quammen, David, "Review of *Famous All Over Town*" from *The New York Times*, April 24, 1983. Copyright © 1983 by The New York Times Co. Reprinted by permission.

RTMARK, Press Release "RTMARK Finds Bucks For Beck Rip-off," February 17, 1998, http://www.rtmark.com. Reprinted by permission of ®™ark, Inc.

Samiljan, Tom. "Building a Desktop Computer" by Tom Samiljan from *Rolling Stone*, June 9, 2000. Copyright © Rolling Stone LLC 2000. All Rights Reserved. Reprinted by Permission.

Santiago, Danny. Reprinted with the permission of Simon & Schuster Adult Publishing Group, from *Famous All Over Town* by Danny Santiago. Copyright © 1983 by Danny Santiago. All rights reserved.

Santiago, Esmeralda, "Skin" as appeared in *Body*, Sharon Sloan Fiffer and Steve Fiffer, editors. An Avon Book, 1999. Reprinted by permission of Esmeralda Santiago.

Scruggs, Jan C. and Joel L. Swerdlow, from *To Heal a Nation*. Copyright © 1985 by Jan C. Scruggs and Joel L. Swerdlow. Reprinted by permission of the authors.

Spiegler, Marc, "Marketing Street Culture: Bringing Hip-Hop Style to the Mainstream." Originally published in *American Demographics*, November, 1996. Updated by the author, November 2000. Reprinted by permission of Marc Spiegler.

Stallcup, Charles, "Your Turn" ("Reader Overdosed on 'Cisneros Edition'") from Editorial Section, *San Antonio Express-News*, November 23, 1997. Copyright © 1997 San Antonio Express-News. Reprinted by permission.

Suarez, Ray, with Ellis Cose, Joie Chem, George de Lama, and Mark Trahant, from transcript "Race Diversity in the Media" (Hour 2). Copyright © Copyright NPR ® 1999. The news report by Ray Suarez was originally broadcast on National Public Radio's "Talk of the Nation®" on July 8, 1999, and is used with the permission of National Public Radio, Inc. Any unauthorized duplication is strictly prohibited.

Taulbert, Clifton L., "Bright Boy from the Delta" from *Watching Our Crops Come In*. Copyright © 1997 by Clifton L. Taulbert. Used by permission of Viking Penguin, a division of Penguin Putnam, Inc.

Turkle, Sherry. Reprinted and edited with the permission of Simon & Schuster Adult Publishing Group, from *Life On the Screen: Identity in the Age of the Internet* by Sherry Turkle. Copyright © 1995 by Sherry Turkle. All rights reserved.

Weinstein, Michael, "A Man's Place" in *The New York Times*, May 16, 1999. Copyright © 1999 by The New York Times Co. Reprinted by permission.

Wied, Nancy de, "Cisneros Put Cart Before the Horse," *San Antonio Express-News*, August 23, 1997. Copyright © 1997 San Antonio Express-News. Reprinted by permission.

Williams, Patricia, "Hate Radio" from *Ms.* Magazine, March/April 1994. Reprinted by permission of *Ms.* Magazine. Copyright © 1994.

Yerkes, Susan, "King William Seeing Red Over Purple," San Antonio Express-News, July 26, 1997. Copyright © 1997 San Antonio Express-News. Reprinted by permission.

Yerkes, Susan, "Now We Know Why It's Called Purple Passion," *San Antonio Express-News*, July 30, 1997. Copyright © 1997 San Antonio Express-News. Reprinted by permission.

Photo Credits

Page 6: Tribune Photo by Jose M. Ororio; **33L:** Van Gogh's Chair by Vincent Van Gogh. © National Gallery, London, NG3862; **33R:** © R.B. Kitaj, courtesy, Marlborough Gallery, New York; **89:** Richard Fremont/Getty Images; **143:** Douglas Kirkland/Corbis; **148 (all):** Photographs from the collection of Clifton L. Taulbert, reprinted from Watching Our Crops Come In published by Viking, copyrights Clifton L. Taulbert 1997; **191:** Conversation Piece by Juan Munoz. Hirshhorn Museum and Sculpture Garden, Smithsonian Institution, Museum Purchase, 1995. Photo by Lee Stalsworth; **224:** Philip Gould/Corbis; **253:** David Turnley/Corbis; **255:** Bill Stover/NYT Pictures; **259 (top, left):** Bill Stover/NYT Pictures; **259 (top right):** Lloyd DeGrane; **259 (bottom left):** Steve Woit; **259 (bottom, right):** Mark Perlstein; **260 (right):** Steve Woit.

Index